Corpus Linguistics
and the Web

LANGUAGE AND COMPUTERS: STUDIES IN PRACTICAL LINGUISTICS

No 59

edited by
Christian Mair
Charles F. Meyer
Nelleke Oostdijk

Corpus Linguistics
and the Web

Edited by
Marianne Hundt,
Nadja Nesselhauf
and Carolin Biewer

Amsterdam - New York, NY 2007

Cover design: Pier Post

Online access is included in print subscriptions:
see www.rodopi.nl

The paper on which this book is printed meets the requirements of
"ISO 9706:1994, Information and documentation - Paper for documents -
Requirements for permanence".

ISBN-10: 90-420-2128-4
ISBN-13: 978-90-420-2128-0
©Editions Rodopi B.V., Amsterdam - New York, NY 2007
Printed in The Netherlands

Contents

Language variation and change

Corpus linguistics and the web

Marianne Hundt, Nadja Nesselhauf and Carolin Biewer

University of Heidelberg

The almost dramatic technological developments since the birth of the first standard corpora for English – Brown and LOB – have resulted not only in a proliferation of corpus analytical tools, but also allowed us to take a major step in terms of corpus size. The standard size of modern corpora is no longer 1 million but rather 100 million words.[1] Why, then, should anyone want to use any material other than carefully compiled corpora? Why take the risk of using databases that are unlikely to meet the requirement of representativeness? There are a number of possible answers to this question:

1. For some areas in corpus-linguistics, even the new mega-size corpora of the BNC-type are still not large enough. Examples would be most kinds of lexicographic research, in particular. The study of lexical innovations or morphological productivity really needs material that goes far beyond even the new mega-corpora. But even the investigation of some of the more ephemeral points in English grammar is not possible on the basis of a 100 million word corpus.

2. Apart from the ICE-project, corpus linguistics has largely focussed on inner-circle varieties of English, and within the inner circle, mostly on British and American English. In other words, for an awful lot of varieties, whenever we want to go beyond the fairly narrow confines of a 1 million word corpus, we need to turn to databases of some kind or other rather than carefully combined corpora. For more exotic varieties of English – like Samoan and Cook Island English, for instance – we do not even have ICE components and are very unlikely so see them in the (near) future.

3. The technological developments themselves have given rise to new text types that the compilers of Brown could not yet envisage – apart from e-mail, there are chat-room discussions, text messaging, blogs, or interactive internet magazines – text types that are interesting objects of study in themselves. Moreover, these are also often text types that will add a new dimension, for instance, to the discussion of written vs. spoken usage because they all use the written medium but are obviously much closer to the patterns that we expect to see in spoken interaction. For some outer-circle varieties, traditional text types such as private letters do not exist in English but e-mail exchanges may be used as a substitute.

Finally, the new text types on the world wide web (www) also add an interesting dimension to the discussion of socio-pragmatic phenomena such as 'crossing' or 'private language in the public domain'.

4. It takes a long time and considerable financial resources to compile standard reference corpora which, ironically, are quickly out of date when it comes to recent or ongoing change.

5. Language use on the www itself may be a major source of influence for ongoing language change. To be able to evaluate the impact that 'weblish' or 'netspeak' are having on our language use we have to gain a better understanding of the (fairly elusive) phenomenon itself. Open questions in this field are whether the English part of the www is dominated by non-native English or by American English, and whether it is closer to oral or written communication.

Of these issues, corpus size is one of the most pressing problems in corpus linguistics. For a lot of interesting research questions, carefully compiled corpora offer either very limited information or no information at all. An obvious strategy is to supplement traditional corpora with other sources of evidence. Apart from ready-made text databases, a logical place to look for such additional but 'messy' data is the web. In fact, it is such an obvious source that even the *Economist* had an article on the subject in January 2005 with the title 'Corpus colossal'. The pressing need for addressing the issue of the world wide web as corpus is also evidenced in the *WaCky Project* initiative – which, on their homepage,[2] is described as an "effort by a group of linguists to build or gather tools to use the web as a linguistic corpus. The acronym stands for Web-as-Corpus kool ynitiative […]." Before we embark on any analysis of the web as corpus, however, we have to pause and consider whether this might not be a bit of a wacky procedure.

First of all, we have to distinguish the two different ways in which the web has been used in corpus-linguistic research (the distinction has been made by de Schryver 2002 and Fletcher 2004 and this volume):

(a) With the help of commercial crawlers or internet-based search engines such as WebCorp, the web can be used as a corpus itself ('Web as corpus') – as a heuristic tool but also in a more systematic way. The heuristic use could be referred to as 'data sniffing', the systematic application as 'data testing'.

(b) The www can alternatively be used as a source for the compilation of large offline monitor corpora ('Web for corpus building').

The main problems with the first approach are that we still know very little about the size of this 'corpus', the text types it contains, the quality of the material included or the amount of repetitive 'junk' that it 'samples'. Furthermore, due to the ephemeral nature of the web, replicability of the results is impossible. Other problems have to do with the way that the commercial crawlers work: they cannot access all web pages because some pages are 'invisible', and – more worrying still – the commercial crawlers have an inbuilt local bias. This poses a real problem if you want to do a manual post-editing of the first several hundred hits of a search, for instance. Commercial crawlers apparently prioritize hits that are closer to the 'home' of the individual user, which may lead to different results depending on whether the web is accessed from Britain, the US or Australia (cf. Fletcher, this volume). Crawlers also build up a profile of the user and since we rarely use crawlers for linguistic searches only, this may produce an additional skewing effect.[3] All this adds up to the rather uncomfortable impression that in the web-as-corpus-approach, the machine is determining the results in a most 'unlinguistic' fashion over which we have little or no control. This is not to say that it cannot be done. And for the study of certain phenomena, in particular neologisms, the web is and probably will be one of our best sources of information. It can also be used fruitfully as a place where we may quickly find back-up for previously more or less anecdotal evidence. When you want to find out whether an adjective like *clampable* – undesirable as it may be on euphonic grounds – is used by native speakers of English or not, the evidence is only a mouse click away. And this is precisely the kind of information that even huge corpora like the BNC do not provide.

A methodologically somewhat safer approach is the use of the web as a source for corpus compilation or corpus building. The method has been applied in the field of historical linguistics by tapping into on-line text archives (cf. Hoffmann 2005 or Nesselhauf, this volume). The www also provides other archives and sources that linguists are beginning to exploit for corpus compilation. In future, this will be even our only way of obtaining reasonable amounts of data for some varieties of English, as pointed out above. There are quite a few advantages that using the www for corpus building has over using the web itself as a corpus: the keywords are control, accessibility, and level of analysis.

> Control: We, as corpus linguists, have more control over what goes into our data base. We may, for instance, want to include only certain text types from a newspaper (sports reportage rather than leading articles). We have a much better idea of the text types that go into our off-line corpus in the first place than if we use the whole web.

> Accessibility: Off-line monitor corpora culled from the web can be used with the standard software tools that we like working with.

> Level of analysis: Off-line monitor corpora can be annotated and thus allow us to do searches that are impossible to do on raw web data.

While for many purposes, using the web as a source for corpus building might be the appropriate approach, a few practical and methodological problems remain. We still need efficient tools that help in the automatic removal of any web-specific formatting which hampers the near-automatic creation of off-line corpora from the web. Tools are also needed for aspects related to meta-information on the web texts we would want to include, such as the genre, authorship (native vs. non-native speaker origin), or the detection of translations from other languages, to name but a few. Some of these goals are still fairly utopian, but it is one of the ways in which corpus linguistic research has to develop. One of the chances in using the www is that some of the challenges we are facing in using the web as corpus or for corpus building will necessarily have to bring us to cooperate closely (once again – or even more closely) with computational linguists.

We will, in future, have to make use of the web as one additional resource to complement the evidence we can extract from our carefully compiled 'standard' corpora. In doing so, it will be unlikely that corpus linguists will forget about the basic principles of corpus compilation. On the contrary, the ongoing discussion and the articles in this volume show that many corpus linguists are still very much concerned with issues such as representativeness, structure, balance, documentation and replicability, especially when it comes to the use of the web as a source of information. These issues now have to be re-addressed from a new angle – it could be argued that the challenge of using the www in corpus linguistics just serves as a magnifying glass for the methodological issues that corpus linguists have discussed all along. Traditional corpus linguists and compu-tational linguists should team up and contribute to this ongoing discussion.

The articles in this volume are, in part, based on papers presented at the symposium *Corpus Linguistics – Perspectives for the Future* that was held at the IWH (*Internationales Wissenschaftsforum*) in Heidelberg in October 2004. The majority of the papers at this symposium focussed on using the web for corpus linguistic purposes in one way or other. A number of articles were later commis-sioned from other leading scholars in the field.

Part one and two of the book focus on practical problems of using the www as corpus or for corpus building. They address the problem of suitable linguistic search tools for accessing the www (Renouf et al. and Fletcher), the question of register variation (Biber and Kurjian), or they probe into methods for culling data from the web (Hoffmann and Claridge). The critical voices in part three (Leech and Kennedy) argue for the improvement of existing corpora and their systematic exploitation. Part four of this book offers a range of case studies that make use of both approaches to the www in corpus linguistics – web-as-corpus and web-for-corpus-building. These studies do not only cover a wide range of topics (morphology, syntax, lexis, synchronic studies of a single variety as well as comparative studies of several varieties, and, finally, diachronic investigations); these pilot studies also show that – despite the many unsolved methodological problems – web data can provide useful additional evidence for a broad range of research questions, especially if combined with results from standard reference corpora.

Finally, we would like to express our gratitude to all those who helped in the production of this volume: the Fritz Thyssen Stiftung and the Stiftung Universität Heidelberg as well as the Internationales Wissenschaftsforum Heidelberg (especially Dr. Theresa Reiter) for enabling us to have the 2004 symposium; the participants of the symposium for their contributions and fruitful discussion; the authors of the commissioned articles for their enthusiasm in joining the project; the editors of the series *Language and Computers* for helpful comments; and last but not least, Anne Buschkühl and Ingrid Fauser for their help in preparing the type script.

Marianne Hundt, Nadja Nesselhauf and Carolin Biewer
Heidelberg
May 2006

Notes

1   Note, however, that the American National Corpus has not been completed, yet. In other words, 100-million-word corpora are the 'standard size' that is aimed at today.

2   http://wacky.sslmit.unibo.it/feed.php.

3   Note that the same problems also apply to the use of more 'linguistic' approaches to using the web as corpus. Even more specialised search software (as for instance WebCorp), to this day, has to rely on commercial crawlers.

References

de Schryver, G.-M. (2002), 'Web for/as corpus: a perspective for the African languages', *Nordic Journal of African Studies*, 11 (2): 266-282. http://tshwanedje.com/publications/webtocorpus.pdf.
Fletcher, W.H. (2004), 'Making the web more useful as a source for linguistic corpora', in: U. Connor and T. Upton. (eds.) *Corpus Linguistics in North America 2002. Selections from the Fourth North American Symposium of the American Association for Applied Corpus Linguistics.* Amsterdam: Rodopi. http://kwicfinder.com/AAACL2002whf.pdf.
Hoffmann, S. (2005), *Grammaticalization and English Complex Prepositions. A Corpus-Based Study.* London: Routledge.
WaCky Project at http://wacky.sslmit.unibo.it/feed.php.

Using web data for linguistic purposes

Anke Lüdeling,

Stefan Evert

Marco Baroni

Humboldt University
Berlin

University of Osnabrück

University of Bologna

Abstract

The world wide web is a mine of language data of unprecedented richness and ease of access (Kilgarriff and Grefenstette 2003). A growing body of studies has shown that simple algorithms using web-based evidence are successful at many linguistic tasks, often outperforming sophisticated methods based on smaller but more controlled data sources (cf. Turney 2001; Keller and Lapata 2003).

    Most current internet-based linguistic studies access the web through a commercial search engine. For example, some researchers rely on frequency estimates (number of hits) reported by engines (e.g. Turney 2001). Others use a search engine to find relevant pages, and then retrieve the pages to build a corpus (e.g. Ghani and Mladenic 2001; Baroni and Bernardini 2004).

    In this study, we first survey the state of the art, discussing the advantages and limits of various approaches, and in particular the inherent limitations of depending on a commercial search engine as a data source. We then focus on what we believe to be some of the core issues of using the web to do linguistics. Some of these issues concern the quality and nature of data we can obtain from the internet (What languages, genres and styles are represented on the web?), others pertain to data extraction, encoding and preservation (How can we ensure data stability? How can web data be marked up and categorized? How can we identify duplicate pages and near duplicates?), and others yet concern quantitative aspects (Which statistical quantities can be reliably estimated from web data, and how much web data do we need? What are the possible pitfalls due to the massive presence of duplicates, mixed-language pages?). All points are illustrated through concrete examples from English, German and Italian web corpora.

1.   Introduction

Different kinds of data are needed for different linguistic purposes. Depending on the linguistic question or problem at hand, a researcher has to identify the data he or she needs. For many research questions, data from a standard corpus like the *British National Corpus* (BNC) are sufficient. But there are cases in which the data needed to answer or explore a question cannot be found in a standard corpus because the phenomenon under consideration is rare (sparse data), belongs to a genre or register not represented in the corpus, or stems from a time that the corpus data do not cover (for example, it is too new). In these cases, the web seems a good and convenient source of data.

In this paper we want to focus on the possibilities and limitations of using the web to obtain empirical evidence for different linguistic questions.[1] In principle, there are several options for using data from the web:

a)   Searching the whole web through a commercial engine:

   I.   One can use the commercial engine, for example Google or AltaVista, directly.
   II. One can add pre- and/or post-processing to the search engine, to refine query results etc. Examples are WebCorp (Kehoe and Renouf 2002) and KWiCFinder (Fletcher 2001).

b)   Collecting pages from the web (randomly or controlled) and searching them locally:

   III. One can construct a corpus automatically by downloading pages from the web. This can be done by running Google queries or by using one's own web crawler (Ghani et al. 2001, Baroni and Bernardini 2004, Träger 2005). The data can then be processed in any way necessary (cleaning up boiler-plate (roughly: the templatic parts of the web page in which certain format-ting information is coded, doing linguistic annotation etc.).
   IV. One can collect a corpus by manual or semi-automatic selection of pages downloaded from the web, according to precisely specified design criteria. This procedure is not different in principle from building a corpus such as the BNC or Brown Corpus, and has the same advantages and disadvan-tages as these (except that there is much more material without strict copy-right on the web, see e.g. Hermes and Benden 2005). An example of such a procedure is described by Hoffmann (this volume).

In section 2, we focus on the direct use of search engines (Option I) since this approach is taken by most researchers (if only for pragmatic reasons) and compare them to traditional corpora. As examples of the latter we look at the publicly available portion of the *DWDS-Corpus*[2] (http://www.dwds-corpus.de/) for German data and the *British National Corpus* (http://www.natcorp.ox.ac.uk/, Aston and Burnard 1998) for English data, both of which contain roughly 100 million tokens. The BNC represents a "traditional" synchronic balanced corpus. It contains samples of British English from a wide range of registers which were published or recorded in the early 1980s. The corpus is distributed together with specialized software for linguistic searches, but the full data are included in the distribution and can also be searched with other suitable tools. The *DWDS-Corpus*, on the other hand, can only be accessed through a web interface that limits the number of search results and the amount of context which can be obtained. It was compiled for lexicographic purposes and consists of 10 sub-corpora, balanced samples from each decade between 1900 and 2000.[3]

The advantages and problems of the other solutions (II - IV) will be discussed in section 3. A conclusion and outlook is given in section 4.

2.   Searching corpora and searching the web

In order to search a corpus, one needs

(a)   a qualitative description of the items to be found that can be operationalized in the form of search conditions;

(b)   a stable corpus (at least for the duration of the data acquisition, but ideally also in the long term, so that experiments can be replicated by other researchers),

(c)   the necessary (linguistic) annotation so that the items of interest can be located according to the search conditions formulated in (a); a tool to perform the search with high precision and recall (a query processor or search engine), and

(d)   the possibility to categorize search results according to meta-information such as genre and age of speaker.

Every corpus search begins with a linguistic problem – the data are either used to explore a linguistic topic or to test a hypothesis that has been formulated by the researcher. As an example, consider the development of (German and English) non-medical *-itis*. A detailed discussion of the structural and quantitative properties of this suffix is given by Lüdeling and Evert (2005). Here, we chose it as an example because it is quite infrequent and there is some evidence that it has only developed recently. Therefore, standard corpora such as the BNC and the *DWDS-Corpus* will likely contain too few instances of non-medical *-itis* to support a thorough analysis.

In addition to medical *-itis,* which means 'inflammation' and combines with neoclassical stems denoting body parts (as in *arthritis* 'inflammation of the joints' or *appendicitis* 'inflammation of the appendix'), many languages have a non-medical version that is semantically derived from medical *-itis* but means something like 'hysteria' or 'excessively doing something', as illustrated in

(1)   Possibly they are apt to become too ambitious – they rarely succumb to the disease of "fontitis" but are only too apt to have bad attacks of "linkitis" and "activitis". *(BNC, CG9:500)*

(2)   Außerdem leide der Mann offensichtlich an Telefonitis, sagte am Donnerstag ein Polizeisprecher. *(DWDS-Corpus, o.A.[pid], Polizeibericht, in: Frankfurter Rundschau 06.08.1999, S. 31)*
'In addition, the man obviously suffers from telefonitis, a police spokesman said on Thursday.'

Types of questions that might be asked with respect to non-medical *-itis* are

- qualitative: With which bases does non-medical -*itis* combine?
- distributional: In which contexts are the resulting complex words used?
- quantitative: Is word formation with non-medical -*itis* productive?
- comparative: What are the differences (in structure or in use) between the English and the German affix? Is one of them more productive than the other?
- diachronic (recent change): When did non-medical -*itis* start to appear and what is its development?

First we need to formulate the search target. For all the research questions listed above we need to find instances of complex nouns ending in non-medical -*itis* in the given language. In most cases, we want to find all the noun *types* but it is not always necessary to obtain a complete list of their occurrences. For the quantitative studies, however, it is essential to identify all instances of each type so that type-token statistics can be computed. For the distributional studies, we also need some linguistic context and in most cases meta-information such as text type or age of speaker. The diachronic study requires a specific kind of meta-information, namely occurrence dates for all *itis*-tokens.

2.1 Reproducibility

In the next step, we need to find a suitable corpus. We do not address aspects of corpus design such as representativeness or balance (see Hunston, to appear), but rather focus on the issue of reproducibility. The corpus should be stable or grow in a controlled way (in the sense of a monitor corpus) so that the results of a study can be validated by direct replication of the experiment. Ideally, it should also be possible to test the *reproducibility* of the results by repeating the experiment on a different corpus that has been compiled according to the same criteria. For traditional corpora this is, at least in principle, possible by constructing a second comparable corpus. While often practically infeasible, it can be simulated by dividing up the corpus into two or more independent parts, to which the individual documents are assigned randomly. Results obtained on one of these parts can then be tested on the remaining parts. For corpora such as the *DWDS-Corpus*, which are only available via a web interface, the partitioning approach is usually difficult to implement (the only options provided by the *DWDS-Corpus* are partitioning by genre or by decade, so that the resulting sub-corpora are not truly comparable).

It should be immediately clear that being able to validate and reproduce findings is essential for any quantitative study, whose relevance depends crucially on the correctness and interpretability of the published numbers. It may be less obvious, though, why these issues also play a role for qualitative studies. Usually, a "qualitative" researcher is interested in finding examples of a specific construction or usage, which are then evaluated against a theory. Any example that exhibits the desired properties and is acceptable to native speakers can be used.

This superficial view is clearly inadequate, considering e.g. the qualitative description of the suffix *-itis*. Any claims made about the set of possible bases are invalidated when a replication (or repetition) of the experiment brings up contradictory examples.[4] Reproducibility is even more important when the interpretation of corpus examples depends on meta-information (which cannot be inferred from a simple example sentence, even by a native speaker) or a larger context (which cannot be included in a published report), as is typically the case for comparative and distributional studies.

When using the web as a corpus – especially when it is accessed through a commercial search engine – it is virtually impossible to test for reproducibility. Obviously, one cannot construct a second comparable corpus, a "shadow web", within the necessary time-frame for a synchronic analysis. While it would in principle be possible to divide the web pages collected by a search engine into random subsets in order to simulate repetition of an experiment, no commercial search engine currently offers such functionality.[5] One plausible solution is to perform experiments on a corpus that is compiled from the web in a controlled way. Then, additional comparable corpora can be constructed in the same way to test reproducibility of the results. This procedure is basically equivalent to regular corpus building and shares its limitations with respect to the amount of data that can be collected, cf. Option III in section 1. Another solution, which can – at least in principle – make use of the full amount of text available on the web, is to build a database of web documents (similar to that of a commercial search engine) that is fully under the control of linguistic researchers. It would then be easy to partition this database into random subsets of any size.

While validation of experiments is in most cases trivial for traditional corpora (provided that the corpus data and the search technology used are publicly available), the web is constantly in flux, and so are the databases of all commercial search engines. Therefore, it is impossible to replicate an experiment in an exact way at a later time. Some pages will have been added, some updated, and some deleted since the original experiment. In addition, the indexing and search strategies of a commercial engine may be modified at any time without notice. For instance, some unsettling inconsistencies have recently been discovered in Google's result counts for common English words. Shortly afterwards, the Google counts for many words (and especially those of more complex queries) began to fluctuate wildly and unpredictably as Google's engineers struggled to remove the inconsistencies.[6] Archiving efforts such as the Internet Archive's Wayback Machine (http://www.archive.org/) cannot solve this problem either. Despite the enormous size of its database,[7] the Wayback Machine covers a much smaller portion of the web than e.g. Google (Bill Fletcher, p.c.). It is difficult to estimate the true relevance of the replication problem: only experience will show how much the results produced by commercial search engines fluctuate over time (e.g. by tracking the web frequencies of different search engines for the same search terms over the course of several years).

A short digression seems to be called for at this point: Some researchers see the brittleness of web data more as an opportunity than as a problem. These researchers repeat their Google searches a few months after the original study. Provided that the results are overall the same, they claim that they have demonstrated the reproducibility of their experiment by repeating it on a different "snapshot" of the web. In doing so, they have succumbed to the statistical fallacy of using a non-independent data set for validation. While there can be no doubt that Google's database changes substantially over the course of a few months, the second snapshot will still contain almost all the web pages from the first one, except for those that were modified or deleted in the meantime.[8] It is therefore very unlikely that search results would change drastically during this time, except when the phenomenon being studied is more or less restricted to newly-indexed web pages (e.g. a new word that is coined and becomes popular in the time between the two experiments). Substantial changes usually indicate that the engine's indexing or search technology has been replaced by a different implementation, as noted above.

2.2 Corpus search

In this section, we look at the problem of locating the desired items in the corpus with high accuracy, the "corpus search". The two aspects of search accuracy are 'precision' (i.e. the search does not return too many "wrong" hits, called 'false positives'; see also Meurers 2005) and 'recall' (i.e. the search does not miss too many correct items, called 'false negatives'). While it is always necessary to achieve minimum levels of precision and recall, the precise requirements – and which of the two is more important – depend on the type of research question. Purely qualitative studies, where every example is evaluated by a native speaker, do not require a very high level of either precision or recall, although the manual work involved may become prohibitively time-consuming if too many false positives are returned. Low recall is problematic only when the search misses important instances that would support or contradict the hypothesis to be tested, and it is mitigated by large corpus size (especially when searching the web as a corpus). For quantitative studies, on the other hand, the correctness of the underlying frequency counts is paramount. Low precision can, in principle, be compensated by checking the result lists manually, provided that this is feasible both technically (i.e. full lists of results are available) and practically (i.e. it does not take too much time). For web data, these conditions are usually not met (see section 3.1). In any case, there is no way of correcting for low recall, which may lead to unpredictable errors in the frequency counts (since it is usually also impossible to estimate the level of recall that has been achieved).

The accuracy of a corpus search depends both on the range and the quality of linguistic annotations (including pre-processing steps such as identification of word and sentence boundaries) and on the search facilities offered by the software that is used. In the following, we will discuss these factors together, since the available annotations and search facilities are usually tightly coordinated: Corpora with rich annotations are often shipped with a specialized search tool that is geared to exactly the type and depth of annotation offered. It makes little sense for the Google database to include annotations that cannot be utilized by its search engine. The main purpose of this discussion is to compare the search possibilities and accuracy of traditional corpora (represented by BNC and *DWDS-Corpus*) with those of the web as a corpus (represented by Google). In doing so, we use the research questions on non-medical *-itis* outlined at the beginning of section 2 as a case study.

The basic requirement is to locate all complex nouns with the suffix *-itis* in the corpus. The corpus search has to be followed by manual inspection of the results in order to distinguish between medical and non-medical *-itis*. Since none of the corpora considered here are annotated with morphological structure,[9] we approximate the desired search condition by matching words that end in the string <itis>, regardless of whether it is a complete morpheme or not. Both the BNC and the *DWDS-Corpus* provide options for searching substrings of words. This method has perfect recall, but it will also return false positives such as *Kuwaitis*. Since both corpora include part-of-speech tagging, precision can be improved by searching only for instances tagged as nouns.[10] After manual validation, we find the following *-itis* nouns in the BNC that are clearly non-medical: *activitis, baggitis, combinitis, compensationitis, dietotectalitis, faxitis, fontitis, idlitis, lazyitis, leaguetableitis, linkitis, Pygmalionitis, ruggitis, taffyitis,* and *toesillitis*. Interestingly, some of them (*toesillitis, ruggitis*) are formed in direct analogy to medical terms and do not conform to the 'doing too much' semantics postulated above. We have now obtained a small set of qualitative evidence that can be used to describe the properties of non-medical *-itis*, such as the fact that non-medical *-itis* combines with native stems or names (medical *-itis* only combines with neo-classical stems). Similar results can be found for German (Lüdeling and Evert 2005).

For a more comprehensive and detailed account, it would be desirable to find more instances of these words (most of them occur just once or twice in the BNC and it is often difficult to derive their precise semantics from the examples) as well as additional *-itis* nouns (so that we can make valid generalizations about the set of possible bases). Using the web as a corpus, we should be able to obtain both substantially more *-itis* types and more tokens for each type.[11] Unfortunately, Google and other commercial search engines do not support any form of substring search, so it is impossible to obtain a list of all *-itis* nouns on the web. Thus, even this qualitative and exploratory study can only be performed on a traditional corpus, not on the web as corpus via a standard search engine. What can be done is to run web searches for the noun types found in the BNC in order to find more instances of them. Interestingly, for *Pygmalionitis* and *toesillitis* Google returns exactly the same example as in the BNC (from a poem and a best man's speech, respectively), though in the latter case it is found on several different web pages, so a frequency of 10 is reported.[12]

In order to perform a quantitative study such as measuring the productivity of non-medical *-itis*, it is essential to have a complete list of types with reliable frequencies, to which a statistical model can then be applied. The frequency data obtained from the BNC and the *DWDS-Corpus* are highly accurate once the "wrong" types have been filtered out manually. Precision can be improved even further when all instances of the remaining types are checked as well, although this is often too time-consuming in practice.

Using frequency data from a search engine ("Google frequencies") is much more problematic. For one thing, all search engines perform some sort of normalization: searches are usually insensitive to capitalization ("poles" and "Poles" return the same number of matches), automatically recognize variants ("white-space" finds *white space, white-space* and *whitespace*) and implement stemming for certain languages (as in *lawyer fees* vs. *laywer's fees* vs. *lawyers' fees*, see Rosenbach, this volume). While such features can be helpful when searching information on the web, they may also distort the frequency counts. It is possible to deactivate some, but not all of these normalizations. However, this requires a detailed knowledge of the query syntax, which may change whenever Google decides to update its software (cf. the remarks on brittleness in section 3.1). Another serious problem has already been demonstrated by the example of *toesillitis* above, where 8 of the 10 pages found by Google are duplicates of the same best man's speech.[13] Such duplication, which is much more common on the web than in a carefully compiled corpus, may inflate frequency counts drastically. Manual checking could in principle be used to correct the frequency counts, both for normalization and for duplication, but it is prohibitively time-consuming (since the original web pages have to be downloaded) and is hampered by artificial limits that Google imposes on the number of search results returned.

2.3   Meta-data

Comparative studies rely on meta-data like mode (spoken vs. written), language, origin (dialect), genre, information about the demographic properties of the speaker, etc. to categorize search results. Statistical tests are then applied to the resulting frequency tables in order to detect systematic differences between the categories. Three requirements must be satisfied so that meaningful answers can be found with this procedure: (i) the corpus must contain a sufficient amount of data from all relevant categories; (ii) the corpus must be annotated with accurate meta-data (which have to be accessible through the search tool); and (iii) the total number of tokens in the corpus that belong to each category must be known. The BNC satisfies all three criteria, since its file headers provide rich meta-data that can be used for a broad range of comparative studies. The *DWDS-Corpus* also contains a certain (though smaller) amount of meta-information, but there is only limited access to this information via its web interface. In particular, requirement (iii) is not fulfilled.

For the web as corpus, it is reasonable to assume that all categories of written language are represented to some extent. However, there are no explicit meta-data, at least not of the kind required for linguistic research. The only possibilities for categorizing (or filtering) search results are by

- language: Google's automatic classifier currently distinguishes between 35 languages;
- domain name: this has sometimes been used to approximate geographic location (national domains) or even dialect (e.g., '.com' vs '.co.uk'), but is an extremely unreliable indicator (www.google.com, www.google. co.uk, www.google.de, www.google.it, etc. all refer to the same cluster of computers[14]), see also Fletcher (this volume) on problems of regional results;
- file format (HTML, PDF, Word, PowerPoint, etc.): this has presumably little linguistic relevance, except for highly specialized studies; and
- date: whether a web page has been updated within the last 3, 6 or 12 months.

In addition to these limitations on the available meta-data and their accuracy, requirement (iii) cannot be satisfied (except by extrapolation from the search results for a large set of very general words).

Diachronic studies can be seen as a particular type of comparative analysis based on a special kind of meta-data, namely date of occurrence (publication or recording). Of the three alternatives considered here, only the *DWDS-Corpus* provides the necessary information to answer a diachronic research question. Using the *DWDS-Corpus*, Lüdeling and Evert (2005) show that the non-medical use of *-itis* (in German) is not new, the first occurrences in the corpus are from 1915 (*Spionitis* 'excessive fear of spies) but that it became much more productive and changed qualitatively in the 1990s. Neither the BNC nor the web could be used for such a diachronic study: Many traditional corpora, such as the BNC, are designed to be synchronic, so that diachronic analysis is only possible when a comparable corpus with material from a different time is available. While the web is an inherently diachronic resource, it has only existed for a short time span so far, and the available date information is highly unreliable. A recent date shown by Google may indicate that a page that has existed for years has only now been discovered by its crawler, or that minor (cosmetic) changes have been made to an old page. Conversely, many recent pages contain copies of novels, plays, poems, songs, etc. that were first published decades or centuries ago.

To summarize: For many linguistic research questions, such as the ones discussed with regard to non-medical *-itis*, there is no perfect corpus at the moment. The BNC is not diachronic and probably (if the productivity findings for German carry over to English) too old. The *DWDS-Corpus*, while it is diachronic and provides occurrence dates, is not yet stable enough and can only be searched through a web interface. While the necessary data is available on the web, there are not enough meta-data, the data are changing constantly, and the commercial search facilities are not useful to linguists. In the next section we therefore want to discuss other options for querying the web.

3.   How to improve on Google

We discussed in some detail the problems of commercial search engines as tools for linguistic analysis. In this section, we shortly review current attempts to "improve on Google", by making web data more suited for linguistic work. We can distinguish between systems that pre-process queries before they are sent to search engines and post-process the results to make them more linguist-friendly; and systems that try to dispense with search engines completely, by building and indexing their own web corpora.

3.1   Pre- and post-processors

Probably the most famous pre-/post-processing system is WebCorp (Kehoe and Renouf, 2002). Other tools in this category include KWiCFinder (Fletcher 2001) and the very sophisticated Linguist's Search Engine (Elkiss and Resnik 2004). Here, we focus on WebCorp, but the main points of our discussion apply (albeit possibly in different ways) to any tool that relies on a commercial search engine as its data source.

WebCorp is a web-based interface to search engines such as Google and AltaVista, where the user can specify a query using a syntax that is more powerful and linguistically oriented than the one of the search engines. For example, it is possible to use wildcards such as * meaning "any substring" (as in: "*ing"). Moreover, WebCorp organizes the results returned by the search engine in a clean "keyword in context" format, similar to that of standard concordancing programs. Just like such programs, WebCorp also offers various result processing options such as tuning the kwic visualization parameters (e.g. larger / smaller windows), the possibility of retrieving the source document, word frequency list generation, computation of collocation statistics, etc.

A tool such as WebCorp makes it easier for linguists to formulate linguistically useful queries to search engines. For example, as we discussed above, search engines do not provide substring search options, e.g. the possibility of looking for all words that end in <itis> ("*itis"). WebCorp, by contrast, supports substring queries (see above). Moreover, WebCorp and the other tools provide post-processing functionalities that are obviously of great interest to linguists (e.g. the possibility of extracting a frequency list from a retrieved page). However, ultimately these tools are interfaces to Google and other search engines, and as such 1) they are subject to all the query limitations that the engines impose, 2) they cannot provide information that is not present in the data returned by the engines, and 3) they are subject to constant brittleness, as the nature of the services provided by the engines may change at any time. It is worthwhile looking at these three problems in more detail.

In terms of the first problem, the most obvious limitation is that search engines do not return more than a small, fixed number of results for a query. WebCorp cannot return more results than the search engine. As a matter of fact,

WebCorp will typically return *fewer* results than the underlying engine, since it has to filter out results that do not match the user's query. For example, the search "*itis" (tried on WebCorp on April 18, 2005) did not return any results although, as we saw above, at least some of the *-itis* words from the BNC are also present in Google's database. The search "I like *ing" (tried on WebCorp on March 27, 2005) returned only 10 matches (3 of them from the same page). What probably happened here is that WebCorp had to query Google for "I like *" or "I like", and then go through the 1,000 pages returned by Google (the maximum for an automated query), looking for the small fraction of pages that contain the pattern "I like *ing". While precision is high (all contexts returned by WebCorp do indeed match the wildcard query), this comes at the cost of very low recall. In this example, recall is so low that it would have been better to use a traditional corpus such as the BNC (where the same "I like *ing" query returned 295 hits).

The situation is made worse by the fact that WebCorp (or any similar tool) does not have control over the Google ranking. If we can only see, say, 10 instances of a certain syntactic construction, we would probably prefer to see a random sample of the pages in which it occurs, or perhaps 10 pages that are "linguistically authoritative". Instead, the set of pages returned from a search engine will be the "best" according to criteria – such as popularity and topical relevance – that are not of particular linguistic interest (see also Fletcher, this volume).

The second problem with pre-/post-processors is that, if some information is not available through the search engine, it is very hard (and often impossible) for tools such as WebCorp to provide it to the user. Thus, most obviously, since the search engines do not allow queries for syntactic information (e.g. part of speech), such queries are not available through WebCorp either. More generally, any "abstract" query that is not tied to a specific lexical (sub-)string will either be impossible or, if the post-processor performs heavy filtering on the search engine output in order to simulate the query (as in the case of the "I like *ing" query above), it will result in very low recall.

Perhaps the most serious problem with systems that rely on search engines is their inherent brittleness. Search companies are constantly up-dating their databases and changing their interfaces. These changes imply that experiments done with a tool such as WebCorp are never truly replicable (because of changes in the databases). For example, the query "I like *ing" was repeated on April 18, 2005 (about 3 weeks after the first experiment) and returned only 8 results instead of 10. More dramatically, none of the functionality supported by the tools is guaranteed to work forever. For example, in March 2004, various features of KWiCFinder stopped working all of a sudden because the underlying search engine (AltaVista) had discontinued support for the relevant functionality (such as proximity queries). As another example, some features of WebCorp depend on the asterisk as a whole word wildcard in Google phrase queries. As of April 2005, it is not clear that Google will continue to support this syntax. Even if it does, the developers of WebCorp stated in recent postings to the Corpora mailing list that they intend to switch to their own search engine, in order to eliminate the brittleness problem (and more generally to avoid reliance on search companies whose priorities, of course, have little to do with helping linguistic research).

3.2 A search engine for linguists

This leads us to an alternative, more drastic way to try and "improve on Google", i.e. building one's own corpus directly from the web instead of relying on an existing search engine. Except for very small corpora, the process of downloading web pages to build the corpus (and any post-processing that is applied) must be automated. If the resulting corpus is in turn made available for querying through a web interface, one can speak of a proper "search engine for linguists" (Volk 2002, Kilgarriff 2003, Fletcher 2004, this volume). In principle, this is the optimal approach to using the web as corpus, given that it provides full control over the data (whose importance has been discussed in section 2). However, crawling, post-processing, annotating and indexing a sizeable portion of the web is by no means a trivial task.

It is telling that, even though the idea of building a linguist's search engine has been around for at least 3 years, to this date the only projects that have produced concrete results involved (relatively) small-scale crawls. For example, Ghani et al. (2001) sent automated queries to the AltaVista engine using words "typical" of specific languages and retrieved the pages found by the engine in order to build corpora of minority languages. Baroni and Bernardini (2004) used a similar approach (relying on Google instead of AltaVista) to create specialized language corpora for terminographical work. Sharoff (submitted) applied the tools developed by Baroni and Bernardini to build general corpora of English, Russian, Chinese and German text that are similar in size to the BNC. Studies of this sort have concrete results (e.g. Baroni and Bernardini's tools are publicly available and have been used in a number of terminological projects; Sharoff's corpora can be queried at http://corpus.leeds.ac.uk/internet.html), they demonstrate how various types of corpora can be created very rapidly using the web, and they provide useful material for the comparison of web data with traditional corpora. However, as one of the main reasons to use the web instead of a traditional corpus is to have access to an enormous database, small-scale corpus creation is not a satisfactory solution.

In what follows, we shortly review the main steps that would be necessary to build a linguist's search engine with a large database, highlighting the problems that must be solved at each step.

3.2.1 Crawling

A crawler is a program that traverses the web by following hyperlinks from one page to another. In our case, the crawler should download pages containing text, such as HTML pages, but also PDF and MS Word documents. The set of URLs used to initialize the crawl and various parameter settings of the crawler (e.g. the number of pages to be downloaded from each domain) will have strong effects on the nature of the corpus being built. Several tools that are freely available can perform efficient crawling (e.g. Heritrix: http://crawler.archive.org), but a broad crawl of the web will require considerable memory and disk storage resources. One argument that is often brought forward in favour of web corpora (as opposed to traditional static corpora) is that they offer language that is constantly "fresh" and open up the possibility of diachronic studies (cf. the discussion in section 2.3). To deliver on these promises, the linguist's search engine should do periodic crawls of the web. Thus, the issues of memory and storage are multiplied by the number of crawls to be performed (efficiency and computational power issues in all the following steps are of course also affected by the need to keep the corpus up-to-date).

3.2.2 Post-processing

Once a set of web pages has been crawled and retrieved, one has to strip off the HTML and other "boilerplate". The character encoding and language of each page must be identified. "Linguistically uninteresting" pages (e.g. catalogues and link lists) must be discarded. Identical and – much more difficult – "nearly identical" pages have to be identified and discarded (according to some criterion for when two pages are too similar to keep them both). None of these tasks is particularly difficult *per se*, and there is a large amount of literature in the Information Retrieval and www research community on topics such as near-duplicate detection (see, e.g., Broder et al. 1997). However, even "solved" problems such as language identification or near-duplicate detection require considerable computational resources and very careful implementations if they have to be applied to very large datasets, such as crawls that contain terabytes of data.

3.2.3 Linguistic encoding

Part-of-speech tagging, lemmatization, possibly automated categorization in terms of topic and other parameters are among the features that could really make the difference between a normal search engine and a specialized linguistic search engine. Again, it is not difficult to find tools to perform such tasks for many languages, but we will need very fast computers, very smart implementations and/or a lot of patience if we have to tag terabytes of data.

3.2.4 Indexing and retrieval

In our experiments, even a very efficient tool for indexing linguistic corpora such as the IMS Corpus WorkBench (CWB, ref. http://cwb.sourceforge.net/) has problems encoding corpora larger than about 500 million tokens. Thus, in order to index a corpus that contains many billions of tokens, one must either develop a new, extremely efficient indexer or design a distributed architecture in which the corpus is split into multiple sections that can be indexed separately. In turn, this complicates the retrieval process, which must pool the relevant information from several indexes. Based on our experience with CWB and large corpora, we also believe that retrieval would be much slower than on Google. However, this would probably not be seen as a major problem, as long as the information that can be retrieved is much more attractive to linguists than what is offered by Google.

3.2.5 Query interface

Powerful languages to retrieve information from a corpus are already available – e.g. the CWB *corpus query processing* language. A language of this sort would probably also be adequate for linguistic queries on the indexed web data, although, once again, particular attention must be paid to issues of efficiency (e.g. if a query is matched by 10 million kwic lines, the query interface has to provide highly efficient functionalities to work with the sheer amount of data that is returned).

4.   Conclusion

A generalization emerges from the analysis of the various steps: While there is no major theoretical / algorithmic roadblock to the realization of a linguist's search engine, its implementation requires major computational resources and very serious, coordinated, high-efficiency programming – a far cry from the "do it yourself with a Perl script on whatever computer is available" approach typical of corpus linguistics.

There are also legal issues to be addressed. It is true that what we as linguists would be doing is not different from what Google and the other search engines have been doing for a decade, apparently without legal hassles. However, there are some worrying differences between linguists and Google: the linguist's search engine will "modify" the original pages (e.g. by adding POS information) in a much more radical way than Google does for cached pages; the linguist's engine would not provide "free advertising" as a high Google placement does; and the typical équipe of linguists is unlikely to have access to the same expensive legal expertise that Google can have. Even if the concrete legal threats are probably minor, they may have negative impact on fund-raising – and, as we just saw, such process is unlikely to be successful without the kind of computational and human infrastructure that requires a lot of funds.

It is very likely that the next few years will see the birth of one or more search engines for linguists. These engines will solve some of the problems we discussed in this paper: They will likely provide sophisticated query options, such as full substring search support ("*itis"), linguistic annotation (e.g. part of speech tagging), reliable meta-data, and they will not suffer from brittleness. In order to achieve these concrete goals, it is probably unavoidable that such engines, at least for the near future, will have to give up some of the most attractive characteristics of Google: Their databases will not nearly be as large nor have comparable cross-linguistic coverage, and (because of efficiency / storage constraints and to avoid brittleness) they will probably not be updated very frequently. Thus, for good or for bad, it is likely that this first generation of linguist's search engines and the underlying web corpora will look like oversized versions of the corpora we know (billions of words rather than hundreds of millions of word), solving some of the sparseness problems of current corpora, but still far away from exploiting all the dynamic linguistic potential of the web.

Despite the problems we highlighted, we are not pessimists. Indeed, two of the authors of this paper are involved in *WaCky* (*Web as Corpus kool ynitiative*, http://wacky.sslmit.unibo.it/), an informal initiative to rapidly build 1-billion-token proof-of-concept web corpora in three languages and a toolkit to collect, process and exploit such large corpora. However, we believe that – in order to go beyond roadmaps and manifestos, towards the concrete creation of a linguist's search engine – it is extremely important to be aware that this is a very difficult task and that this search engine will not be able to solve all the problems of corpus linguists. Too much optimism may lead to sour disappointment and unfair backlashes towards what is undoubtedly one of the most exciting perspectives in corpus linguistics today.

Notes

1   Whether the web can be viewed as a corpus is currently the object of much debate, since corpora are often defined as collections that have specific design criteria. This is not the topic of this paper (but see Kilgarriff and Grefenstette 2003 for a discussion). We are not interested in web data as an object of study (we will not study web English or Google English, for example); we are also not interested in data mining applications like Turney (2001), or other computational linguistic applications that use web data, as for example machine translation (Way and Gough 2003). We will also not argue for the general usefulness of corpora in linguistic research (see e.g. Meurers 2005).

2   This corpus was compiled as a resource for the creation of a large German dictionary, the *Digitales Wörterbuch der deutschen Sprache.*

3   At the moment, the publicly available portion of the *DWDS-Corpus* is slightly different from this core corpus because of legal problems.

4   For our research question (qualitative description of words with non-medical *-itis*) we do not run into the problem of having to judge grammaticality (since we are looking for occurrences of a word formation process

in a changing process). For many other issues the difference between 'occurrence' and 'grammaticality' would have to be discussed.

5   It is also unlikely that such an option will be added in the future because it is irrelevant (perhaps even detrimental) for the search engines' target audience. The only possibility is to filter documents by their file type, language, or the internet domain they originate from (eg '.edu' vs. '.com' vs. '.org'), none of which can be expected to produce comparable subsets of the web (cf. Ide, Reppen and Suderman (2002), who express surprise at the fact that the language found in the domains '.edu' and '.gov' does not correspond to a balanced sample from general American English).

6   See   http://aixtal.blogspot.com/2005/03/google-snapshot-of-update.html and pages referenced there for an entertaining and illuminating account of these events (accessed on 17 April 2005, but if these pages go off-line, you may still be able to retrieve them from Google's cache).

7   In October 2001, the archive had a size of over 100 terabytes and was growing at a rate of 12 terabytes per month (http://www.archive.org/about/wb_press_kit.php, accessed on 17 April 2005).

8   The second snapshot may even include many pages that were deleted and are no longer accessible, but are still available in Google's cache.

9   Much less for allomorphs – so it is not possible to search for non-medical -*itis* directly.

10   Making use of the fully automatic part-of-speech tagging of these corpora may result in a loss of recall, though, especially when there are systematic tagging errors in the data.

11   Keller and Lapata (2003: 467) estimate that the English part of the web indexed by Google is at least 1000 times larger than the BNC.

12   www.google.com, 17 April 2005.

13   The remaining two pages are a different version of the joke on which the speech is based, and a list of common misspellings of the word *tonsillitis* (www.google.com, 17 April 2005).

14   Tested on 17 April 2005 with the nslookup utility.

References

Aston, G. and L. Burnard (1998), *The BNC Handbook.* Edinburgh: Edinburgh University Press.

Baroni, M. and S. Bernardini (2004), 'BootCaT: bootstrapping corpora and terms from the web', in: *Proceedings of the 4th International Conference on Language Resources and Evaluation (LREC-2004)*, Lisbon.

Broder, A.Z., S.C. Glassman, M.S. Manasse and G. Zweig (1997), 'Syntactic clustering of the web', in: *Sixth International World-Wide Web Conference*, Santa Clara, California.

Elkiss, A. and P. Resnik (2004), *The Linguist's Search Engine User's Guide*. Available at: http://lse.umiacs.umd.edu:8080/lseuser (March 29, 2005).

Fletcher, W.H. (2001), 'Concordancing the web with KWiCFinder', in: *Proceedings of the 3rd North American Symposium on Corpus Linguistics and Language Teaching*, Boston. Draft version at http://kwicfinder.com/ FletcherCLLT2001.pdf (March 22, 2005).

Fletcher, W.H. (2004), 'Facilitating the compilation and dissemination of ad-hoc web corpora', in: G. Aston, S. Bernardini and D. Stewart (eds.) *Corpora and Language Learners*. Amsterdam: Benjamins. 275-302.

Fletcher, W.H. (this volume), 'Concordancing the web: promise and problems, tools and techniques'.

Ghani, R., R. Jones and D. Mladenic (2001), 'Mining the web to create minority language corpora', in: *Proceedings of the 10th International Conference on Information and Knowledge Management (CIKM)*, 2001

Hermes, J. and C. Benden (2005), 'Fusion von Annotation und Präprozessierung als Vorschlag zur Behebung des Rohtextproblems', in: B. Fisseni, H.-C. Schmitz, B. Schröder and P. Wagner (eds.) *Sprachtechnologie, mobile Kommunikation und liguistische Ressourcen. Beiträge zur GLDV-Tagung 2005 in Bonn*. Volume 8 of *Computer Studies in Language and Speech*. Frankfurt: Peter Lang.

Hoffmann, S. (this volume), 'From web-page to mega-corpus: the CNN transcripts'.

Hunston, S. (to appear), 'Collection Strategies and Design Decision', in: A. Lüdeling and M. Kytö (eds.) *Handbook of Corpus Linguistics* (HSK / Handbücher zur Sprach- und Kommunikationswissenschaft / Handbooks of Linguistics and Communication Science). Berlin: Mouton de Gruyter.

Ide, N., R. Reppen and K. Suderman (2002), 'The American National Corpus: more than the web can provide', in: *Proceedings of the Third Language Resources and Evaluation Conference* (LREC), Las Palmas, Spain. 839-844.

Kehoe, A. and A. Renouf (2002), 'WebCorp: applying the web to linguistics and linguistics to the web', in: *Proceedings of the WWW 2002 Conference*, Honolulu.

Keller, F. and M. Lapata (2003), 'Using the web to obtain frequencies for unseen bigrams', *Computational Linguistics*, 29 (3): 459-484.

Kilgarriff, A. (2003), 'Linguistic search engine. Abstract', in: *Proceedings of the Workshop on Shallow Processing of Large Corpora 2003*, Lancaster. 412.

Kilgarriff, A. and G. Grefenstette (2003), 'Introduction to the special issue on the web as corpus', in: *Computational Linguistics*, 29 (3): 333-347.

Lüdeling, A. and S. Evert (2005), 'The emergence of productive non-medical *-itis*. Corpus evidence and qualitative analysis', in: S. Kepser and M. Reis (eds) *Linguistic Evidence. Empirical, Theoretical, and Computational Perspectives*. Berlin: Mouton de Gruyter. 350-370.

Meurers, D. (2005), 'On the use of electronic corpora for theoretical linguistics. Case studies from the syntax of German', in: *Lingua*, 115 (11): 1619-1639.

Rosenbach, A. (this volume), 'Exploring constructions on the web: a case study'.

Sharoff, S. (submitted), *Open-Source Corpora: Using the Net to Fish for Linguistic Data.*

Träger, S. (2005), *Korpora aus dem Netz – Die Erstellung eines Fachkorpus aus Webseiten.* MA Thesis, Humboldt-Universität zu Berlin.

Turney, P. (2001). 'Mining the web for synonyms: PMI-IR versus LSA on TOEFL', in: *Proceedings of the 12th European Conference on Machine Learning (ECML-2001).* Freiburg. 491-502.

Volk, M. (2002), 'Using the web as corpus for linguistic research', in: R. Pajusalu and T. Hennoste (eds.) *Tähendusepüüdja. Hatcher of the Meaning. A Festschrift for Professor Haldur Õim.* Tartu: University of Tartu.

Way, A. and N. Gough (2003), 'wEBMT: developing and validating an example-based machine translation system using the world wide web', *Computational Linguistics*, 29 (3): 421-457.

Concordancing the web: promise and problems, tools and techniques[1]

William H. Fletcher

United States Naval Academy

Abstract

The web is an inexhaustible reservoir of machine-readable texts in most of the world's written languages for compiling corpora or consulting directly as a 'corpus'. This paper first surveys some characteristics of the web and discusses the potential rewards and practical limitations of exploiting the web either directly as a linguistic corpus or to compile corpora. Particular attention is paid to search engines, our gateways to the web. The author then reviews several innovative applications of web data to corpus-related issues. KWiCFinder (KF), developed by the author to help realize the web's promise for language scholars and learners, is described and motivated in detail. KF, readily accessible to novices yet powerful enough for advanced researchers, conducts web searches, retrieves matching online documents, and produces an interactive keyword in context concordance of the search terms. This paper then discusses the pitfalls of 'webidence' in serious research and proposes an initial solution. Finally the author reviews the future of the web for corpus research and application.

1. The nature of the web

1.1 Size, composition and evolution

The world wide web is a wondrous place, with an overwhelming range of languages, content domains and media formats. Just how many web pages there are and how they are distributed by language and genre are not easy questions to answer. The web is constantly changing and growing, and even the best estimates can only approximate its extent and composition. Studies of the nature of the web echo the story of the blind men and the elephant: each one extrapolates from its own samples of this ever-evolving entity taken at different times and by divergent means. The most reliable estimates suggest that the number of publicly-indexable web pages in mid-2005 falls in the range of 10 to 20 billion (i.e. thousand million; see e.g. Gulli and Signorini 2005); some speculate that the actual number is far greater.

These ten billion-plus easily accessible pages are only the tip of the iceberg. To be indexable, a page must allow unrestricted public access, and another publicly accessible page must link to it with a standard HTML tag.[2] Far larger is the vast 'invisible' web of content in databases, which cannot be 'crawled' (explored) by an all-purpose 'robot' (crawler program), only explored by entering relevant queries in a form.[3]

How dynamic and volatile the Webscape has become is revealed in an exhaustive year-long study of 154 web sites from the perspective of a search engine (SE) (Ntoulas et al. 2004). This selection of commercial, government, academic and media sites primarily from the U.S. was judged 'representative' and 'interesting', with content that would rank high in a link popularity scheme like Google's PageRank (see below). The authors' software monitored these sites weekly, averaging 4.4 million web pages (65 GB) per crawl. From their analysis over time, they estimate that new pages[4] appear at the rate of 8% per week. Assuming 4 billion total web pages at the time, they extrapolate their figures to 320 million new pages, or roughly 3.8 terabytes (roughly 10^{12} bytes) of new data for the web as a whole each week. Here 'new' does not mean 'additional' or even 'novel': the total number and size of web pages on these sites stayed relatively constant as old pages retired, and only about 5% of the weekly harvest actually represented new content; 50% of the online content remained available a year later. Far greater volatility was documented in the link structure: each week 25% new links were created, and only 20% of links survived a year. Underscoring the importance of sites like the Web Archives' Wayback Machine,[5] the authors speculate from other evidence that only 20% of all web pages are still accessible a year later. While this investigation addresses characteristics of the bulk of the web in deep web sites, not its breadth, it graphically portrays the rapid radical evolution of the net.

Such establishment web sites may remain stable in size, but there seems no end in sight for the colossal growth in number and sheer text volume of self-published and collaborative web sites like blogs (web logs) and wikis (discussion and documentation sites with multiple authors, like Wikipedia), which often feature thoughtful, well-written content. During the first half of 2005, blog articles indexed by Bloglines.com doubled to over 500 million, and Blog-wise.com lists blogs from 190 different countries.

1.2   Languages on the web

Despite the web's overwhelming size and global expansion, English continues to predominate. Studies by Inktomi and Cyveillance (Moore and Murray 2000) in 2000 conclude that at that time over 85% of publicly-accessible web pages were in English. Around the same time, the *Fifth Study of Language and the Internet* (FUNREDES 2001) documents strong growth among the non-English languages in the proportion of web pages relative to English and observes that the number of web pages in the Romance languages and German was roughly proportional to the population of web users with those languages as native tongue. O'Neill et al. (2003) find that the English-language share of the web had dropped to 72% by 2002. In sharp contrast to the web's first decade, recent years have seen no systematic studies based on large-scale general sampling of actual web pages. This hiatus presumably stems from the tremendous resources required and the transient validity of any results. Nevertheless, current data from the principal SEs provide a rough indication of the web page distribution by language. They suggest that English-language documents comprise around two-thirds of the content indexed in early 2005.[6] The large international SEs' bias toward the major European tongues, especially English, probably inflate their position relative to minority and non-Western languages in these data.

Historically Anglophone users and content have overshadowed other languages on the net, but the trend toward diversity is clear and growing. Statistics compiled by Global Reach illustrate this long-term development. In 1996, four-fifths of the 50 million internet users were native speakers of English. By September 2004, Anglophones constituted only 35% of the world's estimated online population of 801 million.[7] Currently the Language Observatory Project and its Cyber Census Survey aim to raise awareness of the digital divide between both languages and writing systems as well as track the distribution of languages online (Mikami and Suzuki 2005), and UNESCO is actively promoting linguistic and cultural diversity on the web. The phenomenal growth in the non-Anglophone segment of the web is spurring expansion of online resources in other tongues, particularly the smaller non-Western ones, to the benefit of those who investigate, teach and learn these languages.

2.   The web as a corpus for investigating and learning languages

2.1   Why use the web as corpus?

The abundant online texts both tantalize and challenge linguists and other language professionals: the web's self-renewing machine-readable body of documents in scores of languages is easy to access, but difficult to evaluate and exploit efficiently. Yet there are powerful reasons to supplement existing corpora or create new ones with online materials.

-    **Freshness and spontaneity:** the content of compiled corpora ages quickly, but texts on contemporary issues and authentic examples of current, non-standard, or emerging language usage thrive online.
-    **Scope and completeness:** existing corpora may lack a text genre or content domain of interest, or else may not provide sufficient examples of an expression or construction easily located online; some very productive contemporary genres (blogs, wikis, discussion forums...) exist only on the net.
-    **Linguistic diversity:** languages and language varieties for which no corpora have been compiled are accessible online.
-    **Cost and convenience:** the web is virtually free, and desktop computers to retrieve and process web pages are available to researchers and students alike.
-    **Representativeness:** as the proportion of information, communication and entertainment delivered via the net grows, language on and of the web increasingly reflects and enriches our tongue.

2.2   Corpus approaches to the web

The term 'web corpus' has been used for at least three distinct concepts: a static corpus with a web interface, one compiled from web pages, and the body of freely available online documents accessed directly as a corpus. We will disregard the first sense and, following De Schryver (2002), distinguish between 'Web *for* Corpus' (WfC), as a source of machine-readable texts for corpus compilation, and 'Web *as* Corpus' (WaC) consulted directly. A well-known descriptive framework for finding and using information distinguishes three basic approaches: 'hunting', or searching directly for specific information, 'grazing', or using ready-made data sets composed and maintained by an information provider, and 'browsing', or coming across useful information by chance (Hawkins 1996). Each approach can serve as a model for corpus building or utilization. In the following sampler of applications of Wf/aC we use the 'hunting' metaphor for SE-mediated access to the web and 'grazing' for systematic data collection on sites predetermined to be productive.

2.2.1 Hunting

Since the dawn of web civilization, Anne Salzman and Doug Mills (2005) have sent their ESL (English as a second language) students on 'Grammar Safaris'. Guided by their online assignments and armed only with a browser and a SE, these learners hunt down web pages with the structures they are studying, then find examples within the documents and copy and paste them into a word processor document to bring to class for discussion. In a comparable approach, Robb (2003) outlines browser-based techniques for researching English usage with Google.

WaC for language learners can be far more sophisticated than such Info-Stone-Age safaris. The Lexware Culler (Dura 2004)[8] enhances Google search with wildcards, part-of-speech variables and automatically generated morphological variants. It retrieves search engine report pages (SERPs) and displays only the snippets (the 10-20 word document extracts on SERPs) which match the user's potentially more specific query. While snippets may be too brief for some purposes and only a few languages are fully supported, Lexware Culler is a powerful proof-of-concept for WaC. One desktop application, WebLEAP (Web Language Evaluation Assistant Program), even automates the search phase for non-native English writers (Yamanoue et al. 2004). As they enter text, it displays Google SERP snippets of keywords to suggest appropriate wordings. WebLEAP also helps users judge text quality by displaying Google's hit counts of sub-sequences of their writings: rare or missing phrases are likely suspect. Chesñevar and Maguitman (2004) have proposed a comparable but more sophisticated solution yet to be implemented. Finally, Squirrel, a metasearch engine in development, promises to help locate suitable texts for language instruction and practice through automatic document classification and metrics of text difficulty and similarity (Nilsson and Borin 2002; Carlson et al. 2005).

Linguistic researchers also follow the hunting model to exploit the web. To compile a dictionary of regional variants of German, investigators trawled the web to complement the traditionally-compiled corpus materials gleaned from other sources (Bickel 2000, Bickel and Schmidlin 2004).[9] Another study contrasts slogans from the 80s and the 00s as metaphors for their respective times; the former survive only in precompiled corpora, while the latter had to be studied via WaC (Gerbig and Buchtmann 2003). Other innovative solutions based on web searching techniques include using the web to disambiguate natural language confusion sets (Banko and Brill 2001), as a resource for example-based machine translation (Grefenstette 1999; Way and Gough 2003), to identify and collect sets of morphologically related lexemes (Tanguy and Hathout 2002), and to estimate frequencies of bigrams unattested in a given corpus (Keller and Lapata 2003). Kilgarriff and Grefenstette (2003) summarize other applications and issues in Wa/fC.

2.2.2 Grazing

In contrast to the safari model, Jeremy Whistle (1999) has his students graze in a pasture where he controls the kind and quality of the fodder. He has selected texts from the French Ministry of Foreign Affairs' online series 'Label France'. Intended for foreigners learning French, these texts are suitable in both language level and content, and obtaining permission from the ministry to incorporate them into an offline corpus for desktop use entailed no difficulties. Typically commercial sites require prior authorization for offline archiving and analysis. Since 1998 Knut Hofland has used his grazing permit from ten Norwegian newspapers to amass almost 400 million words of journalistic prose, identifying over a thousand 'new' words (names, compounds and loanwords as well as neologisms) daily (http://avis.uib.no/). Similarly, GlossaNet (http://glossa.fltr.ucl. ac.be/) monitors 100 newspapers in 12 languages. Its publicly-accessible database is searchable by structure as well as word form, but unfortunately covers only several days' material.

With their explicit or implicit permission, official web sites (e.g. http://www.un.org/documents/) and text archives (e.g. http://gutenberg.org) lend themselves to unrestricted grazing and archiving for offline use. For example, OPUS (Tiedemann and Nygaard 2004), an open source parallel corpus, collects, linguistically annotates and aligns parallel translated texts from the web, primarily from freely available government sources. To extend the very productive focused grazing model from WfC to WaC, search agents like KWiCFinder can restrict searches to known sites with appropriate content and language to harvest texts for online concordancing or offline use.

3.   Search engines past, present and future

3.1   Search engines and searchers

SEs remain key tools to find online documents to compile a corpus, and effective use of offline corpora requires search skills as well. Understanding how SEs work and how they are evolving to improve lay searchers' satisfaction is essential for serious exploitation of the web as a corpus resource. Commerce drives today's web, with significant consequences for online linguistic research. The large general-purpose search sites we must rely on are business ventures, developed and operated at enormous expense. They provide essential services in exchange for advertising fees, and 'paid positioning' is intended to steer searchers away from more relevant 'natural' search results toward advertisers' sites.

The average searcher's interests and requirements are quite different from those of a language scholar or learner. While the former wants to explore a question exhaustively, typical SE users have a specific content-oriented goal such as locating a specific site, finding valid information on a topic, or discovering a source for a web-mediated product or service. In a seminal paper drawing on his experience at AltaVista, Broder (2002) designates these goals as 'navigational', 'informational' and 'transactional' respectively. A user survey and analysis of actual queries at AltaVista (AV) identified the underlying information needs as 20% navigational, 48% informational and 30% transactional, with some overlap between the latter two categories.

Over the last decade, SEs have evolved away from demanding sophisticated searching skills from the user to boost results' relevance. What Broder calls first-generation web search relied upon on-page information – search term salience in text frequency and formatting – and was best suited to full-text search for informational queries. Epitomized by the string-matching power of AV, this represented the state-of-the art through 1997. Second-generation SEs use off-page web-specific information like PageRank, the link popularity ranking introduced by Google in 1998 as an indicator of page quality. By proving effective for both navigational and informational queries, this approach has made Google the market leader. Since the early 2000s, third-generation approaches have attempted to identify the 'need behind the query' to identify relevant results – while providing targeted advertising. According to Broder, semantic analysis and context determination enable rapidly-evolving SE techniques to improve precision (relevance of search results) for all three kinds of queries.

3.2   Consequences of current trends in web search

Investigations of the typical user's preferences and search behavior have strongly influenced online searching.[10] Information seekers immediately confront the crucial problem of Information Retrieval (IR), maximizing both precision and recall, i.e. ideally matching *only* (precision) and *all* (recall) relevant documents.

Two recent articles, Asadi and Jamali (2004) and Evans et al. (2005), sketch how SEs are evolving to address this problem. Continuing in the IR tradition, first-generation SEs supported sophisticated querying to boost result relevance. While AltaVista once imposed no limits on query length or complexity, complex queries were rare, and up to 25% of those submitted to AV were ill-formed and thus returned no results (Silverstein et al. 1999; Körber 2000). Currently, 80%-90% of all SE queries consist of a single word or very brief phrase, usually a noun, very frequently a proper noun, and in languages where this makes a difference, in the nominative form. Searches for other word classes are rare except in phrases.[11] The predominance of short, simple searches and improvements in result ranking schemes have permitted SEs to abandon underused 'geek-seek' features with their high computational overhead such as nested bracketing, wildcards, long queries and large result datasets, and they have incorporated features like proximity, stemming and fuzzy matching into their standard matching algorithms. Unfortunately for language professionals, it is precisely such complex query tools that facilitate targeted online linguistic research.

The query, search and ranking optimization techniques SEs have adopted can either assist or sabotage a scholar's quest. On the positive side, when vague queries match large numbers of disparate documents, some SEs list frequently co-occurring terms for users to select to boost the relevance of results upon re-query.[12] Geographic relevance is a ranking criterion with both pros and cons: SEs guess the users' location by their computer's IP (Internet Protocol) address, then rank results (and display advertising) by presumed proximity to the searcher. While beneficial for marketing, this technique can interfere when investigating a foreign language. For example, when I seek English-language pages via a Dutch internet provider, some SEs rank hits in the Netherlands higher than for the same search via a provider in the U.S. Automatic geographic ranking can undermine a quest for authoritative examples, but optional specification of the region to search would be useful. Finally, all major SEs now take link popularity into account to rank results. This sacrifices diversity in the search results, biasing them toward large, popular sites.[13]

3.2   The future of web search

What will the next big developments in web search bring? Major SEs will soon capitalize on document clustering and display techniques like those developed by Vivisimo, Kartoo, Ujiko and Grokker, which offer more meaningful ways to represent and relate information to organize SERPs than a ranked listing of matching hits.[14] Labels extracted automatically from the document clusters will provide linguists easily accessible, productive mines for lexical associations. Another SE trend is personalizing the process of searching by basing SERP ranking on analysis of patterns in the user's browsing and searching habits, an approach that could improve relevance for language-oriented (re)search. In addition, industry analysts expect significant growth in 'vertical' search, i.e. specialized SEs dedicated to a single content domain or region, which will allow language professionals to target searches more precisely. Desktop search (DS) applications offered by major SEs are integrating offline and online search, eradicating distinctions between document locations and types of information resources. Thanks to their application programming interfaces (APIs), these technologies have tremendous potential as corpus tools.

In the U.S., the major search sites have become the largest growth sector in the information economy, diverting advertising dollars away from print and other media.[15] For the typical searcher, SERPs from all the major search sites are now roughly comparable in relevance and usefulness, so SEs must compete for market share on other grounds. They will continue to improve search functionality and add non-search features to their sites. Any successful enhancement will be copied by other major sites. In the future, user loyalty will derive more from inertia and dependence on other services (e.g. news, video, audio, e-mail, blogging, online photo albums, discussion group hosting) than from perceived search quality.

While SEs have little incentive to address language researchers' specific needs directly, the innovations and services introduced to boost competitiveness will benefit us ultimately. As they expand global coverage, SEs will spur development of natural language processing technology for a growing range of languages. Academic research across the spectrum of search and information science issues will expand, with opportunities for cross-disciplinary collaboration and funding – and employment for our graduates. Having mastered scaling databases to terabytes of data, SEs can now focus on discovering and relating patterns in those data, leading to new linguistic knowledge.

Efforts to build user loyalty by customizing the search experience are resulting in greater power and flexibility for those whose research rides on public SEs. Free APIs enable rapid incorporation of sophisticated search into special purpose application programs. Currently Yahoo offers the most varied API, supporting not only classical web search, but also context search and term extraction from uploaded texts. One can even restrict results to content with a Creative Commons license (http://creativecommons.org), for which the copyright holder clearly specifies the conditions for reuse. Yahoo's My Web services even allow one to build, search and share online archives of web pages, an avenue to WfC requiring minimal technical sophistication for the user. Microsoft's search API allows one to tweak the settings for ranking and matching factors, reducing SE second-guessing which can degrade result quality for a linguist.

4.   Concordancing the web

4.1   KWiCFinder concordancing search agent

During the web's early history SEs were disappointingly ineffectual. AV's launch in December 1995 changed that – and made me an intensive SE user. While I soon developed techniques and programs to maximize efficiency of downloading and evaluating web pages, few students or colleagues adopted my multitasking methods. To expedite finding and reviewing web pages, I programmed 16-bit KWiCFind, which excerpted documents and produced summary reports with keyword in context (KWiC) display, piloted in 1997. After a complete overhaul, 32-bit KWiCFinder (KF) premiered publicly in Fletcher (1999). It has continued to evolve, and can be downloaded free from http://kwicfinder.com/.

4.1.1 KWiCFinder and AltaVista

When I developed KF, AV offered the most powerful full-text matching capabilities. Since AV was acquired and retired[16] by Yahoo! in the spring of 2004, much of that searching power was lost. I will review those capabilities to highlight essential features for efficient search. 'AV-Y' designates Yahoo's limited successor to AV.

AV indexed all words, even function and other high-frequency words ignored by some other SEs which may be the target of a linguistic investigation. AV-Y continues to indicate which web pages contain these 'stopwords', but does not reliably track the co-text, reducing its usefulness for exact phrase matching. Formerly AV distinguished upper- from lower-case and 'special' characters with diacritics from their 'plain' counterparts, and incorporated language-specific knowledge, such as equivalence of *ä* and *ae, ß* and *ss* in German. Major SEs no longer support search by case, and support for query by special characters is either lacking (Google) or inconsistent on most SEs.[17]

Early advocates of WaC will remember AV for its innovation, power and size. It was the first SE to provide true world-wide multilingual coverage, and it introduced document clustering ('Live Topics'), search by language, web page translation (Babelfish) and integrated desktop search. To support narrowly focused searches AV offered Boolean operators including NEAR (i.e. within 10 words of another search term), nested bracketing, and wildcards,[18] and imposed no limits on query length or complexity. It allowed matching any number of documents (current standard practice limits results to 1000 web pages), crucial for random sampling of the web. AV also set off the first SE size war by indexing 16 million pages at launch, while its competitors' databases boasted fewer than two million entries. Finally, AV enabled the first SE-based study in corpus linguistics (Brekke 2000).

Unfortunately AV's innovative search technology was 'locked inside a dying company' which did not support it properly (Schwartz 2004). After surviving several changes of ownership and reorganization, AV-Y's market share has dropped well below 1%, and it might disappear entirely before long. Fortunately a noble successor to AV has appeared on the horizon. Exalead, a new Web SE based in France, supports all of AV's sophisticated features and much more, even offering regular expression pattern matching and desktop search, with an API in the works. Once again the future appears bright for geek seek!

4.1.2   KWiCFinder's enhancements to web search

For precisely focussed queries, KF offers matching strategies beyond AV's capabilities. AV(-Y) automatically matches a plain character in a search term with any corresponding accented character, and lower-case letters also match their upper-case counterparts (e.g. *a* in a search term matches any of *aáâäàãœåAÁÂÄÀÃÆÅ*). In typical web searches these 'implicit wildcards' ensure that paradigmatic and graphic variants of a given word match a single search term, despite factors like sentence-initial capitalization, required, omitted, or misused diacritics, or alternate spellings due to keyboard limitations.

Wildcards simplify entering search terms, but they also lead to irrelevant matches which must be eliminated individually. To address this problem I implemented single-character wildcards: *?* and *%*, which match either one (no more, no less) or zero to one character, respectively. KF's *'sic'* option forces exact match to plain or lower-case characters in a query; without *sic,* the query *polish* matches *Polish* as well. Similarly, KF complemented AV's NEAR Boolean operator, with BEFORE and AFTER operators and specification of the distance between the terms.[19] Extensions like single-character wildcard and *sic* matching do come at a significant price: KF may have to retrieve, analyze and discard many documents matched by the SE which fail the user's finer criteria.

Completely specifying alternate forms makes searches more efficient than wildcard queries, but entering variants is time consuming. KF introduced 'tamecards', a shorthand for alternate forms. For example, the tamecard query *s[iau]ng[,s,ing]* expands to all forms of the verb *sing: sing, sings, singing, sang, sung* (fortunately the nonsense forms *sangs, sungs, sanging, sunging* yield no false matches). The SE is queried for any of these forms, and only exact matches are processed. Since morphological patterns typically apply to many words, tamecards can be saved and pasted into queries as needed. A further refinement is the 'indexed tamecard', in which every *n*th field in curly braces corresponds to the *n*th field in other sets of curly braces within the same search term, so that *{me,te,se} lav{o,as,a}* expands only to reflexive *me lavo, te lavas, se lava.*

Other KF tamecards address orthographic variants with or without hyphens or apostrophes. Search terms with this punctuation are expanded to alternate forms, so *on-line* matches any of the spellings *on-line, on line,* or *online,* and German *ich hab's* matches both *ich hab's* and *ich habs.* This shorthand is particularly useful for English, where national and individual usage varies, and German, now in transition to a new spelling. German reforms permanently separate many words once written as one, while fusing some former phrases into single words and permitting individual discretion in breaking up compounds. Thanks to KF's tamecards, queries like *kennen-lernen* match both old-style *kennenlernen* and reformist *kennen lernen* with a single entry.

Finally KF introduced 'inclusion' and 'exclusion' criteria, terms and conditions either to target a specific content domain or to disqualify documents from consideration. Such terms are added to the SE query to focus a search, but do not appear in KF's KWiC concordance report. Other selection criteria include date, internet domain (a rough guide to country of origin), as well as host, i.e. a specific web server, and URL.

4.1.3 KWiCFinder concordance reports

While processing a query, KF retrieves up to 20 documents a minute, excerpts them and produces a concordance of the key search terms in context, along with information about the source documents. The search reports are encoded in XML (eXtensible Markup Language) and offer a choice of interactive display formats through a set of XSLT (eXtensible Stylesheet Language Transformation) stylesheets. To display a useful report, KF transforms this XML with an XSLT 'stylesheet' to select which information to show, insert text labels and format the result as an HTML document for browser display. To change the display layout or language, a different stylesheet is applied to the same XML data. With knowledge of XSLT and browser scripting techniques, an end user can create new report formats or apply other stylesheets to annotate, merge, prune, or restructure XML search reports.

JavaScript and dynamic HTML enable substantial interactivity in KF's classical KWiC display reports. The user can specify criteria for re-sorting concordances and tallying forms in the co-text. Searching for specific forms tallies and highlights them, and buttons provide rapid navigation between highlighted forms. Concordance lines can be annotated or deleted. Any user modifications to the KF report can be saved as a browser-based stand-alone interactive concordance. This approach points the way to a light-weight cross-platform solution for learner concordancing.

4.1.4 KWiCFinder and web as / for corpus

While the web is no corpus in the classical sense, I regularly access it with KF to research linguistic questions and to develop language instruction materials. Fletcher (2004a) illustrates how with many concrete examples. Concordancing techniques are also beneficial at the text level, to evaluate content and form of web pages matching a query.

KF can also compile an ad-hoc corpus from the web for offline analysis and use. For example, to build a sample web corpus I recently ran up to 20 independent KF searches simultaneously on a home broadband connection. In one morning KF downloaded over 22 thousand web pages (9 GB of HTML) totaling 115 million words and saved them on my hard drive in text format. With techniques and software described elsewhere (Fletcher 2004b), I eliminated 'uninteresting' and duplicate documents, leaving a 38 million word corpus for further processing into a database of *n*-grams and phrase-frames with full-text KWiC concordances available on demand.[20] While this project took almost a day, a targeted corpus of a few million words can be completed in less than an hour.

4.2   WebKWiC

For searchers who prefer not to install KF I developed WebKWiC (WK),[21] a fully browser-based JavaScript application. It takes advantage of Google's 'Document from Cache' feature to automate web page retrieval and markup: Google serves up copies of web pages from its archives, highlighting the search terms with color codes. WK retrieves these cached pages in batches, adding buttons for easy navigation among highlighted terms and windows. WK provides an interface for special character input and gives essential search options greater prominence than does Google's original page. Google is an ideal partner for an entry-level search agent like WK. Its straightforward approach to advanced search with 'implicit Booleans' is easy to learn and widely imitated, so users either come with or acquire readily transferable skills. Since Google indexes major non-Western European / non-Latin orthography languages, WK meets needs which KF does not address.[22]

5.   Webidence as linguistic evidence

We all know the limitations of online information: there is too much ephemeral content of dubious reliability; journalistic, commercial and personal texts of unknown authorship and authority abound; assertions are represented as established fact, and details of sources and research methodology are documented haphazardly at best. For linguistic research even more caution is essential. The internet domains in a URL ('.ca', '.uk', '.de', '.jp', '.com', '.net' etc.) are at best a rough guide to provenance. Furthermore, many web pages are mainly fragments – titles and captions, with the occasional imperative ('click here', 'buy now'). As the lingua franca of the digital frontier, English is both the target and source of contamination: non-Anglophones often translate their web pages into Info-Age pidgin English while fusing creolized web English into texts in their native tongue. Similarly, searches for linguistic examples can lead to work by learners with imperfect mastery of the language or to baffling machine translations. In many online forums, careless or cryptic language and sloppy spelling prevail. With its frenetic pace of development, the web typically values content creation above perfection and tolerates ill-formed language – anyone upset by this is but a click away from relief.

5.1   Search engines as gateways to webidence

In light of these pitfalls we need 'Standards of Webidence' to guide the selection and documentation of online language for linguistic research. We also must understand and beware of SEs' limitations. In particular, hit counts reported by a SE give only a general indication; these numbers cannot prove the prevalence or appropriateness of a given formulation.[23] SEs warn not to trust their figures, and with good reason: generating SERPs receives priority over estimating hit counts, and the exact form and order of search terms affects those counts. For several reasons numbers for the same or equivalent query easily vary up to an order of magnitude.[24] Moreover, SEs report document count, i.e. the number of web pages matching a query, not the actual number of occurrences on those pages. A single document may contain alternate usages, thus appearing in multiple counts, and numerous pages propagate verbatim a formulation originating in a single document, thus multiplying its apparent frequency. Some spurious or unusual usages are traceable to a single source. Fletcher (2004b) evaluates several approaches to filtering out 'noise' resulting from highly repetitive, virtually identical and primarily fragmentary documents.

SE indexing and ranking practices also affect the usefulness of web data. For example, Google proudly states 'Searching 8,058,044,651 web pages', but it does not index all the text on so many pages. For a sizeable subset, analysis is limited to the hyperlink text and target. Moreover, following standard practice, only the first 100,000 words are indexed on any page. Since major SEs provide access to only the first thousand hits, the order of search results is crucial. Exact ranking criteria and weighting are continually tweaked proprietary secrets, but prevalent practice relies heavily on link popularity – the number and reliability of links to a web page, indicative of authority and quality – and term salience expressed as TF/IDF, a metric derived from the ratio of the frequency of a search term (TF) in a given document to the inverse of the total number of documents in which it occurs (IDF). Yahoo and MSN apparently assign relatively more weight to term salience and less to link popularity than Google. For some purposes, however, a linguist requires texts in which a term simply occurs without being salient, as in this example. Recently a Dutch colleague asked what abilities one can *hone* metaphorically in English besides *skills*. The BNC offers only a handful of examples, so I went to the web. The first thousand hits reminded me that in the commercial world *hones* collate with *knives* and *chisels*, *brakes* and *engines*, *stone* and *tile*, but few *abilities* appeared. Repetition made variants of *hone* salient on pages offering such products and services; I had exhausted my quota with few metaphoric results. In contrast, my randomly compiled web corpus (4.1.4) has more relevant examples, and almost none of the concrete use.

5.2   Verifiability: preserving and sharing webidence

Verifiability is a cornerstone of responsible research: evidence for any claim or conclusion must be subject to inspection and alternate analysis by other research-ers. The web's volatility diminishes its credibility for research. Not only do hit counts vary widely due to non-linguistic factors, but the same query on the same search site can return different sets of SERPs, not only from different places or at different times, but even during a single user session. In the best case, the laws of large numbers permit *comparable* results for frequent search terms, but the composition of the actual web pages matched can be quite different.

No web search data are truly verifiable by other investigators, which is one reason why I propose a Web Corpus Archive (Fletcher 2004a). A few principles would represent progress toward that goal for WaC research. Investigators should make all webidence accessible to others for verification or reuse, preferably online. If SE hit counts are used, multiple SEs should be queried with various search term orders, and the queries should be rerun at several week intervals and on different regional versions of the SE to ensure stable counts and tolerable variance; the corresponding SERPs would be retained as webidence. Web pages on which an analysis is based must be preserved and shared, as should other matching pages.

KF facilitates responsible online linguistic scholarship in several ways. One can review large numbers of documents and concordances efficiently. Each keyword is displayed in sufficient context to evaluate its relevance and validity, and the total number of occurrences can be tallied. Web pages can be saved locally for further analysis or independent verification of results. Complementary corpus tools can process these web pages to eliminate repetitive or redundant documents, to analyze lexical patterns, and to compile databases for further exploration and deployment on the web.

6.   The future of the web for / as corpus

Recent developments inspire considerable optimism about the prospects for Wa/fC. Major SEs are introducing services and features that lower the threshold for simple web concordancing and archiving for e.g. translators and language teachers. New SEs even improve on the level of search sophistication we once enjoyed with AV. Thanks to powerful free tools for customizing every aspect of crawling, analyzing, searching and archiving web documents, Wa/fC linguists can focus on their research, not on studying internet protocols and developing software from scratch. At least two research groups – the University of Central England's RDUES WebCorp and the WaCky consortium organized by the University of Bologna-Forlì's SSMILT – are working toward multi-language SEs for linguists, and other Wa/fC projects are underway. The interests of corpus and computational linguists are intersecting in novel ways with those of computer and information scientists, suggesting broader opportunities for fruitful collaboration and funding. As practices evolve to ensure the integrity of web data, it will become fully accepted as a legitimate source for linguistic research. This explosion of activity in Wa/fC a decade after the web's Big Bang promises ongoing innovation and ample rewards as we apply this boundless resource to our endeavors.

Notes

1   Portions of this paper are based on an earlier paper on pedagogical applications of the web as a corpus available online (Fletcher 2001). It was substantially revised and updated in spring 2005 during a sabbatical at the

Radboud University of Nijmegen. The author gratefully acknowledges the RU Language and Speech research group's generous hospitality and the Naval Academy Research Council's partial support of this research.

2   *Indexable* is distinct from *publicly accessible:* search engines (SEs) 'crawl' the web by following links from known sites to pages not yet in their database, first downloading then extracting links from these new pages and following those new links. A site with no incoming links from known sites will never be found, so its pages are not indexable even if publicly accessible. Wikipedia gives an overview of SEs and crawling, and Chakrabarti (2002) demystifies and details their workings.

3   Ntoulas et al. (2005) propose a framework for generating queries to mine deep-web sites which downloads up to 90% of 'hidden' content.

4   From the SE perspective of their paper the authors count *any* changed page as a new page, even if only a single word or the URL changes.

5   The Web Archive (http://web.archive.org) preserves over 40 billion web pages from 1996 on for public access. While not a comprehensive repository, it affords a glimpse into the web's evolution over this period. The Archive also helps preserve and distribute audio, video and print materials.

6   Currently Google, Yahoo, MSN, and Teoma are the only large, well-established independent SEs; others either are smaller or use other providers' databases. Based on the proportion of total page hits reported by leading search engines for common numerals and dates to the number of English pages with those numerals, the percentage of pages in English appeared to fall in the range 60-70% in June 2005. Grefenstette and Nioche (2000) offer a methodologically interesting study estimating the number of words (not web pages) online in various European languages, updated by Kilgarriff and Grefenstette (2003).

7   Data from Global Reach (2004) track the percentages of internet users by language over the period 1996-2004. Other studies of online populations include http://www.internetworldstats.com/ and the forecast of one billion users in 2005 (http://www.c-i-a.com/pr0904.htm).

8   http://82.182.103.45/lexware/concord/culler.html.

9   Description of the project approach and the resulting 'Wörterbuch Nationale Varianten des Deutschen' online at http://www.germa.unibas.ch/deusem/forsch/Prolex/prolex.de.html.

10 Relevant user studies include Silverstein et al. (1999), Körber (2000), and Spink and Jansen's summary article and book-length synthesis (2004a, b). For a recent critical review of the literature see Martzoukou 2004. Bates

(2002) contextualizes information seeking in humankind's behavior and evolution.

11   http://searchenginewatch.com/facts/article.php/2156041 links to sites listing popular query terms; some display sample queries as they are being processed by SEs. http://wordtracker.com delivers a weekly list from various sources by e-mail, and similar services exist for other languages as well.

12   For example, to help users focus queries, AlltheWeb offers lists of terms to select for inclusion or exclusion in a refined query. Similarly, Google allows one to search for pages related to a given hit, and when it finds few hits for a query, it may propose a more frequent alternative with 'Did you mean to search for _____?'

13   Pandey et al. (2005) propose to 'shuffle the stacked deck' by mixing a random sample into popularity-ranked results so less familiar sites gain exposure. For linguistic research the ability to tweak popularity weighting would be most useful.

14   Document clustering discovers features shared by web pages and groups them together by those features; this is distinct from classifying documents by categories determined *a priori*. Additional clustering resources: Carrot2 (http://sourceforge.net/projects/carrot2/, demonstrator at http://carrot.cs.put.poznan.pl/), an open-source search results clustering framework; SnakeT, a personal meta-search engine which clusters on the basis of snippets from SERPs (Ferragina and Gulli 2005).

15   Google's and Yahoo's revenue grew from $2.5 billion in 2003 to $6.5 billion in 2004, and at this writing the total value of Google's stock is far greater than that of any other 'media' company, even though it produces no original content.

16   While the site http://altavista.com still exists, it now uses the Yahoo! search database with greatly reduced full-text search capabilities. Ray et al. (1996) portray the exciting early days at AltaVista.

17   http://forums.searchenginewatch.com/showthread.php?t=6013 explores special-character matching issues exhaustively.

18   Google does offer two kinds of wildcard matching: 'wildwords', where * can match any word in a phrase, e.g. *the * * of* matches 'the lower house of' etc.; the 'synonym' operator ~, which matches alternate forms and semantically similar words, e.g. *~labor* matches 'labour' as well, and *~nation* also matches 'nations' and 'national'.

19   When AV still supported NEAR, it also had the undocumented ability to match pairs of terms within *any* specified range, and it supported BEFORE and AFTER as well, either alone or in combination with proximity.

20   To accelerate web corpus compilation KWiCFinder can skip generating a search concordance and simply download and save matching pages. Free ancillary programs help weed out useless pages: kfWinnow automatically eliminates very short and very long pages (<500 or >20,000 words) and those with very low or high average number of words per paragraph (<10 or >500); kfReviewFiles presents a quick peek at these discarded pages to identify possible keepers; kfNgram compiles lists of frequent words and phrases in the texts; kfNgramDB is a database builder and browser for sophisticated analysis and retrieval of the texts and wordlists.

21   Cf. http://kwicfinder.com/WebKWiC/.

22   Fletcher (2004a) compares and discusses alternatives to KWiCFinder in depth.

23   It is unclear how many linguists understand these limitations. Postings in scholarly forums like Corpora List and Linguist List citing evidence from SE hit counts rarely indicate whether the poster has verified a substantial number of the hits or is even aware of the limitations of this method.

24   Véronis (2005) documents striking discrepancies in Google hit counts for equivalent queries. Factors in such variation are detailed in numerous threads on http://forums. searchenginewatch.com/.

25   Links verified May 2005; those marked with * are no longer at the URL given, but still can be found on the Wayback Machine http://web.archive.org.

References[25]

Asadi, S. and H.R. Jamali (2004), 'Shifts in search engine development: a review of past, present and future trends in research on search engines', *Webology*, 1 (2), Article 6. http://www.webology.ir/2004/v1n2/a6.html.

Banko, M. and E. Brill (2001), 'Scaling to Very Very Large Corpora for Natural Language Disambiguation', ACL 2001. http://research.microsoft.com/~brill/Pubs/ACL2001.pdf.

Bates, M.J. (2002), 'Toward an integrated model of information seeking and searching', *Fourth International Conference on Information Needs, Seeking and Use in Different Contexts*, Lisbon, Portugal, September 11-13, 2002. http://www.gseis.ucla.edu/faculty/bates/articles/info_SeekSearch-i-030329.html.

Bickel, H. (2000), 'Das Internet als Quelle für die Variationslinguistik', in: A. Häcki Buhofer (ed.) *Vom Umgang mit sprachlicher Variation. Soziolinguistik, Dialektologie, Methoden und Wissenschaftsgeschichte. Festschrift zum 60. Geburtstag von Heinrich Löffler.* Tübingen: Francke. 111-124. http://www.germa.unibas.ch/seminar/whoiswho/Publikationen/Variationsling.pdf.

Bickel, H. and R. Schmidlin (2004), 'Ein Wörterbuch der nationalen und regionalen Varianten der deutschen Standardsprache', in: T. Studer and G. Schneider (eds.) *Deutsch als Fremdsprache und Deutsch als Zweitsprache in der Schweiz, Bulletin valsasla*, 75: 99-122. http://www.germa.unibas.ch/seminar/whoiswho/Publikationen/BickelSchmidlin.pdf.

Brekke, M. (2000), 'From the BNC toward the cybercorpus: a quantum leap into chaos?', in: J.M. Kirk (ed.) *Corpora Galore: Analyses and Techniques in Describing English. Papers from the Nineteenth International Conference on English Language Research on Computerised Corpora (ICAME 1998).* Amsterdam and Atlanta: Rodopi. 227-247.

Broder, A. (2002), 'A taxonomy of web search', *ACM SIGIR Forum Archive*, 36 (2): 3-10. http://www.acm.org/sigir/forum/F2002/broder.pdf.

Carlson, L., M. Grönroos and S. Lemmilä (2005), 'Squirrel Two: Experiments on a metasearch engine for CALL', *NODALIDA 15*, Joensuu, Finland, 20-21 May 2005. http://phon.joensuu.fi/nodalida/abstracts/28.shtml.

Chakrabarti, S. (2002), *Mining the Web: Analysis of Hypertext and Semi-Structured Data.* San Francisco: Morgan Kaufmann.

Chesñevar, C.I. and A.G. Maguitman (2004), 'An argumentative approach to assessing natural language usage based on the web corpus', *Proceedings of the European Conference on Artificial Intelligence (ECAI).* Valencia, Spain, 22-27 August 2004. http://fermat.eps.udl.es/~cic/2004/2004_ecai.pdf.

De Schryver, G.-M. (2002), 'Web for / as corpus: a perspective for the African languages', *Nordic Journal of African Studies*, 11 (2): 266-282. http://tshwanedje.com/publications/webtocorpus.pdf.

Dura, E. (2004), 'Concordances of Snippets', *Workshop 'Enhancing and using electronic dictionaries', COLING.* Geneva, August 2004. http://82.182.103.45/Lexware/English/publications/coling04.pdf.

Evans, M.P., R. Newman, T. Putnam and D.J.M. Griffiths (2005), 'Search adaptations and the challenges of the web', *IEEE Internet Computing*, 9 (3): 19-26. http://doi.ieeecomputersociety.org/10.1109/MIC.2005.65.

Ferragina, P. and A. Gulli (2005), 'A personalized search engine based on web-snippet hierarchical clustering', *Proceedings of WWW 2005*, 10-14 May 2005, Chiba, Japan. 801-810. http://www2005.sfc.keio.ac.jp/cdrom/docs/p801.pdf.

Fletcher, W.H. (1999), 'Winnowing the web with KWiCFinder', *CALICO*, Miami University of Ohio, Oxford, OH, 5-9 June 1999.

Fletcher, W.H. (2001), 'Concordancing the web with KWiCFinder', *American Association for Applied Corpus Linguistics, Third North American Symposium on Corpus Linguistics and Language Teaching*, Boston, MA, 23-25 March 2001. http://kwicfinder.com/FletcherCLLT2001.pdf.

Fletcher, W.H. (2004a), 'Facilitating the compilation and dissemination of ad-hoc web corpora', in: G. Aston, S. Bernardini and D. Stewart (eds.), *Corpora and Language Learners*. Amsterdam: John Benjamins. *Studies in Corpus Linguistics* 17. 271-300. http://kwicfinder.com/FletcherTaLC5.pdf.

Fletcher, W.H. (2004b), 'Making the web more useful as a source for linguistic corpora', in: U. Connor and T.A. Upton (eds.) *Applied Corpus Linguistics. A Multidimensional Perspective.* Amsterdam and New York: Rodopi. *Language and Computers - Studies in Practical Linguistics* 52. 191-206. http://kwicfinder.com/AAACL2002whf.pdf.

Fletcher, W.H. (2005), 'Towards an independent search engine for linguists: issues and solutions', *Symposium La Rete come Corpus*, University of Bologna, Forlì, Italy, 14 January 2005. http://kwicfinder.com/WaCForli 2005-01.pdf.

Gerbig, A. and P. Buchtmann (2003), 'Vom 'Waldsterben' zu 'Geiz ist Geil': Figurativer Sprachgebrauch im Paradigmenwechsel von der ökologischen zur ökonomischen Handlungsmotivation', *metaphorik.de* 04, 97-114. http://www.metaphorik.de/04/gerbigbuchtmann.pdf.

Global Reach (2004), *Global Internet Statistics (by Language)*. http://global-reach.biz/globstats/.

Grefenstette, G. (1999), 'The world wide web as a resource for example-based machine translation tasks', *ASLIB, Translating and the Computer 21*, London, Nov 10-11, 1999.

Grefenstette, G. and J. Nioche (2000), 'Estimation of English and non-English language use on the www', *RIAO 2000*, Paris, 12-14 April 2000. http://arxiv.org/ftp/cs/papers/0006/0006032.pdf.

Gulli, A. and A. Signorini (2005), 'The indexable web is more than 11.5 billion pages', *WWW 2005*, May 10-14, 2005, Chiba, Japan. http://www2005.sfc.keio.ac.jp/cdrom/docs/p902.pdf.

Hawkins, D.T. (1996), 'Hunting, grazing, browsing: a model for online information retrieval', *ONLINE* 20 (1). *http://www.onlinemag.net/JanOL/hawkins.html.

Ho, J. (2005), 'Hyperlink obsolescence in scholarly online journals', *Journal of Computer-Mediated Communication*, 10 (3), article 15. http://jcmc.indiana.edu/vol10/issue3/ho.html.

Keller, F. and M. Lapata (2003), 'Using the web to obtain frequencies for unseen bigrams', *Computational Linguistics*, 29 (3): 459-484. http://acl.ldc.upenn.edu/J/J03/J03-3005.pdf.

Kilgariff, A. and G. Grefenstette (2003), 'Introduction to the special issue on the web as corpus', *Computational Linguistics*, 29 (3): 333-347. http://acl.ldc. upenn.edu/J/J03/J03-3001.pdf.

Körber, S. (2000), *Suchmuster erfahrener und unerfahrener Suchmaschinennutzer im deutschsprachigen World Wide Web. Ein Experiment.* Unpublished master's thesis, Westfälische Wilhelms-Universität Münster, Germany.

Martzoukou, K. (2004), 'A review of web information seeking research: considerations of method and foci of interest', *Information Research*, 10 (2), paper 215. http://InformationR.net/ir/10-2/paper215.html.

Mikami, Y. and I. Suzuki (2005), 'The language observatory project and its experiment: Cyber Census Survey. Crossing the digital divide', *SCALLA 2004.* http://www.elda.org/en/proj/scalla/SCALLA2004/mikami.pdf.

Moore, A. and B.H. Murray (2000), *Sizing the Internet.* 10 July 2000, Arlington, VA: Cyveillance, Inc. *http://www.cyveillance.com/resources/7921S_ Sizing_the_Internet.pdf.

Nilsson, K. and L. Borin (2002), 'Living off the land: the web as a source of practice texts for learners of less prevalent languages', *Proceedings of LREC 2002, Third International Conference on Language Resources and Evaluation*, Las Palmas: ELRA. 411-418. *http://fenix.ling.uu.se/lars/ pblctns/lrec2002.pdf.

Ntoulas, A., J. Cho and C. Olston (2004), 'What's new on the web? The evolution of the web from a search engine perspective', *WWW 2004*, ACM Press. 1-12. http://www2004.org/proceedings/docs/1p1.pdf.

Ntoulas, A., P. Zerfos and J. Cho (2005), 'Downloading textual hidden web content through keyword queries', *Proceedings of the Joint Conference on Digital Libraries* (JCDL), June 2005. http://oak.cs.ucla.edu/~cho/papers/ ntoulas-hidden.pdf.

Pandey, S., S. Roy, C. Olston, J. Cho, S. Chakrabarti (2005), 'Shuffling a stacked deck: the case for partially randomized ranking of search engine results', *Proceedings of 31st International Conference on Very Large Databases (VLDB)*, September 2005. http://oak.cs.ucla.edu/~cho/papers/cho-shuffle. pdf.

O'Neill, E.T., B.F. Lavoie and R. Bennett (2003), 'Trends in the evolution of the public web 1998 – 2002', *D-Lib Magazine*, 9 (4) (April). http://www.dlib. org/dlib/april03/lavoie/04lavoie.html.

Ray, E.J., D.S. Ray and R. Seltzer (1996), *The AltaVista Search Revolution.* Berkeley, CA: Osborne-McGraw-Hill.

Robb, T. (2003), 'Google as a quick 'n' dirty corpus tool', *TESL-EJ*, 7 (2), on the internet. http://www-writing.berkeley.edu/TESL-EJ/ej26/int.html.

Salzmann, A. and D. Mills (2005), *LinguaCenter Grammar Safari.* http://www. iei.uiuc.edu/student_grammarsafari.html.

Schwartz, B. (2004), 'Search memories – live from SES San Jose', *Search EngineWatch 'SEM Related Organizations & Events'*, 8 May 2004. http://forums.searchenginewatch.com/showthread.php?t=949.

Silverstein, C., M. Henzinger, H. Marais and M. Moricz (1999), 'Analysis of a very large web search engine query log', *SIGIR Forum*, 33 (1): 6-12. http://www.acm.org/sigir/forum/F99/Silverstein.pdf.

Spink, A. and B.J. Jansen (2004a), 'A study of web search trends', *Webology*, 1 (2), article 4. http://www.webology.ir/2004/v1n2/a4.html.

Spink, A. and B.J. Jansen (2004b), *Web Search: Public Searching of the Web. Information Science and Knowledge Management* 6. Dordrecht: Kluwer.

Tanguy, L. and N. Hathout (2002), 'Webaffix: un outil d'acquisition morphologique dérivationnelle à partir du web', *TALN 2002*, Nancy, 24-27 June 2002. http://www.sciences.univ-nantes.fr/info/perso/permanents/daille/TALN/AC_0072.txt.html.

Tiedemann, J. and L. Nygaard (2004), 'The OPUS corpus - parallel & free', *Proceedings of the Fourth International Conference on Language Resources and Evaluation (LREC'04)*, Lisbon, Portugal, May 26-28. http://stp.ling.uu.se/~joerg/paper/opus_lrec04.pdf.

Véronis, J. (2005), 'Web: Google's missing pages: mystery solved?', Blog entry 8 February 2005. http://aixtal.blogspot.com/2005/02/web-googles-missing-pages-mystery.html.

Way, A. and N. Gough (2003), 'wEBMT: developing and validating an EBMT system using the world wide web', *Computational Linguistics*, 29 (3): 421-457. http://www.computing.dcu.ie/~away/PUBS/2003/way02.pdf.

Whistle, J. (1999), 'Concordancing with students using an "Off-theWeb" corpus', *ReCALL*, 11 (2): 74-80. http://www.eurocall-languages.org/recall/pdf/rvol11no2.pdf.

Yamanoue, T., T. Minami, I. Ruxton and W. Sakurai (2004), 'Learning usage of English KWICly with WebLEAP/DSR', *Proceedings of the 2nd International Conference on Information Technology for Application* (ICITA 2004). http://attend.it.uts.edu.au/icita05/CDROM-ICITA04/papers/14-6.pdf.

Webcorp: an integrated system for web text search

Antoinette Renouf, Andrew Kehoe and Jayeeta Banerjee

The University of Central England, Birmingham

Abstract

The web has unique potential to yield large-volume data on up-to-date language use, obvious shortcomings notwithstanding. Since 1998, we have been developing a tool, WebCorp, to allow corpus linguists to retrieve raw and analysed linguistic output from the web. Based on internal trials and user feedback gleaned from our site (http://www. webcorp.org.uk/), we have established a working system which supports thousands of regular users world-wide. Many of the problems associated with the nature of web text have been accommodated, but problems remain, some due to the non-implementation of standards on the Internet, and others to reliance on commercial search engines, which mediation slows up average WebCorp response time and places constraints on linguistic search. To improve WebCorp performance, we are in the process of creating a tailored search engine, an infrastructure in which WebCorp will play an integral and enhanced role.

In this paper, we shall give a brief description of WebCorp, the nature and level of its current functionality, the linguistic and procedural problems in web text search which remain; and the benefits of replacing the commercial search engine with tailored web-search architecture.

1.   Introduction

The Research and Development Unit for English Studies at the University of Central England, Birmingham is a multi-disciplinary team of linguists, software engineers and statisticians which works to understand and describe language in use, and to apply this knowledge. The language in question has primarily been English, and the applications have primarily been in the fields of information extraction, retrieval and management, but we are also mindful of the needs of linguistic researchers, language teachers and learners, both in English and in other languages.

We regard language as a changing phenomenon, and we thus began early on to build systems to accumulate and process journalistic text chronologically, to complement existing finite, synchronic corpora. When web text emerged in the nineties, we had been analysing evolving, particularly neologistic, language use in very large textual databases for almost a decade. We were thus well placed to appreciate the advantage of web-based text over the increasingly historical entities which stand as representatives of 'current English' – web text would allow the fine-tuning of the picture of what is current usage, providing access to aspects and domains of language which were missing from corpora. Web text presented a serendipitous opportunity, and its many well-rehearsed shortcomings were outweighed by the advantages it offered of access to free, plentiful, up-dated and up-to-date data.

2.   Current WebCorp architecture

The WebCorp project was an experiment to see whether we could develop a system to extract linguistic data from web text efficiently and present a quality of raw and analysed linguistic output that was similar to that derived from finite corpora and which met users' expressed needs. In 1998, we placed a simple prototype web search feedback tool on our website, which requested and received user impressions and requirements. By 2000, when funding allowed full-scale system development to commence, we already had a good idea of the functionality we were interested in providing. The basic tool was expanded to provide a range of functions, within the limits imposed by our dependence on commercial search engines and the processing capacity of our servers. WebCorp architecture as it currently stands is represented in the diagram in figure 1, which also explains the search and analysis routine.

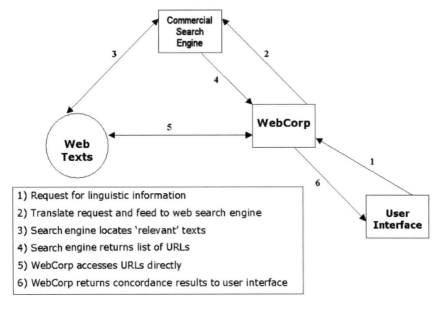

1) Request for linguistic information
2) Translate request and feed to web search engine
3) Search engine locates 'relevant' texts
4) Search engine returns list of URLs
5) WebCorp accesses URLs directly
6) WebCorp returns concordance results to user interface

Figure 1:   Diagram of current WebCorp architecture

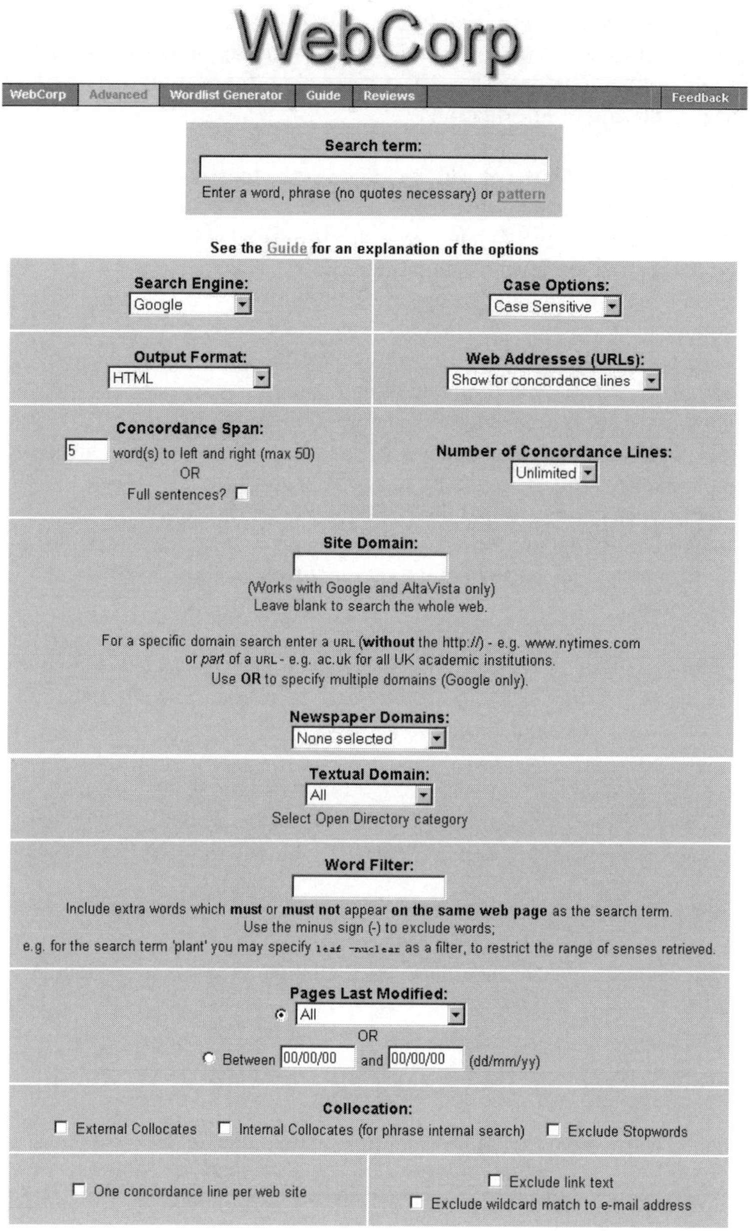

WebCorp

| WebCorp | Advanced | Wordlist Generator | Guide | Reviews | | Feedback |

Search term:

Enter a word, phrase (no quotes necessary) or pattern

See the Guide for an explanation of the options

Search Engine:
Google

Case Options:
Case Sensitive

Output Format:
HTML

Web Addresses (URLs):
Show for concordance lines

Concordance Span:
5 word(s) to left and right (max 50)
OR
Full sentences? ☐

Number of Concordance Lines:
Unlimited

Site Domain:

(Works with Google and AltaVista only)
Leave blank to search the whole web.

For a specific domain search enter a URL (**without** the http://) - e.g. www.nytimes.com
or *part* of a URL - e.g. ac.uk for all UK academic institutions.
Use **OR** to specify multiple domains (Google only).

Newspaper Domains:
None selected

Textual Domain:
All
Select Open Directory category

Word Filter:

Include extra words which **must** or **must not** appear **on the same web page** as the search term.
Use the minus sign (-) to exclude words;
e.g. for the search term 'plant' you may specify leaf -nuclear as a filter, to restrict the range of senses retrieved.

Pages Last Modified:
⦿ All
OR
○ Between 00/00/00 and 00/00/00 (dd/mm/yy)

Collocation:
☐ External Collocates   ☐ Internal Collocates (for phrase internal search)   ☐ Exclude Stopwords

☐ One concordance line per web site

☐ Exclude link text
☐ Exclude wildcard match to e-mail address

Figure 2: WebCorp user interface: http://rdues.uce.ac.uk/wcadvanced.html

The WebCorp user interface (http://rdues.uce.ac.uk/wcadvanced.html) is shown in figure 2. As indicated, WebCorp finds words, phrases and discontinuous patterns through word and wildcard search. It currently offers the following series of options for the filtering of information:

-   a choice of 5 search engines (of which Google is the most-used)
-   upper and lower case distinction
-   site domain to help to specify language variety – can be a specific site (e.g. news.bbc.co.uk) or a top level domain (e.g. '.uk')
-   a choice of 4 newspaper site groups: UK broadsheet, UK tabloid, French news, US news
-   a choice of textual domain based on the Open Directory categorisation, to control language register and probable topic range
-   selection of data-subset according to last date of modification
-   restriction of the number of instances of an item to one per site, to avoid domination and skewing of results by one author or source
-   exclusion of hyperlink text, email addresses and other distracters
-   use of a word filter, to improve recall or precision in research results, by allowing or suppressing particular words occurring in the same text as the main search term.

The basic output format takes the form of concordance lines, in each of which the key term is a one-click link back to its full text of origin. The interface also allows the specification of output format in relation to:

-   mark-up and layout (HTML or plain text, with or without KWIC layout)
-   web addresses (URLs); whether these should be shown in every or any case
-   concordance span, in numbers of words to left and right, or as sentence output
-   total number of concordance lines

The current functionality of the interface will be illustrated in more details in sections 3 and 4.

3.   Types of linguistic information currently retrievable by WebCorp

WebCorp yields large amounts of information about current language use to supplement what is in conventional corpora, but it also opens a window on text domains and types which are not available in corpora, including those which have evolved through its very existence, such as chat room talk. For linguists and language teachers, what WebCorp is uniquely able to provide includes neologisms and coinages, newly-voguish terms, rare or possibly obsolete terms, rare or possibly obsolete constructions, and phrasal variability and creativity, and we shall demonstrate this facility with a few examples.

3.1   New coinages

A coinage which emerged in web-based newspaper text in July 2005 but which will not be encountered in designed corpora for some time is the term *deferred success*. This item of political correctness was coined by a UK teaching union official in 2005, to replace the word *fail* as a verdict on children's school work. An extract of the linguistic information derivable from web text is presented in figure 3, which clearly shows the usage patterns and meaning of the word, and indicates that whilst it is too early to see the routine productive inflection and modification of the basic lexeme that would reveal its assimilation into the language, it is already being used creatively to humorous ends (see lines 3-5), and applied allusively in different, equally topical contexts (6-7).

1.   The word 'fail' should be deleted from the school vocabulary and replaced with the term '**deferred success**', according to a group of teachers.
2.   Ms Beattie had in mind when proposing to a teachers' conference that the word "fail" be jettisoned from the educational lexicon, and replaced with "**deferred success**".
3.   The phrase 'failure is not an option' will be amended to '**deferred success** is one of many possibilities on the table'.
4.   "When you apply for university they are hardly going to say, 'Well you have had some **deferred success** so we'll let you in'."
5.   'Don't call it failure, call it **deferred success**', as the bishop said to the actress.
6.   A bombing mission has ended in failure or, as politically correct teachers are now being urged to say, **deferred success**.
7.   The measure prohibits journalists from describing the situation in Iraq as a 'failure' and orders them to replace it with the term '**deferred success**'.

Figure 3:   Results for search term *deferred success*, filter: UK news

3.2   Rare or obsolete language

Alternatively, the research question may centre on a rare or possibly obsolete item of vocabulary which is not found in existing corpora, and for which confirmation as to its status is sought. An example is the traditional UK colour term *bottle-green*, that seems to have been replaced by such fashion terms as *emerald*. WebCorp nevertheless yields some instances, which are shown in figure 4. This is useful stuff for the linguist, in that it indicates firstly that the term is not totally obsolete, but only rare, and secondly, that it is used in restricted contexts. It is cited metalinguistically as mention rather than use, in an American online dictionary (1); quoted from 19th century writers, Dickens (2) and Washington (3), used in the scientific context of icebergs (4), and used in reference to gem-stones (5), and to school uniform colours in a colonial context (6). All these instances (as indicated by the text sources supplied) could be said to reflect use that is either anachronistic, non-UK, non native-speaking English, or semi-technical.

1. **bottle-green** [a] 1) of a dark to moderate grayish green color (thefreedictionary.com)

2. He had a long wide-skirted bottle-green coat on, and a **bottle-green** pair of trousers
    (*Little Dorrit*, Dickens)

3. bows and arrows...tipped with stone of a **bottle-green** color
    (*Astoria or Anecdotes of an enterprise beyond the Rocky Mountains*, Washington)

4. The **bottle-green** icebergs of antarctica Antarctic icebergs
    (Science Frontiers ONLINE No. 87: May-Jun 1993)

5. all **bottle-green** Tourmalines came almost exclusively from Brazil
    (International Colored Gemstone Association)

6. Hair that touches the collar should be tied up with **bottle-green** hair accessories
    (Camps Bay Primary School code for school uniform, Zambia)

Figure 4:   Results for search term *bottle-green* in web texts

3.3   Phrasal creativity

The phrasal variability and creativity which can be investigated with the use of WebCorp is illustrated with reference to the Chaucerian aphorism *time and tide wait for no man*. This conventional and established idiom can be searched for in its canonical form, but if the linguist wishes to test whether, like most so-called 'frozen expressions', it is in fact modified in use, WebCorp supports this activity. The string may simply be submitted with various key words suppressed. Thus, in figure 5, we see the output of variants forced by the use of the word filter option to suppress the word *tide* in the output.

1. Clear law criminalising identity theft should be introduced as soon as possible. Time, and **cybercrime**, wait for no man.

2. Parliament received a powerful and embarrassing reminder that time and **tights** wait for no man.

3. But time and **semantics** wait for no man and a new volume is deemed necessary

Figure 5:   Results for search pattern *wait for no man*; collocate *tide* suppressed

What figure 5 reveals, among several other interesting facts about phrasal creativity in general, is that a convention of creative modification is for rhyme, assonance or other phonological devices to play a role in the substitution, as in line 1, where *cybercrime* rhymes with *time*, and in 2, where *tights* assonates with both *time* and *tide*. Line 3 shows how semantically-related words are motivated by context, as here with *semantics* in the context of 'a new dictionary volume'.

3.4   Semantically disambiguated information

Ambiguity is a central issue in automated text search. The fact is that, in addition to the obvious issues of polysemy and homography, most terms are multi-referential or multi-contextual (Renouf 1993a) in use, and thus liable to generate low-precision results unless this is controlled, for example by restriction of the textual domain, or by the accompaniment of some contextual or analytical (e.g. grammatical) filter. The WebCorp word filter does the latter, by allowing the searcher to require the presence (or absence) of a disambiguating word on the same page as the search term. This is a simple but often effective means of improving precision, as shown in figure 6, where the polysemous search term *sole* is limited to its piscatorial sense by the simple selection of *fish* as a required contextual item via the word filter.

1.   I expected to get a nice juicy **sole**.
2.   Andy was no more impressed with our syllabus of oeuf mayonnaise, **sole** véronique and sauce Espagnole than I was.
3.   Quotas to cut fishing for **sole** in the English Channel and anchovies in the Gulf of Gascogne, in south-west France, are also of concern.
4.   An extra 1C rise in temperature pushes haddock, cod, plaice and lemon **sole** 200 to 400 miles north, according to the WWF.
5.   I recall the most splendid Dover **sole** at Scotts in Mayfair, assisted by a quite magnificent premier cru Chablis

Figure 6:   Extract of WebCorp output for search term *sole*; context *fish* specified

1.   He and I once met for lunch for the **sole** purpose of continuing an argument
2.   Katiek, what about a cause whose **sole** aim is to label people "evil" and "stupid"?
3.   Its **sole** redeeming feature is that Stalin left their two-hour meeting complaining that Shaw was an awful person.
4.   The **sole** black family on the vast Whinmoor estate in Leeds
5.   Yesterday's summit finally dispelled the illusion that the UN is or can be the **sole** arbiter of war and peace.

Figure 7:   Extract of output for search term *sole*; context *characteristic* specified

In figure 7, the word sole is restricted to the sense of 'unique, only' by the word filter selection of the term characteristic. Curiously, the requirement for its presence somewhere in the text seems to licence the occurrence of some immediate collocates for sole which are compatible with but do not include characteristic itself – namely purpose, aim, feature. This indicates that the filtering word, if not functioning as an actual collocate, can function instead to create a semantic prosody (Louw 1993) which encourages the desired sense of the search term to be realised. This fact of the language is convenient, if not entirely robust.

3.5   External collocate profiles

WebCorp also provides some basic statistical information, in particular about the 'collocational profile' (Renouf, e.g. 1993b) of the word. This is of necessity currently restricted to simple ranked frequency of occurrence in the set of pages visited. Figure 8 shows top-ranked 'external collocates' to complement the concordance lines in figure 7 for the same search term, *sole*, again with the word *characteristic* in its presence. The slightly more extensive output shows that the hypothesis that a single term can be used to focus context type certainly holds in this case: all top immediate collocates for *sole* here are compatible with the required sense.

Word	Total	L4	L3	L2	L1	R1	R2	R3	R4	Left Total	Right Total
purpose	8			2		6				2	6
survivors	2					2				0	2
responsibility	2					2				0	2
survivor	2					2				0	2
raison	2					2				0	2
d'etre	2						2			0	2
aim	2					1	1			0	2
object	2					1		1		0	2
family	2					1	1			0	2

Figure 8:   External collocate output for search term *sole*; context *characteristic* specified

By way of further illustration, figure 9 shows top-ranked 'external collocates' for the phrasal fragment *familiarity breeds*, where the phrasal completive contempt has been suppressed by the word filter, and the word slot on which the query is focussed lies in position R1, outside the pattern submitted. Here, as shown in 3.3. above, phonology and semantics clearly play their role in the substitution.

Word	Total	L4	L3	L2	L1	R1	R2	R3	R4	Left Total	Right Total
content	5					5				0	5
contentment	4					4				0	4
respect	1					1				0	1

Figure 9: Top external collocates for search pattern *familiarity breeds*, with phrasal component *contempt* filtered out

3.6 Key phrases

A simple heuristic (Morley 2005) in WebCorp, involving a series of significant co-occurrence calculations, identifies a set of possible key phrases found within the results. In figure 10, this reveals the more popular alternative phrases which emerge in place of the canonical when the key phrasal element *contempt* is suppressed.

Key Phrases: **familiarity breeds content** **familiarity breeds contentment**

Figure 10: Key phrases for search pattern *familiarity breeds*; *contempt* suppressed

3.7 Internal Collocates

Word	Total	1
money	8	8
apples	6	6
eggheads	4	4
dreams	4	4
marbles	3	3
chips	2	2
bets	2	2
hopes	2	2
chickens	2	2
risks	2	2
fish	2	2

Figure 11: Top internal collocates within search pattern *all your * in one basket*, with collocate *eggs* suppressed

If a study is being conducted of lexical creativity within the phrasal pattern, WebCorp can provide the corresponding 'internal collocate' (Renouf 2003) profile. This is illustrated in figure 11 for the search pattern fragment *all your * in one basket*, where the internal collocates are non-hapax items which substitute for the suppressed *eggs* in wildcard position. These choices, as shown earlier, reveal some of the word play that characterises phrasal creativity in English.

3.8   Language detection

There are three main stages envisaged in the internationalisation of WebCorp (Renouf et al. 2004): handling / representing texts in other languages; refining search by specifying language; and automatic language identification. Of these, we have tackled the first two, since these have been prioritised by our users. The first is achieved by the integration of Unicode/double byte characters into the system. The second is accommodated through the selection of site domain (e.g. '.uk', '.pt'), as a heuristic to control language or dialect variant, and it frequently works quite well, though it is not entirely reliable due to the well-documented cross-fertilisation which goes on between sites in terms of quotation of other languages, mirror-siting, and so on. Automatic language identification has been considered by us but not implemented as yet; it could be achieved by a combination of using the HTTP 1.1 language identification protocol, and by the implementation of one or other method of feature analysis. However, the true challenge comes not in identifying the language of a linguistically homogenous text, but of identifying words and short stretches in a different language within it. There is much knowledge already available in this area for us to draw on in the next stage of WebCorp.

4.   Linguistic post-processing currently available with WebCorp

Post-processing of web-derived results adds time to what is already a slow procedure. Nevertheless, during 2002-3, we added post-processing options to WebCorp. One is the post-extraction alphabetical sorting of results on any specified collocate position. Another is the selection of desired and removal of unwanted concordance lines. We also added simple POS tagging, using the TNT tagger (internal version only).

An important move was the development of a means to conduct diachronic search. Web text protocols for dating are not applied consistently or at all, and at best they are ambiguous, so we devised a set of heuristics for searching for linguistic and other clues within the mark-up and the text itself, which have a measure of success in ordering results. Figure 13 demonstrates this for the word *radicalisation*.

18/08/1999 10:13:27 **1**	a widespread polarisation and	<u>radicalisation</u>	amongst the working class
16/09/1999 15:06:22 **1**	Kurds, Assyrians, Jews) and	<u>radicalisation</u>	of the Cossack movement
13/09/2001 18:19:39 **1**	Genoa – a new	<u>radicalisation</u>	has begun The 300
01/01/2002 00:00:00 **5**	has seen the increasing	<u>radicalisation</u>	of the Muslim position
24/01/2005 00:00:00 **2**	the areas of combating	<u>radicalisation</u>	and preventing terrorism.
09/07/2005 00:00:00 **3**	many factors behind the	<u>radicalisation</u>	of Muslim youth, including

Figure 13: Post-extraction chronological listing of results for *radicalisation*

The first column here shows the date and time (where available) extracted by WebCorp for each of the originating web pages. This is followed by a number indicating the source of the date, where '1' is a server header date (the most reliable mechanism), '2' is a date metatag, '3' is a modification date in the body of the text, '4' is a copyright date and '5' is a date in the URL of the page (see Kehoe 2005 for further explanation).

5.   Remaining problems

As demonstrated, an extensive range of functions have successfully been developed for WebCorp, but given the intrinsic nature of web text, with its unorthodox definition of 'text', heterogeneity of data, lack of reliable punctuation and so on, several of these embody interim solutions and heuristics could benefit from further improvement. Current WebCorp performance also lacks the high degree of processing and storage which is required to meet user needs expressed for simultaneous use by more users, including class-sized groups, grammatical and better collocational analysis, and more sophisticated pattern matching.

The primary constraint on the improvement of WebCorp performance, however, is its reliance on a commercial search engine. The problems posed by this dependence are as follows:

-    the amount of web text searched is limited by time constraints, so that recall can be poor
-    the proportion of potentially relevant web texts that is actually searched is limited (by search engine search criteria such as 'relevance' ranking and the 'indexability' (linking status) of a text), so that
-    a similar small crop of texts is accessed each time, and a given search term garners largely the same results (although not reliably so, in terms of repro-ducibility), due to time-out and misjudged search prioritisation
-    the speed of results is inhibited.

The delay built in by Google-dependent text extraction means that the time required for the linguistic post-processing of text is prohibitive, whether for POS tagging, for date and alphabetical sorting, or other requisite procedures.

There are also unpredictable changes in Google service and even at the best of times, Google is geared to commercial rather than linguistic or academic requirements. As discussed recently on 'Corpora-list' (http:// torvald.aksis.uib.no/ corpora/2005-1/0191.html), this can mean, for example, unreliable word count statistics and limited and inconsistent support for wildcard search.

With an eye to the long-term sustainability of the WebCorp system, we collaborated in 2001-2 with a UK-based search engine company, searchengine.com, who in exchange for linguistic information from us, provided first-hand experience of search engine technology and back-door access to their indexes, which speeded up response time.

6.   The WebCorp Linguistic Search Engine[1]

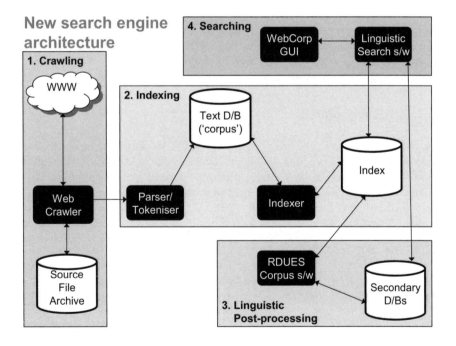

Figure 14:   The new WebCorp Linguistic Search Engine architecture

Our response to the problems anticipated and cited above has been to develop WebCorp with an eye to creating components that can be integrated into an independent, linguistically tailored search engine. We are currently calling this the 'WebCorp Linguistic Search Engine', since WebCorp functionality will be integrated into the new architecture alongside the search engine, and the whole fronted by an enhanced version of the WebCorp GUI. The new architecture is displayed graphically in figure 14. The generic term 'linguistic search engine' is in fact a misnomer, since the search engine, while informed by linguistic knowledge, will not be 'linguistic' as such.

The components of the new linguistic search engine system are as follows:

- web crawler
- parser / tokeniser
- indexer
- WebCorp tools
- WebCorp user front end
- more, also off-line, linguistic processing tools

We have so far developed them individually, as we shall now outline.

6.1   Web crawler

Some five years ago, we developed a crawler module in Perl to select and download articles from UK newspaper websites. These are currently restricted to the *Guardian* and *Independent*, with whom we have had special arrangements. We shall now supplement them with tabloid and other categories of journalism. Not all newspaper sites have full archives like the *Guardian*, so instead of downloading them retrospectively, as we have done hitherto, we shall download the current day's articles daily, to build up the corpus progressively. Our initial estimate is that the newspaper 'domain' accessible through the WebCorp Linguistic Search Engine will contain at least 750 million word tokens. Our newspaper crawler incorporates the following features:

- exclusion lists (i.e. kinds of pages on newspaper sites NOT to download)
- error logging and re-queuing of failed pages
- extraction of date, author, headline and sub-headline
- URL parsing to extract section of newspaper (Sport, Media, etc)
- storage of articles by date (to facilitate diachronic analysis)
- removal of advertising banners and links ('boilerplate')
- stripping of HTML mark-up

We shall continue to use our tailored crawlers for our newspaper 'domain' and for other domains where pages are in a uniform format. We also have a special-ised tool to extract neologisms from online articles in real-time. We shall expand this 'live' system to monitor and record neologisms, although once the web texts are downloaded into corpus format, we will begin to achieve this through the application of our APRIL system (http://rdues.uce.ac.uk/april.shtml), as we have begun to do with *Guardian* articles more recently.

In addition to structured sub-domains, we shall download a very large (multi-terabyte) subset of random texts from the web, to create a mini version of the web itself. Some users will prefer to look at this, much as they do with WebCorp at present, rather than at particular sub-domains. The aim will not in itself be to build either specific sub-corpora or 'collections' of texts from the web, as other people such as Baroni and Bernardini (with BootCaT, 2004) have done, but to find a useful balance and combination of raw data, for instance in selecting random texts within a specific domain.

More generic tools will be required for the creation of this multi-terabyte mini-web, to cope with a variety of page layouts and formats. Several ready-made tools are available freely online, but we are developing a new crawler for our specific task, building upon our experience with the newspaper downloads and making use of other open-source libraries whenever possible.

The new crawler will need to be provided (or 'seeded') with web addresses of where to embark on its crawl of the web). The search process could be completely random. This will not be appropriate, however, when building a structured corpus with carefully selected sub-domains. We shall employ other 'seeding' techniques including the use of Open Directory index, where editors classify web pages according to textual 'domain'. Our crawler will make use of the freely downloadable Open Directory 'RDF dumps' (http://rdf.dmoz.org/), containing lists of URLs classified by domain (or 'category'). We shall also consult human experts, university colleagues from our own and other disciplines, current WebCorp users and other contributors, to catalogue the major target websites in their field, so that these can also be used to seed the crawler. Thus a carefully planned seeding strategy will ensure a well-balanced and linguistically informed corpus.

New features of the crawler which are being developed include better duplicate detection: methods of comparing newly-encountered pages with those already stored in the repository to identify both updated and mirror versions of pages. We are also determined to improve on the date detection mechanism we have already created. Knowledge as to when our crawler first encountered a page may provide a clue as to when it was created, and the discovery of a new version of a page already stored will reveal when it was updated. The existence of our own independent search engine will allow us to conduct date detection off-line, not in real-time as at present. We shall also be able to classify changes and updates from the linguistic perspective, by scrutinising the page for changes in actual content rather than simply in mark-up or layout. Another area on which we have done considerable work, but which we should still like to improve on, is language detection, which could be done by the crawler or at the indexing stage.

6.2 Indexing

The source files will be stored in our standard RDUES format and then processed using specially adapted versions of the parsing, tokenising and indexing software which we have developed over the past 15 years, and run on texts downloaded from newspaper websites for the past 5 years. This will construct the corpus as a series of binary files and indexes. Our past experience indicates that we will be able to store 10 billion word tokens per terabyte of disk storage, including the processed corpus, indexes, raw HTML files (the 'source file archive' in figure 14) and the secondary databases resulting from the linguistic post-processing stage outlined below.

Corpus updates will be incremental. New articles will be added to the newspaper domain daily, while other domains and the large mini-web 'chunk' will be updated at monthly intervals. Corpus processing will take place off-line and the new version of the corpus will 'go live' when processing is complete.

A constantly growing corpus could potentially cause problems when scholars attempt to reproduce previous experiments but find that the corpus composition has changed in the meantime (cf. section 7.2 concerning frequency counts and statistics). For this reason, there will be a mechanism in the WebCorp Linguistic Search Engine allowing users to restrict searches to a specified subset (or 'collection') of texts which can be saved across sessions.

6.3 Linguistic post-processing

We shall be able to run on web texts any of the gamut of tools we can run on our current newspaper corpus. Where necessary, we shall also develop new tools, to provide a comprehensive range of corpus-processing functions. A priority is to exploit the tools created in major projects over the last 15 years, including those which generate collocates, 'nyms' (alternative search terms in the form of sense-related items), neologisms, summaries, document similarity measures, domain identification and so on. The sharing of these specialist language facilities will be a matter of individual negotiation: we shall be looking for relevant collaborative research proposals from potential users.

6.4 Searching

We shall develop new user interfaces, building upon our experience with WebCorp and other tools, such as the step-by-step and advanced APRIL neologisms demos (http://rdues.uce.ac.uk/aprdemo), taking into account user feedback.

All results from the linguistic post-processing will be stored in the secondary databases shown in the figure 14 diagram of system architecture, and there will be new linguistic search software created to access the secondary databases.

7.   Features and benefits of the new tailored web-search architecture

7.1   Increased speed

The system will now function as quickly as Google, but will be able to offer more functionality from a linguistic perspective. In terms of enhanced text quality, there will be a far greater rate of accuracy in respect of duplicate detection, sentence identification and full-text search. Text specification will be significantly improved with regard to domain detection, better date information for diachronic study and reliable language identification. Text search routines will be made more sophisticated with regard to specific domain search and specific URL sets.

7.2   Improved statistics

The web data will no longer be a vast, unquantifiable sea from which the system plucks an amount of data that cannot be evaluated in terms of its significance. The sub-web, or rather webs, which are regularly downloaded will be known entities, and thus reliable statistical counts and measures will be possible – in particular, the current WebCorp limitation to simple frequency counts will cease, and calculation of relative frequency and significance of phenomena such as collocation will commence.

7.3   Improved search

WebCorp search functionality will be vastly improved. This will include wildcard-initial search, wildcard matching for a variable number of intra-pattern search words up to a maximum span, POS specification, and lexico-grammatical specification.

8.   Indicative output from the WebCorp Linguistic Search Engine

There follow some invented examples of the more complex and comprehensive linguistic and statistical analyses that we shall provide for the user once the WebCorp Linguistic Search Engine is up and running, and the post-processing operation will no longer be prohibitively time-consuming. The first two concern refined wildcard pattern search.

8.1   Wildcard-initial words as search terms

Google does not consistently support wildcard pattern search, and when it does, it does not allow wildcard-initial words as search terms. Our system will provide such information, as shown in invented output for the term *athon in figure 15. In addition, it will continue to be possible to specify textual domain (here 'UK broadsheets'), context length (here 'sentences') and dates (here Sept-Dec, 2004).

1. including an ice-cream **scoopathon** and sausage treasure hunt
2. We left home at 10.15 to participate in the annual Right-to-Life **Walk-a-thon**
3. everyone talks about Zellweger's **eatathon** as if she'd been forced to lose a kidney
4. he strutted and tried to look feistier than he managed in that first **scow-lathon**
5. A small army of people descend with cleaning materials for a five-hour **scrubathon**
6. It is one of the 20 tracks on the new **Spearsathon**
7. in October she will publish 'Manners', in time for the mass British **incivilityathon**

Figure 15: Invented results for wildcard-initial search pattern **athon*

8.2 Variable number of words in wildcard position

For a search allowing for variation in number of words in the NP, we shall be able to provide a pattern search wildcard which allows for a specified maximum number of words. For instance, in a study of the 'It-cleft' construction *it was* + PN (proper noun) *(3) + *that*, the *(3) would be a specification of all words in the wildcard position up to a maximum of 3. This would allow a search to yield results such as those shown in figure 16.

(1 word)
1. it was **Blair** that gave him this power
2. it was **Iraq** that started the 1980-1988 war with Iran.
(2 words)
1. it was **Mitchell's reporting** that helped lead to the guilty verdicts
2. it was **Dennis's enthusiasm** that sparked the project to life.
3. it was **Seattle Weekly** that broke the Strippergate story
4. it was **the USA** that helped protect Australia from the Japanese
(3 words)
1. it was **the Muslim community** that could do things itself
2. it was **the Liberal Party** that ended the racist White Australia
3. it was **Cristijan Albers' Minardi** that punctured a left rear and went off the road

Figure 16: Invented results for pattern *it was *(3) that*, with a maximum of 3 words in wildcard position

8.3   POS and lexico-grammatical search

We have already mentioned the POS annotation that we already have in place. This is not apparent in the WebCorp interface, but exists in our internal working software. Once we have established a sub-web processing system, we shall have the leeway in response time to apply it, providing lexico-grammatical search of the kind indicated by the search in figure 16, or indeed in the phrasal creativity searches in figures 9 and 11, where a combination of actual lexical realisations and grammatical categories could in principle have been specified.

9.   Application of additional linguistic applications

9.1   Alternative search terms

As mentioned above, the new search engine will allow us to bolt on past automated systems of linguistic analysis, of which we shall illustrate just two here. One such is the ACRONYM (Renouf 1996) system, which automatically provides Wordnet-type sense-related synonyms or alternative search terms, and thus offers an opportunity for increase in recall. A sample of the ranked output it produces from our *Independent/Guardian* database is presented in figure 17 for the terms *quest* and *questioned*, respectively:

- *quest*: pursuit, search, struggle, odyssey, ambition, endeavour, crusade, obsession, dream, mission
- *questioned*: quizzed, doubted, disagreed, examined, challenged, queried, argued, protested, speculated, lambasted

Figure 17:   Sense-related synonyms / alternative search terms from ACRO-NYM

9.2   Morphological Analysis

We also intend to append the APRIL project morphological analyser (Renouf et al., forthcoming) to the new system. This conducts the morphological analysis of target words, as well as providing plots of the fortunes of the target word or words across time. Figure 18 presents an extract of morphological information of the kind available with the new system – here, new nouns ending in -*ings*, (or rather, nouns occurring for the first time since 1989). Figure 19 presents a time plot to allow the examination of the productivity patterns of the suffix -*esque*, which reveals a slow growth, peaking in 2004.

☐ - re-wordings	re- '-' (wordings)	|NN2|	200404
☐ - cushionings	(cushioning) -s	|NN2|	200404
☐ - dampenings	(dampening) -s	|NN2|	200404
☐ - fritterings	(frittering) -s	|NN2|	200404
☐ - head-tiltings	(head) '-' (tilting) -s	|NN2|	200404
☐ - unfurlings	(unfurling) -s	|NN2|	200404
☐ - brush-wipings	(brush) '-' (wiping) -s	|NN2|	200404

Figure 18: Extract of APRIL results (April 2004): new nouns with suffix *-ings*

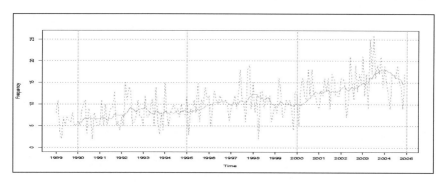

Figure 19: APRIL time plot showing number of new words with the suffix *-esque*

10. Concluding remarks

There is general agreement among those who have devised and implemented automated methods of extracting linguistic research data from the web via a commercial search engine (e.g. our team; Fletcher 2001 and this volume; Resnik and Elkiss 2003), as well as among reviewers of such initiatives (e.g. Lüdeling, Evert and Baroni, this volume; Kilgariff 2003), that the mediated route is less than ideal, particularly for on-line retrieval systems. Having foreseen this problem at the outset, we have worked steadily over the last five years to develop the components required to create a linguistically-tailored and accessorised search engine, and we shall in the coming months assemble an infrastructure that will be progressively incorporated into the WebCorp front-end. We are confident that this will enhance its performance on the fronts outlined above, and allow it to support serious research. Improvements to our system will be incrementally perceptible at http://www.webcorp.org.uk/.

Notes

1　This section draws on material in a previous paper, Renouf, A., Kehoe, A and J. Banerjee (2005).

References

Baroni, M. and S. Bernardini (2004), 'BootCaT: bootstrapping corpora and terms from the web', in: *Proceedings of LREC 2004.* Lisbon: ELDA. 1313-1316.

Fletcher, W.H. (2001), 'Concordancing the web with KWiCFinder', in: *Proceedings of the American Association for Applied Corpus Linguistics Third North American Symposium on Corpus Linguistics and Language Teaching.* Available online from http://www.kwicfinder.com.

Fletcher, W.H. (this volume), 'Concordancing the web: promise and problems, tools and techniques'.

Kehoe, A. (2005), 'Diachronic linguistic analysis on the web with WebCorp', in: A. Renouf and A. Kehoe (eds.) *The Changing Face of Corpus Linguistics.* Amsterdam and Atlanta: Rodopi. 297-307.

Kehoe, A. and A. Renouf (2002), 'WebCorp: applying the web to linguistics and linguistics to the web', in: *Online Proceedings of World Wide Web 2002 Conference,* Honolulu, Hawaii, 7-11 May 2002. http://www2002.org/ CDROM/poster/67/.

Kilgarriff, A. (2003), 'Linguistic search engine', in: *Proceedings of the Shallow Processing of Large Corpora Workshop (SProLaC 2003) Corpus Linguistics 2003,* Lancaster University.

Louw, B. (1993), 'Irony in the text or insincerity in the writer? The diagnostic potential of semantic prosodies', in: M. Baker, G. Francis and E. Tognini-Bonelli (eds.) *Text and Technology. In Honour of John Sinclair.* Philadelphia and Amsterdam: John Benjamins. 157-176.

Lüdeling, A., S. Evert and M. Baroni (this volume), 'Using web data for linguistic purposes'.

Morley, B. (2005), 'WebCorp: a tool for online linguistic information retrieval and analysis', in: A. Renouf and A. Kehoe (eds.) *The Changing Face of Corpus Linguistics.* Amsterdam and Atlanta: Rodopi. 283-296.

Renouf, A. (1993a), 'What the linguist has to say to the information scientist', in: F. Gibb (ed.) *The Journal of Document and Text Management,* vol. 1:2. 173-190.

Renouf, A. (1993b), 'Making sense of text: automated approaches to meaning extraction', in: *Proceedings of 17th International Online Information Meeting,* 7-9 Dec 1993. 77-86.

Renouf, A. (1996), 'The ACRONYM project: discovering the textual thesaurus', in: I. Lancashire, C. Meyer and C. Percy (eds.) *Papers from English Language Research on Computerized Corpora (ICAME 16)*. Amsterdam and Atlanta: Rodopi. 171-187.

Renouf, A. (2003), 'WebCorp: providing a renewable data source for corpus linguists', in: S. Granger and S. Petch-Tyson (eds.) *Extending the Scope of Corpus-Based Research. New applications, new challenges.* Amsterdam and Atlanta: Rodopi. 39-58.

Renouf, A., B. Morley and A. Kehoe (2003), 'Linguistic research with the XML/RDF aware WebCorp Tool', in: Online Proceedings of *WWW2003*, Budapest. http://www2003.org/cdrom/papers/poster/p005/p5-morley.html.

Renouf, A., A. Kehoe and D. Mezquiriz (2004), 'The accidental corpus: issues involved in extracting linguistic information from the web', in: K. Aijmer and B. Altenberg (eds.) *Proceedings of 21ˢᵗ ICAME Conference, University of Gothenburg, May 22-26 2002.* Amsterdam and Atlanta GA: Rodopi. 404-419

Renouf, A., A. Kehoe and J. Banerjee (2005), 'The WebCorp search engine: a holistic approach to web text search', *Proceedings from the Corpus Linguistics Conference Series, Vol. 1, no. 1.* ISSN 1747-9398. URL: www.corpus.bham.ac.uk/PCLC.

Renouf, A., M. Pacey, A. Kehoe and P. Davies (forthcoming), 'Monitoring lexical innovation in journalistic text across time'.

Resnik, P. and A. Elkiss (2003), 'The linguist's search engine: getting started guide', Technical Report: *LAMP-TR-108/CS-TR-4541/UMIACS-TR-2003-109, University of Maryland, College Park, November 2003.*

From web page to mega-corpus: the CNN transcripts

Sebastian Hoffmann

University of Zurich

Abstract

This paper focuses on the technical and methodological issues involved in using data available on the internet as a basis for quantitative analyses of Present-day English. For this purpose, I concentrate on the creation of a specialized corpus of spoken data and outline the steps necessary to convert a large number of publicly available CNN transcripts into a format which is compatible with standard corpus tools. As an illustration of potential uses of such data, the second part of my paper then presents a sample analysis of the intensifier so. *The paper concludes with a brief discussion of the advantages and limitations of this type of internet-derived data for corpus linguistic analysis.*

1.   Introduction

In corpus linguistics, general patterns in language use are described on the basis of large collections of authentic language data. It is therefore no surprise that scholars have been drawn to the world wide web as a potential source of additional data. Indeed, if the catchphrase "Bigger is better!" fully applied to corpus linguistics, the internet would have to be considered a near-perfect source. However, the use of internet-based data clearly raises a number of important issues. In contrast to the carefully compiled and balanced language corpora available today, the internet is a conglomerate of "messy data" whose size, composition and provenance constantly changes and which simply cannot be properly assessed. As a consequence, fundamentals of corpus linguistic method-ology such as the concept of corpus representativeness, the replicability of linguistic findings or the use of normalized frequency counts cannot be easily applied to internet-based data. In addition, search engines such as Google or AltaVista have not been specifically designed for a linguistic analysis of the data and they therefore have serious limitations with respect to the search algorithms offered as well as the way in which the results are presented.[1] Until such issues are convincingly resolved, any scholar who makes use of the whole of the internet as a (single) corpus must proceed with extreme caution when interpreting the observed patterns of language use.[2]

The present paper will focus on a more restricted application of the internet in corpus linguistics by demonstrating how it can be employed as a source for the compilation of specialized corpora. As I will show, such internet-derived corpora offer the researcher an opportunity to greatly expand the range of available data without having to unduly compromise the application of standard corpus linguistic methodology. As a practical illustration of the issues at hand, I have chosen to concentrate on a large database of transcripts which is provided via unrestricted access by the news channel CNN (available at http://transcripts.cnn.com/transcripts/) and which covers the time-span from January 2000 onwards. The transcripts are created by professional transcribers and they are made available to internet users on the day after the actual broadcast. In addition to standard news programmes, this database also contains transcripts from a whole range of other discourse contexts types, including for example interviews (e.g. *Larry King Live*) and debates. Although the CNN transcripts are clearly not fully comparable in nature to such spoken corpora as the *Longman Spoken American Corpus* or the spoken component of the *British National Corpus* (BNC), they may nevertheless be useful to scholars whose research requires much larger amounts of spoken data than is available in standard corpora.

I will first address some of the technical and methodological questions that arise when converting the CNN transcripts into a format which can be searched with the help of standard concordancing software. This will be followed by a sample study of the intensifier *so* carried out on the basis of this dataset. An evaluation of my findings will then allow me to focus on some advantages and limitations of using internet-derived data.

2.   Downloading the originals

The first step towards the creation of a CNN transcripts corpus consisted of downloading the complete set of relevant web pages to a local hard-disk. Given the large number of transcripts available, this of course had to be carried out automatically rather than by manually saving each transcript. A number of software solutions exist for this type of task. I opted for LWP (short for "Library for World Wide Web in Perl"), which is a set of Perl ("Practical Extraction and Report Language") modules that enable automated access to web pages and the information encoded on them.[3]

The actual download proceeded in two steps: First, a simple Perl script generated web addresses (URLs) for all possible dates between January 2000 and August 2004 (e.g. http://transcripts.cnn.com/TRANSCRIPTS/2003.10.21.html for broadcasts aired on 21 October 2003) and saved the corresponding daily overview pages. A second script then parsed these pages for the URLs of individual transcripts and automatically downloaded them to the local hard-disk. In total, 102,579 transcripts amounting to approximately 3.3 gigabytes of data were thus saved in their original HTML-format ("Hyper-Text Mark-Up Language").[4]

3.   Basic conversion

Figure 1 displays the first part of a transcript of a news item reporting an air security breach. It was aired as part of the programme *American Morning* on

October 21, 2003.[5] The participants of the conversation are indicated in capital letters, followed by their individual turns. The extract shown in figure 1 is quite typical of the type of language use found in the CNN transcripts: Rather than consisting of pieces of news that are read off the teleprompter by a single speaker, this transcript is based on a more or less spontaneous dyadic conversation. Also, while the accuracy of the transcription is unlikely to match that of spoken corpora which were specifically created for linguistic analysis, the presence of interruptions and discourse-specific items such as *oh* and *well* in the transcripts suggests that the written representation is relatively close to the actual speech event. Finally, figure 1 also clearly shows that the downloaded web page contains a range of other elements such as advertisements and links to other pages. Such items are of course not of interest to somebody wishing to compile a corpus of transcripts as they would seriously compromise the quality of the data. In a first conversion process, the actual transcript thus had to be isolated from these other elements.

There are various strategies for managing the content of a web site which is providing access to a large number of (formally) similar items. One common solution is to store the information in a database. When a user chooses to access a particular item, a corresponding web page is then dynamically created on the basis of an HTML-template. Unless the template is changed, all of the downloaded web pages will thus be largely identical with respect to their formal features.[6] This in turn will greatly facilitate the task of extracting the relevant information from such web pages. In the case of the CNN transcripts, however, a different strategy is employed: The web pages containing the transcripts appear to have been saved as individual HTML-files on the CNN servers. As a result, layout changes implemented between January 2000 and August 2004 have resulted in drastic changes in the underlying HTML-code. Furthermore, HTML-code is relatively lenient with web content creators in that changes in the order of certain items will not alter the actual appearance of the page in a web browser. In addition, different types of JavaScript elements and internal comments may be part of the code, without affecting the form or order of what is displayed. Finally, the element of human error introduces a further level of inconsistency, and the unexpected repetition of elements or misplaced features may thus add to the formal diversity of the web pages. As a result, automatically extracting the relevant passages from the CNN transcripts pages proved to be less trivial than originally envisaged. A number of delimiting features had to be identified – e.g. the statement beginning with "THIS IS A RUSH TRANSCRIPT" shown in figure 1 – and built into a Perl script. When this script did not encounter the expected format, it created an error message, which in turn allowed me to adapt the script.

SEARCH   The Web   CNN.com   [   ]   [Search]   Powered by YAHOO! search

| Home Page |
| World |
| U.S. |
| Weather |
| Business |
| Sports |
| Politics |
| Law |
| Technology |
| Science & Space |
| Health |
| Entertainment |
| Travel |
| Education |
| Special Reports |

SERVICES
Video
E-mail
Newsletters
CNNtoGO

SEARCH
Web   CNN.com
[   ]
[Search]   Powered by YAHOO! search

TRANSCRIPTS Transcript Providers

[Transcripts]   Return to Transcripts main page

AMERICAN MORNING

Air Security Breach

Aired October 21, 2003 - 07:16   ET

THIS IS A RUSH TRANSCRIPT. THIS COPY MAY NOT
BE IN ITS FINAL FORM AND MAY BE UPDATED.

SOLEDAD O'BRIEN, CNN ANCHOR: A 20-year-old
college student is charged with carrying a concealed
weapon onboard an aircraft -- a federal crime. According
to the FBI, Nathaniel Heatwole admits that he placed box
cutters, bleach, matches and modeling clay that resembled explosives on Southwest jets last
month. The FBI says Heatwole calls his actions civil disobedience, aimed at improving air safety.
And Heatwole attends Guilford College in North Carolina.
One of his professors, Rex Adelberger, joins us this morning from Greensboro.

Good morning to you, sir. Thanks for joining us.

REX ADELBERGER, GUILFORD COLLEGE PROFESSOR: Hi. Good morning to you.

O'BRIEN: Thank you very much.

You're obviously one of Nathaniel's professors. But give me a sense of how well you know him
personally.

ADELBERGER: Well, I've known him since he's been a first-year student at Guilford. I've taught him
in four classes. We worked together setting up -- or rebuilding a ham radio shack that the college
owns. It has a ham radio system. And so, you know, we've talked. I'm one of his academic advisors
He's also a political science major, as well as a physics major.

O'BRIEN: Give us a little insight...

ADELBERGER: So...

O'BRIEN: Oh, I'm sorry. Forgive me for interrupting you there.

ADELBERGER: Yes.

O'BRIEN: I was just going to ask you to give us a little insight into who this young man is.

ADELBERGER: Well, he's -- you know, when you first meet him, you'd think he's very quiet. He's
not one who just sits there and talks all of the time. You have him in class, and he sits in the class

Figure 1:   A CNN transcript as it is displayed in a web browser

4.   Identifying the speakers

The result of the two conversion processes described in the previous section will
be suitable for a whole range of linguistic analyses. However, since the names of
speakers are given in the transcripts, a further conversion process was felt to be
desirable. The texts should be annotated in a way that would make it possible to
perform searches over the CNN transcripts that are restricted to the utterances of

individual speakers. For example, I wanted to have the option of searching everything President George Bush said on CNN. As it turned out, this was not a trivial undertaking.

As the short extract presented in figure 1 showed, the speakers are first introduced with their full name, followed by their function (for example *CNN Anchor* or *Guilford College Professor*). The speaker's name and function are separated by a comma. However, in the same speaker's subsequent utterances, he or she is only referred to by last name. I therefore had to match these later utterances with the first one and assign a unique speaker identification code to them. In addition, this unique code would ideally be the same in all other transcripts in which the speaker is found. In the case of the extract shown in figure 1, this conversion process presented no difficulties. However, it soon emerged that major complications had to be tackled. The case of George Bush can serve as an illustration of some of these difficulties.

The first problem is posed by the fact that a total of eight different versions of George Bush's name exist in the CNN transcripts. They are displayed in table 1. Although *George W. Bush* is by far the most frequent variant, all of them should of course be subsumed under the same unique speaker identification code.[7] In addition to these variants, there are over 120 different combinations of George Bush's name and his function. This diversity is partly a reflection of the developments of recent history: in my data, he starts out as *Governor George Bush*, who then becomes *Presidential nominee*, then *President elect* and finally *President of the United States*.[8] In addition to that, there are also a number of typographical errors and other types of mistakes that add to the multiplicity of labels (e.g. Bush as *White House correspondent* or as *president of the Untied States*). For a human reader, this diversity of course poses no problems, but the computer needs to be instructed about how to deal with them.[9]

Table 1: Eight different ways of referring to the same person

GEORGE W. BUSH	G.W. BUSH
GEORGE. W. BUSH	G. W. BUSH
GEORGE BUSH	GEORGE W.BUSH
GEORGE WALKER BUSH	GEORGE W. BUSH, PRESIDENT OF THE UNITED STATES

Again, I developed a number of heuristics that allowed me to assign a unique speaker identification code to the large majority of speakers, and again there is a margin of error. For example, if Laura Bush and George W. Bush are interviewed in the same transcript and George W. is later referred to only as *Bush* – which is fully transparent to a human reader – the Perl script cannot assign the correct match. In cases like this, the isolated surname was included as a separate identity. While this does of course present a less-than-ideal solution, it is still preferable to assigning utterances to a wrong speaker identification code.

2003.10.21.1tm.05	CNN_S_O'BRIENS	OLEDAD O'BRIEN, CNN ANCHOR: A 20-year-old college student is charged with carrying a concealed wea
2003.10.21.1tm.05	REX_ADELBERGER	REX ADELBERGER, GUILFORD COLLEGE PROFESSOR: Hi. Good morning to you.
2003.10.21.1tm.05	CNN_S_O'BRIEN	O'BRIEN: Thank you very much. You're obviously one of Nathaniel's professors. But give me a sen
2003.10.21.1tm.05	REX_ADELBERGER	ADELBERGER: Well, I've known him since he's been a first-year student at Guilford. I've taught him
2003.10.21.1tm.05	CNN_S_O'BRIEN	O'BRIEN: Give us a little insight...
2003.10.21.1tm.05	REX_ADELBERGER	ADELBERGER: So... I'm sorry. Forgive me for interrupting you there.
2003.10.21.1tm.05	CNN_S_O'BRIEN	O'BRIEN: Oh, I'm sorry. Forgive me for interrupting you there.
2003.10.21.1tm.05	REX_ADELBERGER	ADELBERGER: Yes.
2003.10.21.1tm.05	CNN_S_O'BRIEN	O'BRIEN: I was just going to ask you to give us a little insight into who this young man is.
2003.10.21.1tm.05	REX_ADELBERGER	ADELBERGER: Well, he's -- you know, when you first meet him, you'd think he's very quiet. He's not
2003.10.21.1tm.05	CNN_S_O'BRIEN	O'BRIEN: He has...
2003.10.21.1tm.05	REX_ADELBERGER	ADELBERGER: And he's very good...
2003.10.21.1tm.05	CNN_S_O'BRIEN	O'BRIEN: He has said that what he did was an act of civil disobedience; that he wanted to raise
2003.10.21.1tm.05	REX_ADELBERGER	ADELBERGER: Not that I know about. I've talked -- you know, we've talked in the class that we have
2003.10.21.1tm.05	CNN_S_O'BRIEN	O'BRIEN: If his goal was...
2003.10.21.1tm.05	REX_ADELBERGER	ADELBERGER: It might be...
2003.10.21.1tm.05	CNN_S_O'BRIEN	O'BRIEN: Forgive me, sir. I keep tripping over you. But I want...
2003.10.21.1tm.05	REX_ADELBERGER	ADELBERGER: That's OK, I can...
2003.10.21.1tm.05	CNN_S_O'BRIEN	O'BRIEN: All right, well, thank you. I'm just going to keep going, then. I know that he obvious
2003.10.21.1tm.05	REX_ADELBERGER	ADELBERGER: Yes, I think so. He's too well-prepared and well-thinking a person not to do that. I d
2003.10.21.1tm.05	CNN_S_O'BRIEN	O'BRIEN: No credit, but...
2003.10.21.1tm.05	REX_ADELBERGER	ADELBERGER: And if that's civil disobedience...
2003.10.21.1tm.05	CNN_S_O'BRIEN	O'BRIEN: ... a potential big downside for him, possibly. A quick question for you, and we don't
2003.10.21.1tm.05	REX_ADELBERGER	ADELBERGER: Yes.
2003.10.21.1tm.05	CNN_S_O'BRIEN	O'BRIEN: But I want to know what's been the reaction of the fellow students. Are they supportin
2003.10.21.1tm.05	REX_ADELBERGER	ADELBERGER: All sides -- there are students that think that what he did was absolutely right, and
2003.10.21.1tm.05	CNN_S_O'BRIEN	O'BRIEN: Well...
2003.10.21.1tm.05	REX_ADELBERGER	ADELBERGER: So, there are all three there.
2003.10.21.1tm.05	CNN_S_O'BRIEN	O'BRIEN: Professor Adelberger, I thank you for your time this morning and for providing a littl
2003.10.21.1tm.05	REX_ADELBERGER	ADELBERGER: OK.

Figure 2:   A CNN transcript in its final format

In the case of George Bush, an additional complication is introduced by the fact that his father carries the same name. Distinctive features such as the labels *junior, senior* or *former president* or the additional first name *Herbert* are often not present. For the computer, there is thus virtually no way of determining whether the transcribed words were uttered by George Bush senior in a re-broadcast of an earlier piece of CNN footage or whether they stem from the current president of the United States.[10] As a result, some of the utterances in my corpus currently assigned to George Bush junior may actually stem from his father.

Similar complications also exist for a considerable number of other speakers. For example, as in the case of *Senator Tom Daschle* and *Senator Thomas Daschle*, the first names of speakers often exist in different versions. In order to avoid labelling them as different speakers, a frequency list of all names was compiled and then manually scanned. Obvious cases of variants were then assigned to a single speaker identification code. Considering that there are almost 100,000 different speakers in my data, this can obviously only be done for speakers who appear frequently on CNN. Again we are thus left with a margin of error that would require considerable manual work to improve.

In a last step, part-of-speech information was added to all words in the transcripts with the help of the automatic tagger *EngCG-2* (see Voutilainen 1997). The final result of the various conversion steps can be seen in figure 2. Each line starts with a code which indicates the date and name of the programme. This is followed by the unique speaker identification code and the original speaker name. As an additional distinction, CNN personnel is identified by adding CNN to their names while the other speaker codes are formed by a combination of their first and last names.[11] Functions (such as *president*) are not part of the identification code. The actual utterance forms the final element of each line. The individual items are separated by tab-stops, which facilitates the isolation of the actual utterance from circumstantial information by a search script or concordancer.

5.   Searching the data

While standard concordancing software such as Wordsmith or MonoConc will be able to search the CNN transcripts in the simple text format presented at the end of the previous section, Perl and its powerful regular expression engine can offer a greater level of flexibility and control to a linguist with a moderate level of programming expertise.[12] The effectiveness of Perl for a linguistic analysis of text is further enhanced when it is combined with the relational database system MySQL (see http://www.mysql.com). Thus, I extracted the information available for the individual transcripts and stored them in a number of databases. For example, one database contains the name of the programme, the date of broadcast and the total number of words for each transcript. A second database stores all speaker identification codes, the corresponding full speaker names (including their function, if available) and the total number of words produced by the speakers. Using these databases, it is a simple task to instruct a Perl script to restrict searches to individual speakers, individual programmes or certain time-spans (or a combination of these aspects). Furthermore, these databases also make it possible to automatically compile basic descriptive statistics for search results. On the basis of such information, individual idiosyncrasies and topic-specific preferences of the features investigated can easily be detected.

For many types of linguistic analysis, researchers require access to additional information about the language data studied, and most of the currently available electronic corpora are therefore annotated with metatextual data. For example, with its detailed information about speakers or authors (for example age, sex, social class) and texts (for example text domain, publication date, target audience), the BNC allows scholars to investigate issues of variation from a sociolinguistic perspective. In comparison, relatively little information is available for the corpus of CNN transcripts, and manually annotating the data – for example by adding socio-demographic information for the speakers – would clearly be a daunting task. A limited number of options exist for extending the range of information by way of an automated procedure. Thus, fairly simple heuristics could be employed to differentiate between male and female speakers (for example on the basis of lists of first names). It may also be possible to extract additional information about at least some of the speakers from other sources available on the internet. However, such automated methods would no doubt be subject to considerable error and the findings obtained on the basis of such types of annotation would thus require a particularly careful evaluation on the part of the researcher.

6.   The CNN transcripts corpus – some statistics

Table 2 summarises some of the general properties of the CNN transcripts corpus. With its more than 172 million words uttered by almost 100,000 different speakers in over one hundred different news programmes, this dataset clearly represents an attractive source of data for scholars whose research questions require access to large amounts of spoken data.

Table 2:   The CNN transcripts corpus – an overview

Period covered:	1.1.2000 - 18.8.2004
Total number of transcripts:	102,579
Total number of words:	172,639,697
Number of different speaker identification codes:	99,513
Number of different programme titles:	104
Number of different CNN speakers	2,004
Words spoken by CNN speakers:	97,225,664 (56.3%)

However, a number of important caveats require brief mention here. Given its specialized nature, the language use represented by the CNN transcripts can of course not be directly compared with the range of discourse contexts found in the currently available general spoken corpora. Furthermore, the CNN transcripts corpus is a very unbalanced dataset with respect to the number of words produced by its individual speakers. This is clearly shown by the fact that the 2,004 speakers identified as CNN personnel contribute more than half of the words in the corpus (56.3 per cent). This lack of balance is even further emphasized by table 3, which lists the seven most prominent speakers in the CNN transcripts corpus. With a total of just under 20 million words, these speakers contribute 11.5 per cent of the whole corpus.

Table 3: Most prominent speakers in the CNN transcripts corpus

Speaker identification code	Number of words
CNN_W_BLITZER	5,099,573
CNN_L_KING	3,035,656
CNN_J_WOODRUFF	2,765,619
CNN_B_HEMMER	2,460,969
CNN_D_KAGAN	2,394,666
CNN_P_ZAHN	2,110,491
GEORGE_W._BUSH	2,009,847
	19,876,821

Another important point to consider is the degree of naturalness or orality of the language use found in the CNN transcripts. Obviously, quite a proportion of the words uttered will have been read off a teleprompter. However, since no indication of this is given in the transcripts, it is impossible to (automatically) distinguish between these extracts and others which were spoken freely with very little – if any – preparation. Some programmes are of course more likely to contain spontaneous speech, but this is not a categorical distinction.

As a final point, it also needs to be stated that a considerable number of speakers in the CNN transcripts are non-native speakers of English. However, unless the corpus is annotated with additional socio-demographic information, it is not possible to reliably distinguish between utterances made by native and non-native speakers.

7. A sample study: the intensifier *so*

Notwithstanding the caveats mentioned in the previous section, a large corpus of news programme transcripts can of course still be very useful for a whole range of linguistic analyses. First of all, given that the transcripts are published on the

CNN web site on the day after the airing of the programme, they naturally contain extremely recent use of English. Very few changes are required to apply the conversion scripts to newly available transcripts and it is thus in principle possible to study "Present-day English" in an almost literal sense. A corpus of CNN transcripts can therefore be used to describe aspects of current language use and to trace developments in recent English.[13]

Scholars who are interested in morphological productivity, for example, will find ample opportunity to examine new coinages in the lexicon of English. Another type of investigation could focus on discourse strategies in different contexts. The programme *Larry King Live* alone is represented with 10.5 million words and we can observe Larry King with a whole range of different interview partners. Such data could for example be used to look at the interface between power and language.[14] In the present context, I would like to focus on a syntactic topic and investigate to what extent the CNN transcripts corpus can contribute to the study of relatively new uses of the intensifier *so*.

The standard use of this intensifier is shown in example (1), where *so* intensifies the adjective phrase *happy*.

(1)   Thank you, Harris. We've been reading of high security, Bernie, there in Mexico City. We're *so happy* to see that so far, all is smooth and happy. (2000.01.01.se.07, CNN_J_WOODRUFF)

A recent study by Tagliamonte and Roberts (2005) demonstrates that this intensifying use of *so* is on the rise. The authors claim that in some discourse contexts, *so* even outnumbers *very* and *really* in American English today.

A different, but not completely unrelated type of use of *so* is shown in (2):

(2)   On Social Security privatization, Bush seems to make a political gamble that people under about 35 *so mistrust* Social Security *that* they're going to go for these private accounts. (2000.05.19.ip.00, E.J._DIONNE)

This is a *so ... that* construction in which the *that*-clause expresses a result. Quirk et al. (1985:1109) briefly mention variants such as (2) in a note and remark that in these cases *so* is not an intensifier but a manner adverb. The authors also state that this is a feature of formal language and that *that* cannot be omitted in constructions like (2). Huddleston and Pullum (2002: 968), conversely, do not see any problem with omitting *that* in such sentences. This view appears to be closer to actual usage as sentences such as (3) are indeed found in my data:

(3)   Nick in St. Croix, "Bush replace Cheney? Not necessary. Edwards *so outshines* Kerry it makes him look and sound like Herman Munster." (2004.07.08.ltm.05, CNN_J_CAFFERTY)

While Quirk et al.'s distinction between intensifier and manner adverb works well for sentences like (2), it clearly breaks down in example (4). Here, we do have a result clause, but the verb *knew* is certainly also intensified.

(4)   Eat my heart out! I *so knew* he was going to last that I put a very huge bet on his being there to the last dogs lie. (2000.01.27.cf.00, MARY_ MATALIN)

In the majority of sentences in my data, however, no result clause is present and the intensifying *so* simply precedes the verb. A typical instance is shown in (5):

(5)   I know, Betsy, you *so respect* the decision your husband made, even though it's making life much more difficult for you. (2003.03.07.ltm.13, CNN_P_ZAHN)

In the CNN transcripts, a total of 289 such instances were retrieved. Although this is of course a relatively low number for a corpus of 172 million words, it nevertheless points to the fact that this type of intensifying use of *so* has attained a certain level of currency in Present-day American English.

Further insight into the use of this construction can be gained by looking at the kind of verbs that are intensified. Indeed, a number of recurring collocations can be found, the most frequent of which is *so appreciate*, as shown in (6):

(6)   Heidi, Amber, we *so appreciate* your being with us. And Bill, thank you as well. (2002.08.14.cct.00, CNN_C_CHUNG)

Table 4:   Intensifying *so* before a verb – collocations with five or more instances in the CNN transcripts. (Inflected forms are grouped together under the base form of the verb).

Collocation	Number of instances
so appreciate	32
so want	13
so dominate	8
so offend	7
so hate	7
so enjoy	7
so upset	6
so dislike	5
so admire	5
so cherish	5
so love	5

A total of 32 instances of *so appreciate* are found in my data. Other collocations with at least five instances are listed in table 4. It is noteworthy – but perhaps not surprising – that quite a few of those contain a verb that expresses emotional states (*appreciate*, *want*, *dislike*, *enjoy*, *admire*, etc.).

There are, however, also a considerable number of instances that are less typical than those shown in table 4. This is well exemplified in sentences (7) to (9):

(7)   And he was such a tender-hearted, great guy, he just *so understood* my spirituality and lack of religiosity. He *so got* that. (2004.05.21.lkl.01, KATHIE_LEE_GIFFORD)

(8)   So many people say they felt that they knew her because she *so wore* her personality on her sleeve. (2002.03.30.bn.07, CNN_F_WHITFIELD)

(9)   Well, you know what? It *so drove* me crazy for 10 years, how to find a man. (2003.01.10.lol.07, E._JEAN_CARROLL)

In cases like this – particularly (8) and (9) – the issue of the scope of intensification comes into play: In both cases, what is intensified is not the verb but instead the whole predication.

Tagliamonte and Roberts (to appear) claim that that the rise of intensifying *so* in American English is at least partly influenced by the popularity of the TV series *Friends*. They restrict their investigation to *so* before adjectives, but it may not be a coincidence that the CNN transcripts contain one extract from this TV series which shows an extreme case of verbal intensification with the help of *so*:[15]

(10)   MATT_LEBLANC   Oh, man! you are *so wearing* that bracelet.
         MATTHEW_PERRY   I so am.
         MATT_LEBLANC   You have any idea what this will do for your sex life?
         MATTHEW_PERRY   Well, it would probably slow it down at first, but once I get used to the extra weight, I'll be back on track. (2002.08.22.lkl.00)

The instance of *so* shown in (10) appears to be an extension of the more common use exemplified in (5) to (9) above and it may indeed make more sense to regard it here as some kind of pragmatic marker. While quantitative statements are not possible on the basis of this data, my findings clearly suggest that the use of the intensifier *so* is undergoing considerable changes in Present-day American English.

Since the names of the speakers are indicated in the transcripts, it is also possible to determine if anyone in particular contributes to the spread of this innovative use of *so* on CNN. As it turns out, Larry King is quite prominent here. In fact, I received the impression that his speech also contains a number of other interesting features. A more detailed look at the three million words he contributes to the corpus may therefore prove interesting. However, this would lead to the more general question whether or not corpus linguistics should be interested in investigating the language of an individual speaker rather than a cross-section of speakers.

To end this sample study about intensifying *so*, I would like to briefly focus on yet another different use, namely that before *not*. The most frequent representative is the expression *so not true*, as exemplified in (11):

(11)   So many people think that nice people finish last, and it's so not true. (2002.12.25.ltm.09, PHYLLIS_GEORGE)

While Quirk et al. (1985) do not mention this use at all, Huddleston and Pullum (2002: 807) state in a footnote that "[t]his is a relatively new construction, characteristic of the informal speech of younger speakers." Interestingly, they restrict it to predicative adjective phrases such as the one shown in (11). However, my data suggests that this use of *so not* is becoming more productive. As support for this impression, consider sentences (12) to (15), which display *so not* intensifying a past participle, a lexical gap, and two noun phrases:

(12)   What do you think explains that widespread looting and why do you think that was *so not* predicted prior to the fall of Baghdad? (2003.05.19.ltm.14, CNN_B_HEMMER)
(13)   I just - I wanted them a little brighter. I want them a little brighter, and they're still *so not*. (2003.06.23.ltm.10, DINA_WISE)
(14)   They might have felt bad for her, and they figured once she recovered from that, she'd be a hot babe. But she is *so not* a hot babe. (2004.01.15.ltm.06, LOLA_OGUNNAIKE)
(15)   And you know what, and think about Mike Tyson, he's the definition of excessive. I mean, this is *so not* a shock, at least to me. (2003.08.04.lt.04, HARVEY_LEVIN)
(16)   I don't know. I'm *so not* the expert on these kinds of things. (2002.03.27. lkl.00, JODIE_FOSTER)

As shown in figure 3, this intensifying use of *so* before *not* appears to be on the increase. However, overall frequencies are exceedingly low – a total of 55 instances can be retrieved in 172 million words – and far more data would be required to substantiate this impression more reliably.

7.   Evaluation and conclusion

In this paper, I have illustrated the individual steps that were necessary to convert the web pages displaying the CNN transcripts to a format which can be searched with standard concordancing software. I have drawn attention to a number of difficulties (both technical and methodological) and although considerable care has been taken to optimize the conversion process, the result is not an ideal corpus and would thus require extensive manual checking in order to make it even more reliable.

While the result of my labours cannot be considered on a par with balanced corpora like the BNC, my sample study demonstrates that a linguistic analysis on the basis of the CNN transcripts corpus can offer interesting and relevant results. As with all corpus linguistic work, the drawbacks of the data need to be known and taken into account when the results are interpreted.

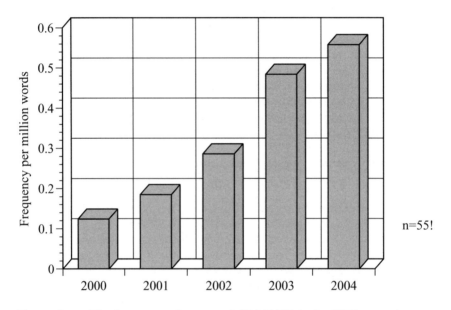

Figure 3:   The frequency of *so not* + AdjP/NP/VP in the CNN transcripts

When comparing insights gained from the CNN transcripts with what can be obtained via a Google search, a few relevant points can be raised: First of all, an internet-derived corpus of 172 million words is clearly a large dataset – still a mega-corpus by today's standards – but it is obviously (and in many ways) only a small fraction of what is available on the web. For example, a Google search for *so not true* conducted in April 2005 retrieved 15,800 web pages and a further 4,860 hits in the newsgroups archive.[16] In contrast, the CNN transcripts only contain 10 instances. Obviously, the CNN transcripts are much more restricted than the whole of the internet with respect to the text types represented, and the low number of instances for *so not true* is certainly a reflection of the fact that news broadcasts contain a relatively small proportion of highly informal conversation. Far-reaching conclusions about the status of the *so not* construction as an element of (spoken) grammar would therefore require further investigation on the basis of other (internet-derived?) data.

However, the limitations of the CNN transcripts can also be considered advantages: I know (or can easily find out) what is in the CNN transcripts and I can interpret the (fully replicable) results accordingly. Furthermore, as the compiler of the corpus, I am in control over what might be added in the future. Its size is known and reliable relative frequencies can be calculated, which still form the standard for comparisons across different linguistic categories. Also, as it was possible to create a part-of-speech tagged version of the corpus, I was able to search my data for syntactic constructions that would be extremely hard to retrieve using only the kind of lexical searches that Google allows.

In sum, I hope to have demonstrated that internet-derived data like the CNN transcripts corpus can indeed be successfully employed to complement available corpora for an analysis of Present-day English. The procedures described in this paper can thus serve as a convenient approach to bridging the gap until more linguistically viable methods of searching the (whole of the) internet have been developed.

Notes

1   This is also true for WebCorp (http://www.webcorp.org.uk/), which offers a more linguistically oriented interface to Google and AltaVista searches but which is still beset by the same kind of general search limitations (cf. Lüdeling et al., this volume).

2   For a more optimistic interpretation of these issues, see Kilgarriff and Grefenstette (2003).

3   A comprehensive introduction to LWP and its flexible set of features is found in Burke (2002).

4   This kind of automated retrieval procedure can put considerable strain on the server from which the files are downloaded. It may therefore be advisable to write delays into the Perl script (e.g. a wait of 10 seconds between page accesses) to spread the load placed on the web server over a longer period of time.

5   This information is also encoded in the URL of the transcript. For example, the transcript displayed in figure 1 is found at http://transcripts.cnn.com/TRANSCRIPTS/0310/21/ltm.05.html, where *ltm* refers to *American Morning*.

6   This is for example the case for the archives of the Indian newspaper *The Statesman* (http://www.thestatesman.net).

7   For some of these variants, the only difference is found in the use of punctuation marks and spaces. While these can of course not be considered different names in the strict sense, a simple script will determine two strings of characters to be distinct elements even if the difference is only

constituted by a single space character. In order to avoid this potential source of distortion of the data, the conversion scripts had to be designed in a way that would account for a certain level of typographical variation.

8   In some of these labels, the function of the speaker precedes his or her name. Typical examples of this are *general, governor, president, professor, reverend* and *senator*. A list of these items was compiled on the basis of a frequency list of all names in order to make sure that the conversion scripts do not identify them as being part of the first names of the speakers.

9   It could also be argued that it would be advisable to retain the distinction between the different stages of a person's career. Does the same person produce different linguistic output as a governor and as president of the United States? While I do not want to suggest that such potential differences are very often relevant, it is still worth pointing out that the decisions taken by a corpus compiler will necessarily influence the kind of results that can be obtained from the data.

10   This situation will of course even be worse once George Bush junior will also be labelled as *former president*.

11   For a considerable number of speakers, the distinction between CNN personnel and other contributors could not be conclusively determined. For example, in earlier transcripts Wesley Clark frequently appears as *GENERAL WESLEY CLARK, SUPREME ALLIED COMMANDER*. In more recent transcripts, however, he is referred to as *GENERAL WESLEY CLARK, CNN MILITARY EXPERT*.

12   For an introduction to regular expression searches, see Friedl (2002).

13   In addition, a corpus of CNN transcripts is of course an interesting archive from the point of view of content as it covers many important events of recent history, including the terrorist attacks of 9/11 and the second Iraq war.

14   See for example Locher (2004), who uses transcripts of presidential election debates to investigate aspects of power and politeness in disagreements.

15   This extract was shown during an interview with the actor Matthew Perry on *Larry King Live*.

16   Six months earlier, the same search had only retrieved 5,750 web pages. However, the situation is very different in the newsgroup archive, where the earlier search in fact retrieved a slightly larger number of hits than in April 2005 (4,860 vs. 4,630). This inconsistency in search results lends strong support to the claim that internet-based findings must be interpreted with great care.

References

Burke, S.M. (2002), *Perl & LWP*. Sebastopol, CA: O'Reilly.

Friedl, J.E.F. (2002), *Mastering Regular Expressions*, 2nd edn. Sebastopol, CA: O'Reilly.

Huddleston, R. and G.K. Pullum (2002), *The Cambridge Grammar of the English Language*. Cambridge: Cambridge University Press.

Kilgarriff, A. and G. Grefenstette (2003), 'Introduction to the special issue on the web as corpus', *Computational Linguistics*, 23 (3): 333-347.

Locher, M.A. (2004), *Power and Politeness in Action. Disagreements in Oral Communication*. Berlin and New York: Mouton de Gruyter.

Lüdeling, A., S. Evert and M. Baroni (this volume), 'Using web data for linguistic purposes'.

Quirk, R., S. Greenbaum, G. Leech and J. Svartvik (1985), *A Comprehensive Grammar of the English Language*. London: Longman.

Tagliamonte, S. and C. Roberts (2005), '*So weird; so cool; so innovative*: the use of intensifiers in the television series *Friends*', *American Speech*, 80 (3): 280-300.

Voutilainen, A. (1997), 'The EngCG-2 tagger in outline', available online: http://www.ling.helsinki.fi/~avoutila/cg/doc/engcg2-outline/engcg2-outline.html (accessed: 11.4.2005).

Constructing a corpus from the web: message boards

Claudia Claridge

University of Kiel

Abstract

This paper investigates the challenges and chances involved in creating a corpus of message board (or internet forum) language, in particular one that also reflects the regional varieties of English. Message boards as an asynchronic and public form of computer-mediated communication function as an 'electronic agora' (Largier 2002: 287), in so far as they are used for a variety of functions ranging from the more private to the more public, including the discussion of highly topical socio-political subject-matter. Thus, content orientation, evaluation and interactive argumentation are potential characteristics of this text form. Firstly, the technical aspects of corpus compilation will be highlighted, examining such matters as how to transform the web interface into a suitably annotated corpus, how to adequately represent the sequencing/relatedness of messages and how to establish regional speaker identities. Secondly, a pilot study on interaction and stance markers will examine how these are realized and distributed in this genre, and whether there are any regional differences in their use.

1.   Introduction

Computer-mediated communication (CMC), especially the web-based public variety, has the potential to influence and partly transform the nature of public debate by uniting people with shared values and goals in a common cause – regardless of their separation in space and (potentially) time. For example, Gurak (1996) has shown how an extensive web debate was successful in leading to the withdrawal of a disputed product by the Lotus company. While such striking success is probably the exception, internet message boards or forums do often deal with non-trivial topics, such as the right to abortion (Largier 2002), the connection between BSE and CJD (Richardson 2001), or General Pinochet's detention in London (Tanner 2001), and as such play a role in establishing, stabilizing or challenging (received) public opinion on serious issues. Largier (2002: 287) has termed this new form, which has sociological, cultural and political implications, an 'electronic agora'. Needless to say, it also has implica-tions and poses challenges for communication studies and linguistics.

Message boards or forums (to be used interchangeably in this paper), which are the focus of this study, are different from other forms of CMC in various respects. They are dialogic (or better: polylogic) and conversational in style like email or chat, but in contrast to these they are completely public. Emails are exchanged between two individuals, a small group, or at most, via lists, a few hundred or thousand subscribed participants (e.g. Linguist List); they are not meant for or accessible to the public at large. Chat takes places in designated chat rooms, and is conducted by registered users; thus, it also establishes entrance limits for the general public. Forums, on the other hand, are part of the public world-wide-web space, look like 'normal' web sites[1] and can be visited and read by any internet user at any time, in the same way as people would read an online newspaper, for example. Forum conversations may be available on the web long after they took place. Marcoccia (2004: 117, 135, 140) has therefore called them a hybrid between interpersonal and mass communication, and pointed out how Goffmann's model of ratified participants *vs.* eavesdroppers and overhearers is being overturned: eavesdroppers, i.e. simple readers, not senders, of messages, become (accepted as) ratified participants.[2] Like email (lists), but unlike chat, forum interaction is asynchronous: the conversations are potentially long-drawn-out, discontinuous, and do not necessarily constitute the only or even the major activity of the participants at a given time (cf. Marcoccia 2004: 117). As to content, email lists are usually restricted in some way, either to a professional (sub)group or to a specific area of interest (and the group united by it), while chat is usually not intended for serious, content-centred discussion but has a more pronounced phatic character. In contrast, forums often offer a wide range of topics, not rarely of a serious, controversial nature, forming an open public-opinion platform, and thus they invite browsing for information.

The dialogic, interactive nature of the above-mentioned forms of CMC has led to an early tendency in research to investigate them with a view to oral linguistic features. However, they are all clearly written texts, in form and in conception, and this needs to be taken into account (cf. Largier 2002: 290, 292; Marcoccia 2004: 116). Forms of CMC are indeed registers or genres of their own, or even, as Crystal (2001: 238) claims, a fourth independent system besides speech, writing and gesture with its own medium-specific characteristics. Lewin and Donner (2002) have shown that features so far typically ascribed to CMC interaction, among them some oral features,[3] are in fact not very frequent in message boards and thus not constitutive for the register as a whole, although their frequency may vary according to board and topic. Collot and Belmore (1996) have approached Bulletin Board Systems (= forums) by using Biber's (1988) multidimensional factor analysis. They found their CMC corpus to score fairly highly not only on Dimensions 1 and 6, which contain features typical of spoken, unplanned discourse, but also on Dimensions 4 and 5, which are concerned with persuasion and abstract information, i.e. are more characteristic of planned and written discourse. Such studies point to the fact that the unique extralinguistic features of CMC have produced an equally unique mix of linguistic characteristics – in other words, that it constitutes a new text type or genre.

While various studies have investigated forum language[4] and some have constructed corpora for this purpose, no sound textual basis for enabling further research has been created so far. Nor is there any publicly available corpus of forum interactions. The main purpose of this contribution is therefore to highlight the need for such a corpus and to discuss the necessities and problems in constructing it. This will be complemented by some preliminary thoughts on the linguistic investigation of forum interactions.

2.   Creating a corpus

Web-based forums are not searchable text in the corpus-linguistic sense,[5] which means that they need to be transformed in some way in order to be analysable as a normal off-line corpus. From a purely practical point of view, it is certainly undesirable for every researcher to start from scratch, in particular as the transformation process can be fairly cumbersome and work-intensive. Furthermore, such one-off approaches leave us with diverse studies on smallish corpora, which might not be fully comparable. Another point concerns the diachronic perspective: the internet is a locus of change, certainly from a technical angle but also from a linguistic one. A corpus set-up with fixed parameters and established transformation mechanisms (html > marked-up corpus) would offer the possibility of creating a diachronic view on message boards.

A message board corpus needs to take appropriate account of the characteristics of this genre. Richardson (2001: 57), who investigated newsgroups, identified four important characteristics of CMC: interactive, international, interested, and intertextual ('four I's'). While 'interested' (the fact that the text content is clearly coloured by the senders' identities, values and concerns) is a characteristic to be kept in mind mainly for corpus analysis, the remaining three already play a role in corpus construction. 'Interactive' means that corpus compilation and mark-up should pay attention to senders, their roles and characteristics (e.g. number of participants, gender, 'heavy' senders), and to the exchange structure of the electronic conversation (e.g. who is replying to whom, chronology). In some ways, such a corpus thus has similar needs to those of a corpus of spoken language. 'International' likewise involves the participants, this time specifically their nationality and mother tongue, as well as the fact that the internet offers the opportunity for transnational contact. While this opens up interesting perspectives for cross-cultural pragmatics, it can cause problems for studying the English language on the web: the question of how to identify and deal with non-native speakers, potentially differentiated into ESL and EFL speakers, will need to be addressed in corpus compilation. In the context of English, or any other multinational language, 'international' can also mean including the variety perspective, i.e. the aspect that message boards offer the opportunity to obtain comparable and up-to-date dialogic material from several varieties of English. Richardson's (cf. ibid.: 62) last point, 'intertextuality', refers to the fact that messages on such boards are composite texts, in so far as they include other (published) texts or prefabricated standard text chunks, establish connections via hyperlinks and quote part or all of other messages. The question is how much to include of such material and in what easily distinguishable ways. All of these aspects will be discussed in more detail below.

As a starting point, the following basic corpus parameters were decided upon: (i) *international*: inclusion of forums from different English-speaking countries, initially only from those where English is the first language; (ii) *interactive*: inclusion of longer conversations (threads) as the basic text units in order to make it possible to study interaction;[6] and (iii) *interactive* (/*interested*): coverage of a broad range of conversational topics, as far as possible those with potential for controversy-laden debate. Different topics – in addition to different forums from each country – can help to ensure the representation of speakers from diverse backgrounds and with varied outlooks.

2.1   The data

In order to investigate the possibilities and problems inherent in creating such a corpus, a small pilot version was constructed. For this pilot, four message boards or forums were used as data sources, to represent four varieties:

> Great Britain: BBC message boards (URL: http://www.bbc.co.uk/messageboards)
> USA: *The Atlantic* online: Forum Post and Riposte (URL: http://www.theatlantic.com/pr/)
> Australia: TVAus.com (URL: http://www.tvaus.com.au/)
> Canada: About.com: Canada online (URL: http://forums.about.com/abcanadaonline/messages) (an additionally thread was taken from http://www.icangarden.com)

The selected forums are quite diverse in affiliation, makeup and outlook, which can be taken as typical of message boards on the internet. While the BBC and Atlantic forums are affiliated to existing mass media, the others are independent sites. TVAus, for example, describes itself on the website as a "non-profit Australian forum that has no ties to any commercial companies or organisations whatsoever." Only one of them is thematically restricted (to gardening),[7] while the others have a variety of sections (e.g. 'science and nature', 'news, current affairs and politics') where many topics (e.g. Prince Charles and Camilla's wedding, the killing of seals) are treated. Membership in the Atlantic forum is reserved to Atlantic subscribers and the site partly focuses on discussion of *The Atlantic*'s print and online articles. There are no such restrictions for the other selected forums; however, it is necessary to register as a user in order to take part in discussions on all of the sites.

The surface presentation is markedly different between the selected sites (cf. screenshots in the appendix). While the BBC, the Atlantic, and Icangarden are text-heavy, Canada online and, especially strikingly, TVAus are more colourful, containing pictures, icons and other graphics. If one considers this together with the topics discussed, one could construct a 'soberness hierarchy' of roughly the following nature: Atlantic/Icangarden – BBC – Canada online – TVAus.[8] The latter is a good illustration of Shank's (1993, quoted from December 1996: 15) claim that on-line communication is neither oral nor written, but in fact semiotic. The ease of following a discussion is different on the boards: while it is possible to see whole threads at once on the BBC, the Atlantic and Icangarden, and at least large chunks (10-20 messages) on TVAus, Canada online presents only one message per screen, thus masking the conversation structure. The BBC graphically marks the structure of the conversation (by nested indenting), while Canada online includes an explicit *to*-line in the header, indicating the intended addressee of the message.

Between them, the selected forums provide a fairly broad representation of internet message boards. The pilot corpus collected from them has the following characteristics:

Table 1: The pilot corpus – composition

	Total	Atlantic	BBC	Canada online	TVAus
Tokens	89.874	15.365	27.147	18.597	28.765
Types	9.160	3.264	4.175	3.337	3.866
Threads	30	6	10	7	7
Messages	796	145	265	159	227
Senders	232	41	95	36	60
Attributed Gender*:					
female	70	8	20	10	32
male	81	10	34	14	23
uncertain	81	23	41	12	5

(*Cf. below for discussion.)

The data was collected in January/February 2005 and contains ongoing or only recently completed conversations. Ongoing of course implies that fragments of conversations are sampled, but this formulation – just like calling others completed – might be misleading: while threads always have a clear beginning, they do not end in a structured (or otherwise determined) way, instead simply stopping without any signals, due to lack of interest. One thread on TVAus, for example, has a second-to-last message dated Aug. 29, 2004 (not replied to) and (at the time of copying) a last message dated Jan. 30, 2005, both by the same person, who is apparently trying to revive the discussion. Threads of manageable/medium size should be chosen, i.e. ideally not smaller than 15 messages and not bigger than 40 (cf. listing in the appendix); however, this is not always feasible, as boards and topics differ with regard to their activity level. On the one hand, threads should allow for a reasonable amount of interaction and development of topic, but on the other hand, the over-representation in the corpus of (perhaps) a very small group of recurrent senders should be avoided. There are two more points of importance. First of all, some of the indicated messages are not in fact there (i.e. with text). Some were deleted, presumably by the forum moderator(s), without a reason being provided. It is not clear to me whether these were seen by any members before deletion or not; if so, their absence represents an unfortunate disruption of the conversational sequence. Secondly, other messages were deleted by myself because they were there twice, e.g. in the BBC thread "Was Nurnberg trial unfair?". A similar case occurred on the Atlantic where one poster was not aware of a length restriction on postings and was automatically cut off several times before he managed to send his message in two 'installments'.

The word counts (tokens) in table 1 partly reflect the amount of usable material, i.e. number and size of threads (e.g. small quantity for the Atlantic), or the cumbersomeness of extracting the text (e.g. Canada online). Another aspect which distorts the picture is the fact that everything is included in the count, even though repeated material (quoted from previous mails) and also non-interactive material (such as pasted articles from online papers) ultimately needs to be factored out. The amount of quoting varies between the forums: while 7% of messages on the Atlantic and 9% each on Canada online and the BBC contain quoted material, 44% of all TVAus messages make use of quotes, which further-more are fairly long in contrast to the other sites. The average length of messages is 87 words (Atlantic), 107 (BBC), 112 (Canada online) and 139 (TVAus), but while this stays practically the same after extracting quotes from the Atlantic and the BBC material, the average figure drops to 105 words for Canada online and to 101 words for TVAus. This could mean that TVAus discussions are more (overtly) interactive, with people paying more attention to what others say, or perhaps (rather) that senders simply need to make the structure clearer, as there is no other indication as to whom the message is a reaction to, unlike the case with Canada online or the BBC. The quote-induced repetitiveness also explains the lower type figure compared to the BBC. A last point to mention in the context of word counts is that so far they have been based on the senders' own uncorrected writing, i.e. missing spaces between words will influence the token figure and spelling mistakes/typos (e.g. *enormous/enourmous, entertained/enternained*) the type figure.

As can be seen from table 1, there are clearly more messages than send-ers.[9] This is to be expected, as an interesting thread usually only develops if senders do not restrict themselves to one message, but interact repeatedly. How-ever, a certain number of senders are also present in more than one thread. Mar-coccia (2004: 135) identified three kinds of participant roles, one of which – simple readers – I have already mentioned above; the other two are 'casual senders' and 'hosts', the later participants who contribute a large number of messages and act like moderators or leaders of the discussion. These are also the contributors that often start new threads. Forum sites may provide information about these user types by indicating the number of postings so far, the time of joining the forum or the like. While the BBC and TVAus provide this information together with the message on the screen, and with Canada online it is available by clicking on the member profile, it is not given by the Atlantic website. It is also interesting how this situation is reflected in the present corpus. People who are active in several threads on one forum are most common on TVAus (33% of all), followed by Canada online (28%) and the Atlantic (27%), while they are uncommon on the BBC (7%). These figures say something not only about the people themselves (their degree of web activity, their interests), but also about how close-knit a community a given forum constitutes, i.e. how well people know each other. This is of interest when studying their interaction with each other. In the present corpus, some of the senders, especially on TVAus, seem to know each other fairly well from common participation in several threads. As to the number of posts sent by individuals, the majority are represented by 2-5 postings on the Atlantic (54%), the BBC (52%) and Canada online (50%), while these come to only 38% on TVAus. People with 6-10 postings make up 7% (Atlantic), 8% (BBC), 17% (TVAus) and 22% (Canada online), while heavy posters (11 and more) are in the minority in all the forums represented here (2% (BBC), 5% (TVAus), 5.5% (Canada online), 7% (Atlantic)). The remainder are represented by one posting in the corpus. The speaker composition of the corpus thus mirrors the situation on the web to a certain extent (casual vs. heavy senders), which is desirable in order to be representative of the genre, while the highly active senders are nevertheless not overpresented, which might unduly bias the corpus data.

Another interesting aspect with regard to the speakers is their gender. This presents problems, however, because of the well-known practice of aliases and nicknames. The gender information given in table 1 is based on names and on self-information. Real-sounding names, such as *Judith Spencer* or *Carl Jones*,[10] were accepted as evidence here on the basis of which to attribute gender, even though they might be just as invented as nicknames, such as *mook-e* or *iratecanadian*, and the address might of course be used by someone else than the person indicated. Perhaps more reliable, though still not necessarily correct, is self-information, for example that given fairly consistently by TVAus together with every message; this accounts for the low number of 'uncertains' there, which refer to people refusing to reveal their gender. Some forums provide personal information via member profiles in the background, where one again finds information supplied by the members themselves and perhaps also information about their 'forum history'. Gender is usually one of the categories to be optionally filled in.[11] The most reliable gender information, however, may be that provided in the context of a message itself, in which case it relates to or situates the argument made; this is attested in the corpus, for example in a discussion on the acceptability of male childminders (BBC) and in another discussion about the question whether men are going soft (TVAus). As table 1 shows, female senders are not necessarily underrepresented: if the attributions are taken at face value, there are overall only 11 fewer than men, and on TVAus they even outnumber men. If one looks at the speech actually produced (i.e. message text excluding quotes), women provide on average longer messages than men on Canada online and the BBC, but 20% and 30% shorter ones on TVAus and the Atlantic, respectively. Needless to say, gender differences are still of high linguistic interest, as are interactional differences in CMC contexts (e.g. Herring 1996). Thus, the encoding of gender to as great an extent as possible is certainly a desirable element in such a corpus.

As one of the corpus parameters listed above is the representation of four English varieties, the nationality, location and mother tongue of the senders are very important aspects. Not surprisingly, explicit linguistic information is not given anywhere. While forums can of course be indicative of a certain nationality – cf. their name (TVAus, Canada online) or their affiliation (BBC) – they are nevertheless open to everybody. Organisations/sites that are well-known and have a certain reputation, e.g. the BBC, have a higher likelihood of extra-national contributors is higher than more localized message boards (e.g. Welsh sites). The BBC thread "Was Nurnberg Trial unfair?", for example, contains messages by one German speaker (cf. the statement in one message "We had *here in Germany* some discussions about that in the time before the reunification in 1990" (BBC 8,12) and potentially by two further non-native speakers (Jozef, Miguel/Michal). As this example illustrates, certain topics may attract international participation, while others, such as those of a clearly national or even only local relevance (e.g. BBC, The housing issue), rather discourage this; thus, the choice of threads with topics of restricted regional interest can help control this sender characteristic. One Canadian was found to post on TVAus, if the sender's own place information ("Quebec, Canada") is to be believed. Two further interesting cases can be detailed from TVAus, where one finds the sender Aussies-online stating "Having a French background [...]" / "But having spent more time in Australia than in France, [...]" (TVAus 6, 50) and zivko contributing such information as "i am serbian and part of my family lives in Kosovo [...]" / "my biculturality and aussie identity" (TVAus 2, 18). Excluding international and 'mixed-language' contributors would be representative neither of the internet/CMC situation nor of immigrant societies such as Australia or the USA. In so far as the corpus is supposed to also be representative of English varieties, however, such contributors should not be too frequent and of course should be clearly identifiable via the mark-up. More precise geographical information, which might become relevant with increasing size of such a corpus, is sometimes also provided, but again not consistently and not always in a useful way. To take TVAus as an example, 39 of 60 senders give no (usable) information, but sometimes give more or less funny descriptions (e.g. 'hiding in the rafters') or are too vague ('West Coast' – of which country?); others are very precise (Berkshire Park NSW, Victoria), while some give more generalized but still useful information (Queensland, Western Australia). All in all, the sender information provided on forum sites can be regarded as sufficient in order to create a usable corpus.

2.2   Creating 'text' and mark-up

After the general discussion of the data and its characteristics above, I will now highlight some aspects of the actual corpus creation. As mentioned above, the forums are diverse: there are differences with regard to the text-to-graphics ratio (and the information content of the graphics), the amount of the 'conversation' presented on one page, the (non)indication of the structure of the conversation or the (way of) providing participant information on the surface level. The transformation thus goes beyond the simple extraction of text (which would lose a large amount of information), but rather needs to take care of the other characteristics in a non-ad-hoc and unified way as well. Similar things need to be treated similarly, such as information on senders or internal conversation structure, so that texts from different forums become searchable in the same manner and thus truly comparable.

As regards the transformation of web pages into treatable text, this was possible by simply copying and pasting of whole threads in the case of the BBC, the Atlantic and IcanGarden (which contain hardly any graphic elements) and of each message individually in the case of Canada online. The subsequent treatment of the text was fairly straightforward in all cases. For TVAus, with its elaborate graphic surface, the underlying source code needed to be copied for each 10/20-message bit of thread and then semi-manually transformed into plain text. The latter was necessary as some graphics carry important information on this forum, such as the gender of the sender, which is represented by icons such as ⚥ (= ♀). Other graphics carry propositional or interactional meaning in the conversation, e.g. ☺, which indicates that the sender is confused about something.

The hierarchical structure of the corpus is the following: forum – thread – message. Thus, quotes from the corpus can be given as in the above examples, e.g. 'TVAus 2,18' = thread 2, message 18 (one forum equals one file). Structure and necessary extralinguistic information is given by mark-up, in order to make the information provided by forums comparable and searchable. The message is the basic textual unit. Let me give three very short examples as illustration:

(1)   <message topic="Rear window" no="4" ad="3"> <person gender="male">david bowman</person> <place="unknown"> <time="2 Feb 2005 16: 33"> <mbinfo posts="32">
<body><p>I have just received an email saying he received an academy fellowship in 1971!!!!</p></body></message> (BBC 1,4)

(2)   <message topic="The 2004 elections: Political fallout" no="16"><person gender="unknown">New York Rat</person> <place="unknown"> <time="05:06pm Nov 22, 2004">
<sig>Every reform is only a mask under cover of which a more terrible reform, which dares not yet name itself, advances. (R. W. Emerson)</sig>
<body><p><quote>Identifying Characteristics of Fascist Regimes </quote>..(according to Jacob R.) </p>
<p>These characteristics sound too much like the characteristics of most human social arrangements according to both history and anthropology. Maybe the human species is fascist by nature. </p></body></message> (Atlantic 1,16)

(3)   <message topic="Are Men Going Soft?" no="45"><person gender="male" desc="Square eyes">Squarz</person> <place="unknown" desc="West Coast"> <time="11:32 pm 20 Jan 2005"> <mbinfo joined="04 Jan 2004" posts="4117" avday="10.37" greats="43" warnings="0">

<body><p>Aussies-Online wrote: <quote>Women don't understand anything about men.</quote></p>
<p>Great eh !!! <visual meaning="eusa_dance"></p></body></message>
(TVAus 6,45)

The <message> bracket contains information on the thread (topic) and the position (number, ad) within this, and on the speaker, as well as the message text
itself (enclosed by <body>), which in turn can be structured into paragraphs
(<p>) and contain quotes (cf. 2, 3). Additionally, the message can include one or
more signature elements (<sig>, cf. (2)), i.e. automatic attachments to any message a given writer sends, which have been kept outside of the body. Such prefabricated signatures have been included in the corpus only once for every sender,
i.e. if a sender provided more than one message, signatures were deleted from the
second posting onwards.

The chunk preceding the body needs further explanation. As to the thread
topic, this has been kept constant throughout, even though there may be smallish
differences in spelling or phrasing (apparently due to people not always using the
automatic reply function). Number of message was already present on some
forums, and provided for others by myself. One further structural indication,
namely which other message it is a reply to, is contained in the <ad> tag, which
in the case of (1) was supplied by me on the basis of the indenting structure of the
website (BBC; on Canada online this information is explicitly given on the
website and could be taken over). (2) and (3) are still missing this <ad> tag here
because the TVAus and Atlantic forums on the whole do not allow for its provi-
sion for all messages. However, the structure of threads and the relationship
between messages can be partly reconstructed on the basis of quotes used in the
messages; this will make the <ad> tag possible in some cases. The remaining
personal section highlights differences between the forums, with TVAus giving
by far the most detailed information. The sender is indicated by (nick)name used
and if possible (cf. 1, 3) gender is supplied; TVAus additionally has a self-
description for each sender (3), which has been included. The place of residence
of the sender is given, again if provided somewhere on the website (in 1-3 it is
marked as unknown); descriptions such as "West Coast" in (3) (only TVAus) are
included, however. The time of sending the message is given, an piece of information which is present on all the sites; as the above examples show, the syntax
used on the sites differs and will need to be regularized. <mbinfo> stands for
message board-related information, as far as provided, which ranges from nothing
on the Atlantic to a considerable amount on TVAus (cf. 3); the latter provides the
time of joining the forum, messages/posts sent so far by that person, the average
posting rate per day, an evaluative category of 'great' messages and, of potentially more interactional relevance, the number of warnings a sender has received
for violating netiquette or forum rules. While it may not be immediately obvious
in every case why some shred of information provided by the forum/the sender
may be relevant, it has been thought useful to include it in order not to close off
any research avenues.

Turning now to the body of the message itself, the quoted material mentioned above is always indicated by <quote> mark-up. Currently, no distinction is made in the mark-up with regard to whether the quote is from within the same thread (as in 2, 3), from another thread of the same forum (e.g. occurring on TVAus) or from non-forum material; perhaps such a marker should be introduced. Hyperlinks are not dealt with by the mark-up at the moment, but ideally the marker used should include a summary of what is being referred to. A last point concerns visual material included in the messages, which comes in basically three shapes: (i) purely additional, decorative material – to be dealt with by a <gap> element; (ii) supportive material related to the content/argument (e.g. a diagram providing the murder rate statistics for Canadian provinces) – also to be dealt with by <gap> element, but with a description of the relevant content; and (iii) graphic elements with emotive/interactive meaning, as in (3) above (<visual>). These latter make an important contribution to the message and thus need to be retained. It is possible to use their html syntax when constructing the code, e.g. for <img src="images/smiles/icon_*biggrin*.gif" alt="*Very Happy*" border="0"/> the italicized elements can be used within the <visual> marker. The type of meaning transported by these elements is basically attitudinal – providing an appropriate link to the final section of this paper.

3.   Some thoughts on involvement, interaction, and attitude

Information exchange, evaluation, and interaction are aspects that play a significant role in forum communication, probably to a varying extent on different sites. Information, in the objective sense, may be the least important (and is often inaccurate, cf. Gurak 1996: 272), as the exchange of views/opinions has been found to be more prominent (cf. Herring 1996: 82, on professional email groups) and is rated as more relevant by users (Largier 2002: 287). Views clearly involve personal evaluation. According to Largier's (2002: 296) online poll, 80% of users expect a reaction to their postings, so interaction and a show of respect for individual contributions are rated highly. Thus, the investigation of interactive features and of attitudinal and emotional aspects seems a useful first approach to message boards. The following remarks are intended to highlight some interesting aspects and problems in this area.

A fairly straightforward approach to personal involvement and interactiveness is of course the investigation of pronoun usage. The overall figures for *I* and *you* are 2,090 (23.3/1,000) and 960 (10.7/1,000), respectively, which far exceed the figures for written corpora (e.g. FLOB: 4.9 and 2.9, respectively) but do not quite reach those for spoken language, in particular spontaneous conversation (e.g. WSC: 25.1/19.3, BNC demographic: 39.0/31.3).[12] While involvement, marked by *I*, is clearly evident, directly approaching the other participants (*you*) seems to be comparatively less important, as the gap between first and second person is wider than in other corpora. Comparing the four forums is also interesting: cf. table 2.

Table 2:   Pronoun use (frequency per thousand words in brackets)

	Atlantic	BBC	Canada online	TVAus
I	231 (15)	748 (27.6)	363 (19.5)	748 (26)
me	17 (1.1)	59 (2.2)	49 (2.6)	96 (3.3)
my	49 (3.2)	153 (5.6)	91 (4.9)	135 (4.7)
myself	2 (0.1)	7 (0.3)	3 (0.2)	5 (0.2)
you	99 (6.4)	419 (15.4)	215 (11.6)	227 (7.9)
your	31 (2)	146 (5.4)	46 (2.5)	62 (2.2)

As these counts contain all the quoted material, the real figures will be somewhat lower for TVAus in particular and also for Canada online. The Atlantic appears to be the least involved and interactive forum of all four on this count. Nevertheless, views (as opposed to pure facts) are characteristic of this message board as well; they are simply expressed in a less personalized way (which needs further investigation). Contributors on both the Atlantic and TVAus seem least overtly concerned with the other senders, while the BBC comes out as the most interactive forum by far. These figures are probably the result of the overall nature of the forums (and what people regard as their purpose) and also especially of the threads selected. For example, there are two threads on the BBC (Male Childminders – who'd av em […]; Wedding) which concern very personal(ized) problems, so that senders actually need to directly refer to the sender who has the problem. There is one similar case on Canada (Cancer treatment), but all the other threads make the use of *you* a less immediate need. This raises the question whether threads should be the basic units in such a corpus, instead of forums, as is the case here. Threads offer the possibility of investigating the effect of topic (in the widest sense) on linguistic usage. TVAus points to another reason for lower *you*-counts: widespread quoting, introduced by the standard email formula 'X wrote:', can reduce the occurrence of *you* without in fact being less addressee-oriented and interactive.

Involvement or the personalisation of views can also be expressed more emphatically (beyond the occurrence of subject *I*) by such means as *personally, as far as I'm concerned, (as) to/for me*, etc., which occur 61 times. *Personally* (19 occurrences) in (4) is emphasizing as well as restrictive and contrasting.

(4)   PErsonally (sic) Jonathon I do think you are being treated unfairly and possible being discriminated against because of your gender but child minding is a service industry that parents can choose!!!!! (BBC 9,11)

Additionally, it is an interesting element in so far as it may be variety-specific to a certain extent. It occurs most commonly on the BBC, to a lesser extent on TVAus and not at all on Canada online and the Atlantic. In other words, it might represent a usage that is not typical of North American varieties, but the present data basis is of course too small to be truly indicative (in comparison, while it does not occur in the spoken Santa Barbara Corpus either, it can be found in the written Frown corpus, both of which represent US American English.)

The expression of attitudes and feelings can be lexical or grammatical(ized), and additionally also semiotic in message boards. In contrast to Lewin and Donner's (2002: 29) claim that the text-based forum language 'cannot convey emotion and tones', users of CMC have long found a solution to this problem. Those elements which have (only) been regarded as genre-specific or as indicative of the oral and/or creative nature of CMC need to be considered here and integrated into the feature pool for general linguistic investigation. The well-known acronyms (e.g. *lol*) belong here,[13] as well as the above-mentioned visual elements (166 elaborate types on TVAus alone, plus the more 'primitive' types of smileys and the like, e.g. :-) or 5b below), which reflect the emotional state of the sender. Other elements include the multiple use of some punctuation marks (? , !), layout features like capitalization, italics, bold-face, and the use of the asterisk for emphasis belong here. In writing, all of these elements have acquired the characteristics of a linguistic sign and thus need to be considered in the investigation. While one exclamation/question mark indicates utterance type, the presence of more than one, as in *Oh my God!!! how confused can you get????* (TVAus 3,12) clearly marks an emotional attitude or increased interactiveness (surprise, shock, disbelief, desperation, get reader's attention etc.). Both signs can be used simultaneously and repetitions range from two occurrences to as many as seventeen! Multiple exclamation marks are more common than question marks (118 *vs.* 76) and they are on the whole more common on Canada online, followed by TVAus, while they are extremely rarely used on the Atlantic (only 4 occurrences). In contrast to the punctuation features (which need interpretation as to the precise emotion that is expressed by them), the more clearly restricted acronyms *lol* and *rofl* together occur only 20 times (especially on Canada online; not at all on the Atlantic). Capitalization as in (5a), especially with expressions that already carry intensification (e.g. *very hard*), is a particularly striking way to inject one's personal attitude into the message – and one that can actually annoy other people, as the reaction in (5b) shows.

(5)   a. all I am saying is that she is being selfish in this PARTICULAR regard). You have to be pretty forgetful to forget that its not YOUR wedding and maybe that your children don't want to do things exactly as you do. (…) It's VERY HARD to hear your mum criticised … (BBC 10,19)

        b. Fairy Do you have to use CAPITALS all the time for emphasis? There are other ways you know - **bold**, *italics* and ***bolditalics*** to name but three :o/ (BBC 10,21)

All these aspects should be considered together with lexical and grammatical means when investigating expression of attitudes, feelings and evaluation in this text type. Lexical means, for example, include directly evaluative items such as verbs of (dis)liking (with first-person subjects). The direct expression of fairly strong love and hate, especially the former, is not uncommon and seems to somewhat exceed the incidence in other corpora.[14] This may of course be connected to the selection of topics, e.g. films/TV shows, eating, body piercing, which elicit such statements rather readily. Lexico-grammatical means also comprise elements that have been identified as style and content disjuncts (Quirk et al. 1985: 615), as domain, modal, evaluative and speech act-related adjuncts (Huddleston and Pullum 2002: 765-75) and as epistemic, attitudinal and style stance markers (Biber et al. 1999: 972ff, Conrad and Biber 1999). A quick survey of a very restricted set of evaluative, epistemic/modal and style/speech-act items, concentrating on adverbs (-*ly*), relatively standardised prepositional phrases (e.g. *from X's perspective, in short*), epistemic verbs (e.g. *think, doubt*) and *if*-clauses (e.g. *if I'm not mistaken*), revealed a fairly similar picture to Conrad and Biber's (1999) findings. The epistemic group is by far the most frequent one, with 12 instances per 1,000 words, followed by the evaluative group with 2.2 instances and the style/speech-act group with a mere 0.5 instances (with the sequence of the last two being the reverse of that in Conrad and Biber 1999). Clearly marking the epistemic status of statements is apparently of rather high importance, which may be connected to the perceived doubtfulness of web-based information. In contrast, it seems somewhat surprising that the evaluative items are used so rarely, but a more comprehensive search might change the picture here – and of course one needs to add the semiotic means mentioned before. As with *personally* above, one can also find instances here that might be preferred by certain varieties. The epistemic item *surely*, for example, again seems to be preferred by BBC contributors, i.e. British English users, and only occurs once each on TVAus and the Atlantic, whereas *sure* (also used as an adverb in the non-British forums) is distributed much more evenly between the forums.

4.   Conclusion

I have tried to point out the need for a corpus of forum language. I hope to have shown that it is necessary to regard forums as constituting a text type of their own, whose investigation should go beyond the quasi-contrastive analysis vis-à-vis speech. A more thorough investigation of the unique group of features determining this text type and also of the variation within this variety makes it necessary to have more than ad-hoc forum corpora for isolated studies. First, solid corpus-linguistic research in this area needs a standardized and annotated textual basis. Secondly, studies done on forum language should become comparable, which requires comparability of the data basis. And thirdly, studies/results should be replicable and falsifiable, which can only be achieved by making such a corpus publicly available. The final section has pointed out some respects in which the item pool will need to be expanded when investigating such phenomena as involvement and attitude, and also how a variety-sensitive forum corpus can assist in finding or corroborating variety-specific usages. As forum language is both intermediate between written and oral forms and always recent through continuous posting, it may even provide a more up-to-date window to linguistic variation than the language represented in other corpora.

Notes

1   This excludes usenet forums.

2   Forum users are aware of this possibility and comment on it, cf. *i will not detail it for obvious safety reasons for the people concerned as this is a public forum and theoretically google-searchable, [...]* (TVAus 2,18) and *I was mainly concerned that you might give the wealthy an excuse to dismiss environmentalism. That's if anybody but us ever reads these boards* (BBC 4,18).

3   They counted as specifically oral features (i) pause fillers (e.g. *hmm, well*) and transcribed sounds (e.g. *heh*), (ii) lack of intersentential connectors (e.g. *however*). (Interestingly, Collot and Belmore 1996 (cf. below) found a fairly high instance of such connectors.) Some of their other features, none of which is frequent, can also be seen as more oral in nature (omission of subjects / verbs, run-on sentences, greetings, use of names) or as compensation for the lack of sound / face-to-face contact (emoticons, orthographic emphasis, multiple punctuation marks).

4   It is not easy to collect all the relevant contributions because a variety of terms (message board, forum, bulletin boards, conferences, newsgroups etc.) or descriptions (electronic language, internet communication, CMC etc.) have been used to describe this form.

5   I exclude here the possibility of researching forum language with the help of WebCorp or with commercial search engines, as this is problematic for various reasons.

6   While Collot and Belmore (1996) also used 'conferences' as the basis for their corpus, Lewin and Donner's (2002) corpus consists of 200 decontextualized messages obtained by taking every fourth message from five different bulletin boards and including each writer only once.

7   This variety of forum is not uncommon on the web. Some types of restriction might help in finding more clearly localized groups of senders.

8   Cf. also the self-description of TVAus: "Where TV meets a bunch of Internet nerds."

9   Establishing the identity and thus the number of senders needs some care as well, as people might contribute under (slightly) different names or addresses, such as BuntingJ and jimbuntin1 (Canada online) or Jonathan Kemp and Jon_33 (BBC). See also Hoffmann (this volume).

10   All names / aliases quoted in this paper are the ones given on the web; no anonymization is carried out in the corpus as the people in question have gone public voluntarily.

11   Other types of information to be found there can include location of sender, age, birthday, occupation, interests, astrological sign etc. Every forum will have a slightly different set, and the consistency and reliability with regard to filling it in will vary as well.

12   Contractions had to be checked especially carefully here, as in the case of *I*, but not *you*, apostrophe-less spellings occurred (*Im, Ill* etc.). *You* includes two occurrences of *ya* (Atlantic, TVAus); no other non-standard forms were found.

13   Acronyms beyond the 'standard' set are also used, e.g. *TBH* = *to be honest* or *WTF* = what the ****, both relevant for attitude and emotion.

14   There are 99 instances (1.1 per thousand) of expressions containing *love, like, hate, can't stand* etc.

References

Biber, D. (1988), *Variation across Speech and Writing*. Cambridge: Cambridge University Press.

Biber, D., S. Johansson, G. Leech, S. Conrad and E. Finegan (1999), *Longman Grammar of Spoken and Written English*. London: Longman.

Collot, M. and N. Belmore (1996), 'Electronic language: a new variety of English', in: S. Herring (ed.) *Computer-Mediated Communication: Linguistic, Social and Cross-Cultural Perspectives*. Amsterdam and Philadelphia: Benjamins. 13-28.

Conrad, S. and D. Biber (1999), 'Adverbial marking of stance in speech and writing', in: S. Hunston and G. Thompson (eds.) *Evaluation in Text*. Oxford: Oxford University Press. 56-73.

Crystal, D. (2001), *Language and the Internet*. Cambridge: Cambridge University Press.

December, J. (1996), 'Units of analysis for internet communication', *Journal of Communication*, 46 (1): 14-38.

Gurak, L.J. (1996), 'The rhetorical dynamics of a community protest in cyberspace: what happened with Lotus MarketPlace', in: S. Herring (ed.) *Computer-Mediated Communication: Linguistic, Social and Cross-Cultural Perspectives*. Amsterdam and Philadelphia: Benjamins. 265-277.

Herring, S. (1996), 'Two variants of an electronic message schema', in: S. Herring (ed.) *Computer-Mediated Communication: Linguistic, Social and Cross-Cultural Perspectives*. Amsterdam and Philadelphia: Benjamins. 81-106.

Hoffmann, S. (this volume), 'From web-page to mega corpus: the CNN transcripts'.

Huddleston, R. and G.K. Pullum (2002), *The Cambridge Grammar of the English Language*. Cambridge: Cambridge University Press.

Largier, C. (2002), 'Aspekte der Debatte in argumentationsorientierten Internet-Foren: die Abtreibungsdebatte in Frankreich und Deutschland', *Deutsche Sprache*, 30: 287-306.

Lewin, B.A. and Y. Donner (2002), 'Communication in internet message boards', *English Today*, 18 (3): 29-37.

Marcoccia, M. (2004), 'On-line polylogues: conversation structure and participation framework in internet newsgroups', *Journal of Pragmatics*, 36: 115-145.

Quirk, R., S. Greenbaum, G. Leech and J. Svartvik (1985), *A Comprehensive Grammar of the English Language*. London: Longman.

Richardson, K. (2001), 'Risk news in the world of internet newsgroups', *Journal of Sociolinguistics*, 5 (1): 50-72.

Tanner, E. (2001), 'Chilean conversations: internet forum participants debate Augusto Pinochet's detention', *Journal of Communication*, 51: 383-404.

Appendix

1. Message boards and Threads (messages per thread in brackets)

The Atlantic
1 politics and society: The 2004 elections: Political fallout (23)
2 politics and society: Faculty diversity: should there be quotas? (21)
3 film and television: Is "The Daily Show" a good news source? (35)
4 books and literature: The Influence of Henry Adams (21)
5 arts and culture: Speak to Us of Eating and Drinking! (20)
6 education and teaching: November Issue: "Now, for Tonight's Assignment" (24)

Canada online
1 I Can Garden: Slugs (18)
2 Tsunami: Did certain people also help (21)
3 Disgracing the Canadian flag (37)
4 Canada's Murder Rate (32)
5 Canada/US border customs (16)
6 Cancer treatment (11)
7 Canada's child care system (21)
8 Health Care (7)

BBC
1 movies: Rear Window (17)

2 movies: Steve Martin – funny or not? (19)
3 environment: Selfish? (25)
4 environment: The housing issue (27)
5 international news: A blue finger to Europe (25)
6 home news: low pay and welfare (26)
7 green room: Britions (sic) are Ignorant over the EU (22)
8 history: wars and conflicts: Was Nurnberg Trial unfair? (33)
9 parenting: childcare: Male Childminders – who'd av em... (38)
10 relationships: Wedding (33)

TVAus
1 News, current affairs and politics: No Apology For Habib (32)
2 News, current affairs and politics: America To Hold Terrorist Suspects Without Evidence For Life (26)
3 Miscellaneous shows: Dr. Phil (30)
4 Movies: Shrek 2 (31)
5 Reality shows: The restaurant (19)
6 General: Are Men Going Soft? (54)
7 General: Body Piercing (36)

2. Screenshots

Atlantic

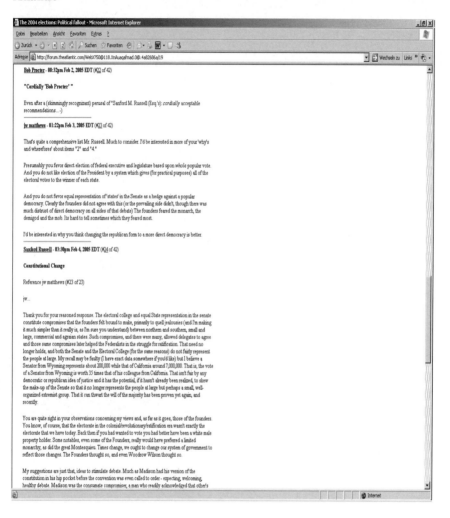

BBC

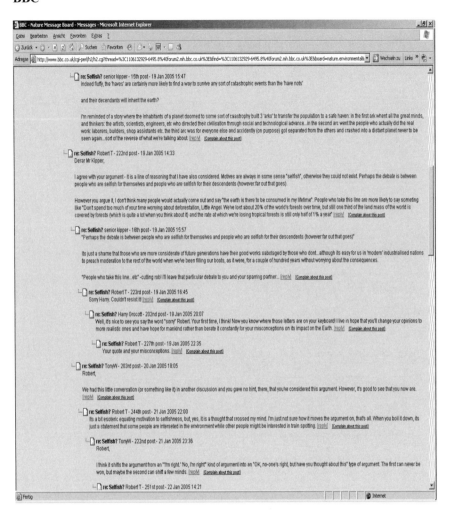

Canada online

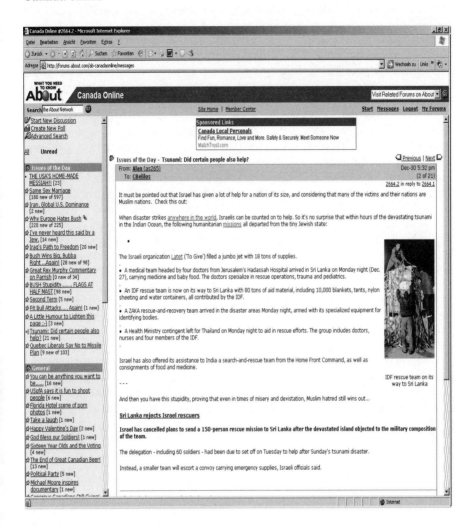

TVAus

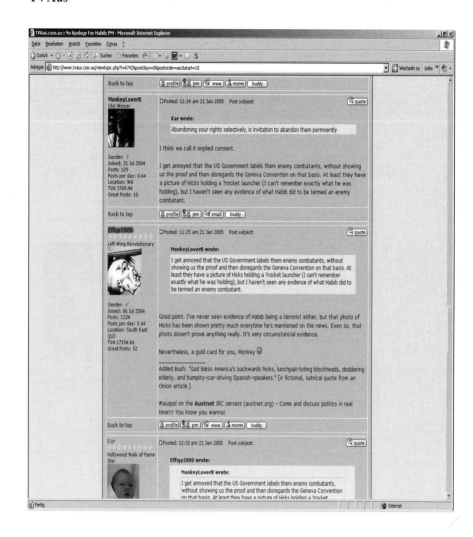

Towards a taxonomy of web registers and text types: a multi-dimensional analysis

Douglas Biber and Jerry Kurjian

Northern Arizona University, Flagstaff, Arizona

Abstract

This paper uses multi-dimensional analysis to investigate the extent to which the subject categories used by Google are linguistically well-defined. A 3.7 million word corpus is constructed by a stratified sample of web pages from two Google categories: 'Home' and 'Science'. The corpus is tagged (using the Biber Tagger) and factor analysis is carried out, resulting in four factors. These factors are interpreted functionally as underlying dimensions of variation. The 'Science' and 'Home' categories are compared with respect to each dimension; although there are large differences in the dimension scores of texts within each category, the two Google categories themselves are not clearly distinguished on linguistic grounds. The dimensions are subsequently used as predictors in a cluster analysis, which identifies the 'text types' that are well defined linguistically. Eight text types are identified and interpreted in terms of their salient linguistic and functional characteristics.

1.   Introduction

Although the world wide web is a tremendous resource of information for students and other end-users, we actually know surprisingly little about its size and composition. Lawrence and Giles (1998, 1999) compared the results of several search engines and estimated the size of the web (in 1999) to be 800,000,000 web pages. By 2004, Google alone indexed c. 8 billion pages (www.google.com). Approximately 70% of the pages on the web are in English, with Japanese, German, Chinese, French, and Spanish also being relatively common (Xu 2000).

Lawrence and Giles (1999) also estimated the breakdown by topic area (in 1999); pages from the commercial domain comprised the overwhelming majority of the web (83%), followed by scientific/educational (6%), health (3.8%), personal (2.2%), and societies (2%). Pornography, community, government, and religion accounted for relatively small proportions. Breakdowns of this type usually depend on the domain identifier used by web pages (e.g. '.com', '.edu') or the general topical categories used by search engines.

Linguists have recently begun to use the web for their own more specialized research purposes, as a corpus for studies of linguistic variation and use (see, for example, the special issue of *Computational Linguistics* (2003) edited by Kilgarriff and Grefenstette). For both general users and linguists, the advantages of the web are obvious: it provides a massive amount of information and linguistic data, readily accessible to anyone with a computer.

Since the late 1990s, linguists have been using the web as a resource to investigate issues of linguistic variation, and as a source of training data for computational applications in natural language processing (NLP) (see, e.g., Kilgarriff 2001; Kilgarriff and Grefenstette 2003; Smarr 2002; Volk 2002).

Linguists like Rohdenburg (this volume) and Mair (this volume) investigate issues of gram-matical variation and change using internet data in comparison to the patterns observed from standard corpora. Other research teams have focused on problems and issues surrounding web searches and the development of search engines that are more responsive to the needs of linguists than the standard search engines (see, e.g., Lawrence and Giles 1998, 1999; Renouf 2003; Fletcher 2004b)

Several studies in NLP have focused on the application of web searches to issues in lexicography, resolving ambiguous word senses, and studying the frequency of senses and collocations for rare words (e.g. Mihalcea and Moldovan 1999; Rigau et al. 2002; Santamaría et al. 2003., and Keller and Lapata 2003). Fewer studies in NLP have used web data to aid parser performance (e.g. Volk 2001, who collected probabilistic data on prepositional phrase attachment), but several studies have used the web for translation applications (e.g De Schryver 2002; Resnik and Smith 2003; Kraaij, Nie and Simard 2003).

Finally, the web has become increasingly popular as a resource for language teaching, especially for ESL/EFL (see e.g. Frand 2000, Pearson 2000, Ooi 2001, Fletcher 2004b). For example, researchers at the University of Illinois have developed 'Grammar Safari', a web tool for data-driven language learning activities (deil.lang. uiuc.edu/web.pages/grammarsafari.html).

1.1   Methodological problems with the web as corpus

The major problem with most web searches is the uncertainty about the kinds of documents that have been included. It is difficult to evaluate the usefulness of information obtained on the web without knowing the nature of the source web pages. Linguistic research using the web as a corpus is similarly hampered by the lack of knowledge about the source texts. As Meyer et al. (2003: 241) note, "The web, however, is really a very different kind of corpus: we do not know, for instance, precisely how large it is or what kinds of texts are in it."

The identification of 'register' (or genre) is an especially important consideration for linguistic research based on the web. Several recent studies have shown that identification of register is crucially important for linguistic research on language variation and use: most linguistic features are used in different ways and to different extents across registers. For example, the *Longman Grammar of Spoken and Written English* (Biber et al. 1999) documents the systematic patterns of variation for a wide range of grammatical features across registers. Identification of register/genre is similarly important for NLP in computational linguistics, improving the performance of word disambiguation software, taggers, parsers, and information retrieval tools (see Kessler et al. 1997, Sekine 1997, Gildea 2001, Karlgren 2000, and Roland et al. 2000).

With most standard corpora (such as the *Brown Corpus* or the *British National Corpus* (BNC)), register categories are readily identifiable and can therefore be used in linguistic studies. However, research based on the web lacks this essential background information. As Kessler et al. (1997) point out: "the problems of genre classification don't become salient until we are confronted with large and heterogeneous search domains like the World-Wide web." Kilgarriff and Grefenstette (2003: 342) similarly note that "the lack of theory of text types leaves us without a way of assessing the usefulness of language-modeling work [in relation to the web]."

Several studies discuss methods and issues for assembling a representative corpus from the web (e.g. Dewe, Karlgren, and Bretan 1998; Fletcher 2004a, b; Rusmevichientong et al. 2001; Jones and Ghani 2000). Most of these studies also note methodological problems with using the web as a corpus, and the need for further research to determine the register (or genre/text type) of web pages (see also Brekke 2000, Kwasnik et al. 2001, Rehm 2002).

Most linguistic studies based on the web as corpus use standard search engines (such as Google) or web crawlers developed by individual researchers. Unfortunately, there is no direct way to identify the registers of the source web pages used in such linguistic searches, making it difficult to interpret linguistic distributional patterns, difficult to determine the relevance of a document for information retrieval purposes, and difficult to know the usefulness of examples as models for language learning purposes (see, e.g., Jansen, Spink, and Saracevic 2000; Pearson 2000).

To address these problems, some studies have begun to develop methods for the automatic classification of web pages (e.g. Glover et al. 2002, Karlgren and Straszheim 1997, Rehm 2002). Several methods have been devised to try to circumvent this problem for the purposes of linguistic research. For example, several studies attempt to achieve control over dialect and register by using a specific internet domain, such as the '.edu' or the '.gov' domains. Other studies have used search engine topical domains to structure the investigation (e.g. the 'Science' or 'Home' domain in Google). Relatively few studies have recognized the need for register/genre classifications of web documents (e.g. Crowston and Williams 2000; Kwasnik et al. 2001; Roussinov et al. 2001). Dewe, Karlgren, and Bretan (1998) conducted a set of perceptual experiments to determine the salient genres recognized by users of the web, and then developed computational tools (using both linguistic and non-linguistic text features) to automatically categorize web pages, with an error rate of one out of four texts. However, this study was relatively small and inconclusive.

Although these approaches provide some degree of control, they do not address the more basic question of what a general web search actually represents. As Kilgarriff and Grefenstette (2003: 343) note: "Once we move to the web as a source of data, and our corpora have names like 'April03-sample77', the issue of how the text type(s) can be characterized demands attention." In fact, even restricted categories, like the '.edu' domain or the 'Home' Google category, include a wide range of disparate registers (ranging, for example, from personal web pages to dense informational research articles). This problem becomes extreme when we consider the full range of pages included in the web. As a result, linguistic patterns observed on the web can vary radically – and seemingly randomly – from one search to the next. The fundamental problem is that we have no reliable methods for identifying the kinds of texts included in a general web search. In fact, there is an even more basic underlying problem: we do not at present know what range of registers exists on the web. As Karlgren (2000, chapter 15) puts it: "to build retrieval tools for the Internet, [...] the choice of genres to include is one of the more central problems: there is no well-established genre palette for Internet materials."

In the present paper, we report on pilot research that tests the feasibility and productivity of a new approach to these issues: identifying the characteristics of web 'text types': text categories that are defined on linguistic bases; once identified, the situational characteristics of those text types can be analyzed. The results of a 'text type' approach are contrasted with the approach typically used in previous research: analyzing the linguistic characteristics of the text categories that are pre-defined on the web (usually based on existing search engine categories, such as Google domains like 'Home' and 'Science').

The two approaches have different strengths and weaknesses. The search engine approach has the advantage of convenience, using text categories that already exist on the web. However, as the following descriptions show, those text categories are not well defined for the purposes of linguistic research. In contrast, we show that the 'text type' approach results in text categories that are linguistically coherent and distinguishable (although the sociolinguistic interpretation of these categories is more abstract).

1.2   Overview of the present study

For the purposes of the present study, we constructed a corpus of web documents that represents two Google categories: 'Home' and 'Science'. The corpus was also designed to represent the major sub-categories within each of these two top-level categories (e.g. 'apartment living', 'consumer information', and 'cooking' within the 'Home' category). The entire corpus was automatically tagged (using the Biber tagger), and Multi-Dimensional analysis was used to identify the underlying linguistic parameters of variation among these texts. The linguistic characteristics of the Google categories were compared with respect to each 'dimension', showing that the Google categories are not well defined linguistically.

Then in the second major analytical step, we analyzed the same corpus of web documents to identify the 'text types' that are distinguishable with respect to their linguistic characteristics. It turns out that these text types are readily interpretable in functional terms, even though they cut directly across the pre-defined Google categories. Finally, in the conclusion, we raise the possibility of a third approach, identifying the range of 'registers' that exist on the web (i.e. text categories that are distinguishable in terms of their purpose and situational characteristics), and then analyzing the linguistic characteristics of those registers. Although a register approach would be labor-intensive (because the register category of each document must be determined by hand), the resulting linguistic patterns are immediately interpretable in sociolinguistic terms. We argue that combining the three approaches would enable a comprehensive linguistic taxonomy of web documents.

2. Methodology

2.1 Constructing the corpus of web documents

Building a representative sample of web documents is not trivial. The most obvious approach is to choose a few top-level pages and then simply follow the links. However, the vast majority of links on the web lead to commercial web pages, and so a corpus constructed under this approach would not represent the range of linguistic variation found on the web.

To adjust for this problem, we deliberately began with two top-level Google categories ('Home' and 'Science') and identified the full range of 2nd-tier categories:

> Home:
> Apartment Living, Consumer Information, Cooking, Do-It-Yourself, Domestic Services, Emergency Preparation, Entertaining, Family, Gardening, Home Automation, Home Business, Home Buyers, Home Improvement, Homemaking, Homeowners, Moving and Relocating, News and Media, Personal Finance, Personal Organization, Pets, Rural Living, Seniors, Shopping, Software, Urban Living
> Science:
> Agriculture, Anomalies and Alternative Science, Astronomy, Biology, Chats and Forums, Chemistry, Conferences, Earth Sciences, Educational Resources, Employment, Environment, History of Science, Institutions, Instruments and Supplies, Math, Methods and Techniques, Museums, News and Media, Philosophy of Science, Physics, Publications, Reference, Science in Society, Social Sciences, Software, Technology, Women

From each of these 2nd-tier categories, we chose two web-sites, the first and the last links from the Google list of linked websites. Sites near the top of the list were nearly always large 'authoritative' commercial or governmental sites; sites toward the end of the list were usually smaller, more personal sites. (See Fletcher 2004b and this volume for a full discussion of related issues.)

An automatic browser, written in Python and incorporating the Harvest-Man spider (see http://www.python.org/pypi/HarvestMan), was developed to download web pages from these websites (see Kurjian 2004 for a complete description of the browser). The software downloaded c. 200 web pages per site and then every fourth web page was selected. Thus, each website contributed approximately 50 web pages, so that each sub-category contributed approximately 100 web pages to the corpus. For the present study, we subsequently excluded documents shorter than 200 words, because they were not long enough to reliably represent the distribution of many linguistic features. Finally, after tagging the corpus (see below), we excluded 'problematic' documents consisting mostly of nouns, prepositions, or adjectives. These documents were usually lists or indexes of some kind; in future research, we will develop methods that allow for the inclusion of documents of this type. As table 1 shows, the resulting corpus had 1400 documents sampled from 63 web sites for 'Home' (1.68 million words) and 1576 documents sampled from 81 web sites for 'Science' (2.06 million words).

Table 1:   Composition of the corpus of web documents

Composition of the corpus		
	'Home'	'Science'
total documents	2426	2678
documents > 200 words	1765	1905
unproblematic documents (i.e. < 50% nouns; < 40% prepositions; < 40% adjectives)	1400	1576

Corpus used for subsequent analyses			
	# of documents	# of words	average length of document
'Home'	1400	1.68 million	1201 words
'Science'	1576	2.06 million	1308 words
Total	2976	3.74 million	

2.2   Analyzing the linguistic characteristics of web documents: multi-dimensional analysis

Each web document was automatically 'tagged' for a large number of linguistic features using the Biber grammatical tagger. The current version of this tagger incorporates the corpus-based research carried out for the *Longman Grammar of Spoken and Written English* (Biber et al. 1999). The tagger identifies a wide range of grammatical features, including word classes (e.g. nouns, modal verbs, prepositions), syntactic constructions (e.g. WH relative clauses, conditional adverbial clauses, *that*-complement clauses controlled by nouns), semantic classes (e.g. activity verbs, likelihood adverbs), and lexico-grammatical classes (e.g. *that*-complement clauses controlled by mental verbs, *to*-complement clauses controlled by possibility adjectives).

Multi-dimensional (MD) analysis was subsequently used to identify the major patterns of linguistic variation among discourse units. MD analysis is a methodological approach that applies multivariate statistical techniques (especially factor analysis and cluster analysis) to the investigation of register variation in a language. The approach was originally developed to analyze the range of spoken and written registers in English (Biber 1986, 1988). There are two major quantitative steps in an MD analysis: (1) identifying the salient linguistic co-occurrence patterns in a language; and (2) comparing spoken and written registers in the linguistic space defined by those co-occurrence patterns. In a third step, it is possible to identify groupings of texts – 'text types' – that are maximally similar in their multi-dimensional profiles (see Biber 1989, 1995); in the present case, these grouping represent web text types.

As noted above, MD analysis uses factor analysis to reduce a large number of linguistic variables to a few basic parameters of linguistic variation. In MD analyses, the distribution of individual linguistic features is analyzed in a corpus of texts. Factor analysis is then used to identify the systematic co-occurrence patterns among those linguistic features – the 'dimensions' – and then texts and registers are compared along each dimension.

Appendix I gives the full factorial structure for the analysis in the present study. Only 41 of the original 120+ linguistic features were retained in the final factor analysis. Several features were dropped because they were redundant or overlapped to a large extent with other features. For example, the counts for common verbs, nouns, and adjectives overlapped extensively with the semantic categories for those word classes, even though the counts were derived independently. In other cases, features were dropped because they were rare in these web documents or because they did not co-occur in important ways with other features in these texts (e.g. semantic classes of phrasal verbs). Some of these features were combined into a more general class. For example, three features that incorporate a passive verb phrase were originally distinguished: agentless passives, passives with a *by*-phrase, and non-finite passives as nominal post-modifiers. These features were combined into the general category of 'passive verbs' in the final analysis.

The solution for four factors was selected as optimal. Taken together, these factors account for only 24% of the shared variance, but they are readily interpretable, and subsequent factors accounted for relatively little additional variance.

3.   Interpreting the factors as 'dimensions' of variation

Table 2 summarizes the important linguistic features defining each dimension (i.e. features with factor loadings over + or - .3). Each factor comprises a set of linguistic features that tend to co-occur in the texts from the web corpus. Factors are interpreted as underlying 'dimensions' of variation based on the assumption that linguistic co-occurrence patterns reflect underlying communicative functions.

That is, particular sets of linguistic features co-occur frequently in texts because they serve related communicative functions. Features with positive and negative loadings represent two distinct co-occurrence sets. These comprise a single factor because the two sets tend to occur in complementary distribution. In the present analysis, though, there are few features with negative loadings on any of the factors.

Table 2:   Summary of the factorial structure

Dimension 1: Personal, involved (stance-focused) narration

Features with positive loadings: past tense, mental verbs, *that*-deletions, 3rd person pronouns, 1st person pronouns, certainty/mental verb + *that*-clause, certainty adverbials, communication verbs, communication verb + *that*-clause, perfect aspect, likelihood/mental verb + *that*-clause, other adverbial clause, pronoun *it*, indefinite pronouns, noun + *that*-clause

Features with negative loadings: nouns

Dimension 2: Persuasive/argumentative discourse

Features with positive loadings: present tense, possibility modals, main verb *be*, predicative adjectives, conditional adverbial clauses, linking adverbials, necessity modals, demonstrative pronouns, prediction modals, split auxiliaries

Features with negative loadings: nouns, past tense

Dimension 3: Addressee-focused discourse

Features with positive loadings: 2nd person pronouns, progressive verbs, desire verb + *to*-clause, group/institution nouns, activity verbs, WH clauses

Features with negative loadings: prepositions, passive verbs

Dimension 4: Abstract/technical discourse

Features with positive loadings: nominalizations, abstract nouns, long words, cognitive nouns, topic adjectives, attributive adjectives

Features with negative loadings: concrete nouns

Dimension 1 in the present study combines some of the major linguistic features and functions associated with the first two dimensions in the Biber (1988) study. Many of these features reflect personal involvement and the expression of personal stance (e.g. 1st person pronouns, certainty/mental verb + *that*-clause, certainty adverbials, likelihood/mental verb + *that*-clause). However, these features co-occur with a set of features used for narration, such as past tense verbs, 3rd person pronouns, perfect aspect verbs, and communication verb + *that*-clause. This dimension can be interpreted as 'Personal, involved narration'.

The corpus used for the 1988 MD study of spoken and written registers included many conversations (face-to-face and telephone); these were highly interactive but generally did not include narratives. At the same time, the 1988 corpus included many excerpts from novels and fictional short stories. These texts relied heavily on stereotypical narrative features, but they were not at all personal in orientation. As a result, the factor analysis in the 1988 study included two distinct dimensions: one for personal involvement/interaction, and one for narrative discourse. In contrast, these two functions tend to co-occur in our web corpus: the narrative web documents in our corpus also tend to be highly involved and personal; and the personal/involved web documents tend to be narratives. As a result, these two feature sets and underlying functions are collapsed on to a single dimension in the present study.

Dimension 2 is interpreted as 'Persuasive/argumentative discourse'. This dimension includes many of the defining features grouped on Dimension 4 in the 1988 MD analysis: conditional adverbial clauses, possibility modals, necessity modals, prediction modals, and split auxiliaries.

Dimension 3, interpreted as 'Addressee-focused discourse', has no direct counterpart in the 1988 MD analysis. The major features on this dimension include 2nd person pronouns, progressive aspect verbs, desire verb + *to*-clause (e.g. *want to, need to*), group/institution nouns (e.g. *bank, church, hotel, hospital, household, college, institution, home, house, lab, laboratory, community, company, government, university, school, congress, committee*), and activity verbs (e.g. *buy, sell, make, go, give, take, come, use, leave, show, try, work, bring, send*). This combination of features seems to often serve advice-giving or other directive functions in web documents.

Finally, Dimension 4 consists entirely of features associated with technical vocabulary and complex noun phrases, used for the dense packaging of information into texts: nominalizations, abstract nouns, long words, cognitive nouns, topic adjectives, attributive adjectives. (This set of features is very similar to the negative co-occurring features on Dimension 1 in the 1988 MD analysis.) These features co-occur in texts with a technical, informational focus, leading to the interpretation as 'Abstract/technical discourse'.

4. Comparing the multi-dimensional characteristics of Google categories

It is possible to compare the multi-dimensional characteristics of texts and registers by computing *dimension scores* for each text: that is, a summation of the individual features with salient loadings on a dimension (see Biber 1988: 93-97). The individual feature counts are first standardized so that each feature has a comparable scale, with a mean of 0.0 and a standard deviation of 1. (This standardization is based on the overall means and standard deviations for each feature in the web corpus.) Then, 'dimension scores' are computed by summing the standardized frequencies for the features comprising each of the four dimensions.

Table 3: Tests of statistical significance and strength (General Linear Models procedure in SAS) for differences between the 'Home' and 'Science' categories.

Dimension	F value	probability	strength of the differences (r^2)
1: Personal narration	37.88	$p < .001$	1.3%
2: Persuasive discourse	79.29	$p < .001$	2.6%
3: Addressee-focused	719.54	$p < .001$	19.5%
3: Abstract/technical	348.45	$p < .001$	10.5%

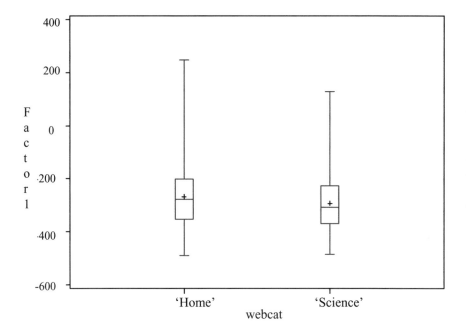

Figure 1: Range of Dimension 1 scores for web documents in the 'Home' and 'Science' categories (showing the median and the interquartile range)

Once a dimension score is computed for each text, the mean dimension score for each register can be computed. Plots of these mean dimension scores allow linguistic characterization of any given register, comparison of the relations between any two registers, and a fuller functional interpretation of the underlying dimension. Standard statistical procedures (such as the General Linear Models procedure in SAS) can be used to further analyze the statistical significance of differences among the mean dimension scores.

Statistical comparison of the two top-level Google categories in our corpus ('Home' and 'Science'), summarized in table 3, shows that there were significant differences with respect to all four dimensions; however, the r^2 values show that these differences were extremely weak (accounting for less than 5% of the total variance for most dimensions). That is, there are large linguistic differences among the web documents in the corpus, but those differences are mostly <u>not</u> systematically related to Google categories. For example, less than 5% of the linguistic variation along Dimensions 1 and 2 can be accounted for by knowing whether a document came from the 'Home' or 'Science' category.

Figure 1 plots the range of Dimension 1 scores for the web documents in these two categories, showing the extremely high degree of overlap. Similarly, table 4 shows that there are significant differences among the 2nd-tier Google subcategories, but these differences are also weak (20% - 30% of the dimension score variances). In sum, these statistical findings showed that the Google categories are not linguistically well-defined, because there is an extreme range of linguistic variation among the documents included in any category.

Table 4: Tests of statistical significance and strength (General Linear Models procedure in SAS) for differences among the 25 sub-categories under 'Home'

Dimension	F value	probability	strength of the differences (r^2)
1: Personal narration	16.45	p < .001	20.8%
2: Persuasive discourse	13.04	p < .001	17.2%
3: Addressee-focused	22.62	p < .001	26.5%
3: Abstract/technical	28.05	p < .001	30.9%

5. Identifying and interpreting web 'text types'

Most MD studies have been undertaken to investigate the patterns of variation among 'registers': varieties of language that are defined by their situational (i.e. non-linguistic) characteristics (see Biber 1994). At one level, the Google categories and subcategories used to construct our web corpus (listed in 2.1 above) can be considered as registers that are defined by reference to general topical domains. However, the documents included in these categories vary considerably with respect to their purposes, interactiveness, personal involve-ment, and production circumstances. As a result, there is an extreme range of linguistic variation among the documents within each of these categories, while the categories themselves are not well distinguished linguistically.

A complementary perspective on textual variation is to identify and interpret the text categories that are linguistically well defined, referred to as text types. Text type distinctions have no necessary relation to register distinctions. Rather, text types are defined such that the texts within each type are maximally similar in their linguistic characteristics, regardless of their situational/register characteristics. However, because linguistic features have strong functional associations, text types can be interpreted in functional terms.

Text types and registers thus represent complementary ways to dissect the textual space of a language. Text types and registers are similar in that both can be described in linguistic and in situational/functional terms. However, the two constructs differ in their primary bases: registers are defined in terms of their situational characteristics, while text types are defined linguistically.

In the MD approach, text types are identified quantitatively using Cluster analysis, with the dimensions of variation as predictors. Cluster analysis groups texts into 'clusters' on the basis of shared multi-dimensional/linguistic characteristics: the conversations grouped in a cluster are maximally similar linguistically, while the different clusters are maximally distinguished. This approach has been used to identify the general text types in English and Somali (see Biber 1989, 1995).

Cluster analysis is an exploratory statistical technique that groups web documents statistically, based on the scores for all four dimensions. The FASTCLUS procedure from SAS was used for the present analysis. Disjoint clusters were analyzed because there was no theoretical reason to expect a hierarchical structure. Peaks in the Cubic Clustering Criterion and the Pseudo-F Statistic (produced by FASTCLUS) were used to determine the number of clusters. These measures are heuristic devices that reflect goodness-of-fit: the extent to which the texts within a cluster are similar, while the clusters are maximally distinguished. In the present case, these measures had peaks for the 8-cluster solution.

Table 5:   Summary of the cluster analysis

Cluster	Frequency	Maximum Distance from Seed to Observation	Nearest Cluster	Distance Between Cluster Centroids
1	428	27.83	4	14.72
2	490	22.09	3	17.24
3	599	24.33	2	17.24
4	503	25.36	1	14.72
5	620	21.50	1	18.22
6	244	30.02	3	18.06
7	21	23.32	5	22.22
8	71	24.09	6	19.52

Tables 5 and 6 provide a descriptive summary of the cluster analysis results. Table 5 shows the number of web documents grouped into each cluster, together with other statistics (such as the nearest cluster, and the dispersion of documents within each cluster). Table 6 gives the mean dimension score for each cluster. The clusters differ notably in their distinctiveness: the smaller clusters are more specialized and more sharply distinguished linguistically. For example,

Cluster 7 has only 21 documents, but these texts are distinguished by their extremely large positive scores on Dimension 4 ('Abstract/technical discourse'). Similarly, Cluster 8 includes only 71 documents, characterized by their extremely large positive scores on Dimension 1 ('Personal narration'), together with moderately large positive scores on Dimension 3 ('Advice') and negative scores on Dimension 4. At the other extreme, Clusters 1-4 are all large (over 400 documents in each of them) and characterized by intermediate scores on all four dimensions.

Table 6:   Mean dimension scores for each cluster

Cluster	Dim. 1 Personal	Dim. 2 Persuasion	Dim. 3 Advice	Dim. 4 Technical
1	-3.84	-7.38	-9.03	-6.72
2	4.20	5.64	-3.31	7.07
3	5.44	6.93	5.77	-7.46
4	-6.48	-4.76	4.29	-1.71
5	-9.18	-9.56	-8.10	10.54
6	14.18	17.48	17.49	-6.41
7	-9.65	-9.44	-9.36	32.72
8	28.30	7.04	11.51	-12.53

Figure 2 plots the multi-dimensional profile for Clusters 1-4, showing how these four clusters have relatively intermediate dimension scores on all four dimensions. In contrast, figure 3 plots the multi-dimensional profile for Clusters 5-8, showing how each of those four clusters has marked characterizations on one or more of the dimensions. Based on those notably large positive or negative dimension scores, these four clusters can be assigned functional labels, reflecting their interpretations as web 'text types':

Cluster 5: 'Informational Discourse'
Cluster 6: 'Persuasive Advice'
Cluster 7: 'Technical Discourse'
Cluster 8: 'Personal Narrative'

Table 7 shows that some web documents from both Google categories are grouped into each web text type, although the web text types are not distributed evenly across Google categories. For example, 481 of the 1576 web documents from the 'Science' category (30.5%) are grouped into the Informational Discourse text type (Cluster 5), while only 139 of the 1400 documents from the 'Home' category (9.9%) are grouped into this web text type. A few text types show a strong association with one of the Google categories. For example, 19 of the 21 documents in the 'Technical discourse' type (7) are from the 'Science' category, while 52 of the 71 documents in the 'Personal narrative' type are from the 'Home' category. In general, though, the eight web text types are composed of documents from both 'Home' and 'Science' Google categories.

The web text types also cut across the Google sub-categories included in our corpus. For example, the 71 documents in the 'Personal narrative' type (8) came from 16 different Google sub-categories. The cluster analysis grouped these documents into a single text type because they all had similar linguistic character-istics (e.g. frequent past tense verbs, mental verbs + *that*-clauses, first person pronouns, third person pronouns, and communication verbs). The 244 documents from the 'Persuasive advice' text type are even more widespread across the corpus, coming from 34 different Google sub-categories. These documents all share the defining characteristics of relatively high scores on Dimensions 2 and 3 (e.g. possibility and necessity modals, conditional clauses, second person pronouns, and desire verbs + *to*-clauses).

The clusters can be interpreted as web text types, because each cluster represents a grouping of web documents with similar linguistic profiles. Taken together, tables 5-7 and figures 2-3 provide the basis for the interpretation of each web text type. (These interpretations are refined by consideration of individual documents from each type.) The interpretive labels proposed above summarize those interpretations.

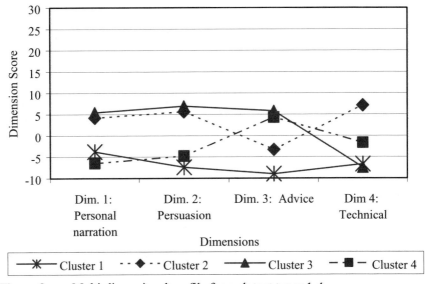

Figure 2:   Multi-dimensional profile for web text types 1-4

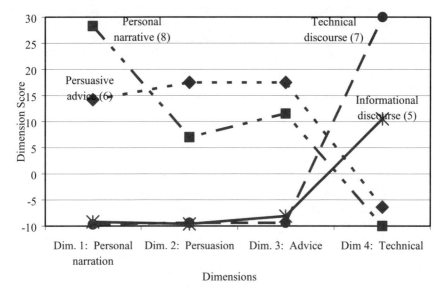

Dim. 1: Personal   Dim. 2: Persuasion   Dim. 3: Advice   Dim 4: Technical
narration

Dimensions

Figure 3:   Multi-dimensional profile for web text types 5-8

Table 7:   Breakdown of 'Home' and 'Science' web documents across the 8
text types

CLUSTER	Web Category		Total	Text Type
	'Home'	'Science'		
1	150	278	428	
	10.7%	17.6%		
2	149	341	490	
	10.6%	21.6%		
3	385	214	599	
	27.5%	13.5%		
4	344	159	503	
	24.5%	10.1%		
5	139	481	620	Informational discourse
	9.9%	30.5%		
6	179	65	244	Persuasive advice
	12.7%	4.1%		
7	2	19	21	Technical discourse
	0.1%	1.2%		
8	52	19	71	Personal narrative
	3.7%	1.2%		
Total	1400	1576	2976	
	100%	100%		

Text Samples 1, 2, and 3 illustrate the range of linguistic variation within Google sub-categories. All three samples are from the 'Family' subcategory of 'Home'. However, Sample 1 is from the 'Personal narrative' web text type (Type 8); Sample 2 is from the 'Persuasive advice' web text type (Type 6); and Sample 3 is from the 'Informational Discourse' web text type (Type 5).

Text Sample 1:
Google categories: 'Home'; 'Family'.
Text Type: 'Personal Narrative'
The biggest help in my experience of foster care was a three year old. Shalece taught me so much about how to love truly and without asking anything in return. She taught me what it means to be family, when from the day I walked into her house, I was her big sister. She never let me forget that – even when I had to leave. To this day she is excited when I come to see her. She has never let me down. I love and trust her more than anyone else. Her parents were also of great help to me, but they could never have reached me like that tiny little girl with the large heart did from day one. Some day when she is old enough to understand, I think I will show her this to let her know I really feel grateful to her. I think people have a hard time seeing that from me.

Text Sample 2:
Google categories: 'Home'; 'Family'.
Text Type: 'Persuasive Advice'
What is the Mom Team??
The Mom Team is an organization that is dedicated to assisting, training and supporting others who would like to work from home with their own business.
What kind of business is it?
All members of the MOM Team are simply customers of a wonderful company where we save time, money, provide a safer environment for our homes and improve our health.
It was just announced this morning that for the month of June, you can join our awesome group and begin living the dream of working from home for only ONE DOLLAR!! This is incredible and we didn't want you to miss the opportunity to take advantage of this awesome promotion.
How much income can I earn?
It's up to you. You can earn a few hundred dollars a month or even thousands each month depending on you and your own personal goals.
What do I need to be able to run this business from my home?
You need a computer (or access to one), a telephone, and a willingness to become part of our team and use our proven system.

How much does this cost to get started?
You can get started for just $29.00 US.

Text Sample 3:
Google categories: 'Home'; 'Family'.
Text Type: 'Informational Discourse'
General Science Information
Amino Acids – Symbols, formulas and 3D images.
Bird Species – Pictures and scientific names will help improve your identification skills. Includes herons, sparrows, warblers, woodpeckers, owls and more.
Chemicool Periodic Table – Search and learn about the elements.
Entomology for Beginners – the basics of insect study.
Grasshopper – science links and a list of cool museums to visit.
Human Anatomy 1994 – These x-rays have labeled body parts.
K-12 WWW Links – links to sites for answers to any science question.
Mad Scientist Network, The – answers to science questions.
Microworlds – This interactive tour uses graphics, photos and text to explore the structure of materials.
SciEd
Science Bytes, from UT
Science Education Gate-Way – K-12 science education resource center for teachers and students with learning adventures in Earth and Space science from a NASA-sponsored partnership of museums, researchers and educators.
Science Learning Center – Access to exhibits, publications, museums and more.

6. Conclusion

As noted in the introduction, the usefulness of the web as a corpus for linguistic research is currently limited by difficulties in identifying the text category of web documents. As a result, it is often difficult to interpret the results of a web search, because we are not able to determine what the search sample of documents actually represents.

In the present paper, we have compared the feasibility and productivity of two analytical approaches to this problem. The first simply relies on categories that are pre-defined on the web, specifically Google search engine categories in our pilot study. The second approach relies on web 'text types': text categories that are defined on linguistic bases.

The analyses presented here have shown that search engine categories are not well defined for the purposes of linguistic research. In contrast, the 'text type' approach was highly successful in identifying text categories that could be interpreted on both linguistic and situational grounds.

In future research, we plan to consider a third general approach to these issues, analyzing the range of web 'registers': text categories that are defined on non-linguistic bases (for example with respect to parameters like communicative purpose and goals, interactivity, audience, general topical domain). The first analytical step in this approach would be to identify the range of registers that end users can reliably distinguish on the web (e.g. reports, commercial advertisements, FAQs, blogs, chat rooms). In a second analytical step, we would code the register of each document in a web corpus. Then, in the final step, the linguistic characteristics of those registers can be analyzed and compared.

These three approaches have different strengths and weaknesses. The first approach has the advantage of convenience, using text categories that already exist on the web. However, as shown here, these text categories are not generally useful for the purposes of linguistic research. The second (text type) approach results in text categories that are linguistically coherent and distinguishable. However, the sociolinguistic interpretation of those categories is sometimes abstract, because they often cut across recognizable register categories. The third (register) approach is labor-intensive (because the register category of each document must be determined by hand), but the resulting linguistic patterns are immediately interpretable in sociolinguistic terms.

The final goal of this line of research is a detailed description of the text categories that comprise the web. Given the results of our pilot research, we plan to rely primarily on register and text type analyses in our future research. By merging the two perspectives, based on analysis of a large and diverse sample of web documents, we hope to identify text categories that are well defined with respect to both situational and linguistic criteria.

References

Biber, D. (1986), 'Spoken and written textual dimensions in English: resolving the contradictory findings', *Language*, 62: 384-414.

Biber, D. (1988), *Variation across Speech and Writing*. Cambridge: Cambridge University Press.

Biber, D. (1989), 'The typology of English texts', *Linguistics*, 27: 3-43.

Biber, D. (1994), 'An analytical framework for register studies', in: D. Biber and E. Finegan (eds.) *Sociolinguistic Perspectives on Register*. New York: Oxford University Press. 31-56.

Biber, D. (1995), *Dimensions of Register Variation: A Cross-Linguistic Perspective*. Cambridge: Cambridge University Press.

Biber, D., S. Johansson, G. Leech, S. Conrad and E. Finegan (1999), *Longman Grammar of Spoken and Written English*. London: Longman.

Brekke, M. (2000), 'From the BNC toward the cybercorpus: a quantum leap into chaos?', in: J.M. Kirk (ed.) *Corpora Galore: Analyses and Techniques in Describing English*. Amsterdam: Rodopi. 227-247.

Crowston, K. and M. Williams (2000), 'Reproduced and emergent genres of communication on the world-wide web', *The Information Society*, 16: 201-215.

De Schryver, G. (2002), 'Web for/as corpus: a perspective for the African languages', *Nordic Journal of African Studies*, 11: 266-282.

Dewe, J., J. Karlgren and I. Bretan (1998), 'Assembling a balanced corpus from the internet', in: *Proceedings of the 11th Nordic Conference on Computational Linguistics* [reprinted in Karlgren 2000; chapter 15].

Fletcher, W.H. (2004a), 'Making the web more useful as a source for linguistic corpora', in: U. Connor and T.A. Upton (eds.) *Applied Corpus Linguistics*. Amsterdam: Benjamins. 191-206.

Fletcher, W.H. (2004b), 'Facilitating the compilation and dissemination of ad-hoc web corpora', in: G. Aston, S. Bernardini and D. Stewart (eds.), *Corpora and Language Learners*. Amsterdam: Benjamins. 271-300.

Fletcher, W.H. (this volume), 'Concordancing the web: promise and problems, tools and techniques'.

Frand, J. (2000), 'The information-age mindset: changes in students and implications for higher education', *EDUCAUSE Review*, 35: 14-24.

Gildea, D. (2001), 'Corpus variation and parser performance', in: *Proceedings of the Conference on Empirical Methods in NLP*, Pittsburgh.

Glover, E.J., K. Tsioutsiouliklis, S. Lawrence, D.M. Pennock and G.W. Flake (2002), *Using Web Structure for Classifying and Describing Web Pages*. WWW2002, Honolulu.

Jansen, B.J., A. Spink and T. Saracevic (2000), 'Real life, real users, and real needs: a study and analysis of user queries on the web', *Information Processing and Management*, 36: 207-27.

Jones, R. and R. Ghani (2000), 'Automatically building a corpus for a minority language from the web', in: *Proceedings of the Student Workshop of the 38th Annual Meeting of the Association for Computational Linguistics*, Hong Kong. 29-36.

Karlgren, J. (2000), *Stylistic Experiments for Information Retrieval*. PhD dissertation, University of Stockholm.

Karlgren, J. and T. Straszheim (1997), 'Visualizing stylistic variation', in: *Proceedings of the 30th Hawaii International Conference on Systems Sciences*, IEEE. Maui, Hawaii.

Keller, F. and M. Lapata (2003), 'Using the web to obtain frequencies for unseen bigrams', *Computational Linguistics*, 29: 459-484.

Kessler, B., G. Nunberg and H. Schütze (1997). 'Automatic detection of text genre', in: *Proceedings of ACL and EACL*. Madrid. 39-47.

Kilgarriff, A. (2001), 'Web as corpus', in: P. Rayson, A. Wilson and T. McEnery (eds.) *Proceedings of the Corpus Linguistics 2001 Conference*, Lancaster University, *UCREL Technical Papers*, 13: 342-344.

Kilgarriff, A., and G. Grefenstette (2003), 'Introduction to the special issue on the web as corpus', *Computational Linguistics*, 29: 333-347.

Kraaij, W., J.-Y. Nie and M. Simard (2003), 'Embedding web-based statistical translation models in cross-language information retrieval', *Computational Linguistics*, 29: 381-419.

Kurjian, J. (2004), *Towards a Representative Corpus of the Web*. Ms, San Diego State University.

Kwasnik, B., K. Crowston, M. Nilan and D. Roussinov (2001), 'Identifying document genre to improve web search effectiveness', *Bulletin of the American Society for Information and Technology*, 27: 23-26.

Lawrence, S. and C.L. Giles (1998), 'Searching the world wide web', *Science*, 280: 98-100.

Lawrence, S. and C.L. Giles (1999), 'Accessibility of information on the web', *Nature*, 400: 107-109.

Mair, C. (this volume), 'Change and variation in present-day English: integrating the analysis of closed corpora and web-based monitoring'.

Mihalcea, R. and D. Moldovan (1999), 'A method for word sense disambiguation of unrestricted text', in: *Proceedings of the 37th Meeting of the ACL*, College Park, MD. 152-158.

Ooi, V.B.Y. (2001), 'Investigating and teaching genres using the world wide web', in: M. Ghadessy, A. Henry and R.L. Roseberry (eds.) *Small Corpus Studies and ELT*. Amsterdam: Benjamins. 175-203.

Pearson, J. (2000), 'Surfing the internet: teaching students to choose their texts wisely', in: L. Burnard and T. McEnery (eds.) *Rethinking Language Pedagogy from a Corpus Perspective*. Franfurt am Main: Peter Lang. 235-239.

Rehm, G. (2002), 'Towards automatic web genre identification: a corpus-based approach in the domain of academia by example of the academic's personal homepage', in: *Proceedings of the 35th Hawaii International Conference on System Sciences*, Hawaii.

Renouf, A. (2003), 'WebCorp: Providing a renewable data source for corpus linguists', in: S. Granger and S. Petch-Tyson (eds.) *Extending the Scope of Corpus-Based Research*. Amsterdam: Benjamins. 39-58. (www.webcorp.org. uk).

Resnik, P. and N.A. Smith (2003), 'The web as a parallel corpus', *Computational Linguistics*, 29: 349-380.

Rigau, G., B. Magnini, E. Agirre and J. Carroll (2002), 'Meaning: a roadmap to knowledge technologies', in: *Proceedings of COLING Workshop on a Roadmap for Computational Linguistics*, Taipei, Taiwan.

Rohdenburg, G. (this volume), 'Determinants of grammatical variation in English and the formation / confirmation of linguistic hypotheses by means of internet data'.

Roland, D., D. Jurafsky, L. Menn, S. Gahl, E. Elder and C. Riddoch (2000), 'Verb subcategorization frequency differences between business-news and balanced corpora: the role of verb sense', in: *Proceedings of the Workshop on Comparing Corpora, 38th ACL*, Hong Kong.

Roussinov, D., K. Crowston, M. Nilan, B. Swasnik, J. Cai and X. Liu (2001), 'Genre based navigation on the web', in: *Proceedings of the 34th Hawaii International Conference on System Sciences*, Hawaii.

Rusmevichientong, P., D.M. Pennock, S. Lawrence and C.L. Giles (2001), 'Methods for sampling pages uniformly from the world wide web', in: *Proceedings of the AAAI Fall Symposium on Using Uncertainty within Computation*. 121-128.

Santamaría, C., J. Gonzalo and F. Verdejo (2003), 'Automatic association of web directories to word senses', *Computational Linguistics*, 29: 485-502.

Sekine, S. (1997), 'The domain dependence of parsing', in: *Proceedings of the Fifth Conference on Applied Natural Language Processing*, Washington, DC. 96-102.

Smarr, J. (2002), 'GoogleLing: the web as a linguistic corpus', online at http://www.stanford.edu/class/cs276a/projects/reports/jsmarr-grow.pdf.

Volk, M. (2001), 'Exploiting the WWW as a corpus to resolve PP attachment ambiguities', in: *Proceedings of Corpus Linguistics 2001*, Lancaster, England.

Volk, M. (2002), 'Using the web as corpus for linguistic research', in R. Pajusalu and T. Hennoste (eds.) *Tähendusepüüdja: Catcher of the Meaning*. University of Tartu.

Xu, J.L. (2000), 'Multilingual search on the world wide web', in: *Proceedings of the Hawaii International Conference on System Science* (HICSS-33), Maui, Hawaii.

Appendix: Statistical output from the factor analysis of web documents

Table I.1:   Eigenvalues for the first four factors

	Eigenvalue	Difference	Proportion	Cumulative
1	13.3512011	7.7380702	0.1203	0.1203
2	5.6131309	1.3716806	0.0506	0.1708
3	4.2414504	0.8778715	0.0382	0.2091
4	3.3635789	0.4455549	0.0303	0.2394

Table I.2:   Inter-Factor Correlations

	Factor 1	Factor 2	Factor 3	Factor 4
Factor 1	1.00000	0.30424	0.12491	-0.28968
Factor 2	0.30424	1.00000	0.40607	-0.23135
Factor 3	0.12491	0.40607	1.00000	-0.32306
Factor 4	-0.28968	-0.23135	-0.32306	1.00000

Table I.3:   Rotated factor pattern (Promax rotation)

	Factor1	Factor2	Factor3	Factor4
Factor 1 Features:				
Positive:				
Pasttnse	0.72836	-0.43369	-0.01412	-0.17364
Mentalv	0.52866	0.13219	0.48879	0.15881
that_del	0.50498	-0.05699	0.36928	0.07394
pro3	0.49600	-0.08733	-0.00962	-0.07585
pro1	0.48887	-0.08592	0.34927	-0.03674
fact_vth	0.48566	-0.04446	0.13415	0.06093
Factadvl	0.45301	0.17506	0.10033	0.01065
Commv	0.43627	0.07929	0.09676	0.25554
nonf_vth	0.40773	0.02291	-0.04169	0.11524
Perfects	0.39889	-0.06459	-0.14479	-0.05132
lkly_vth	0.36778	0.03769	0.13411	0.12921
sub_othr	0.32987	0.22566	-0.01789	-0.12808
It	0.30174	0.28261	0.01546	-0.08610
Pany	0.30568	0.09452	0.21751	-0.05129
all_nth	0.29096	0.14375	-0.09966	0.19167
Negative:				
nouns	-0.55720	-0.56705	0.05097	-0.00803
Factor 2 Features:				
Positive:				
Pres	-0.12339	0.70658	0.31404	0.00979
pos_mod	-0.07749	0.54539	0.10962	-0.01457
be_state	-0.07289	0.53928	-0.07286	-0.03374
pred_adj	0.08771	0.50047	-0.25191	-0.01912
sub_cnd	-0.15665	0.44997	0.24364	-0.08142
Conjncts	0.26246	0.43751	-0.28103	0.03171
nec_mod	-0.00040	0.40637	0.03438	0.08383
Pdem	0.25025	0.37207	-0.02913	0.00227
prd_mod	-0.02157	0.35976	0.04518	0.06094
spl_aux	0.19739	0.32415	-0.22371	0.10236
Negative:				
Nouns	-0.55720	-0.56705	0.05097	-0.00803
pasttnse	0.72836	-0.43369	-0.01412	-0.17364
Factor 3 Features:				
Positive:				

pro2	-0.20975	0.23060	0.67108	-0.08567
Vprogrsv	0.10331	-0.03972	0.40924	0.04331
dsre_vto	0.13164	0.04493	0.40622	0.05607
Groupn	0.05023	-0.17888	0.36500	0.13152
Actv	0.13322	0.16240	0.32304	-0.15965
wh_cl	0.16565	0.07859	0.28940	0.05465
Negative:				
Prep	0.18466	-0.05765	-0.48977	0.14476
Allpasv	-0.02260	0.22100	-0.45995	0.05585
Factor 4 Features:				
Positive:				
N_nom	-0.12713	-0.09568	0.09601	0.80425
Abstrctn	0.00280	0.15802	0.08745	0.65036
Wrdlngth	-0.19665	-0.21485	-0.10344	0.66341
Cognitn	0.22940	0.17306	-0.03108	0.41358
Topicj	0.10630	-0.00567	-0.07613	0.36909
adj_attr	-0.20110	-0.12845	-0.22417	0.36133
Negative:				
Concrtn	-0.27499	0.10500	-0.05841	-0.34322

New resources, or just better old ones? The Holy Grail of representativeness

Geoffrey Leech, Emeritus Professor

Lancaster University

Abstract

This paper runs counter to the majority of papers in this volume in focusing on the argument that, while welcoming opportunities to use new resources and methods, we should not neglect to improve and refine the resources and methods we already have.

The path of progress in corpus linguistics is strewn with unfinished business. Because no other realistic course is available, corpus linguists have understandably been following the path of practicality, pragmatism and opportunism. By and large, we have built up the resources and techniques of the present generation by taking advantage of what is already available and what can be relatively easily obtained. Our research efforts have consequently been limited and skewed by what resources we have been able to lay our hands on.

In this paper, I illustrate the skewing effect with reference to corpus design and composition, focusing on the desiderata of representativeness, 'balancedness' and comparability. After arguing that we need to give more consideration to these basic requirements, I briefly address the issue of representativity (a term used to mean 'the degree to which a corpus is representative') in relation to the use of the world-wide web as a source of corpus data, both with respect to 'the web as corpus' and with respect to 'corpus building from www-material'.[1]

1. Introduction

In one sense corpus linguists appear to inhabit an expanding universe. The internet provides a virtually boundless resource for the methods of corpus linguistics. In addition, there is continuing growth in the number and extent of text archives and other text resources. If we consider corpora of the English language, one of the noticeable achievements has been the production of new historical textual resources,[2] so that gradually gaps in a mosaic of increasing coverage of historical varieties of the language are being filled in. This is greatly to be welcomed, obviously. Such are the increased opportunities for examining data of authentic usage in studying English that it may seem churlish to focus on what we lack, rather than on what new riches we can enjoy. On the other hand, there are still some weak spots in the coverage of natural language by existing corpora: notably in limitations in both quality and quantity of spoken language data, and in data from some of the newer electronic language media (e-mails, text messages, internet relay chat, and so forth).

2.   Problems and challenges

One of our goals for the future should be to extend or refine existing resources: in other words, we need to strengthen the empirical foundations of corpus linguistics, not only in corpora but in the means to exploit them. There are many areas where corpus linguistics is not making appreciable progress. Strategies of stepwise refinement (for example, in corpus design and in POS-tagging) are known about, but are not activated. To take an example where research is skewed by what resources we can lay our hands on: Gaëtenelle Gilquin (2002) examined articles relating to grammar in the *International Journal of Corpus Linguistics* (IJCL) 1996-2001, and found that 68 per cent of these concentrated on word-based studies. Of the corpora used, 28 per cent were untagged 'raw' corpora, 43 per cent were POS-tagged corpora, and 29 per cent were parsed corpora. This suggests that the ways people use corpora have not caught up with the possibilities of sophisticated corpus analysis. The full potential of even limited annotation, that of part-of-speech tagging, has not been realised. Of course one can investigate English grammar using an untagged corpus, but this in general means that one can only investigate narrow areas of grammar where abstraction and generalization across lexical items are limited. Gilquin argued that we need a Holy Grail – the software capable of achieving a useful parsing of any corpus we want to investigate. So far an accurately working corpus parser has eluded us – although considerable human effort has been invested in the production of exceedingly useful parsed corpora, such as ICE-GB.

3.   The holy grail of representativeness

An even more basic issue at the foundations of corpus linguistics is: Have we been building the right kind of corpora?

It is generally accepted that one of the desiderata for a corpus is that it be REPRESENTATIVE, but in practice, this requirement has not been treated as seriously as it should be. A seminal article by Biber (1993) has frequently been cited, but no attempt (to my knowledge) has been made to implement Biber's plan for building a representative corpus. He came to the conclusion that the construction of such a corpus should "proceed in cycles: the original corpus design [...] followed by collection of texts, followed by further empirical investigation of linguistic variation and revision of the design" (1993: 243). Although corpus linguists (including myself) often pay lip-service to representativeness, there has been relatively little productive debate on Biber's or anyone else's method of determining representativeness. However, one starkly negative contribution has been a paper by Váradi (2001), who dismisses the whole concept of representativeness as defined by Biber, and by implication claims that corpus linguistics is in a similar position to the emperor with no clothes. Much of the apologetics in favour of corpus linguistics stresses its immense advantages in providing a sound empirical base upon which to formulate linguistic generalizations, explore variation, and test linguistic theories. But – looking at the matter with Váradi's sceptical eye – unless the claim that a corpus is representative can be substantiated, we cannot accept such findings. Without representativeness, whatever is found to be true of a corpus, is simply true of that corpus – and cannot be extended to anything else.

This is more serious than academic point-scoring. There is a crucial difference between claiming that such-and-such is the case in a corpus, and that the same such-and-such is the case in a language. By definition, a sample is representative if what we find for the sample also holds for the general population (Manning and Schütze 1999: 119). Putting this in operational terms, 'representative' means that the study of a corpus (or combination of corpora) can stand proxy for the study of some entire language or variety of a language. It means that anyone carrying out a principled study on a representative corpus (regarded as a sample of a larger population, its textual universe) can extrapolate from the corpus to the whole universe of language use of which the corpus is a representative sample.[3] But as things stand at present, can we even claim a 'face validity' (to use a language testing term) for the representativeness of the corpora we work with?

This is, of course, taking a parole- or performance-based orientation towards language. For Chomsky and those taking his position, a corpus can only yield information about E-language (externalized language), and is therefore seen as irrelevant to the study of language per se, I-language (internalized language):

> Linguistics should be concerned with I-language and knowledge of
> I-language, that is with truths about the mind/brain, putting aside
> the irrelevant concept of E-language, however construed.
>
> (Chomsky 1987: 45)

But for a corpus linguist, who specializes in the investigation of E-language, I take it that the goal of inquiry is to arrive, through the study of language in use, at a better understanding of some language, both in the sense of E-language and in the sense of I-language. The two are not in totally unconnected knowledge-domains, as Chomsky seems to assume. Rather, E-language is a crucial, indispensable manifestation of I-language. Yet the obvious point is that a corpus is a sample of E-language, not of I-language. The totality of a relevant textual universe of E-language is what is being sampled. For example, in the case of the *Lancaster-Oslo/Bergen* [LOB] *Corpus* (Johansson et al. 1978) the textual universe was the totality of published material produced by adult native speakers of British English published in the UK in 1961. This is a very large but finite textual universe, consisting of a finite number of texts of finite length. The same can be claimed about other corpora: the total textual universe of spoken utterances in the US in 1991 (say) is larger and more diffuse than the total textual universe of published texts of the same year. But it is still a finite (though mind-bogglingly large) set of utterances. It is true that lack of knowledge prevents us from enumerating the texts in this textual universe, and it is also true that the linguistic domain of what is 'English' has some unclear boundaries. But this is a perfectly coherent and intelligible idea of what is being sampled, and I see no reason for Chomsky's claim that E-language is an 'epiphenomenon at best' (Chomsky 1986: 25), suffering from "complex and obscure socio-political historical and norma-tive-teleological elements" (Chomsky 1991: 31).[4] Against this background, the claim that a corpus be representative of the textual universe of which it is a sample gains a sharper focus.

It is true that the textual universes associated with a modern language with a large number of native speakers, such as English, can be immense; but no more bafflingly immense than the universe of the material cosmos, about which physicists construct intelligible theories.

4.   What is a balanced corpus?

Another often-mentioned desideratum of a corpus is that it should be BALANCED, but there have been few attempts to explain what this requirement means. In my understanding, for a corpus to be balanced is an important aspect of what it means for a corpus to be representative. This 'balanced' quality has frequently been claimed for corpora such as the *Brown Corpus* or the *British National Corpus* (BNC) or ICE-GB, which have been carefully designed to provide sufficient samples of a wide and 'representative' range of text types. But balancedness is very difficult to demonstrate, even for such painstakingly constructed corpora. An obvious way forward is to say that a corpus is 'balanced' when the size of its subcorpora (representing particular genres or registers) is proportional to the relative frequency of occurrence of those genres in the language's textual universe as a whole. In other words, balancedness equates with proportionality. But no serious attempt was ever made to ensure that the genres in the Brown Corpus or the BNC were proportional in this sense. Váradi maintains that a corpus like the Brown Corpus is not representative in this sense, although its design was clearly intended to achieve some kind of proportionality, with some text categories being assigned many more text samples than others. He points out the immense difficulty of determining the proportional amount of text appropriate for just one text category, that of Humour, containing 9 of the 500 2,000-word texts in the corpus:

> For the BROWN corpus to qualify as a representative sample of the totality of written American English for 1963[5] for humorous writing, it would have to be established that humorous writing did make up 1.8% of all written texts created within that year in the US.
>
> (Váradi 2001: 590)

It is instructive here to go back to the earliest discussions of corpus representativeness I am aware of, those that appeared in the volume edited by Bergenholtz and Schaeder (1979). Two contributors to that volume illuminated the problem of representativeness in very different ways. Rieger (1979: 66) paradoxically claimed the pointlessness of achieving it:

> [...] a random sample of the feature in question can only be designated representative when so much is known about the universe from which it comes that the formation of this sample is no longer needed.[6]

Bungarten (1979: 42-3) took a less negative stance, pointing out that even if we cannot achieve a representative corpus, there is a lesser degree of success worth achieving, what he usefully calls "an exemplary corpus":

> A corpus is exemplary, when its representativeness is not demonstrated, although less formal arguments, like evident coherence, linguistic judgements of competent researchers, specialist consensus, textual and pragmatic indicators, argue that the corpus may reasonably function as representative.[7]

Interestingly, it was in the same edited volume that Nelson Francis, chief begetter of the *Brown Corpus*, came up with a definition of a 'corpus' that included representativeness. A corpus, according to him, was 'a collection of texts assumed to be representative of a given language, dialect, or other subset of a language, to be used for linguistic analysis' (Francis 1979: 110). The tell-tale word here, of course, is 'assumed': there is nothing in the design of the Brown Corpus to guarantee representativeness. Instead, it seems that the Brown Corpus fits more snugly into the category Bungarten calls exemplary. Francis goes into some detail about the method of arriving at the composition of the Brown Corpus:

> [...] we convened a conference of such corpus-wise scholars as Randolph Quirk, Philip Gove, and John B. Carroll. This group decided the size of the corpus (1,000,000 words), the number of texts (500, of 2,000 words each), the universe (material in English, by American writers, first printed in the United States in the calendar year 1961), the subdivisions (15 genres, 9 of 'informative prose' and 6 of 'imaginative prose') and by a fascinating process of individual vote and average consensus, how many samples from each genre (ranging from 6 in science fiction to 80 in learned and scientific).
>
> (ibid.: 117)

Unfortunately, the deliberations of these corpus-wise scholars have not come down to us: we do not know how far considerations of 'balance' led to their conclusion that 80 text samples were needed for the learned genre, and only 6 for that of science fiction. Although design of corpora has made considerable advances since that time, what makes a corpus 'balanced' or 'unbalanced' has remained obscure.

There is one rule of thumb that few are likely to dissent from. It is that in general, the larger a corpus is, and the more diverse it is in terms of genres and other language varieties, the more balanced and representative it will be.

However, perhaps we can do a little better than this. I would like to reconsider the value of proportionality in defining a balanced corpus. Biber (1993 – see also Biber et al. 1998: 247) rejected proportionality, on the grounds that it would mean sampling of speakers and writers from the language community in proportion to their membership of demographic classes (e.g. by age, gender, socioeconomic groupings, etc.), and this would lead to a highly *skewed* corpus, from the point of view of representing the whole range of linguistic variation, 90 per cent of the corpus consisting of conversation. Biber assumed that 90% of linguistic activity is conversational, and that conversation on the whole has relatively little variation compared with other varieties of language. He noted that other varieties of language would receive little representation (e.g. statutes, TV news) since only a tiny proportion of the language community is engaged in producing such texts.

However, Biber elsewhere observes that there are three elements of language use that could enter into the sampling procedures. There are (a) the speakers and writers – the *initiators* of texts; (b) the hearers and readers – the *receivers* of texts; and (c) the *texts* themselves. I maintain that the representation of texts should be proportional not only to their initiators, but also to their receivers. After all, decoding as well as encoding is a linguistic activity. Thus a radio programme that is listened to by a million people should be given a much greater chance of being included in a representative corpus than a conversation between two people, with only one listener at any one time. I propose, therefore, that the basic unit to be counted in calculating the size of a given textual universe is not the text itself, but an initiator-text-receiver nexus, which we can call an ATOMIC COMMUNICATIVE EVENT (ACE). When a radio programme is listened to by a million people, there is only one text, but a million ACEs.

Since proportionality is widely considered to be the basis for representative sampling, Váradi (2001) criticizes Biber's (1993) decision to reject proportionality on the grounds of the estimation of greater 'importance' of certain genres (such as TV new broadcasts) in contrast to others (private conversations). Biber argues:

> It would [...] be difficult to stratify a demographic corpus in such a way that it would insure representativeness of the range of text categories. Many of these categories are very important, however, in defining a culture.
>
> (Biber 1993: 245)

To which Váradi's riposte is:

> One of the fundamental aims of Corpus linguistics as I understand it is to show up language as it is actually attested in real life. However, Biber seems to argue that in designing a corpus one should apply a notion of importance that is derived from a definition of culture. … this throws the door wide open to subjective judgment in the compilation of the body of data that is expected to provide solid empirical evidence for language use.
>
> (Váradi 2001: 592)

However, I would suggest that 'importance' does not have to be subjective. A conceptually simple way of measuring the importance of a text, for purposes of corpus building, is how many receivers it has. It is true that some corpus builders in the past have introduced evaluative criteria, judging, for example, a broadsheet newspaper (in the UK) to be more important or influential than a tabloid one; a novel which wins a national prize for literature to be more important than a pulp-fiction best-seller; or speakers belonging to socio-economic groups A and B to be more corpus-worthy than members of lower socio-economic groups D and E. However, this élitism is entirely spurious in a corpus intended for linguistic analysis.[8] In contrast, the criterion of size of readership / audience is free of evaluative bias. One of its results, no doubt unpalatable to corpus-builders with a sense of taste, is that tabloid newspapers are more likely to be included in a representative corpus than so-called quality or broadsheet newspapers. But this is something one has to put up with in the interests of representativeness.

It will not have escaped notice that the notion of an ACE as the basic unit of a textual universe, hence of sampling from a textual universe, is largely impractical. For the majority of samples we might want to include in a balanced corpus, we just have no way of knowing the number of texts, let alone the number of ACEs, in the relevant textual universe. The composition of the LOB Corpus was a particularly favourable case.[9] It was possible to use bibliographical sources to arrive at a relatively complete list of publications in the UK during the year 1961 to be used as a sampling frame. But no sampling on the basis of readership was attempted, and could not have been attempted for the corpus as a whole. It is true that some of the readership figures are relatively easy to come by – for example, the circulation of national newspapers – but for the large majority of publications, they are not. For most books, if we knew the number of copies purchased, we would be able to estimate the number of readers. But in general such information is not publicly available. A valuable source of information in the UK (and there are similar sources in other countries) is provided by the PLR (Public Lending Right) organization, which samples books borrowed from public libraries. But on the whole, the difficulties of determining the size of the textual universe and its sub-universes from which a corpus is to be sampled are formidable.[10]

One additional difficulty is the variable length of texts. Text lengths, as well as text readerships, would have to be determined in order to calculate the likelihood that a sample of a given text should be included in a sample corpus.

Thus a tabloid newspaper such as *The Sun* (in the UK) contains fewer words per issue than a broadsheet newspaper such as *The Independent*. This should give *The Independent* greater sampling privilege which would partially offset the smaller circulation of that paper.

It is reasonable to ask: Is there any point in pursuing the goal of a balanced corpus, where 'balanced' is understood to mean 'ACE-proportional' as it has been explained here? I will defend this concept of ACE-proportionality, while recognizing that it is a Holy Grail even more unattainable that Gilquin's working corpus parser. My arguments are these. First, the fact that something cannot be precisely specified or calculated does not detract from its actuality as something worth aiming at. Secondly, there are ways of mitigating the difficulty. (a) It is possible to estimate text usage, even where one cannot determine the quantity absolutely. (b) It makes sense to consider representativeness and balancedness in terms of a scale of approximation to the ideal. (c) Above all, representativeness (or, as I will prefer to call it, representativity) is a scalar phenomenon. Even if the absolute goal of representativeness is not attainable in practical circumstances, we can take steps to approach closer to this goal on a scale of representativity.[11] For example, the impossible calculations I referred to above can be estimated through the judgement of the corpus compilers combined with whatever objective measures may be available.[12]

In practice this is how people appear to have designed 'balanced' corpora in the past. The term 'judgement' here refers to the ability professionally competent members of a speech community seem to have in recognizing the relative prevalence of different genres, just as they may recognize their prevalent linguistic features. The 'corpus-wise' linguists who arrived at the composition of the Brown Corpus no doubt used this kind of judgement. A low degree of representativity, corresponding to Bungarten's 'exemplary corpus', can be attained by such informal means. A higher degree of representativity may be attained by using EXTERNAL (sociocultural)[13] criteria as formalized in a systematic typology of genres, as proposed by Biber (1989) among others. The aim here is to ensure that the widest practicable range of text categories within the textual universe is sampled. But we should perhaps emphasise the desirability of both breadth and depth in the typology: not only must the range be broad enough to include all genres at a primary level of classification, but the granularity of the typology must be sufficient to ensure that sampling includes delicate subcategories.

At a higher level still, representativity can be enhanced by a concerted effort to improve the proportionality of samples. This is, however, where I take a different route from Biber (1993: 248-55), who, having rejected proportionality, pursues a quantitative INTERNAL analysis of genres according to their linguistic characteristics. His plan is to carry out a multidimensional frequency analysis of register variation (see Biber and Kurjian's contribution to this volume), and to develop a corpus which is representative of the full range of linguistic variation that occurs in the textual universe. Analysis of variation can reveal those registers where the corpus gives insufficient evidence of variation, and needs to be supplemented by additional textual material (longer textual samples, or more samples). By a cyclic research programme, the corpus can be gradually enlarged and modified until all variation in language use is sufficiently represented.

Perhaps Biber's method is just another way of achieving balance. It will mean that language varieties are to be represented in the corpus in proportion to their heterogeneity, rather than in proportion to their prevalence of use in the whole textual universe. Arguably, this is not representativeness, but another corpus desideratum: heterogeneity. It is a different way of drawing the map of the varieties of usage. But the goal is similar: that once the map has been drawn, and the parameters of variation confirmed, the results of a corpus analysis can be extrapolated to data outside the corpus, and ultimately to the whole universe of language use.

How far is Biber's goal of an optimally heterogeneous corpus comparable to the ACE-proportionality theory of representativeness? It could have different results: for example, poets experiment endlessly with language, and the poetry genre is likely to show immense heterogeneity. But poetry might not score particularly highly in terms of volume of usage: poetry books do not tend to have a wide readership, nor poetry magazines a high circulation. So this might lead to a relatively low representation of poetry in a corpus modelled on ACE-proportionality, whereas it would lead to a high representation according to the heterogeneity criterion.

Biber's method, like the ACE-proportionality, is extremely difficult to implement. One of the difficulties is that the size of text samples depends on the amount of text required to manifest a stable pattern of variation. With frequent grammatical characteristics, small text samples of 1,000 words are sufficient; however, as Biber admits, some linguistic features, such as a *that*-clause functioning as subject, are rare, and for these, much larger text samples would be needed. More dauntingly, if one considers collocations, lexico-grammatical combinations, granularity of linguistic classifications in grammar, in phonology, in semantics, etc., the number of linguistic features that might enter into a thorough study of variation is vast and open-ended. Some of these features would be very rare. The size of text samples needed would vary according to the linguistic feature under consideration, and for some rare features enormous text samples would be needed. There would be no 'fits all sizes' corpus. Biber et al. (1998: 250) understandably comment that a great deal of work needs to be done in improving corpus design along these lines, and other difficulties, such as those of speech transcription, copyright clearance, or time and financial constraints, mean that compromises have to be made.

5.   Comparable corpora

A third yardstick for successful corpus building is the construction of COMPARABLE CORPORA (also sometimes called 'matching' corpora): a set of two or more corpora whose design differs, as far as possible, in terms of only one parameter: the temporal or regional provenance of the textual universe from which the corpus is sampled. Thus, if comparability is achieved, one is entitled to assume that a significant contrast between one comparable corpus and another in terms of linguistic frequency is likely to be due to the variability between the two corpora – of time or region – rather than variability within one corpus or within the other. The original example of comparability was that of the Brown and LOB corpora, which were intended to match one another in all respects apart from that of the country of origin (the USA versus the UK).

The requirement of comparability depends at least partly on that of representativity: comparable corpora permit precise comparisons between two varieties or states of a language, but only if the corpora are reasonably representative of their respective varieties. One might add, too, that comparability, like representativity, can be conceptualized as a scale, rather than as a goal to be achieved 100 per cent. The design profiles of the Brown and LOB corpora differed rather slightly, but enough to cause some doubt about whether we had truly attained a comparison of like with like.[14]

As is well known, a number of comparable corpora have been built on the Brown model, including the Frown [Freiburg-Brown] and FLOB [Freiburg-LOB] Corpora which match Brown and LOB respectively in being American and British matching corpora on the Brown model, but sampled from texts published in 1991 / 1992, rather than 1961. Hence the four corpora Brown, LOB, Frown and FLOB are each comparable in two dimensions, dialectal and diachronic: between American and British English, and between 1961 and 1991 / 1992. Another well-known example of comparable corpora is the *International Corpus of English* [ICE], where a corpus model (with stratified sampling from both written and spoken English) has been instantiated in different regional subcorpora such as ICE East Africa, ICE Great Britain, ICE India, ICE New Zealand, ICE Phillipines, ICE Singapore – these are the six varieties so far publicly available.

While it makes sense to achieve success in both representativeness and comparability, there is a sense in which these two goals conflict: an attempt to achieve greater comparability may actually impede representativity and vice versa. Nicholas Smith and I have encountered this problem in a mild form while building a 'prequel' to the LOB and FLOB corpora: a corpus on the familiar Brown model but with texts sampled from the years 1931±3 (i.e. 1928-34). Our most immediate research objective was to compare grammatical frequencies between 1931±3 and 1961, and to see how far they would enable us to project further into the past the trends already observed in the differences between the 1961 and 1991 corpora. But we encountered a problem with the sampling.

Rather like the wave and particle theories of light, representativeness and comparability, though each has its own validity, are ultimately incompatible ways of looking at corpus design. As one nears to perfection in comparability, one meets with distortion in terms of representativeness, and vice versa. In the LOB sampling, books and periodicals were randomly sampled[15] within the predetermined text categories, from comprehensive lists of publications from the year 1961 (using the *British National Bibliography Cumulative Index 1960-64* and *Willings Press Guide*). When Christian Mair's Freiburg team set about building a 1991 equivalent of LOB, they aimed to achieve a one-to-one match between individual 2,000-word text samples in LOB and FLOB. This meant choosing, for example, from the same periodicals if these happened to be in print both in 1961 and in 1991. Random sampling would not have achieved such a close match, and so would have jeopardized the comparability of the two corpora. For example, the compilers of the 1991 corpus "deliberately excluded papers which are circulated in vast quantities without charge. Although they are a sign of the times, we ranked the comparability of LOB '91 to LOB '61 higher in priority than the possible alternative goal, viz. to create the accurate picture of the British printed press right now" (Sand and Siemund 1992: 120). In other words, comparability was prioritized at the expense of synchronic representativity. The Lancaster team have decided to follow this precedent in compiling the (so far incomplete) Lancaster1931 corpus. If we had followed the procedures of LOB, we would have carried out random sampling which would, for instance, have resulted in provincial newspapers from different cities being included in the Press categories A-C, and possibly the addition of new styles of publication (such as free newspapers) which had no equivalent in LOB.

This brings me to a more fundamental challenge to comparability: GENRE EVOLUTION (discussed in Leech and Smith 2005). It is increasingly being recognized that the genres on which stratified sampling of many corpora is based are themselves subject to change. New genres emerge; old genres decay (see Biber et al. 1998: 252). As a case in point, we had problems filling the slots in the *Lancaster1931 Corpus* for science fiction and sociology texts – two sub-genres that were emergent at that time. One can argue that when these sub-genres are given the same degree of prominence in the 1931 corpus as in the 1961 corpus (where they were given 6 and 5 two-thousand-word samples respectively), they are overrepresented. Moreover, even some of the so-called sociology texts available in 1931 were arguably of a different genre, following more in the tradition of humanistic and philosophical discourse than in that of the then fledgling discourse of social science. We had to consider sample texts case by case, but in general followed the principle of text-by-text matching with LOB as far as possible. This policy, if adopted for an earlier corpus sampling publications in (say) 1901 or 1871, would clearly confront the compiler with more severe problems of genre definition, leading to increasing sacrifice of comparability to representativeness or vice versa, as one moved further into the past. The problems described here of maintaining diachronic comparability also arise with synchronic comparability. An example is the rearrangement of fiction text categories in the Australian Corpus of English, another corpus on the Brown model, where two new categories, Historical Fiction and Women's Fiction, were introduced, compensating for a dearth of Australia-published fiction in other categories.

The above discussion of representativeness, balance and comparability might lead the reader to reject these concepts as being ill-defined, problematic, unattainable. My attitude is different from this. I have tried to show that these are important considerations, and even if we cannot achieve them 100 per cent, we should not abandon the attempt to define them and achieve them. We should aim at a gradual approximation to these goals, as crucial desiderata of corpus design. It is best to recognize that these goals are not all-or-nothing: there is a scale of representativity, of balancedness, of comparability. We should seek to define realistically attainable positions on these scales, rather than to abandon them altogether.

6.   Conclusion: internet implications

I will finally turn to the theme of this book, and attempt to show how the reflections above have a bearing on the issue of using the web as a corpus. First, consider representativeness. One idea is that the web-as-corpus makes the notion of a representative corpus redundant. Potentially, the whole of the web can be searched with a search engine, so a sample corpus is unnecessary: we have the whole textual universe at our disposal. However, it is clear that this ideal situation does not exist. A search engine like Google employs algorithms which are totally mysterious to the average user (but see Fletcher's contribution to this volume, section 3.1). Google provides nothing like a complete search of the web, and reports such as that by Jean Véronis[16] show how unstable and inconsistent are the counts that one gets from Google, at least at the present time. What we get is an enormous sample of the web, but how representative it is remains a mystery. The consensus seems to be that frequency information obtained from Google is at present seriously misleading.

What must be excluded from the above judgement, of course, are well-defined custom-made corpora based on particular websites, such as the CNN corpus and the SPEA-Corpus introduced by Hoffmann and Hundt and Biewer in their respective chapters of this book.

A second question, with regard to representativeness, is: Can we see the web (or the sample of it we access in searching with a web browser) as somehow representative of English language use as a whole; or at least of written English language use? Can the proportional sense of a 'balanced corpus' be applied to it? It is true that the web gives access to a very wide range of genres, some of them well-established in the written medium, such as academic writing and fiction writing; others newly-evolving genres closer to speech, such as blogs. However, it is also true that the web by definition gives little or no access to private discourse, such as everyday conversation, telephone dialogues, and the like. (Indeed, the very notion of 'privacy' is sometimes challenged by www-mediated communication.) Searching with a search engine provides no access to spoken or manuscript data. There are major areas seriously underrepresented, if they are represented at all. It is also likely that certain varieties, such as academic writing, are overrepresented. The multi-media and HTML format of web pages is also likely to exercise its own constraints and preferences in the use of language. The web in English is its own textual universe, with huge overlaps with the non-electronic textual universe of the English language. It is a textual universe of unfathomed extent and variety, but it can in no way be considered a representative sample of language use in general.

Turning to the concept of comparability: it is obvious that the web provides nothing like the exact comparability of text selection for different periods or different regions of the world. On the diachronic axis, it is even impossible to tell when a particular text or text extract was written; similarly, on the synchronic axis, knowledge of the provenance of a text is minimal. Whether the author was a native speaker, for example, is usually unknown. On the other hand, searching on the country codes in URLs can provide convincing gross frequency contrasts between national varieties, as in the case of *different from, different than,* and *different to* illustrated in Mair's contribution to this book. If we are interested in rough-and-ready rather than more precise frequency data, and observe sufficiently striking contrasts, the web can offer revealing results, which can be confirmed by replication.

Even without such qualities as representativeness, a corpus retains the merit, in Váradi's terms, in showing up "language as it is actually attested in real life". In providing evidence for neologisms, new word usages, and collocations the web wins out against other corpora because of its sheer size and because it is always being updated. Hence it is useful, and may have even become indispensable, for lexicography and for lexico-grammatical investigations. The absence of any linguistic annotation such as POS tagging means that grammatical and semantic investigations are limited, in the ways indicated by Gilquin (2002). They have to rely on searches based on orthographic lexical form, which is not to say they are unimportant. Perhaps the future will bring 'intelligent search engines' which consign this restriction to history (see Fletcher's and Renouf et al.'s contributions to this volume for steps in this direction). Meanwhile, while the internet is an added resource of immense potential, it does not remove the need to improve and update other textual resources, and does not render obsolete the corpus compiled according to design and systematic sampling.

Notes

1   I am grateful to Nick Smith for helpful discussions on some topics covered in this paper. I am also grateful to the editors of this volume for their comments, which resulted in improvements to the paper.

2   Just a few of the new historical corpora arising from recent work are the *Penn-Helsinki Parsed Corpus of Middle English* (PPCME2), the *Penn-Helsinki Parsed Corpus of Early Modern English* (PPCEME), extensions of the ARCHER corpus (*A Representative Corpus of Historical English Registers*), the *Corpus of Early English Correspondence Sampler* (CEECS), the *Corpus of Late 18th Century Prose,* the *Corpus of English Dialogue* (1560-1760), the *Corpus of Nineteenth Century English* (CONCE), and the *Zürich Corpus of English Newspapers* (ZEN). In addition, proprietary resources like *The Times Digital Archive,* the *OED quota-*

tions database, and the Chadwyck-Healey literature collections provide further extensive and rich full-text resources for the history of English.

3   Of course not all corpora are samples. Some corpora contain the complete extant textual material belonging to a certain language or language variety. Examples are the *Corpus of Shakespeare's Works*, the *Corpus of Hellenistic Greek*, the *Corpus of twentieth-century newspapers in Basque* (see the UZEI *Systematic Compilation of Modern-Day Basque* – EEBS). Particularly in the case of languages long dead, the corpora of data that have come down to us are the result of chance survivals, of course contain no spoken language, and are usually heavily biased towards certain periods, genres, and authors. Porter and O'Donnell (2003: 121) observe that for Hellenistic Greek, "in the 55 million words in the Thesaurus Linguae Graecae database, around 10 million of those words are by the fourth-fifth century writer John Chrysostom." In the case of such closed exhaustive corpora, the issue of representativeness clearly cannot be seriously addressed.

4   These two quotations from Chomsky are found in Váradi (2001: 587).

5   The year '1963' here is presumably an error for '1961'.

6   „[...] eine Stichprobe hinsichtlich des betrachteten Merkmals nur dann als *repräsentativ* ausgezeichnet werden kann, wenn über die Grundgesamtheit, aus der sie stammt, so viel bekannt ist, daß es eben dieser Strichprobenbildung gar nicht mehr bedarf." (See Mark Sebba's web page http://www.ling.lancs.ac.uk/staff/mark/cwbc/cwbcman.htm.)

7   „Ein Korpus ist exemplarisch, wenn seine Repräsentativität nicht nachgewiesen ist, andererseits weniger formale Argumente, wie evidenter Zusammenhang, linguistische Urteile des kompetenten Forschers, fachlicher Konsensus, textuelle und pragmatische Indikatoren, für eine sinnvolle Vertreterfunktion des Korpus plädieren." (Also quoted on Mark Sebba's web page.)

8   Interestingly, the BNC falls foul of the accusation of élitism on two of these counts, although the intentions behind these decisions were not élitist. The numbers of speakers sampled for the demographic (conversational) subcorpus from the lowest socio-economic classes D and E were equal to those from classes A and B, although if they had been sampled in proportion to population, they would have been larger. This apparent 'élitist' deviation from proportionality was reportedly due to a difficulty data-collecting researchers experienced in persuading members of classes D and E to record their own conversations and to take part in the data collection. In the interests of economy, the easier way out was chosen: the samples from each class were equalized. Another 'élitist' deviation from proportionality was the higher representation of broadsheet ('quality') newspapers in the BNC than of tabloid newspapers. The reason for this was that

permission could not be obtained from certain newspapers to include their material in the corpus.

9   The reason for choosing LOB as a particularly favourable case, rather than Brown, is that the Brown texts were sampled from local libraries in Providence, R.I., where Brown University is located, and therefore contains a representation of US publications in 1961 that is limited to the holdings of these libraries.

10   Anticipating the discussion in section 6, it is worth noting that focus on text reception is actually an advantage of the web as corpus, since access data are recorded on many web pages.

11   This view is taken by Mukherjee (2004: 114): "Absolute representativeness is an unattainable ideal, but specific procedures may help in getting closer to this goal [...]."

12   The following is an afterthought, added after this paper had been completed and submitted. The criterion of ACE-proportionality can, without much simplification, be reduced to a criterion of receptive proportionality. The argument is as follows. The number of ACEs (communicative events defined in terms of a single addresser and a single addressee) represented by a text is the product of the number of addressers and the number of addressees of that text. However, in all canonical cases the number of addressers (whether in speech or in writing) is just one. (Cases of multiple addressers are, of course, found in choral speech and in co-authorship of written texts, but these cases are confined to rather special circumstances: by far the majority of published texts, for example, have a single author.) Hence the number of ACEs per text reduces, without much distortion, to the number of receivers of a text. Research on proportionality therefore reduces to language reception research, which can be conducted along the sociological lines, taking a demographic sample and investigating (by means of diaries, questionnaires, etc.) the amount of time spent in listening to different categories of speech and reading different categories of written text. In the design of the *Czech National Corpus* this kind of language reception research was employed to determine proportions of different genres of written text (Čermák and Schmiedtová 2003: 212). To undertake a fully-fledged research project of this kind as a prerequisite to compiling a balanced corpus would be rather expensive and time-consuming, but not beyond the bounds of possibility. It would also be valuable for other research domains, such as literacy research.

13   The terms 'external' and 'internal' here follow the usage of Sinclair (1996), for whom text classification can be based either on external 'sociocultural' or internal 'text linguistic' criteria. Biber (1993) made use of a similar distinction.

14   For example, the Western and Adventure Fiction category (N) in Brown contained many more Western Fiction texts than the LOB Corpus, as such works were rarely published in the UK.

15   Problems of copyright clearance meant that random sampling was not adhered to in all cases.

16   Cf.   http://aixtal.blogspot.com/2005/02/web-googles-missing-pages-mystery.html.

References

Bergenholtz, H. and B. Schaeder (eds.) (1979), *Empirische Textwissenschaft: Ausbau und Auswertung von Text-Corpora*. Königstein: Scriptor.

Biber, D. (1989), 'A typology of English texts', *Linguistics*, 27: 3-43.

Biber, D. (1993), 'Representativeness in corpus design', *Literary and Linguistic Computing*, 8 (4): 243-257.

Biber, D. and J. Kurjian (this volume), 'Towards a taxonomy of web registers and text types: a multi-dimensional analysis'.

Biber, D., S. Conrad and R. Reppen (1998), *Corpus Linguistics: Investigating Language Structure and Use*. Cambridge: Cambridge University Press.

Bungarten, T. (1979), 'Das Korpus als empirische Grundlage in der Linguistik und Literaturwissenschaft', in: H. Bergenholtz and B. Schaeder (eds.). *Empirische Textwissenschaft: Ausbau und Auswertung von Text-Corpora*. Königstein: Scriptor. 28-51.

Chomsky, N. (1986), *Knowledge of Language: Its Nature, Origin and Use*. New York: Praeger.

Chomsky, N. (1987), *Generative Grammar: Its Basis, Development and Prospects*. Kyoto: Kyoto University of Foreign Studies.

Chomsky, N. (1991), 'Linguistics and cognitive science: problems and mysteries', in A. Kasher (ed.) *The Chomskyan Turn*. Oxford: Blackwell, 26-53.

Čermák, F. and V. Schmiedtová (2003), 'The Czech National Corpus: its structure and use', in: B. Lewandowska-Tomaszczyk (ed.), *PALC 2001: Practical Applications in Language Corpora*. Frankfurt am Main: Lang. 207-224.

Fletcher, W.H. (this volume), 'Concordancing the web: promise and problems, tools and techniques'.

Francis, W.N. (1979), 'Problems of assembling and computerizing large corpora', in: H. Bergenholtz and B. Schaeder (eds.) *Empirische Textwissenschaft: Ausbau und Auswertung von Text-Corpora*. Königstein: Scriptor. 110-123.

Gilquin, G. (2002), 'Automatic retrieval of syntactic structures: the quest for the Holy Grail', *IJCL*, 7 (2): 183-214.

Hoffmann, S. (this volume), 'From webpage to mega-corpus: the CNN transcripts'.

Hundt, M. and C. Biewer (this volume), 'The dynamics of inner and outer circle varieties in the South Pacific and East Asia'.

Johansson, S., G. Leech and H. Goodluck (1978), *Manual of Information to Accompany the Lancaster-Oslo/Bergen Corpus of British English, for Use with Digital Computers*. Department of English, University of Oslo.

Leech, G. and N. Smith (2005), 'Extending the possibilities of corpus-based research on English in the twentieth century: a prequel to LOB and FLOB', *ICAME Journal*, 29: 83-98.

Manning, C.D. and H. Schütze (1999), *Foundations of Statistical Natural Language Processing*. Cambridge, MA: MIT Press.

Mukherjee, J. (2004), 'The state of the art in corpus linguistics: three book-length perspectives', *English Language and Linguistics*, 8 (1): 103-119.

Porter, S.E. and M. O'Donnell (2003), 'Theoretical issues for corpus linguistics and the study of ancient languages', in: A. Wilson, P. Rayson and T. McEnery (eds.), *Corpus Linguistics by the Lune*. Frankfurt am Main: Lang. 119-137.

Renouf, A., A. Kehoe and J. Banerjee (this volume), 'WebCorp: an integrated system for web text search'.

Rieger, B. (1979), 'Repräsentativität: von der Unangemessenheit eines Begriffs zur Kennzeichnung eines Problems linguistischer Korpusbildung', in: H. Bergenholtz and B. Schaeder (eds.) *Empirische Textwissenschaft: Ausbau und Auswertung von Text-Corpora*. Königstein: Scriptor. 52-70.

Sand, A. and R. Siemund (1992), 'LOB – 30 years on ...', *ICAME Journal*, 16: 119-122.

Sinclair, J. (1996), *Preliminary Recommendations on Corpus Typology*. EAGLES Document EAG—TCWG—CTYP/P. http://www.ilc.cnr.it/ EAGLES96/ corpustyp/corpustyp.html.

Váradi, T. (2001), 'The linguistic relevance of corpus linguistics', in: P. Rayson, A. Wilson, T. McEnery, A. Hardie and S. Khoja (eds.) *Proceedings of the Corpus Linguistics 2001 Conference*. Lancaster University: UCREL Technical Papers 13. 587-593.

An under-exploited resource: using the BNC for exploring the nature of language learning

Graeme Kennedy

Victoria University of Wellington

Abstract

At a time when the use of the world wide web as a source of data for linguistic description is beginning to be explored by corpus linguists, this paper considers insights which can be gained from an existing structured corpus, and possible implications for our understanding of the nature of language learning. The British National Corpus (BNC) is used as a source of data to explore semantic relations which may underlie certain multi-word sequences identified in the corpus. The analysis focuses on collocations containing verbs or amplifiers. It is suggested that the richness of the data in the BNC is still somewhat under-exploited for the description of English, and for exploring the nature of language learning and teaching.

1.   Introduction

One of the great linguistic mysteries continues to be what it is we learn when we learn a language. An easy answer could be that we learn grammar and lexis, and how to perform speech acts. In theory, the more familiar we are with the grammar of a language, and the more words we know, the more fluently we can perform these speech acts. Linguists and language teachers have, of course, long recognised that lexis involves more than single words, and that we tend to string sequences of words together and use these same multi-word sequences repeatedly as prefabricated units. This formulaic characteristic of speech has a notable literature, dating back to the beginning of the 20th century. There has been little consistency in approach or terminology, however, with some 40 different terms for multi-word sequences being identified by Wray (2002), and others. The most widely used term has probably been 'collocation'. A particular irony has been that formulaic speech has sometimes been condemned as 'cliché' when recognised and used by native speakers, while the ability to use such sequences is simultaneously considered a mark of fluency among second or foreign language learners.

Much of the work on collocation has been focused on particular sequences of words which, it has been argued, have become lexicalised and behave like individual words: e.g. *bring up* 'raise'; *at the present time* 'now'; *I see what you mean* 'understand'. The focus has been on the phenomenon of the word sequence itself or on syntactic constructions based on canonical structures or patterns. Developments in corpus linguistics have made it increasingly easy to identify such collocations, and to count how often they occur in text, thus making it possible to describe their likelihood of occurrence in particular genres, or more generally in a language. Statistical procedures such as the Mutual Information (MI) measure (Church and Hanks 1990) have taken corpus-based analysis beyond frequency counting by establishing ways of measuring the strength of the bond between adjacent or near adjacent words. In describing collocations not just as adjacent words, or in terms of patterns, it has also become possible to uncover semantic principles or processes which may lie behind many collocational phenomena. This paper explores a small number of such semantic processes which appear to characterise some of the recurring multi-word sequences in the BNC, and which may be relevant for second and foreign language learning.

2.   The world wide web as a corpus

Forty years ago, corpus linguists were particularly concerned with corpus design and compilation. Initially, one million-word corpora were considered to be state-of-the-art, although it soon became apparent that for studies of all but the most frequent words very much larger corpora would be necessary for lexical studies. Large corpora of hundreds of millions of words are now available, even though some of them are not constructed to be representative of a language, but rather are simply large, sometimes opportunistic databases of newspapers or other readily available sources of text. In this context, the world wide web has taken on particular significance. Estimated by some commentators to have contained over 200 billion words of text by the end of 2004, the web has been perceived by a number of scholars as promising to provide an even richer resource from which to sample texts from many different genres. On the face of it this may appear to be an attractive prospect for the scientific study of language. However, bigger is not necessarily better when it comes to using a corpus for linguistic description, and the web has yet to prove that it has advantages over the carefully constructed large corpora and databases which corpus linguists have become familiar with.

For a start, the web as a corpus is unlikely to be representative of spoken language; it is often unclear as to the authorship of the text with the result that it is not always possible to even determine whether a particular text has been compiled by fluent or native speakers of the language; there can be issues of copyright; even with sampling, analysis of the web as a corpus can produce unmanageable amounts of data which do not necessarily lead to different insights from those derived from much smaller, structured or monitor corpora. Further, it sometimes seems that there is a tendency among corpus linguists to move on to working with larger or newer corpora even when there is much valuable work still to be done with smaller or older corpora whose resources have not been fully exploited.

A case in point is the rich resource of the BNC (Burnard 1995). It is large enough, at 100 million words, to undertake the study of all but the least frequent lexis in context, and superb interfaces such as those developed by Lehmann et al.

(2002), have made it easy to manage analyses of the BNC, a corpus which still has much to reveal about the English language and how it is used.

3. *Lose, lost, find* and *found* in the BNC

Few corpus linguists will need any persuading that intuitions about how English works do not always coincide very well with corpus-based evidence. For example, when native speakers of English are asked to suggest a word related to *lose* many of them suggest the antonym *find*. *Lose* and *find* seem to be semantically associated (cf. *give-take, give-keep, show-hide, rise-fall, like-dislike, come-go, come-bring*). When these same native speakers are asked what words they would expect to use after the word *lose* they typically give answers such as *keys, wallet, purse, credit card, passport,* or occasionally *the plot*. The words they would expect to use after *find* include *answer, a bargain, keys,* 'something that was lost'. The BNC however, shows that speakers of British English also associate *lose* and *find* with quite different words.

There are huge numbers of tokens of the verb forms *lose, lost, find* and *found* in the BNC. In the following analysis these types have not been lemmatised, so as to highlight the effect of verb form on collocation. The rank order of the 40 most frequent collocates of each of these four verb forms are set out in table 1 in the appendix.

It can be seen that losing *weight, sight, jobs, control, money,* and *temper* rank high in the frequency with which they are used in the BNC, with *lose* and *weight* occurring together 238 times in the 100 million words of the corpus. *Find* and *way* similarly occur together 1063 times in the BNC.

Using a different measure of collocational association, the Mutual Information (MI) measure (Church and Hanks 1990), a different picture emerges. The 40 strongest collocational associations, as revealed by the MI measure are set out in table 2, where each of the items in the list of collocates of *lose, lost, find,* and *found* has a collocational value in the adjacent column, representing the strength of the association in the corpus between the keywords (*lose, lost, find, found*) and the most strongly associated words in the corpus (see table 2 in the appendix).

Although the MI measure tends to favour or emphasize collocations containing low frequency words, it is nevertheless one useful indication of the strength of association between two (or more) words in a corpus. The MI measure compares the actual frequency of co-occurrence of two words with the predicted frequency of co-occurrence of the two words if each were randomly distributed in the corpus.[1] If there is a genuine association between the two words, then the joint probability of occurrence, f (n,c), will be much larger than chance and consequently the MI will be >0. The BNCWeb interface can provide MI values automatically for any collocation in the corpus.

Comparing frequency of occurrence of collocations with strength of the collocational bond, we can see in tables 1 and 2 that the most frequent collocations are not necessarily the strongest, and that MI associations coincide to only a limited extent with the list of associations based on frequency of occurrence.

Further, in table 2, while *temper* and *virginity* both associate strongly with *lose* and *lost*, *tempers* (pl) is not in the *lost* list, and *self-control* and *concentration* associate strongly with *lose* but are not in the top 40 collocates of *lost*. It seems that we do not mind saying that we lose self-control, but we are less inclined to report it as having occurred. On the other hand, in table 2 *wickets* and *marbles* associate strongly with *lost* but are not so strongly associated with *lose*. Over 60 percent of the words in table 2 associated with *lose* or *lost* occur with only one of these words. Looking at the collocates of *lose* more closely, among the top 40, only *financially* and *valuable* are not nouns.

Turning now to the word *find* in table 1, the most frequent collocate in the BNC is the noun *way*, but overall there is a higher proportion of adjective collocates than noun collocates. Table 2 shows that 23 out of 40 of the strongest collocates of *find* are adjectives. The other 17 are all nouns or reflexive pronouns. That is, there is a very different pattern of grammatical associations compared with *lose*. Tables 1 and 2 suggest that we tend to *lose* nouns and *find* adjectives. In the case of *found* 20 out of the 40 collocates listed are adjectives.

It is worth noting that in the BNC there is a striking lack of parallelism between *lose* and *find*: We *lose our footing*, but we *find our feet* (not our *footing*). Similarly, We *lose the plot*, but we don't *find the plot* and we *lose our tempers* but we can't find them again.

4. Amplifier collocations in the BNC

Analysis of the verb forms *lose, lost, find* and *found* suggests that collocations may not be formed only with lemmas but also with individual types. This is borne out when we examine data on the use of amplifiers modifying adjectives and past participles in the BNC. In their corpus-based grammar of English, Biber et al. (1999: 545) show that the most frequent amplifier-adjective collocations in British English conversation include *very good, very nice, quite good, pretty good, quite nice, really good, really nice,* and *too bad*. In American English conversation the same collocations occur frequently, and in addition, we find frequent use of *real good, real quick, really bad,* and *too bad*. In British and American English conversation frequently used amplifiers include *very, so, really, too, real, completely, absolutely, totally, extremely, highly, entirely, fully, incredibly, perfectly, strongly, terribly, damn* and various expletives.

Biber et al. (1999: 564) note that, "[s]peakers and writers have a variety of degree adverbs to choose from in modifying adjectives", and while some are not interchangeable "[…] in many cases, there is little semantic difference between the degree adverbs. Thus the adverbs could be exchanged in the following pair of sentences with little or no change of meaning: *That's **completely** different. It's **totally** different.*"

It is true that some amplifiers such as *completely* and *totally* may seem to be synonymous. However, the BNC shows that even apparently synonymous amplifiers seem to prefer to keep different company. Examples from each of the three main sub-groups of amplifiers (maximizers, boosters and downtoners) described by Quirk et al. (1985) will be considered in turn.[2]

4.1 Maximizers

Table 3 (see appendix) contains the 40 most strongly bonded words (as determined by the MI measure) associated with four maximizers in the BNC *(completely, fully, totally, utterly)*. Other maximizers not dealt with in this analysis include *absolutely, entirely, perfectly,* and *dead.*

Each maximizer in table 3 tends to collocate strongly with quite different words. Thus *completely* collocates most strongly with *refitted* with a collocational value of 6.09, while *fully* collocates most strongly with *fledged.* Whereas the four maximizers in table 3 may all appear to be roughly synonymous, they each bond strongly with different adjectives and participles. But there is more to it than this. The information in table 3 shows more general semantic and grammatical characteristics can be involved in the collocations.

- *Completely* tends to be associated with 'abolition' (e.g. *eradicated, wrecked, destroyed, eliminated, gutted*); 23% have a negative prefix; 10% have an *out-* or *over-* prefix; 78% of the collocates have an *-ed* suffix.
- *Fully* has exclusively positive associations; 13% of the adjectives have an *-able* or *-ible* suffix; 78% of the collocates have an *-ed* suffix.
- *Totally* tends to have mainly negative associations (e.g. *unsuited, lacking, insane*); 65% of the adjectives have a negative prefix; 45% of the collocates have an *-ed* suffix.
- *Utterly* has negative associations in 75% of the collocations (e.g. *desolate, stupid, ruthless, miserable*); 38% of the collocates have an *-ed* suffix.

4.2 Boosters

When we consider the boosters which are used frequently in British English, (including badly, clearly, considerably, deeply, enormously, extremely, greatly, heavily, highly, incredibly, particularly, really, severely, terribly, very) it is again apparent that each of them tends to collocate strongly with quite different words. As was the case with maximizers, almost any booster can in theory be associated with almost any adjective or verb. In reality, there are probabilities of occurrence, and learning and using these contributes greatly to fluency. The collocational associations of four English boosters in the BNC are shown in table 4 in the appendix.

- *Extremely* tends to be associated more with adjectives which have negative associations (e.g. *difficult, risky, wasteful, dangerous*) than positive (e.g. *versatile, valuable, fruitful, lucrative*); 20% of the adjectives end in *-ful*; 15%

have a negative prefix; only two of the collocates end in *-ed* (*distressed* and *agitated*).

- *Greatly* mainly has positive associations, with the exception of *outnumbered, alarmed* and *distressed*; there are no negative prefixes; all 40 collocates end in *-ed*; 40% have the /id/ allomorph.
- *Incredibly* tends to be associated with adjectives which express 'subjective judgement' (e.g. *sexy, naïve, handsome, brave, clever, boring, beautiful*); some have a *-y* suffix (e.g. *lucky, funny, sexy, easy*); only three of the collocates have an *-ed* suffix.
- *Really* has with both positive (e.g. *cute, nice, funny, tasty*) and negative associations (e.g. *scary, pathetic, horrible, vile*); 25% of the collocates have *-y* suffixes; 13% end in *-ing*; 15% end in *-ed*.

4.3   Downtoners

Collocations associated with four downtoners in the BNC are shown in table 5 in the appendix.

- *A bit* seems to be particularly associated with aberration or negative polarity (e.g. *iffy, haywire, groggy, dodgy, pricey, fussy, weird, tricky, messy, scruffy*). 55% of the examples in the table end in *-y*. Collocations 41-100, which are not printed in table 5, also have predominately negative associations.
- *Pretty* tends to be used with adjectives having negative associations in about half of the collocates listed in table 5. A grim picture is painted: *horrendous, hopeless, awful, boring, dull, depressing, fed up*. Outside the top 40, many other adjectives with negative associations such as *rotten, pathetic, lonely, bad* may be found with *pretty*. Only one word (*uncomfortable*), however, has a negative prefix.
- *Rather* is associated with adjectives having negative polarity (e.g. *nondescript, ungainly, jaundiced, seedy, self-indulgent, grubby, pompous*).
- *Relatively* is notable for 55% of the associated adjectives having a negative prefix, while maintaining positive polarity (e.g. *inexpensive, unproblematic, uncontroversial*). After the top 40, the next in line include similar words such as unaffected, unspoiled, innocuous.

Thus, in addition to supporting the view that words associated with maximizers, boosters and downtoners may be usefully characterized in collocational terms, the data presented here suggest that certain grammatical and semantic factors may also be involved in determining collocational associations.

2.   Collocations and language learning

In light of data such as these it has been suggested in Kennedy (2003) that corpus linguistics can contribute to language learning and teaching not only through direct applications of distributional information to curriculum content, but also by informing teachers about what it is their learners are learning.

Corpus linguistics is well-placed to reveal more about the nature and role of formulaic speech, and to take further the pioneering work of linguists and language teaching theorists, including Palmer (1933). Firth (1957), Halliday and Hasan (1976), Nattinger (1980), Pawley and Syder (1983) and Sinclair (1991), who are among those who kept reminding applied linguists of the importance of formulaic speech. However, in recent years, language teachers have rarely been able to incorporate a focus on lexis or multi-word sequences within the dominant pedagogical paradigm of communicative language teaching.

The collocations I have described reveal only a miniscule part of the learning which is necessary in order to become a fluent user of a language. A substantial part of linguistic competence appears to be based on a huge store of memories of previously-encountered words and groups of words stored in units of use. Research in cognitive science (Kirsner 1994) has shown that the frequency with which we experience words and groups of words significantly influences the extent to which these linguistic items are associated, stored and retrieved from memory. Through repeatedly coming across the same words occurring together in the same order, implicitly-learned linguistic 'patterns' or 'constructions' are stored (e.g. *Do you want any more? I think I'll go to bed; There's nothing worth watching on TV tonight*).

The more frequently we are exposed to these units of use (which typically consist of tone units of up to about seven syllables), the faster we can process them, and the more 'fluent' we become (Bybee and Hopper 2001).

One of the issues which continue to be explored within applied linguistics is the relative importance of implicit knowledge of the kind I have referred to, and explicit knowledge. Implicit knowledge is, in part at least, the vast amount of information we acquire unconsciously about a language simply through exposure to the language being used in speech and writing. For example, few learners are taught that in English we are likely to *completely* forget to ring people, not just *forget*. (If we simply *forget* we may be perceived as not caring; if we *completely forget* then regret may be implied); trucks are rarely just *laden*, but tend to be *heavily* (or *fully*) *laden*; we might *become deeply suspicious,* or *highly,* (rather than *heavily*), *skilled*; we are more likely to be *incredibly lucky* than *highly lucky*; we thank people *very much* and not just *much,* and so on. Such collocations are an unstated part of the implicit curriculum for language learners.

Learning explicit knowledge, on the other hand, is learning with aware-ness. It includes the very large amount of information which typically forms the basis for the second language curriculum, the words, patterns and functions which are taught as a set of assumptions about what we need to know in order to become fluent users of a language. A curriculum typically includes explicit instruction on the language code (phonology, grammar and vocabulary); how to perform certain speech acts (e.g. how to use *excuse me* as an apology in the US, and as a request in Britain); how to develop proficiency in the skills of listening, speaking, reading or writing, and appreciation of culture.

In addition to the explicit curriculum, learners are unconsciously acquiring experience of which linguistic items typically occur in the company of other items. This curriculum probably cannot be explicit, and is indeed typically hidden, but nevertheless it still has to be learned if fluency is to be achieved. Of course, the acquisition of collocations is nowhere near the whole story. Sinclair (1991) reminded us that regularity in language as the basis for meaning arising from text comes from both an 'open choice' or grammatical principle, and an 'idiom' or formulaic principle. Formulaic sequences are not easy to learn, because of the operation of subtle and complex linguistic factors of the kind illustrated here. Further, on the one hand there is a frequency metric making particular collocations familiar, and on the other hand a metric based on strength of bonding, as revealed by the MI measure.

While recognizing that it is not easy, even if possible, to teach explicitly the kind of complexity revealed by the corpus, the challenge for language teachers is how to devise a curriculum which maximizes the opportunities for learners to get enough experience of collocations in use in order to internalise them. It should be clear from tables 1 to 5 that some of the collocations which contain the strongest bonds, as measured by the MI score, are in fact infrequent, and should not be a pedagogical priority (e.g. *lose momentum, lose entitlement, find solace, found strangled*). From a pedagogical viewpoint, it is, of course the most frequently-occurring collocations which normally need to be learned first. Some explicit instruction in frequently-occurring collocations taught as vocabulary is therefore almost certainly worthwhile. These collocations can range from the highly frequent (e.g. *very good, really good*) to less frequent types such as *completely clear, highly skilled,* or *clearly visible.* The most infrequent collocations, however strong the bonding, are almost certainly best left for implicit learning.

The most important outcome of corpus-based insights into what language learning entails may be in consciousness-raising for teachers. A language imposes its own implicit curriculum on learners, although it is a curriculum that is normally hidden from us, and may be different from what we think is being learned. Corpus-based research has challenged language educators to work out how to maximize the exposure needed for learners to acquire probabilistic implicit knowledge which cannot easily be taught explicitly. The encouragement of autonomous language learning, especially through reading, is obviously very important to help maximize exposure to language in use. In addition, data of the kind considered here can, of course, reveal something of the cognitive processes which lie behind language learning and use, and which enable us to become fluent language users.

Acquisition of collocational patterns by language learners might eventually be based on analysis of texts from the web, achieved through filters enabling the downloading of text from the internet. The analysis could also be useful as a blueprint for distinguishing between native and non-native web pages. In the meantime, research on balanced corpora can contribute the necessary ground work for developing the tools that might eventually help us tackle the world wide web as a source for building huge monitor corpora.

Notes

1   It is calculated as follows: MI = log2 ((f (n,c) x N) / (f(n) x f(c)) where f(n,c) is the collocation frequency, f(n) is the frequency of the node word, f(c) is the frequency of the collocate, and N is the number of words in the corpus.

2   See Kennedy (2003) for a fuller analysis of maximizers and boosters.

References

Biber, D., S. Johansson, G. Leech, S. Conrad and E. Finegan (1999), *Longman Grammar of Spoken and Written English*. London: Longman.

Burnard, L. (ed.) (1995), *Users Reference Guide to the British National Corpus*. Oxford: Oxford University Computing Services.

Bybee, J. and P. Hopper (eds.) (2001), *Frequency and the Emergence of Linguistic Structure*. Amsterdam: John Benjamins.

Church, K.W. and P. Hanks (1990), 'Word association norms, mutual information and lexicography', *Computational Linguistics*, 16: 22-9.

Firth, J. (1957), *Papers in Linguistics, 1934-1951*. London: Oxford University Press.

Halliday, M.A.K. and R. Hasan (1976), *Cohesion in English*. London: Longman.

Kirsner, K. (1994), 'Second language vocabulary learning: the role of implicit processes', in: N. Ellis (ed.) *Implicit and Explicit Learning of Languages*. London: Academic Press.

Kennedy, G. (2003), 'Amplifier collocations in the British National Corpus: implications for English language teaching', *TESOL Quarterly*, 37: 467-87.

Lehmann, H-M., S. Hoffmann and P. Schneider (2002), *BNCWeb*. Zürich: Englisches Seminar, Universität Zürich.

Nattinger, J. (1980), 'A lexical phrase grammar for ESL', *TESOL Quarterly*, 14: 337-44.

Palmer, H.E. (1933), *Second Interim Report on English Collocations*. Tokyo: Kaitakusha.

Pawley, A. and F. Syder (1983), 'Two puzzles for linguistic theory: nativelike selection and nativelike fluency', in: J. Richards and R. Schmidt (eds.) *Language and Communication*. London: Longman.

Quirk, R., S. Greenbaum, G. Leech and J. Svartvik (1985), *A Comprehensive Grammar of the English Language*. London: Longman.

Sinclair, J. (1991), *Corpus, Concordance, Collocation.* Oxford: Oxford University Press.
Wray, A. (2002), *Formulaic Language and the Lexicon.* Cambridge: Cambridge University Press.

Appendix

Table 1:   Rank order frequencies of content word collocates of four verb forms in the BNC

	LOSE	freq.	LOST	freq.	FIND	freq.	FOUND	freq.
1	weight	238	interest	91	way	1063	guilty	709
2	sight	148	jobs	78	difficult	856	also	705
3	jobs	135	sight	77	themselves	798	themselves	583
4	job	113	way	74	people	474	difficult	561
5	control	104	weight	70	hard	442	way	538
6	money	103	control	66	new	438	only	510
7	temper	91	job	66	very	411	very	393
8	interest	90	get	65	something	387	dead	373
9	touch	53	never	63	ways	294	hard	336
10	time	44	touch	60	work	287	new	327
11	confidence	41	temper	59	place	258	later	248
12	people	38	time	58	time	235	often	248
13	way	38	days	54	easy	201	never	230
14	right	37	sense	51	often	195	evidence	206
15	power	35	confidence	49	just	191	always	202
16	face	31	completely	49	anything	189	among	201
17	pounds	31	battle	46	never	181	time	199
18	track	31	money	46	useful	177	body	191
19	everything	30	only	46	only	176	just	191
20	sense	30	now	43	easier	172	still	179
21	heart	27	lives	42	such	171	people	177
22	grip	26	almost	42	always	170	soon	176
23	home	26	nearly	41	right	170	place	164
24	quickly	25	stolen	41	suitable	170	impossible	161
25	sleep	25	seat	40	somewhere	166	nothing	161
26	contact	24	forever	39	now	165	now	152
27	ability	23	everything	38	job	159	work	139
28	business	23	men	37	interesting	154	necessary	138
29	easily	22	seats	36	solution	151	man	137
30	patience	22	something	35	quite	147	something	134
31	support	22	love	33	better	144	useful	132
32	identity	21	balance	32	again	142	quite	125
33	head	20	faith	31	soon	138	such	125

34	something	20	power	31	well	137	study	123
35	baby	19	ground	31	good	136	back	121
36	credibility	19	life	30	probably	136	looking	120
37	value	19	war	30	here	130	police	118
38	balance	18	count	29	things	130	almost	116
39	concentration	18	pounds	29	money	124	lying	115
40	hope	18	ability	26	best	123	survey	114

Table 2:   Mutual Information values of content word collocates of four verb forms in the BNC

	LOSE	MI value	LOST	MI value	FIND	MI value	FOUND	MI value
1	temper	5,76	irretrievably	7,04	objectionable	4,18	envying	4,89
2	virginity	5,56	virginity	6,36	off-putting	4,14	guilty	4,59
3	self-control	5,44	footing	6,14	solace	4,02	resenting	4,23
4	tempers	5,13	temper	5,94	distasteful	3,67	distasteful	3,91
5	weight	4,81	paradise	5,17	loopholes	3,57	hanged	3,72
6	sight	4,58	tragically	5,05	takers	3,43	congenial	3,71
7	footing	4,54	hopelessly	5	backers	3,41	solace	3,61
8	credibility	4,45	wickets	4,98	pickings	3,41	repugnant	3,58
9	patience	4,39	marbles	4,96	amusing	3,41	correlate	3,56
10	individuality	4,38	knack	4,86	disconcerting	3,4	niche	3,52
11	jobs	4,12	mists	4,83	congenial	3,37	strangled	3,5
12	grip	4,1	nerve	4,75	yourself	3,36	herself	3,49
13	financially	3,94	narrowly	4,7	frustrating	3,32	repulsive	3,45
14	nerve	3,83	forever	4,4	ourselves	3,29	straying	3,45
15	entitlement	3,83	bearings	4,06	difficult	3,27	unnerving	3,41
16	touch	3,56	sight	4,01	repulsive	3,26	appendix	3,35
17	momentum	3,47	seats	4,01	helpful	3,25	incriminating	3,32
18	innocence	3,32	patience	4	contentment	3,23	gratifying	3,31
19	confidence	3,26	seat	3,96	unconvincing	3,16	rescuers	3,28
20	appetite	3,22	grip	3,95	niche	3,16	incomprehensible	3,24
21	identity	3,15	thread	3,94	outlet	3,14	wandering	3,22
22	track	3,11	appetite	3,84	irresistible	3,13	infuriating	3,2

23	inches	3,1	stolen	3,82	themselves	3,13	commonly	3,19
24	job	3,09	credibility	3,78	culprits	3,11	experimentally	3,16
25	votes	3,05	antiquity	3,78	puzzling	3,11	unpalatable	3,13
26	consciousness	3,03	jobs	3,73	unattractive	3,09	myself	3,12
27	concentration	3,01	completely	3,71	enclosed	3,08	unfit	3,1
28	chains	2,85	leg	3,65	fulfilment	3,04	takers	3,1
29	seats	2,84	strikes	3,62	easier	2,98	wanting	3,07
30	monopoly	2,79	admiration	3,61	suitable	2,94	stabbed	3,03
31	control	2,76	consciousness	3,46	depressing	2,93	postmortem	3,02
32	liberty	2,76	lives	3,44	distressing	2,92	objectionable	3
33	sleep	2,68	balance	3,39	inconceivable	2,91	tiring	2,96
34	interest	2,67	touch	3,38	lodgings	2,9	disconcerting	2,94
35	faith	2,66	temporarily	3,33	unacceptable	2,87	amusing	2,94
36	licence	2,59	seat	3,28	myself	2,84	himself	2,93
37	excess	2,59	momentum	3,27	agreeable	2,81	fossils	2,88
38	tissue	2,56	totally	3,26	irritating	2,81	puzzling	2,88
39	valuable	2,53	weight	3,25	solutions	2,78	dead	2,86
40	money	2,5	nearly	3,24	intolerable	2,78	contentment	2,86
41	precious	2,5	damaged	3,21	somewhere	2,77	expedient	2,82
42	a great deal	2,5	impetus	3,19	pretext	2,77	traces	2,81
43	ability	2,41	millions	3,18	hilarious	2,76		

Table 3:   Forty strongest MI values with selected MAXIMIZERS in the BNC

	COMPLETELY	MI value	FULLY	MI value	TOTALLY	MI value	UTTERLY	MI value
1	refitted	6,09	fledged	7,77	unsuited	6,23	desolate	5,42
2	inelastic	5,85	conversant	6,9	unprepared	5,89	disgraceful	5,31
3	outclassed	5,69	battened	6,37	illegible	5,65	irresponsible	4,8
4	redesigned	5,51	clothed	6,22	unsuitable	5,61	ruthless	4,8
5	refurbished	5,42	air-conditioned	6,06	impractical	5,6	compelling	4,61
6	overhauled	5,35	deductible	5,82	uncharacteristic	5,58	miserable	4,55
7	eradicated	5,33	elucidated	5,77	illogical	5,57	ridiculous	4,18

8	disorientated	5,27	configured	5,7	unacceptable	5,55	horrified	4,1
9	renovated	5,18	compre-hended	5,61	unconnected	5,51	helpless	3,96
10	mystified	5,16	automated	5,49	devoid	5,49	divorced	3,84
11	sequenced	5,08	washable	5,27	unintelligible	5,38	exhausted	3,82
12	gutted	4,91	equipped	5,24	symmetric	5,35	alien	3,73
13	revamped	4,86	programma-ble	5,22	unfounded	5,34	appalling	3,71
14	uninterested	4,76	operational	5,19	untrue	5,33	deserted	3,71
15	untrue	4,76	sighted	5,19	unmoved	5,27	useless	3,68
16	overshadowed	4,66	dilated	4,92	unjustified	5,25	convincing	3,62
17	healed	4,59	rigged	4,91	oblivious	5,18	foolish	3,62
18	submerged	4,59	staffed	4,83	incompre-hensible	5,16	charming	3,62
19	untouched	4,41	utilized	4,83	unrelated	5,16	opposed	3,6
20	cured	4,34	briefed	4,83	unconcerned	5,15	unexpected	3,51
21	lifeless	4,33	integrated	4,82	eclipsed	5,11	transformed	3,45
22	unrelated	4,26	computerized	4,73	immersed	4,99	shocked	3,4
23	wrecked	4,25	exploited	4,65	unrealistic	4,97	defeated	3,38
24	ignored	4,22	matured	4,61	unaware	4,97	absorbed	3,33
25	baffled	4,22	carpeted	4,58	engrossed	4,91	destroyed	3,21
26	disregarded	4,21	adjustable	4,55	inadequate	4,87	confused	3,04
27	bald	4,14	inclusive	4,53	fucked	4,85	worn	3,04
28	destroyed	4,11	informed	4,43	unexpected	4,77	mad	2,97
29	numb	4,11	aligned	4,4	one-sided	4,76	inadequate	2,94
30	self-contained	4,1	computerised	4,36	bemused	4,73	silent	2,91
31	obscured	4,06	compatible	4,35	lacking	4,65	dependent	2,91
32	devoid	4,05	manned	4,34	incapable	4,6	devoted	2,85
33	irrelevant	4,03	justified	4,26	insane	4,59	stupid	2,77
34	overgrown	4,02	licensed	4,26	alien	4,59	remote	2,72
35	eliminated	4,01	loaded	4,26	dependent	4,59	brilliant	2,71
36	automated	3,92	implemented	4,22	submerged	4,58	impossible	2,7
37	insane	3,91	turbulent	4,22	irrelevant	4,55	failed	2,65
38	forgotten	3,91	articulated	4,2	pissed off	4,53	convinced	2,59
39	absorbed	3,9	glazed	4,2	dispropor-tionate	4,51	false	2,47
40	ignorant	3,9	assimilated	4,19	baffled	4,46	felt	2,24

Table 4:   Forty strongest MI values with selected BOOSTERS in the BNC

	EXTREMELY	MI value	GREATLY	MI value	INCREDIBLY	MI value	REALLY	MI value
1	hard-working	3,9	facilitated	5,21	sexy	4,7	chuffed	3,36
2	time-consuming	3,88	appreciated	5,07	naïve	4,53	naff	3,15
3	versatile	3,86	outnumbered	5,03	handsome	3,75	pissed off	3,1
4	rare	3,83	admired	4,95	boring	3,73	scary	2,92
5	arduous	3,71	exaggerated	4,94	brave	3,67	weird	2,86
6	valuable	3,71	enhanced	4,93	exciting	3,65	groovy	2,86
7	difficult	3,66	enlarged	4,81	lucky	3,55	annoying	2,58
8	frustrating	3,65	benefited	4,76	stupid	3,55	uptight	2,54
9	distressing	3,61	strengthened	4,64	efficient	3,47	tacky	2,51
10	wasteful	3,56	simplified	4,63	clever	3,42	wacky	2,49
11	knowledge-able	3,55	elongated	4,62	complicated	3,34	cute	2,41
12	unhelpful	3,51	indebted	4,62	dangerous	3,21	nice	2,31
13	durable	3,49	influenced	4,56	thin	3,2	funny	2,29
14	distressed	3,47	expanded	4,5	fast	3,12	nasty	2,29
15	fruitful	3,42	improved	4,47	beautiful	2,99	annoyed	2,29
16	risky	3,41	hindered	4,43	tired	2,86	pathetic	2,25
17	fortunate	3,4	differed	4,28	expensive	2,84	tasty	2,2
18	helpful	3,39	accelerated	4,25	funny	2,77	grown-up	2,17
19	unwise	3,35	reduced	4,09	powerful	2,77	obnoxious	2,11
20	wary	3,35	diminished	4,08	soft	2,64	horrible	2,06
21	costly	3,35	underesti-mated	4,08	slow	2,5	boring	1,98
22	reactive	3,32	amplified	4,06	detailed	2,4	amazing	1,97
23	painful	3,3	impressed	4,06	successful	2,36	upset	1,95
24	doubtful	3,29	respected	4,03	difficult	2,34	scared	1,93
25	lucrative	3,25	hampered	4,01	simple	2,33	bothered	1,93
26	annoying	3,25	elaborated	4,01	strong	2,28	fed-up	1,91
27	hazardous	3,24	contributed	3,99	easy	2,27	naughty	1,9
28	agitated	3,24	varied	3,96	blue	2,25	disgusting	1,87
29	stressful	3,21	alarmed	3,94	complex	2,21	degrading	1,86
30	useful	3,18	assisted	3,93	low	2,13	bad	1,84
31	economical	3,16	increased	3,92	interesting	2	vile	1,82
32	unpopular	3,16	exacerbated	3,91	hard	1,83	stupid	1,81
33	damaging	3,15	honoured	3,84	short	1,82	skinny	1,8
34	grateful	3,15	boosted	3,65	high	1,4	juicy	1,8

35	uncomfort-able	3,13	distressed	3,49	important	1,3	silly	1,74
36	dangerous	3,1	aided	3,48	large	0,75	hilarious	1,72
37	cautious	3,1	relieved	3,39	long	0,67	hurt	1,72
38	unpleasant	3,09	altered	3,33	small	0,66	sexy	1,72
39	unlikely	3,08	widened	3,32	good	0,46	excited	1,71
40	tedious	3,08	encouraged	3,31	little	0,4	frightening	1,71

Table 5: Forty strongest MI values with selected DOWNTONERS in the BNC

	A BIT	MI value	PRETTY	MI value	RATHER	MI value	RELATIVE-LY	MI value
1	iffy	5,97	horrendous	3,8	nondescript	4,42	painless	5,35
2	haywire	5,78	hopeless	3,48	ungainly	4,09	inexpensive	5,2
3	peaky	5,73	boring	3,45	racy	4,05	unimportant	5,17
4	cheesed off	5,67	straight-forward	3,26	jaundiced	3,74	inelastic	5,02
5	groggy	5,57	dull	3,11	nebulous	3,64	unproblem-atic	4,88
6	tipsy	5,03	awful	3,07	one-sided	3,63	unscathed	4,84
7	miffed	5,01	fed up	3,05	uninspiring	3,54	straight forward	4,78
8	dodgy	4,97	sure	3,02	seedy	3,51	untried	4,76
9	far-fetched	4,92	depressing	2,98	flippant	3,49	undifferenti-ated	4,72
10	pricey	4,75	horrible	2,97	staid	3,49	unsophisti-cated	4,71
11	edgy	4,41	neat	2,93	sheepish	3,48	insignificant	4,64
12	chilly	4,36	nasty	2,9	self-indulgent	3,46	unexplored	4,61
13	grumpy	4,2	disgusting	2,85	stilted	3,46	unconstrained	4,59
14	apprehen-sive	4,15	useless	2,8	ponderous	3,43	straightfor-ward	4,51
15	lax	4,1	weird	2,71	girlish	3,39	uncommitted	4,44
16	daft	4,07	dreadful	2,71	cloudy	3,38	uncontrover-sial	4,38
17	louder	4,05	silly	2,67	ill-defined	3,38	infrequent	4,37
18	wobbly	4,04	obvious	2,64	spooky	3,36	inexperienced	4,36
19	scary	4,01	miserable	2,61	perfunctory	3,34	undeveloped	4,22
20	messy	3,89	tough	2,59	unnerving	3,33	well-off	4,19
21	tricky	3,87	decent	2,58	sedate	3,3	labour-intensive	4,15
22	fussy	3,8	grim	2,54	unimaginative	3,3	affluent	4,13

23	dizzy	3,8	rough	2,51	forbidding	3,27	uneventful	4,1
24	hazy	3,78	impressive	2,48	patronizing	3,26	homogeneous	4,08
25	scruffy	3,76	uncomfort-able	2,45	florid	3,26	prosperous	4,06
26	rusty	3,68	stupid	2,45	haphazard	3,25	undemanding	4,05
27	weird	3,65	clever	2,45	cumbersome	3,23	powerless	4,03
28	naughty	3,64	busy	2,41	colourless	3,22	undisturbed	3,97
29	boring	3,62	good	2,39	pompous	3,18	autonomous	3,96
30	awkward	3,59	quick	2,38	coy	3,16	modest	3,89
31	pissed (off)	3,59	well	2,35	wobbly	3,15	uncompli-cated	3,88
32	dicey	3,54	smart	2,32	drab	3,14	harmless	3,87
33	confusing	3,48	confident	2,31	stuffy	3,13	inactive	3,82
34	hesitant	3,43	convincing	2,27	grubby	3,12	immobile	3,82
35	annoying	3,42	crowded	2,24	tatty	3,12	well off	3,82
36	silly	3,36	upset	2,23	prim	3,09	untouched	3,8
37	misty	3,36	cool	2,11	fetching	3,09	trivial	3,77
38	warmer	3,29	odd	2,07	intimidating	3,06	stable	3,73
39	dubious	3,28	pleased	2,01	vague	3,05	standardized	3,72
40	shaky	3,25	desperate	1,99	eccentric	3,03	cheap	3,7

Exploring constructions on the web: a case study[1]

Anette Rosenbach

University of Düsseldorf

Abstract

This paper presents a case study on grammatical variation that exemplifies both possibilities and limits of using data drawn from the web in linguistic research. In particular, the impact of animacy (of the modifier) on the choice between s-genitives such as driver's licence *and noun+noun constructions (*driver licence*) will be tested. It will be shown that this type of variation is extremely difficult to study on the basis of 'traditional' electronic corpora since these do not contain a sufficient number of crucial tokens. In this case, therefore, the web provides a unique data resource for investigating a phenomenon which otherwise could barely be studied at all in a corpus. At the same time, however, this paper will also discuss various obstacles we may run into when using web data. Most crucially, it will be shown that – at least in the present case – the WebCorp software provides a more reliable means of retrieving data from the web than Google. The findings and conclusions of the present case study are embedded within a general discussion on using web data in linguistic research.*

1. Introduction

The web has found its way into linguistics by now. It provides a data pool which is larger than any other corpus and thus constitutes an immensely rich and interesting new data resource – but also a challenging one.[2] The concerns of many linguists about the use of web data have recently found expression in Brian Joseph's editorial notes in *Language*:

> [W]e seem to be witnessing [...] a shift in the way some linguists find and utilize data – many papers now use corpora as their primary data, and many use internet data. These are clearly changes that are technologically induced, and in an era in which google is now a common verb, why not? I feel compelled to add, though, *caveat googlator*! In the culling of data from Medieval Greek texts for my dissertation, [...], I ran across some examples [...] that I felt were best treated as having been altered, [...] Thus I considered them to be attested but ungrammatical – some examples obtained on the internet in papers I read now strike me as quite the same, that is, possibly produced by nonnative speakers, or typed quickly and thus reflecting performance errors, and so on. I have no doubt that we will learn how to deal with this new data source effectively [...]. (Joseph 2004: 382)

This paper is an attempt to meet the hope expressed by Brian Joseph that "we will learn how to deal with this new data source effectively." I will present a case study on grammatical variation which demonstrates some of the problems we may run into when using data from the web. At the same time I hope to show how such problems may be overcome. I will proceed as follows: I will first give a brief overview of linguistic research on constructions done in the web (section 2). I will then move on to the case study, based on data drawn from the web (section 3). And finally I will briefly go into the implications of the findings from the present study for the use of web data in corpus linguistics in general (section 4).

2. The world wide web in linguistic research

As any corpus, the web can be used for ascertaining two types of evidence, i.e. qualitative and quantitative evidence. Qualitative evidence is used to show that a certain form or construction is attested; quantitative evidence addresses the question of 'how many' of these forms / constructions can be found in a corpus.[3] These two types of evidence pose different problems for the researcher in general. Drawing such data from the web, in this respect, is similar to 'normal' corpus data, though there are some problems that are specific to web data.

In the following section (2.1), I will briefly address one central problem in using qualitative evidence from the web, and then move on to give some examples of web-based linguistic research. The case study presented in section 3 will then illustrate the use of quantitative evidence from the web.

2.1 Attested but ungrammatical?

Showing that a certain form / construction is indeed attested in a corpus is one thing, showing that it is grammatical another. The use of dubious data from the web is the major concern expressed by Brian Joseph in section 1. He worries that web data may be used for linguistic analysis that might rather fall under the label 'attested but ungrammatical'. The very fact that we simply do not know where our data comes from in the case of web data (in contrast to electronic corpora) certainly constitutes the major obstacle for using such data, besides the ever shifting nature of the data pool, which makes any analysis basically non-replicable. According to Meyer et al. (2003: 243, citing Pleasants 2001), for example, the majority of English web pages (52.5%) originate from non-native speakers of English. And a search conducted on November 19th, 4 o'clock, will reveal results that are different from a search conducted, say, two hours later.

Leaving such general problems aside for a moment, the question remains how to judge whether something is truly ungrammatical. There are certainly very clear cases of typographical errors that can and must be discarded in an analysis; moreover, non-native speaker errors shouldn't enter the analysis of a language, but in many cases the judgment seems to be in the eye of the beholder: what is ungrammatical for one person (or linguist, for that matter) may be perfectly grammatical for others (it may be a regional / dialectal feature, or representing an instance of a recent change). Careful analysis is needed to tease apart true 'garbage' from unusual but nonetheless grammatical features. That is, in such cases we must collect further evidence instead of simply discarding such data from the outset as 'attested but ungrammatical' (see also Manning 2003: 292-294 for such an argument and an illustrative example).

2.2   A (brief) overview of web-based linguistic research

In the following I will give some examples (which by no means are meant to represent an exhaustive list) to illustrate the range of linguistic research conducted on the basis of the web, exemplifying both the use of qualitative and quantitative evidence from the web.

For one, web data is nowadays increasingly used to challenge received wisdom in linguistic theory in quite an enlightening way. For example, Baayen (2003) demonstrates that the prototype example of a completely unproductive suffix in English, namely the *-th* suffix as in *warmth*, is not as unproductive as usually assumed and that new coinages such as *coolth* (as in 2) or *greenth* can be found on the web.

(1)   Coolth, once a nonce word made on analogy with warmth, is now tiresomely jocular: The coolth of the water in the early morning is too much for me [...] (http://www.bartleby.com/68/5/1505.htm)

In a similar vein, Bresnan and Nikitina (2003) show that some constructions that have previously been regarded as clearly ungrammatical with dative NP syntax, such as verbs of manner of speaking, do occur – and are grammatical, as in (2):[4]

(2)   Shooting the Urasian a surprised look, she muttered him a hurried apology as well before skirting down the hall.
       (http://www.geocities.com/cassiopeia.sc/fanfiction/findthemselves.html)

While the examples mentioned so far illustrate the use of qualitative evidence drawn from the web, the web has also come to be used for quantitative arguments. Mazaud (2004), for example, uses Google frequencies as an indication for the degree of lexicalisation of collocations, (in her case, phrasal premodifiers such as *cash-and-scrip* or *question and answer*,) which are not listed in dictionaries but which are most certainly not nonce formations. In this case, higher Google frequencies are supposed to correlate with a higher degree of lexicalisation.

In addition, web data has also been shown to be particularly well suited to track very recent and on-going change, as demonstrated in a case study of *let's* by de Clerck (2003). De Clerck looked for particle-like uses of *let's* (as in *let's us*, *let's don't*) which are evidence for the increased grammaticalization of *let's*. While he could only find a handful of scattered examples in the current electronic corpora of English, he was able to retrieve quite a few interesting examples searching the web, and the figures were even high enough to identify notable differences between American and British English.[5]

All these examples illustrate the use of the web as a corpus. However, it should be kept in mind that the web cannot be used as a data pool as a whole, but that specific tools are needed to extract (portions of) data from the web, and different tools will reveal different results. The most accessible tools for data extraction from the web are certainly the general search engines such as Google or AltaVista, though these are not specifically made to fit the purpose of linguistic research. A software that is tailored for linguistic research is WebCorp (http://www.webcorp.org.uk; see also Renouf 2003 and Renouf et al., this volume). WebCorp operates on search engines such as Google, though it accesses only small potions of the web. Its great advantage in contrast to a search engine such as Google is that it organizes its output in the form of concordances, which makes it far easier to browse manually through the data. But even WebCorp cannot search for abstract constructions. That is, as with all syntactically unannotated corpora, it can only search for specific collocations but not for, say, all indirect objects of ditransitive verbs. Recently, however, a tool has been developed that can do searches involving syntactic structure, i.e. the Linguist's Search Engine (see Elkiss and Resnik 2004 for further details).

Note, finally, that the web has also come to be used for experimental studies. For example, the WebExp software (http://www.webexp.info/) makes it possible to elicit grammaticality judgments (e.g. by the magnitude estimation task) and production data as e.g. in sentence completion experiments (see e.g. Keller 2000). The basic difference to 'conventional' experiments is that in this case subjects perform their task on the web instead of a laboratory. WebExp is plat-form independent (Java-based), which makes it particularly apt for running experiments via the Web. So far, its technical possibilities are still limited in contrast to laboratory experiments, but the developers of WebExp have recently released a new modified version (WebExp2) and are currently working on including auditory stimuli and the possibility to measure reaction times on-line.

3.　Case study: Variation between *s*-genitives and noun+noun constructions

This case study is part of a larger research project on the gradience between *s*-genitives and noun+noun (N+N) constructions. Therefore, my starting point was a specific linguistic phenomenon and a specific research question for which I wanted to deduce evidence, rather than starting from the tool(s) available and see what kind of phenomena can be tested with it, and how. It will be shown that for the present purpose, the web provides an excellent alternative to test the hypotheses at hand, because 'traditional' electronic corpora do not provide a sufficiently high number of tokens for quantification. At the same time, this case study will illustrate how we can study 'constructions' on the web – a linguistic unit which is notoriously difficult to study in corpora, unlike, for example, lexicographic phenomena. And finally, it will demonstrate how we can deduce (reliable) quantitative data from the web.[6]

3.1 The phenomenon: structural and functional preliminaries

The variation between *s*-genitives (*the girl's eyes*) and *of*-genitives (*the eyes of the girl*) is a well-known case of grammatical variation in the literature (see e.g. Altenberg 1982; Quirk et al. 1985; Jucker 1993; Leech et al. 1994; Anschutz 1997; Biber et al. 1999; Rosenbach 2002). Note, however, that *s*-genitives can also vary with N+N constructions, as in *driver's licence* vs. *driver licence*, and the present paper will address the question of what governs the variation between these two constructions by using data drawn from the web.

As in any study of grammatical variation it is crucial to determine the variants before we start with the empirical analysis. That is, what are the constructions that can truly vary? Note that not just any *s*-genitive can be expressed by an N+N construction, and vice versa. Also note that we have to distinguish two types of *s*-genitives, which superficially look alike, but which at a closer look have different semantic properties, as illustrated in table 1.[7]

Table 1: Specifying vs. classifying s-genitives

specifying *s*-genitives (*the girl's eyes*)	classifying *s*-genitives (*driver's licence*)

possessor:
   • [+ referential]
   • referential anchor: 'whose X?'
   • function: determination
	possessor (modifier):
	   • [- referential]
	   • non-referential anchor: 'what type of X?'
	   • function: classification

In specifying *s*-genitives (*the girl's eyes*) the possessor is referential, referring to a specific person, and its function is to referentially anchor the referent of the NP, i.e. it has determiner function. In contrast, the possessor – or more precisely the modifier – in classifying *s*-genitives (*driver's licence*) is not referential and does not specify whose license it is but rather what type of licence. Its function therefore is nominal classification. In N+N constructions such as *cat food* the modifier (*cat*) has essentially the same classifying function as the modifier in classifying *s*-genitives, i.e. it restricts the denotational class of the head noun: The modifier *cat* specifies what type of food it is and not whose food.

It is important to note that specifying *s*-genitives vary with *of*-genitives (*the girl's eyes* ~ *the eyes of the girl*) but usually not with N+N constructions (**the girl eyes*).[8] It is only classifying *s*-genitives that can vary with N+N constructions (*driver's licence* ~ *driver licence*). Note that classifying *s*-genitives and N+N constructions are not only semantically equivalent but also share the same structural properties, as illustrated in table 2.

Table 2:   Word order in English NPs

determination	modification	classification	head
the girl's	*green*		*eyes*
a	*new*	*driver's*	*licence*
a	*new*	*driver*	*licence*
reference-restriction	qualification	denotation-restriction	denotation

While the possessor in specifying *s*-genitives (*the girl's green eyes*) is always in the leftmost position in the NP, the modifier in classifying *s*-genitives (*driver's licence*) and N+N constructions (*driver licence*) is adjacent to the head. That is, *driver's licence* and *driver licence* are semantically and structurally equivalent, and they only differ as to whether they contain a possessive *'s* or not.

Now, the crucial question is: what governs the absence or presence of possessive *'s* in such cases? The grammars of English do recognize this type of variation (if mostly in passing) but conclude that it is essentially variation in spelling (cf. e.g. Quirk et al. 1985:328, note a; Biber et al. 1999: 295). In contrast, I will show that the choice between *s*-genitives and N+N constructions is not a matter of (essentially random) orthographical variation but subject to deeper constraints. My analysis will focus on one factor, namely the animacy of the modifier. Animacy is known to be one of the major determinants of English genitive variation in that animate possessors tend to prefer the *s*-genitive (*John's book*) while inanimate possessors are preferably realized by the *of*-genitive (*the roof of the house*). In the following I will investigate whether animate modifiers also have a preference for occurring in the *s*-genitive, while inanimate modifiers prefer the construction without the *'s*. That animacy is a decisive factor here has also been argued by Taylor (1996: 303-304), though, to the best of my knowledge, this has never been tested empirically. In addition, I will test whether there are any differences as to the impact of animacy between British and American English. As shown in previous research, the *s*-genitive is on the increase in Present-day English with inanimate possessors (Jahr Sorheim 1980; Raab-Fischer 1995; 1997, 1998; Rosenbach 2002, 2003), and in this development American English is more advanced than British English (cf. Hundt 1997, 1998; Rosenbach 2002, 2003). While these studies focussed on the frequency of the *s*-genitive vis-á-vis the *of*-genitive, the present study looks at this question from the angle of the variation of *s*-genitives and N+N constructions. I assume that animacy affects the choice of the *s*-genitive vis-á-vis the N+N construction in the same way, as it affects the choice of the *s*-genitive as compared to the *of*-genitive.

Now, the crucial question is: how can we test these hypotheses at all in corpora, and why should the web be a better corpus than traditional electronic corpora in this case ?

3.2 Methodology

In the ideal case we would have to select all *s*-genitives and all N+N constructions which are mutually interchangeable. In the present case, however, a crucial problem for any corpus-based investigation is that the range of contexts where these two constructions truly vary is very small. The most common (and in fact prototypical) *s*-genitives are specifying *s*-genitives (*John's book*), but, as mentioned before, these do not vary with N+N constructions. On the other hand, N+N constructions are an extremely productive feature of Present-day English, but not all of them can be realized by a corresponding *s*-genitive. For example, as argued by Taylor (1996: 303), the *s*-genitive is not possible with patient modifiers (*child molester*, but not **child's molester*) or appositional modifiers (*a woman doctor* is not equivalent to *a woman's doctor*). Therefore, even if we were able to extract all *s*-genitives and all N+N constructions from a corpus (which is only possible in a syntactically annotated corpus),[9] we would run into considerable practical problems, because we would then have to manually go through the mass of raw data and then sort out all such categorical contexts before we get to the small number of those constructions that can be legitimately compared in a quantitative study, which is quite a task. For this reason, I decided to focus the analysis on some preselected collocations where variation is possible in principle. I selected 10 collocations with a human modifier and 10 collocations with an inanimate modifier, as shown in table 3.

Focussing on certain collocations as representatives of a syntactic construction is a common procedure in corpus linguistics in cases where we cannot search for all relevant constructions in a corpus.[10] Ideally, we would have to test these collocations in 'traditional' corpora first before exploring them on the web, given the rather shaky nature of web data as discussed in section 2 above. This is the procedure followed by Rohdenburg and Mair in their contributions to this volume (see also e.g. Keller and Lapata 2003).[11] In the present case, however, this procedure was not possible, because electronic corpora just do not contain enough data to yield a sufficient number of tokens for the items tested in the first place. Searches on the ICE-GB, the BNC sampler, the FLOB and the FROWN corpus (each of which contains about 1 million words), gave the following figures (cf. table 5). For reasons of space, table 4 only shows the results for animate modifiers.

As is apparent from table 4, for most collocations there are no occurrences at all, and for those that produce any results (like *passenger's seat* vs. *passenger seat*), the figures are extremely low.

Table 3:　Collocations with a human and with an inanimate modifier

animate (human) modifiers	inanimate modifiers
<ul><li>*lawyer's fees* vs. *lawyer fees*</li><li>*butcher's knife* vs. *butcher knife*</li><li>*baby's nappy* vs. *baby nappy*</li><li>*women's magazine* vs. *women magazine*</li><li>*doctor's office* vs. *doctor office*</li><li>*passenger's seat* vs. *passenger seat*</li><li>*mother's milk* vs. *mother milk*</li><li>*driver's licence* vs. *driver licence*</li><li>*master's degree* vs. *master degree*</li><li>*men's suit* vs. *men suit*</li></ul>	<ul><li>*museum's shop* vs. *museum shop*</li><li>*elevator's doors* vs. *elevator doors*</li><li>*car's engine* vs. *car engine*</li><li>*window's panes* vs. *window panes*</li><li>*room's door* vs. *room door*</li><li>*table's drawer* vs. *table drawer*</li><li>*church's tower* vs. *church tower*</li><li>*hotel's lobby* vs. *hotel lobby*</li><li>*bed's headboard* vs. *bed headboard*</li><li>*chair's frame* vs. *chair frame*</li></ul>

Table 4:　Token frequency of collocations (with animate modifiers) in some electronic corpora of English

collocation	ICE-GB	BNC (sampler)	FROWN	FLOB
lawyer's fees	-	-	-	-
lawyer fees	-	-	-	-
butcher's knife	-	-	-	-
butcher knife	-	-	-	-
baby's nappy	-	-	-	-
baby nappy	-	-	-	-
women's magazine	-	-	-	-
women magazine	-	-	-	-
doctor's office	-	-	1	-
doctor office	-	-	-	-
passenger's seat	-	-	1	1
passenger seat	-	2	3	1

mother's milk	-	-	-	-
mother milk	-	-	-	-
driver's licence	-	-	-	-
driver licence	-	-	-	-
master's degree	-	-	2	-
master degree	-	-	-	-
men's suit	-	-	-	-
men suit	-	-	-	-

So what are the frequencies of these collocations in the web? Table 5 gives the frequencies from a Google search, focussing on two test items only, but the difference to the results obtained from the electronic corpora in table 4 becomes immediately apparent.

Table 5: Frequencies of collocations in the web (based on Google search)

Collocations	Google
lawyer's fees	10,800 (11.7%)
lawyer fees	81,700
doctor's office	228,000 (43.8%)
doctor office	293,000

These items, which were not even represented once in the corpora (cf. table 4, except *doctor's office*, which occurred once in the FROWN corpus), occur extremely often in the web. This clearly shows that Google can retrieve a (more than) sufficiently large number of tokens for the present purpose. However, the question remains how reliable these figures are. If we compare the frequencies obtained from a Google search with the corresponding frequencies from a search on WebCorp (cf. table 6), the differences are striking.

Table 6: Frequencies of collocations in the web – contrasting Google vs. WebCorp

Collocations	Google (12/10/2004)	WebCorp (based on Google, 12/10/2004)
lawyer's fees	10,800 (11.7%)	316 (74.2%)
lawyer fees	81,700	110
doctor's office	228,000 (43.8%)	411 (94.1%)
doctor office	293,000	26

First of all, we can notice that the WebCorp frequencies are overall much lower than the Google frequencies. Although the WebCorp search was conducted on the basis of Google, it only accesses parts of the web, resulting in lower figures. A second – and more crucial – difference between the Google and

WebCorp frequencies is that they reveal dramatically different relative frequencies for the two constructions. Whereas in Google the relative frequency of the *s*-genitive is much smaller than that for the corresponding N+N construction (e.g. 11.7 % for *lawyer's fees* and 43.8% for *doctor's office* vs. 88.3% for *lawyer fees* and 56.2% for *doctor office*), in WebCorp the distribution is precisely the other way round, with *s*-genitives being consistently more frequent than the corresponding N+N construction. To make sense of these differences I had a closer look at the respective outputs. It turned out that Google does not discriminate properly between the forms with and without '*s*. Checking manually through the first output pages of Google, it became apparent that the Google results for the *s*-less variant included variants with '*s*. For example, a search for *lawyer fees* included instances of *lawyer's fees* as in (3):

(3)　Posted on Wed, Mar. 31, 2004. SUPERVISOR OF ELECTIONS OFFICE |CHARGES Oliphant rebuffed on **lawyer's fees**. BY STEVE HARRISON sharrison@herald.com.　(http://www.miami.com/mld/miamiherald/news/local/states/florida/counties/broward_county/8316043.htm)

Note that from the point of view of the 'normal' (i.e. non-linguist) Google user this makes perfect sense: When searching for items such as *lawyer fees* a user wants to get all relevant hits, and these include those for *lawyer's fees*, because they both mean the same. In fact, Google explicitly states that it ignores such orthographical variation – it just is not concerned with the subtle distinctions linguists make in their analyses. This explains then, at least in part, why in Google the relative frequencies of the two variants differ so dramatically from the WebCorp frequencies.[12] WebCorp, in contrast, searches for the *exact* search term and is sensitive to the difference of *lawyer's fees* vs. *lawyer fees*. I checked every single token, and in no case did a search for one construction type include results of the other. I therefore decided to use WebCorp instead of Google for extracting web data in this case study. This had the further (practical) advantage that I could quite comfortably browse through the results. Although the WebCorp outputs were much more accurate than the Google outputs, some further cases remained which had to be eliminated (cf. examples (4) to (6)).

(4)　*baby nappy*: there is always a nurse there willing to help me out with a crying **baby**, **nappy** change or burp [...]
(5)　*mother milk*: [...] and her sisters help their **mother milk** the cows, which [...]
(6)　*lawyer's fees:* You say that this hot shot **lawyer's fees** are 5% of the original total sum which was $60 million.

Examples (4) and (5) are truly illegitimate examples. Example (6) illustrates a case where the *s*-genitive *lawyer's fees* is not a classifying but a specifying *s*-genitive. Note that this expression is inherently ambiguous (or polysemous) with respect to a specifying and classifying reading. It can refer both to a type of fees (classifying reading), as well as to the fees of a specific lawyer (specifying reading). In (6), however, the possessor is clearly specifying, as the (singular) demonstrative *this* and the adjective *hotshot* refer to the (singular) possessor *lawyer* and not to the (plural) head *fees*. In this specifying reading, however, it does not represent a choice context (**this hot shot lawyer fees*), as discussed above. All such clearly specifying uses of *s*-genitives had to be eliminated from the analysis.

I regard the WebCorp outputs as samples of the websites accessed by Google. Regrettably, the compilers of WebCorp leave it unspecified in their user's manual on which basis the data selection is made. However, even if the samples are not based on a random but on a more principled selection, the selection criteria for all tested collocations will be essentially the same. Therefore I take the relative frequencies obtained from WebCorp for the single items to be comparable, although the question of the representativeness of the data remains.

3.3   Analysis and results

Searches for the single collocations (with and without *'s*) were conducted on WebCorp for '.uk' and '.com' domains. Restricting searches to these domains at least to some extent controls for results from non-native speakers of English, and at the same time it allows to compare British and American English.[13] I then went manually through the output concordances and eliminated cases of illegitimate examples and/or non-choice contexts. On the basis of the remaining tokens, the relative frequencies of the *s*-genitive and the N+N constructions were calculated for each single collocation.

Before presenting the results, recall the predictions for the distribution of the two constructions made in section 3.1. If the variation between *s*-genitives and N+N constructions mirrors the variation between the *s*-genitive and *of*-genitives, then

-    the *s*-genitive should be more frequent with animate modifiers, while the N+N constructions should be favoured with inanimate modifiers, and
-    American English should allow more *s*-genitive with inanimate modifiers than British English.

Figure 1a gives the results for the '.com' domains, figure 2a the results for the '.uk' domains, collapsed for all collocations.

The results confirm the predictions as to the impact of animacy. For both American ('.com') and British English ('.uk') the *s*-genitive is more frequent with animate modifiers than the corresponding N+N constructions (z, p = 0.013672 for the '.com' domains; z, p = 0.009766 for the '.uk' domains). Likewise, for inanimate modifiers the N+N construction is preferred to the *s*-genitive. Note, however, that for inanimate modifiers only the results for the '.uk' domains yield statistical significance (z, p = 0.003806), while for the '.com' domains the differences found turn out to be not statistically significant (z, p $= 0.160156$). Some of the collocations showed the reverse effect, however ('.uk' domains: *passenger's seat* for animate modifiers, and *car's engine* for inanimate modifiers; '.com' domains: *butcher's knife* for animate modifiers, and *car's engine*, *museum's shop*, and *bed's headboard* for the inanimate modifiers). Since each single collocation entered the statistical analysis (Wilcoxon signed rank test), the analysis of the inanimate modifiers in the '.com' domains did not turn out to be significant.

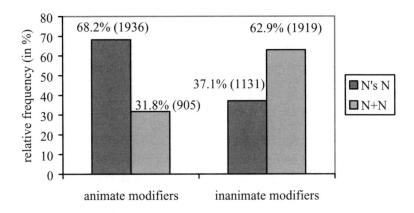

Figure 1a: Animacy of modifier in '.com' domains

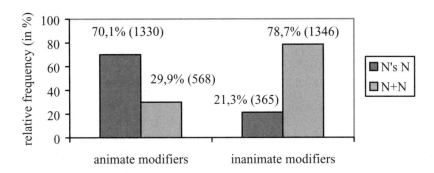

Figure 1b: Animacy of modifier in '.uk' domains

Figure 2 directly compares the results for the '.uk' and '.com' domains:

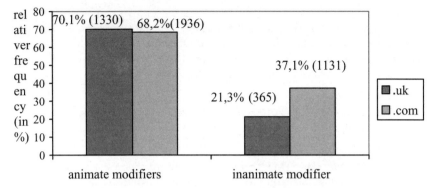

Figure 2:   American ('.com') vs. British ('.uk') websites: relative frequency of the *s*-genitive according to the animacy of the modifier

While the two varieties virtually do not differ in the relative frequency of the *s*-genitive with respect to animate modifiers (*z*, p = 0.695313), there is a striking difference with inanimate modifiers. The US ('.com') domains show a significantly higher proportion of *s*-genitives with inanimate modifiers than the UK ('.uk') domains (*z*, p = 0.001953).[14]

The results therefore indicate that animacy is a decisive factor in the variation between *s*-genitives and N+N constructions, and that animacy affects the choice of *s*-genitives vs. N+N constructions in a very similar way to the one in which it affects the choice between *s*-genitives and *of*-genitives. In both cases, the *s*-genitive is preferred with animate modifiers / possessors, and in both cases, the *s*-genitive is more commonly used in American than in British English.

Note, however, that in addition to the two variants analysed so far, there are also two other variants. Apart from the singular variants as in *lawyer's fees* and *lawyer fees* we can also find equivalent forms in the plural, i.e. *lawyers' fees* and *lawyers fees*, with no apparent difference in meaning.[15] What does the distribution look like if we consider all four variants? When attempting to perform this analysis, however, I came across a practical problem not uncommon with WebCorp. For some reason it was not possible to retrieve the corresponding data for all collocations.[16] Figure 3 therefore only shows the distribution of all four variants for those collocations where results for each single variant could be retrieved. Since the number of matching collocations between the '.uk' and the '.com' domains was too low for any meaningful statistical comparison, the analysis was restricted to the '.com' domains, resulting in 8 items tested for animate modifiers and 9 items tested for inanimate modifiers.[17] The results, collapsed for all collocations, are shown in figure 3.

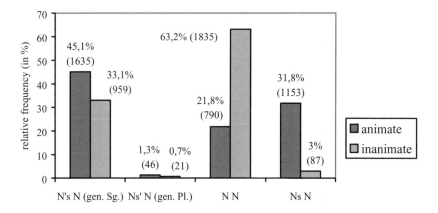

Figure 3:   Relative frequency of the 4 variants (singular and plural variants of the *s*-genitive and N+N constructions) according to animacy of the modifier for '.com' domains.

As is apparent from figure 3, for the singular variants *s*-genitives are still more frequent with animate modifiers (e.g. *driver's licence*) than with inanimate modifiers (e.g. *hotel's lobby*), (*z*, p = 0.117188). Likewise, N+N constructions are more frequent with inanimate modifiers (e.g. *hotel lobby*) than with animate ones (e.g. *driver licence*) (*z*, p = 0.097656). Note, however, that both are only strong tendencies and neither result is statistically significant. As far as the plural variants are concerned it can be observed that genitive plural constructions (as in *drivers' licence*) are in general very infrequent with both animate modifiers (1.3%) and inanimate modifiers (0.7%) and can be largely ignored here. N+N constructions with a plural modifier, however, are amazingly frequent, especially with animate modifiers (*drivers licence, mens suit*). It is, however, not clear what the status of the *-s* is in such constructions.

Plural adnominals as such are not uncommon in English (*arms dealer, airways clearance, drugs problem*), cf. e.g. Johansson (1980) or Biber et al. (1999: §8.3.2). But are these really genuine plurals in our cases here? Just note the occurrence of *womens magazine* and *mens suit* where the *-s* definitively cannot be a plural, since the modifiers are already marked for plural (in irregular forms). Moreover, the very fact that these constructions do occur far more often with animate modifiers (31.8%) than with inanimate modifiers (3%) is striking. With respect to animacy, therefore, plural N+N constructions pattern like *s*-genitives and not singular N+N constructions. This suggests that these plural N+N constructions might be *s*-genitives, with writers simply omitting the apostrophe. Such omissions are not uncommon on the web. Even for specifying *s*-genitive, where the apostrophe must be present, such omissions can be found. For an omission of the apostrophe in the specifying *s*-genitive *the man's car*, for example, altogether 121 hits were found in Google for the '.com' domains, 17 for the '.uk' domains (see (7) for an illustrative example).

(7) The crow flies off Jared's shoulder and lands on the hood of **the mans car**, pecking at the paint job. "Murderer." A gun flashes in the car's head-lights.
www.abahb.crowfans.com/Misc/fiction/tempusfugitus.html

However, I assume that other, linguistic, reasons are responsible for the high frequency of plural N+N constructions, rather than mere sloppiness. Since in spoken language the genitive singular (*lawyer's fees*), genitive plural (*lawyers' fees*) and the plural attributive form (*lawyers fees*) are all homophonous, speakers may be mixing up the plural and the genitive forms in these cases. It is only in written language that a distinction exists, and this distinction itself is so subtle as to only consist of the (presence and location of the) apostrophe. In addition, it does not make too much of a difference semantically whether to use the -*s* as a plural or a possessive marking a generic possessor. The concepts of plurality and genericity are closely connected. Note, for example, that the expression *a driver's licence* translates into 'a licence for drivers' (and not 'a driver'). Given these formal and functional overlaps, it is reasonable to assume that speakers are mixing up these constructions, and the amazingly frequent cases of plural N+N constructions simply reflect speakers' uncertainty about the status of this form, and the results are therefore evidence for the gradient nature of *s*-genitives and N+N constructions.

3.4 Summary

The present case study has shown that the variation between *s*-genitives (*lawyer's fees*) and corresponding N+N constructions (*lawyer fees*) is not simply an instance of random, orthographical variation but subject to deeper constraints in that the animacy of the modifier determines the choice of construction. While animate modifiers favour the *s*-genitive, inanimate modifiers occur more often with a N+N construction. Furthermore, the results indicate that American English uses more *s*-genitives with inanimate modifiers than British English. In this respect, the results for this type of variation mirror the results for English genitive variation, where animate possessors also prefer the *s*-genitive to the *of*-genitive (*John's book*, rather than *the book of John*). In this type of variation it has also been shown that the *s*-genitive is nowadays used more frequently with inanimate possessors and that in this development American English is more advanced than British English (Hundt 1997, 1998; Rosenbach 2002, 2003). At a closer look it turned out that apart from the singular variants there are also plural variants of the constructions, all of which are essentially equivalent. An interesting theoretical question emerging from this is that of the status of the -*s* in plural N+N construc-tions (*drivers licence*, *womens magazine*) is. The quantitative results show that these constructions pattern like *s*-genitives with respect to animacy. This indicates that they are genitives rather than N+N constructions, though more detailed investigations are in order here. Another solution, for example, is to regard them as linking elements, as for example (tentatively) suggested by Taylor (1996: 307).

4.   Conclusion

In general, the larger idea behind this case study is the hypothesis that there is gradience between *s*-genitives and noun+noun constructions (cf. also Taylor 1996:§11; Rosenbach 2005, forthcoming), though such theoretical issues have not been foregrounded in the present paper. Rather, this case study on grammatical variation was meant to illustrate some of the possibilities as well as limitations when using the web to study constructions. A phenomenon was presented which could otherwise barely be studied adequately in corpora of English since these are not sufficiently large and for which the web therefore provides an excellent alternative data resource. For this reason the web data cannot be backed up by corresponding data from traditional electronic corpora. Note, however, that the studies by Rohdenburg (this volume) and Mair (this volume, 2006) indicate that web frequencies correlate fairly well with frequencies from electronic corpora. More specifically, Keller and Lapata (2003) have shown that the web frequencies for N+N constructions (among other constructions) are highly correlated with both BNC frequencies as well as with frequencies obtained from an experimental study (plausibility judgments) conducted on the items tested. All this indicates that despite all problems (e.g. lack of replicability, problem of representativeness, unclear data sources) the web can be used for obtaining quantitative data.

I have further contrasted the use of Google and the use of WebCorp to retrieve the data from the web. Here an interesting result is that relying on Google frequencies in the present case would considerably skew the results, since it is not sensitive to the absence and presence of the *'s* in the constructions in question. In this sense then, the present case study demonstrates that using Google frequencies can be very misleading, pace Meyer et al.'s conclusion that "[...] search engines provide at least a rough guide to the relative frequency of a given linguistic construction" (2003: 247). This is not to say, however, that the present case study argues against the use of Google in general. Rather, it is important to note that it depends on each individual case whether it is necessary at all to draw data from the web, and if so, which way of data retrieval is the best. Different phenomena and research questions will require different tools and methods. Moreover, the present case study illustrates the importance of looking at each single token to eliminate illegitimate examples. Also in this respect, WebCorp is to be preferred to Google: it produces a far smaller (and hence more manageable) output, and organizes it in the form of concordances that can much more easily be browsed through (and printed) than the single Google pages / hits. Alternatively, when using Google one might go individually through the first results, count the illegitimate examples, and from these generalize to the overall ratio of 'bad' examples, as suggested by Mair (2004). It should be stressed once again that the decision on the precise procedure crucially depends on the phenomenon at hand. In the present case I found it necessary to have a look at every single token to clearly identify legitimate variants; in other cases it may be sufficient to approximate the frequencies from Google samples.

Despite the advantages of WebCorp as discussed above, we should, however, also bear in mind that WebCorp is not without problems, either. Apart from practical problems (it is relatively slow and often breaks down for no apparent reason), it remains unclear what the basis for the data selection from the web is.

In general, one way to improve the reliability of frequency results obtained from the web may be to retrieve the same data set with the same search tool at various time intervals, as e.g. suggested by Christian Mair at the Heidelberg symposium. In this case we would compare different (synchronic) 'snapshots' of the web, similarly to comparing two corpora from different periods (as e.g. the FLOB from the 1990s and the LOB corpus from the 1960s). If repeated searches at different point in times lead to essentially the same results, this will strengthen their reliability (by showing that they are not simply an artefact of a particular search at a given point in time).[18] That is, we can show that it does not matter for our results whether we conduct a search on Monday or Friday, for example. What this procedure, however, does not – and cannot – test is whether the results obtained depict 'real' phenomena, or whether they are an artefact of the specific websites accessed. As pointed out by Anke Lüdeling (p.c.), ideally one would have to extract data from different samples of web pages that are truly independent (i.e. the data in one sample must not show up in the data from another sample) to show that the results obtained from one search is really representative for web results in general.[19] Note, that both procedures test different questions and require different statistical tools (for repeated measures, and for comparisons of independent groups, respectively). It is highly desirable that such analyses will be conducted in future research to further demonstrate (or not) the reliability and representativness of web data.[20]

Notes

1   I am grateful to the participants at the Heidelberg symposium on 'Corpus Linguistics – Perspectives for the Future" for stimulating feedback, and especially to Anke Lüdeling for discussion on the web as a corpus. A special thanks goes to Reinhart Willers (Rechenzentrum, University of Düsseldorf) for his generous help with the statistical analysis and to the editors for their meticulous editing of the present article.

2   For useful overviews on the web as corpus, see e.g. Meyer et al. (2003), Kilgariff and Grefenstette (2003), or Lüdeling et al. (this volume).

3   Krug (2004) emphasizes the importance of and need for qualitative evidence in the light of the increasing use of quantitative data in (historical) corpus linguistics. Note, however, that neither quantitative nor qualitative is a privileged type of evidence per se. Rather, it depends on the specific research question at hand which type of evidence is used and evoked by a researcher. For example, hypotheses building on the frequency on constructions ('X is more frequent than Y.') certainly demand quantitative evidence, while other hypotheses may be better explored qualitatively. For further explication of these two types of evidence, see e.g. Penke and Rosenbach (2004).

4   Bresnan and Nikitina's (2003) work is part of a recent development in theoretical (and especially formal) linguistics to ground theoretical syntax on a more solid empirical base, challenging merely introspective grammaticality judgements and increasingly using corpora to test hypotheses. See also Mukherjee (2004: 116) for observing that "corpora have penetrated into linguistic theories and fields of application in which corpus data had been largely ignored until recently."

5   For further examples that demonstrate the usefulness of the web for the investigation of recent developments in language, see also the contributions of Hoffmann, Mair, Mondorf, and Rohdenburg in this volume, as well as Krug (2004).

6   Note from the outset that the focus of this paper will be on methodological issues, relating to the general question of how linguists may use the web as a corpus, rather than on the deeper theoretical issues underlying the case study itself.

7   For the use of the terms, see Biber et al. (1999: 294-295).

8   In earlier English, however, such *s*-less genitives were not uncommon (see e.g. Rosenbach 2002: 205-208, and references given therein).

9   Note that even in syntactically annotated corpora the problem of how N+N constructions are coded remains. If they are coded as compounds (i.e. words), they are not retrievable at all. Given that it is notoriously difficult to decide whether N+N constructions are words or phrases (see e.g. Bauer 1998, or Huddleston and Pullum 2002: 448-451; Giegerich 2004), any syntactic query would necessarily have to rely on the – often – quite arbitrary decision of the annotators.

10   Note that in a way this procedure is also comparable to an experimental setting, where the researcher focuses on a set of test items to test the given hypothesis. While, however, in an experiment the dependent variable is

elicited, in the corpus approach it stems from non-elicited, spontaneous data.

11   In the same vein Mair made a plea for "a concerted strategy for corpuslinguists which rests on the parallel development of 'small and tidy' and 'big and messy' corpora" (2006: 365).

12   As pointed out by Douglas Biber at the Heidelberg symposium, it is striking that even if subtracting the frequencies for the *s*-genitives in the Google searches from the results for the N+N constructions, N+N constructions still by far outnumber *s*-genitives, so the problem remains why the Google and WebCorp results differ so greatly in the distribution of the two variants. I suspect that there are further ways in which Google's ignorance towards orthographical variation is reflected in the data, but I am not in a position to specify these. In the present case I preferred to rely on the WebCorp frequencies, because I was able to manually check through every single example here; a procedure which certainly is not an option for the tens and hundreds of thousands results obtained from the Google searches. An alternative, as for example suggested by Mair (2004), would be to manually check through the first pages of the Google output and then generalize from the number of illegitimate examples in this sample to the number of illegitimate example in the whole output.

13   Note, however, that presumably the .com domains do not reflect proper American usage as accurately as the .uk domains reflect British usage, since they may subsume the websites of many (non-American) international companies and/or institutions. The results should be seen and interpreted with this proviso.

14   Note that it is possible that with inanimate modifiers there is no true equivalence between the *s*-genitive and a corresponding N+N construction. I suspect that the *s*-genitive here entails a specific possessor/modifier, while in the N+N construction the modifier is unspecific. That is, in 'the car's engine' speakers may tend to conceptualize a specific car, while in 'the car engine' the focus is on the type properties of 'car'. This would correspond to Taylor's (1996) claim that constructions with '*s* entail a more referential possessor than constructions without the '*s*. If so, then the *s*-genitive variant in these cases would be a specifying *s*-genitive, which, as argued above, is strictly speaking not a proper variant to a N+N construction. As long as there is no clear syntactic (or contextual) evidence for the clearly specifying status of s-genitives with inanimate modifiers, however, those were included in the analysis. As such, the fact that with inanimate modifiers/possessors the *s*-genitive tends to be specifying, is highly interesting theoretically. Since this paper focuses on methodologi-

cal questions, however, such theoretical issues must be left unaddressed here. This issue is further addressed in Rosenbach (2005).

15   Johansson (1980) shows that in some cases a plural attributive may differ in meaning from a modifier in common case, as e.g. *school adviser* vs. *schools adviser*, where subjects tended to interpret the latter as 'an adviser to a range of schools / for more than one' while the common case form received a singular interpretation. That is, in this case the plural form indicated some plural concept.

16   This appears to be a general problem of WebCorp. During the summer of 2004 the compilers made it clear that the software was under construction and that therefore retrieval may be impeded. However, only a few days after WebCorp was fully launched again in late September 2004, essentially the same retrieval problems occurred. Either searches were not completed, or not performed at all. Considering that WebCorp searches as such do take considerably more time than a corresponding Google search, and considering that for an analysis of variation as in the present case always *all* the variants of a collocation must be tested at a time, this poses a serious practical problem in the application of WebCorp, despite all its other advantages. It also turned out that for the plural variants, WebCorp did not consider the variation between the spelling with apostrophe and without. That is, the results for the search term *drivers licence* included the results for *drivers' licence*. This had to be sorted out manually.

17   The collocations excluded were: *lawyer('s) fees – lawyers(') fees* and *mother('s) milk – mothers(') milk* for animate modifiers, and *bed('s) headboard – beds(') headboard* for inanimate modifiers.

18   True is that in the case of the web the websites accessed at different times would not be identical but vary. However, from a statistical point of view, in the case of repeated measures there always will be some differences. Even when testing the very same subjects at time x and time y, strictly speaking, those subjects will not be 'the same' in both measurements (at the later measurement they will be older, have had different experiences, etc.). In those cases, however, statisticians would regard these differences as 'noise' that can be tolerated. The differences found in such repeated measurements of web data would likewise fall under 'noise' here (Reinhart Willers, p.c.). Although this 'noise' might be considerable in this procedure (repeated measurements of web data), it is worthwhile tolerating it for the benefit of testing the reliability of the results.

19   Representativeness of the data, however, is always a problem, even in a carefully assembled corpus. As Kilgariff and Grefenstette (2003: 340) put it: "The Web is not representative of anything else. But neither are other

corpora, in any well-understood sense." So, maybe rather than representativeness in the strict sense it is our ignorance about our data base which is at stake here.

20 For a first step towards this goal see e.g. Mair (2006) who has been conducting several searches on some selected collocations since December 2002. See specifically Mair (2006: 367, figure 4) for an illustrative "regiochronological profile of a collocation in a major portion of the English-language Web."

21 This is the URL as given in Meyer et al. (2003), where this source was quoted. When trying to access this website on 24/11/2004, however, the site could not be found.

References

Altenberg, B. (1982), *The Genitive v. the Of-Construction. A Study of Syntactic Variation in 17th Century English*. Malmö: CWK Gleerup.

Anschutz, A. (1997), 'How to choose a possessive noun phrase construction in four easy steps', *Studies in Language*, 21 (1): 1-35.

Baayen, R.H. (2003), 'Probabilistic approaches to morphology', in: R. Bod, J. Hay and S. Jannedy (eds.) *Probabilistic Linguistics*. Cambridge, Mass: MIT Press. 229-287.

Bauer, L. (1998), 'When is a sequence of two nouns a compound in English?' *English Language and Linguistics,* 2 (1): 87-119.

Biber, D., S. Johansson, G. Leech, S. Conrad and E. Finegan (1999), *Longman Grammar of Spoken and Written English*. London and New York: Longman.

Bresnan, J. and T. Nikitina (2003), *On the gradience of the dative alternation*. Ms., Stanford University. (http://www-lfg.stanford.edu/bresnan/).

De Clerck, B. (2003), 'The syntactic and pragmatic analysis of *let's* in present-day British and American English', Paper given at the symposium *Syntactic functions – focus on the periphery*, Helsinki, November 13-15, 2003.

Elkiss, A. and P. Resnik (2004), *The Linguist's Search Engine User's Guide*. Institute for Advanced Computer Studies, University of Maryland, College Park, MA. (http://lse.umiacs.umd.edu:8080/lseuser/).

Giegerich, H. (2004), 'Compound or phrase? English noun-plus-noun constructions and the stress criterion', *English Language and Linguistics*, 8 (1): 1-24.

Hoffmann, S. (this volume), 'From webpage to mega-corpus: the CNN transcripts'.

Huddleston, R. and G. Pullum (2002), *The Cambridge Grammar of the English Language*. Cambridge: Cambridge University Press.

Hundt, M. (1997), 'Has BrE English been catching up with AmE over the past thirty years?', in: M. Ljung (ed.) *Corpus-based Studies in English: Papers from the 17th International Conference on English Language Research on Computerized Corpora (ICAME 17)*, Stockholm, May 15-19, 1996. Amsterdam: Rodopi. 135-151.

Hundt, M. (1998), *New Zealand English Grammar. Fact or Fiction. A Corpus-Based Study in Morphosyntactic Variation*. Amsterdam and Philadelphia: John Benjamins.

Jahr Sorheim, M.-C. (1980), *The S-Genitive in Present-Day English*. Thesis, Department of English, University of Oslo.

Johansson, S. (1980), *Plural Attributive Nouns in Present-Day English*. Malmö: CWK Gleerup.

Joseph, B. (2004). 'The editor's department: on change in Language and change in language', *Language,* 80 (3): 381-383.

Jucker, A. (1993), 'The genitive vs. the of-construction in newspaper language', in: A. Jucker (ed.) *The Noun Phrase in English. Its Structure and Variability*. Heidelberg: Carl Winter. 121-136.

Keller, F. (2000), *Gradience in Grammar: Experimental and Computational Aspects of Degrees of Grammaticality*. PhD Dissertation, University of Edinburgh.

Keller, F. and M. Lapata (2003), 'Using the web to obtain frequencies for unseen bigrams', Special issue on 'The web as corpus', *Computational Linguistics*, 29 (3): 459-484.

Kilgariff, A. and G. Grefenstette (2003), 'Introduction to the special issue on the web as a corpus', Special issue on 'The web as a corpus', *Computational Linguistics*, 29 (3): 333-347.

Krug, M. (2004), 'Historical corpus linguistics and beyond', Paper presented at the International Symposium *Corpus Linguistics – Perspectives for the Future*, University of Heidelberg October 21-23, 2004.

Leech, G., B. Francis and X. Xu (1994), 'The use of computer corpora in the textual demonstrability of gradience in linguistic categories', in: C. Fuchs and B. Victorri (eds.) *Continuity in Linguistic Semantics*. Amsterdam: John Benjamins. 57-76.

Lüdeling, A., M. Baroni and S. Evert (this volume), 'Using web data for linguistic purposes'.

Mair, C. (2004), 'Ongoing change and variation in World Englishes: findings from tagged corpora and web-based monitoring', Paper presented at the International Symposium *Corpus Linguistics – Perspectives for the Future*, October 21-23, 2004, University of Heidelberg.

Mair, C. (2006), 'Tracking ongoing grammatical change and recent diversification in present-day standard English: the complementary role of small and large corpora', in: A. Renouf (ed.). *The Changing Face of Corpus Linguistics: Papers from the 24th International Conference on English Language Research on Computerized Corpora (ICAME 24)*. Amsterdam: Rodopi. 355-376.

Mair, C. (this volume), 'Change and variation in present-day English: integrating the analysis of closed corpora and web-based monitoring'.

Manning, C.D. (2003), 'Probabilistic syntax', in: R. Bod, J. Hay and S. Jannedy (eds.) *Probabilistic Linguistics*. Cambridge, Mass.: MIT Press. 289-341.

Mazaud, C. (2004), *Complex Premodifiers in Present-Day English: A Corpus-Based Study*. PhD dissertation, University of Heidelberg.

Meyer, C.F., R. Grabowski, H.-Y. Han, K. Mantzouranis and S. Moses (2003), 'The World Wide Web as Linguistic Corpus', in: P. Leistyna and C.F. Meyer (eds.) *Corpus Analysis. Language Structure and Language Use*, Amsterdam and New York: Rodopi. 241-254.

Mondorf, B. (this volume), 'Recalcitrant problems of comparative alternation and new insights emerging from internet data'.

Mukherjee, J. (2004), 'The state of the art in corpus linguistics: three book-length perspectives' (review article), *English Language and Linguistics*, 8 (1): 103-119.

Penke, M. and A. Rosenbach (2004), 'What counts as evidence in linguistics? – An introduction', in: M. Penke and A. Rosenbach (eds.) *What Counts as Evidence in Linguistics? – The Case of Innateness*. Special issue of *Studies in Linguistics*, 28 (3): 480-526.

Pleasants, N. (2001), 'Languages of the web', *ClickZ Today*, May 11, 2001. (http://www.clickz.com/int_mkt/global_mkt/article.php/841721).[21]

Quirk, R., S. Greenbaum, G. Leech and J. Svartvik (1985), *A Comprehensive Grammar of the English Language*. London and New York: Longman.

Raab-Fischer, R. (1995), 'Löst der Genitiv die of-Phrase ab? Eine korpusgestützte Studie zum Sprachwandel im heutigen Englisch', *Zeitschrift für Anglistik und Amerikanistik*, 43 (2): 123-132.

Renouf, A. (2003), 'WebCorp: providing a renewable data source for corpus linguists', in: S. Granger and S. Petch-Tyson (eds.) *Extending the Scope of Corpus-Based Research*. New York: Rodopi. 39-58.

Renouf, A., A. Kehoe and J. Banerjee (this volume), 'WebCorp: an integrated system for web text search'.

Rohdenburg, G. (this volume), 'Determinants of grammatical variation in English and the formation / confirmation of linguistic hypotheses by means of internet data'.

Rosenbach, A. (2002), *Genitive Variation in English. Conceptual Factors in Synchronic and Diachronic Studies*. Berlin and New York: Mouton de Gruyter.

Rosenbach, A. (2003), 'Aspects of iconicity and economy in the choice between the s-genitive and the of-genitive in English', in: G. Rohdenburg and B. Mondorf (eds.) *Determinants of Grammatical Variation in English*. Berlin and New York: Mouton de Gruyter. 379-411.

Rosenbach, A. (2005), *How Constructional Overlap Gives Rise to Variation (and Vice Versa): Noun+Noun Constructions and S-Genitive Constructions in English*. Ms., University of Düsseldorf.

Rosenbach, A. (forthcoming), 'Descriptive genitives in English: a case study on constructional gradience', *English Language and Linguistics*, 10 (1).

Taylor, J. (1996), *Possessives in English*. Oxford: Clarendon.

Determinants of grammatical variation in English and the formation / confirmation of linguistic hypotheses by means of internet data[1]

Günter Rohdenburg

University of Paderborn

Abstract

My paper discusses in turn some of the effects produced in English by four kinds of (universal and) functionally motivated tendencies:

(a)   the complexity principle which states that in the case of more or less explicit constructional options the more explicit one(s) tend to be preferred in cognitively more complex environments

(b)   a hierarchy of clause embeddings for extraction contexts which stipulates, for instance, that unmarked infinitives are more difficult to extract out of than marked infinitives

(c)   the horror aequi *principle which involves the widespread (and presumably universal) tendency to avoid the use of formally (near-)identical and (near-)adjacent grammatical elements or structures*

(d)   the tendency (motivated by the quantity principle) for the variants scarved *and* leaved *to be more strongly attracted to plural contexts than their rivals* scarfed *and* leafed.

The present study involves two kinds of corpus-linguistic resources, the internet data supplied by Google, and the large corpus collection available at Paderborn. The Google data are used mainly for the heuristic purposes of constructing and testing relevant hypotheses. Considering a wide variety of grammatical variation phenomena it is seen that the results of lexically and grammatically much more specific Google analyses are generally paralleled by the findings of contextually more open and much more laborious searches in controlled newspaper corpora.

1.   Introduction: illustrating the methodology

My paper highlights the interaction between two kinds of corpus-linguistic resources, the internet data supplied by Google, and the large corpus collection available at Paderborn. The Google data are used mainly to provide a quick check on theories, assumptions and hunches suggested by the literature or simply by previous experience. It is on the basis of promising results in such pilot studies that it is decided to carry out a more general, much more laborious and time-consuming analysis in a sufficiently large collection of (mainly) newspaper corpora.

The grammatical variation phenomena to be discussed include the following:

the variable use of selected prepositions
the rivalry between infinitival and gerundial complements
the rivalry between marked and unmarked infinitives
the variable use of adverbially marked manner adverbs
the root allomorphy of derived adjectives like *leafed* / *leaved* or *scarfed* / *scarved*

The distributional patterns observed are accounted for in terms of four kinds of (presumably universal and) functionally oriented tendencies, the complexity principle, an extraction hierarchy in embedded clauses, the *horror aequi* principle, and the iconically motivated quantity principle. I shall start, however, by using a specifically English constraint to introduce the methodology pursued in this paper.

Consider the examples in (1a-b), which concern *many* and *much* as intensifiers of the quantifier *fewer*.

(1)   a. Nowadays our newspapers carry many / much fewer ads.
        b. They had many / much fewer (of these features).

The rivalry between the two is the result of a long drawn out replacement process leading from the exclusive use of *much* in earlier centuries to the predominant use of *many* in formal written English today.[2] This prompts the following question: Are there any environments delaying or speeding up the ongoing change? Informal observations had suggested to me that *much fewer* occurred more freely in cases like (1b), where – unlike the determinative use in (1a) – there is no nominal head following *fewer*. The hunch was confirmed within minutes by the *Google* search summarized in table 1.

Table 1:   The use of *many* and *much* as intensifiers of *fewer* in the internet data provided by Google (date: September 17, 2004)

		I *many*	II *much*	III total	IV percentage of *many*
1	all examples	68,300	40,700	109,000	62.7%
2	*fewer in*	252	2,140	2,392	10.5%
3	*fewer of*	683	1,430	2,113	32.3%
4	*fewer at*	43	76	119	36.1%

Table 1 gives the percentages of *many fewer* for two contextual categories. Rows 2-4 represent the use without a nominal head (as in (1b)), and row 1 refers to all examples, a category which predominantly contains examples including a nominal head. Notice that the type without a nominal head has been isolated by the addition of various prepositions. As is seen in table 1, it is indeed the absence of a nominal head that has delayed the advance of *many fewer* considerably.

These findings certainly suggest that a much more laborious search in a controlled newspaper corpus should be worth our while. The results of such an analysis are shown in table 2. Not surprisingly, table 2 reveals an increased use of *many*, but otherwise reconfirms the basic split between the two kinds of syntactic environment.

Table 2: The use of *many* and *much* as intensifiers of *fewer* in selected British newspapers (t90-t00, g90-g00, d91-d00, M93-M00)[3]

		I	II	III	IV
		many	*much*	total	percentage of *many*
1	determinative use of *fewer* (= presence of nominal head)	263	13	276	95.3%
2	nominal use of *fewer* (= absence of nominal head)	112	20	135	83.0%

2. Implications of the complexity principle

This brings us to the first of four universal functional constraints, the complexity principle. The principle represents a correlation between two dimensions, cognitive complexity and grammatical explicitness, and it has been described as follows:

> In the case of more or less explicit constructional options the more explicit one(s) will tend to be preferred in cognitively more complex environments (cf., e.g., Rohdenburg 1995, 1996, 2002, 2003a).

2.1 Number contrasts

Previous research has identified a great variety of grammatical manifestations of cognitive complexity. This section considers the contrast between singular and plural nouns in examples such as (2a-b).

(2) a. She has difficulty (in) finding a suitable apartment.
　　 b. She has difficulties (in) finding a suitable apartment.

In examples like these the prepositional gerund is being replaced at present by the directly linked one (Rohdenburg 2002: 80-82). The complexity principle implies that the cognitively more complex plural should show a special affinity for the more explicit prepositional variant. The hypothesis is put to the test in table 3 with two verbs, the less frequent *find* and the more frequent and informal *get*.

Table 3:   Prepositional and directly linked gerunds involving the verbs *find* and *get* dependent on and immediately following *he has difficulty / difficulties* in the internet data provided by Google (date: September 27, 2004)

	I *in*	II Ø	III total	IV percentage of *in*
A 1 *he has difficulty + finding*	56	220	276	20.2%
2 *he has difficulty + getting*	36	383	419	8.6%
1 + 2 total	92	603	695	13.2%
B 1 *he has difficulties + finding*	7	6	13	53.8%
2 *he has difficulties + getting*	9	16	25	36%
1 + 2 total	16	22	38	42.1%

Both analyses and all others we have conducted so far confirm our expectations. The plural use typically preserves a larger share of prepositional gerunds than the singular use. And not surprisingly, the erosion process is less far advanced with *find* than with *get*. Turning now to table 4 we find that the Google analysis parallels the earlier evidence found in *The Guardian*. The only difference is that the older type of construction, the prepositional gerund, is (again) retained much better in the formal and British medium than in the internet data.

Table 4:   Prepositional and directly linked gerunds depending on (and immediately following) *he has difficulty / difficulties* in selected parts of *The Guardian* (cf. Rohdenburg 2002: 80-81)

	I *in*	II Ø	III total	IV percentage of *in*
A *he has difficulty + -ing* (g92-g93)	77	264	341	22.6%
B *he has difficulties + -ing* (g90-g94)	32	38	70	45.7%

2.2   Tense contrasts

Another markedness hierarchy analyzed in recent research (cf., e.g., Rohdenburg 2002: 80-81) involves the contrast between past and present tense expressions as in examples (3a-b).

(3)   a. It depends (on / upon) what you want.
   b. It depended (on / upon) what you wanted.

Here we are dealing with another ongoing process of prepositional erosion (Rohdenburg 2003a: 215-216, 232-235). And we would expect the cognitively more complex past tense (as in (3b)) to be more likely to delay the change. The hypothesis was firmly established by means of a googling session lasting not much longer than an hour.

Table 5: Prepositional and zero links introducing interrogative clauses dependent on (and immediately following) *it depends* and *it depended* in the internet data provided by Google (date: September 29, 2004)

	I *on/upon*	II Ø	III total	IV percentage of *on/upon*
1	*it depends + wh* *(what/how/which/whether/* *when/where/who(m)/why)*	443,574	131,736	575,310	77.1%
2	*it depended + wh* *(what/how/which/whether/* *when/where/who(m)/why)*	7,065	1,150	8,215	86.0%

Table 5 shows that the loss of the preposition is indeed less far advanced in the past tense than in the present. These findings are again reconfirmed (in table 6) in our newspaper corpus.

Table 6: Prepositional and zero links introducing interrogative clauses dependent on (and immediately following) *it depends* and *it depended* in selected British newspapers

	I *on/upon*	II Ø	III total	IV percentage of *on/upon*
1	*it depends + wh* (t90-t92, g90-g91, d91-d94)	189	203	392	48.2%
2	*it depended + wh* (t90-t01, g90-g00, d91-d00, M93-M00)	79	18	97	81.4%

Notice that this time the erosion process appears to be much further advanced in the British newspaper corpus. My explanation for this role reversal is as follows: Most of the internet data are presumably American in origin, and even informal American English is clearly lagging behind formal British English in this area. While the zero variant is already the majority option in British quality papers in the case of *it depends* (cf. table 6), it is only found in 12 to 13 percent in *The Washington Times* or the *Detroit Free Press*.

2.3   Not-negated complements

This section focuses on the rivalry between infinitives and gerunds as in examples (4a-b).

(4)   a. He advised to do / doing it in advance.
       b. He advised not to do / not doing it in advance.

In constructions like these dependent on the verbs *advise* and *recommend* and lacking a personal object, the older infinitival variant has been largely replaced by the gerundial complement.[4] Independent research carried out by Uwe Vosberg (2003a/b, 2005) leaves no doubt that the *to*-infinitive represents a more explicit sentential structure than the gerundial complement. In addition, *not*-negated complements have been shown to be attracted to maximally explicit sentential structures (Rohdenburg 1995). This suggests that the ongoing replacement process should be delayed in cases like (4b) involving *not*-negated complements. The hypothesis was put to the test by means of Google with a total of seven selected verbs (cf. table 7).

Table 7:   Nonfinite complements involving selected verbs (*pay, buy, get, sell, ignore, have, be*) dependent on the verb form *advises* (+ *not*) in the internet data provided by Google (date: April 6, 2004)

		I *to*	II *-ing*	III total	IV percentage of *-ing*
1	*advises not ~* (*not*-negation)	170	68	238	28.6%
2	*advises ~* (remaining cases)	1,066	2,509	3,575	70.2%

Table 8:   Nonfinite complements dependent on (the verb) *advise* (used without a personal object) in present-day British corpora

		I *to*	II *-ing*	III total	IV percentage of *-ing*
1	*not*-negation (BNC, t90-01, g90-00, d91-00, M93-00)	23	11	34	32.4%
2	remaining cases (BNC, t90, t95, t00, g90, g95, g00, d91, d95, d00, M93, M95, M00)	10	387	397	97.5%

As we had expected, the replacement process is clearly less far advanced in the case of *not*-negated complements. Again, these results are paralleled (in table 8)

by an extensive newspaper analysis. The only difference is that here the gerund has almost completely replaced the infinitive in other than *not*-negated complements.

3. Extracting postverbal elements out of complement clauses

We move on to consider extractions out of complement clauses as in (5a-b).

(5) a. This is a problem which₁ I don't know how to tackle Ø₁.
b. *This is a problem which₁ I don't know how I should / could / can / might tackle Ø₁.

In a pioneering article, John Hawkins (1999) has shown that, cross-linguistically, finite complements as in (5b) are more difficult to extract out of than non-finite ones as in (5a).[5] According to Hawkins, such contrasts are motivated by a processing tendency which consists in minimizing the filler-gap domain. In (5a-b), the filler-gap domain corresponds to the distance between the relative pronoun (*which*) and the site of the relativized subordinate clause object (marked by the zero symbol).

3.1 Marked and unmarked infinitives after *help* (itr.)

Hawkins' finding represents an important step in an attempt to establish a hierarchy of clause embeddings for extraction contexts.[6] But there are many other contrasts that still have to be sorted out. We start by looking at the contrast between marked and unmarked infinitives as in examples (6a-b).

(6) a. They helped (to) establish this system.
b. This is the system which they helped (to) establish.

Example (6b) represents an extraction context, and (6a) exemplifies the remaining cases. Table 9 analyzes the rivalry between the two infinitives in the internet data with six selected verbs. The analysis distinguishes between two contrasting kinds of structures, extraction contexts as in (6b) and all remaining environments. The results leave no doubt that the marked infinitive is preserved much better in extraction contexts than elsewhere. This analysis was accomplished in less than two hours.

On the basis of these findings, similar analyses taking up over a week were carried out on the American and British newspaper collections available at Paderborn. Some of the results are shown in table 10. Table 10 confirms the existence of a clear-cut split between the two kinds of context for both national varieties. In addition to and in keeping with previous research, we find that American English is much further advanced in this area than British English.[7]

Notice that the evidence in tables 9 and 10 happens to be diametrically opposed to the predictions made by Hawkins' processing theory.

Table 9: Marked and unmarked infinitives of selected transitive verbs (*found, build, get up, construct, initiate, design*) dependent on *he + helped* (used intransitively) in the internet data provided by Google (date: December 29, 2003)

		I *to-* infinitive	II Ø (unmarked infinitive)	III total	IV percentage of *to*-infinitive
1	*which he helped* + infinitive	1,054	2,587	3,641	28.9%
2	remaining uses of *he helped* + infinitive	7,331	31,693	39,024	18.8%

Table 10: Marked and unmarked infinitives of transitive verbs dependent on *I helped* (itr.) in selected American and British newspapers

		I *to*	II Ø	III total	IV percentage of *to*
A	L92-95, W90-92, DFP 92-95				
	1 extractions	7	21	28	25%
	2 rest	15	141	156	9.6%
B	t90-00, g90-00, d91-00, M93-00				
	1 extractions	48	30	78	61.5%
	2 rest	168	237	405	41.5%

3.2 Infinitival and gerundial complements after *committed* (adj)

The remaining contrast to be studied involves marked infinitives versus prepositional gerunds as in (7a-b).

(7) a. We are committed to maintain / maintaining this position.
  b. This is a position which we are committed to maintain / maintaining.

Here, too, the gerund has been replacing the infinitive for at least 100 years. Hawkins' theory does not allow for these variants to be ranked in any straight-forward way. However, a large number of case studies carried out by Uwe Vosberg and myself have shown that extractions out of (marked) infinitival complements have always tended to be strongly preferred over those out of gerundial complements (cf., e.g., Vosberg 2003a/b, 2005; Rohdenburg forthcoming a/b). Consider in this respect the Google analysis shown in table 11.

Table 11 analyzes two contrasting contexts: Row 1 features extractions, and row 2 mostly involves canonical sentence structures. It is seen immediately that the advance of the gerund is delayed in extraction contexts. A strikingly similar picture emerges in table 12 representing the British newspaper corpus. The only difference is that here the replacement process has almost reached completion in canonical sentence structures.

Table 11: Nonfinite complements involving selected transitive verbs (*pay, buy, undertake, develop, maintain, do*) dependent on *we are committed* in the internet data provided by Google (dates: September 4/28, 2004)

		I infinitive	II -*ing*	III total	IV percentage of -*ing*
1	*which we are committed to* ~	59	124	183	67.8%
2	all uses of *we are committed to* ~	3,489	46,65 1	50,14 0	93.0%

Table 12: Nonfinite complements involving transitive verbs dependent on the adjective *committed* in selected British newspapers[9]

		I infinitive	II -*ing*	III total	IV percentage of -*ing*
1	extractions (t90-01, g90-g00, d91-d00, M93-00)	50	78	128	60.9%
2	remaining cases (2nd quarters of t90, t94, t00, g90, g94, g00, d91, d94, d00, M93, M97, M00)	20	610	630	96.8%

4. Implications of the *horror aequi* principle

The third constraint is provided by the *horror aequi* principle, which has been defined as follows:

> [...] the *horror aequi* principle involves the widespread (and presumably universal) tendency to avoid the use of formally (near-)identical and (near-)adjacent grammatical elements or structures [...].
>
> (Rohdenburg 2003a: 205)

4.1   Marked and unmarked manner adverbs

Using this perspective, let us now compare the examples in (8a-b).

(8)   a. She seemed to behave (very / quite) different(ly).
      b. She seemed to behave clearly / extremely / markedly / completely different(ly).

We know that the explicit marking of manner adverbs is lacking or incomplete in many non-standard and informal varieties of English (cf., e.g., Hughes and Trudgill 1979:19). In view *of horror aequi* (in 8b), we would expect unmarked cases of *different* to be more common in examples like (8b) than in cases like (8a). Consider now the Google analysis presented in table 13, which gives the respective percentages of adverbial marking for the two kinds of context distinguished in (8a-b).

Table 13:   Adverbial marking of the manner adverb *different(ly)* immediately following (the verb) *behave* (+ intensifier) in the internet data provided by Google (date: September 20, 2004)[8]

		I -*ly*	II Ø	III total	IV percentage of *differently*
A	BEHAVE *different(ly)*	203,810	6,285	210,095	97.0%
B	*behave very different(ly)*	9,980	274	10,254	97.3%
C	BEHAVE *clearly different(ly)*	16	25	41	39%
D	BEHAVE *extremely different(ly)*	36	25	61	59.0%
E	BEHAVE *markedly different(ly)*	57	38	95	60%

Table 14:   Adverbial marking of the manner adverb *different(ly)* immediately following (the verb) forms in -*ed* / -*ing* (+ intensifier) in selected American newspapers

		I -*ly*	II Ø	III total	IV percentage of -*ly*
A	-*ed* + *different(ly)* (L92, DFP92-95, W90-92)	476	4 (DFP)	480	99.2%
B	-*ed*/-*ing* + *very/quite different(ly)* (L92-95, DFP92-95, W90-92)	31	-	31	100%
C	-*ed*/-*ing* + -*ly different(ly)* (L92-95, DFP92-95, W90-92)	16	6	22	72.7%

Rows C-E are affected by *horror aequi* while rows A-B are unaffected. We can see at a glance that the hypothesis is clearly confirmed by the Google data. Similar analyses were then carried out in the British and American newspaper corpora. In the British newspapers, there are no *horror aequi* effects, since virtually all relevant examples contain the suffix *-ly*. By contrast, as shown in table 14, American newspapers do show a moderately strong tendency to leave out the suffix in *horror aequi* contexts like (8b).

4.2   Infinitival and gerundial complements after *cease*

Consider next the complement choices associated with the verb *cease* as set out in (9a-c).

(9)   a. to cease   to-infinitive / **-ing**
       b. ceasing   **to-infinitive** / -ing
       c. ceased/ceasing/Ø cease   to-infinitive / -ing

In this case, the infinitive has only been replaced to a limited extent by the gerundial complement. In (9a-c) the options favoured by the *horror aequi* principle have been highlighted. Consider now the Google analysis shown in table 15.

Table 15:   Nonfinite complements involving three selected verbs dependent on (and immediately following) the verb *cease* in the internet data provided by Google (date: September 28, 2004)

		I *to*	II *-ing*	III total	IV percentage of *-ing*
A	*do*				
	1 *to cease*	760	4,960	5,720	86.7%
	2 *ceasing*	2,090	43	2,133	2.0%
	3 rest	21,260	10,623	31,883	33.3%
B	*pay*				
	1 *to cease*	91	747	838	89.1%
	2 *ceasing*	748	11	759	1.4%
	3 rest	5,733	5,315	11,048	48.1%
C	*commit*				
	1 *to cease*	26	256	282	90.8%
	2 *ceasing*	82	1	83	1.2%
	3 rest	508	220	728	30.2%

Table 15 distinguishes between three categories of the superordinate verb *cease*, the *to*-infinitive, the *-ing* form and all remaining cases. It is seen that the behaviour of these categories conforms indeed to the expectations raised by *horror aequi*: The advance of the gerund is most pronounced after the *to*-infinitive and least noticeable after the *-ing* form itself. The remaining verb forms, which do not involve any *horror aequi* effects, represent transitional rates of change. These analyses did not take much more than an hour to carry out and tabulate. Turning now to the corresponding newspaper analysis in table 16, we find that it parallels the Google results in all essential respects. Notice, in particular, that the few cases of -*ing* forms immediately following *ceasing* tend to represent various stages of lexicalization.

Table 16:   Nonfinite complements dependent on (the verb) *cease* in two British newspapers

		I *to*	II -*ing*	III total	IV percentage of -*ing*
A	t92-t94 1 *to cease*	19	88	107	82.2%
	2 *ceasing*	69	3 (*trading*: 2, *under- writing*: 1)	72	4.2%
	3 rest	1,233	269	1,502	17.9%
B	M93-M94 1 *to cease*	-	17	17	100%
	2 *ceasing*	10	1 (*trading:* 1)	11	9.1%
	3 rest	263	47	310	15.2%

In addition to the avoidance strategy involving alternative complements, there is the possibility of resorting to largely equivalent nominal complements in certain situations. Compare, for instance, the examples in (10a-b).

(10)   a. to cease paying subsidies to farmers
       b. to cease (the) payment of subsidies to farmers

Table 17:   Nonfinite complements involving the verb *pay* and corresponding direct objects dependent on (the verb) *cease* in the internet data provided by Google (date: September 28, 2004)

		I *to*	II -*ing*	III (*the*) payment	IV total	V percentage of -*ing*	VI percentage of (*the*) *payment*
1	*to cease*	91	747	660	1,498	49.9%	44.1%
2	*ceasing*	748	11	179	938	1.2%	19.1%
3	rest	5,733	5,315	1,821	12,869	41.3	14.2%

In theory, the indirect avoidance strategy in (10b) could be used to the same extent after *to cease* or *ceasing*. However, the gerundial complement still represents the generally dispreferred sentential option, and this is why we may expect the nominal alternative to be favoured especially after the marked infinitive where the gerund is most frequent. The evidence shown in table 17 clearly confirms our hunch. The direct object is used much more commonly after *to cease* than *ceasing*.

This brings us to the corresponding newspaper analysis in table 18, which displays strikingly similar tendencies in both *The Times* and the *Daily Mail*.

Table 18: Nonfinite complements and direct objects dependent on (the verb) *cease* in two British newspapers

	I *to*	II *-ing*	III direct object	IV total	V percentage of *-ing*	VI percentage of direct objects
A t92-t94 1 *to cease*	19	88	86	194	42.6%	44.6%
2 *ceasing*	69	3 (*trading*: 2 *under- writing*: 1)	15	87	3.4%	17.2%
3 rest	1,233	269	144	1,646	16.3%	8.7%
B M93-M94 1 *to cease*	-	17	17	34	50%	50%
2 *ceasing*	10	1 (*trading*: 1)	2	13	7.7%	15.4%
3 rest	263	47	21	331	14.2%	6.3%

5.   Iconic motivations

This section is concerned with the adjectives in (11a-c), whose root allomorphy derives from that of the corresponding nouns.

(11)   a. *hoof*   –   *hooves/(hoofs)*   →   *hoof/ved*
       b. *scarf* –   *scarves/(scarfs)*   →   *scarf/ved*
       c. *leaf*   –   *leaves*   →   *leaf/ved*

Notice that the nouns in (11a-c) use the irregular plural either exclusively (*leaves*) or in roughly 90% or 98% (with *hooves* and *scarves*, respectively) in British newspapers. In a previous article (Rohdenburg 2003b), I have shown that the distribution of the variants *scarfed* / *scarved* in a large newspaper corpus is motivated by the iconic quantity principle (Givón 1991). The longer variant *scarved*, which uses the marked and characteristically plural allomorph, shows a striking affinity for plural contexts. Compare the examples in (12a-b).

(12)   a. in company with a headscarfed woman
       b. several thousand blue-scarved people

Thus, while (*head*)*scarfed* is favoured slightly in singular contexts like (12a), (*head*)*scarved* is definitely preferred in examples like (12b). The contrast between singular and plural contexts is regularly confirmed in Google analyses such as the following:

Table 19:   The rivalry between the adjectival variants *headscarved / head(-)scarved* and *headscarfed / head(-)scarfed* immediately preceding the forms *woman / women* in the internet data provided by Google (date: September 11/12, 2004)

	I -v-	II -f-	III total	IV percentage of -v-
1 *woman*	36	34	70	51.4%
2 *women*	215	59	274	78.5%

At the time, I felt unable to account in a similar way for the rivalry between *leafed* and *leaved*. It was only after I had subjected a large number of potential head nouns to a Google analysis that I began to see a similar pattern emerging in at least part of the lexicon. Compare the evidence in table 20, which focuses on five pre-selected nouns.

Table 20:   Attributive adjectives consisting of *leaved* and *leafed* immediately preceding selected nouns in the internet data provided by Google (dates: December 30, 2003/October 3, 2004)

	I leaved	II leafed	III total	IV percentage of *leaved*
1 a) *type* (sg.)	151	100	251	60.2%
b) *types* (pl.)	342	128	470	72.8%
2 a) *flower* (sg.)	87	91	178	48.9%
b) *flowers* (pl.)	172	59	231	74.5%
3 a) *daisy* (sg.)	163	12	175	93.1%
b) *daisies* (pl.)	11	3	14	78.6%
4 a) *anemone* (sg.)	255	10	265	96.2%
b) *anemones* (pl.)	5	3	8	62.5%
5 a) *violet* (sg.)	906	71	977	92.7%
b) *violet* (pl.)	31	26	57	54.4%

Rows 1a-5a represent singular uses and rows 1b-5b involve plural nouns. It is immediately obvious that we are dealing here with two contrasting classes of head noun. *Type* and *flower* representing generic or general nouns display the expected pattern, where *leaved* is clearly preferred with plural nouns. By contrast, the highly specific nouns in rows 3a/b-5a/b show a reversal of this pattern. Notice in addition that while plural uses strikingly outnumber singular ones with both *type* and *flower*, they are extremely infrequent with the specific nouns in 3a/b-5a/b.

On the basis of these findings, similar analyses were conducted in British and American newspapers.[10] The results in table 21 for American English are particularly illuminating. There is an equally striking split between singular and plural uses in the case of generic / general nouns like *type, plant, flower, bush* and so on. Here, too, the plural is more common than the singular. With the more specific nouns, however, plural uses are clearly outnumbered by the singular, and here we find a slight reversal of the distributional pattern characteristic of generic / general nouns.

Table 21: Attributive adjectives consisting of *leaved* and *leafed* preceding two classes of head nouns in selected American newspapers (L92-L95, W90-W92, DFP92-95)

	I *leaved*	II *leafed*	III total	IV percentage of *leaved*
A generic / general nouns (*plant, tree, variety, bush, shrub* etc.)				
1 singular uses	12	29	41	29.3%
2 plural uses	40	22	62	64.5%
B other than generic / general nouns				
1 singular uses	48	39	87	55.2%
2 plural uses	15	14	29	51.7%

6.   Conclusion

In conclusion, we have seen across a wide range of grammatical variation phenomena that the lexically and grammatically much more specific Google analyses generally parallel the findings of contextually more open searches in controlled newspaper corpora. These striking parallels may be explained by the fact that the distributional patterns observed in both kinds of corpus-linguistic resources are very largely / predominantly determined by various functionally motivated and presumably universal tendencies.

Despite the general messiness of internet data and the lack of sophisticated search tools, even the present stage of internet searches provides several important advantages over traditional corpus analyses.

–   Owing to the enormous speed at which it operates Google allows the analyst to carry out a succession of pilot studies within a very short time exploring such issues as the following: a) Is it worth pursuing a particular hunch at all? b) Is it worth analyzing a promising research question in a corpus of a particular size or do we need a very much larger corpus which we haven't got?

– Owing to the gigantic database supplied by the internet, we can explore ever more fine-grained problems, and by employing the minimal pair procedure we are enabled to disentangle an increasingly wide variety of contextual and lexical constraints.

– Owing to the lower degree of formality found in much of the internet data, we are given a chance to explore a large number of issues that tend to be rare or absent in more formal written corpora and in the available spoken ones. A relevant example is provided by the absence of adverbial marking with manner adverbs.

Notes

1   This study was carried out within the Paderborn research project *Determinants of Grammatical Variation in English*, which is supported by the German Research Foundation (Grant Ro 2211/1-3).

2   A more detailed diachronic and synchronic analysis of this phenomenon is under preparation.

3   The abbreviations of the corpora used in this and the following tables are explained in the list of Primary Sources supplied at the end of this article.

4   Most grammars dealing with this phenomenon seem to assume that the replacement process has reached completion (cf., e.g., Sammon 2002: 150).

5   Cf. also Ross (1974: 117) and Joseph (1980: 360ff), who contrast the transformational potential of finite complements with that of more flexible non-finite ones.

6   Further support for this part of Hawkins' extraction hierarchy is provided by Mair (1993).

7   Previous analyses of the contrast between marked and unmarked infinitives after *help* (± object) in British and American English include the following: Kjellmer (1985); Mair (1995, 2002); Rohdenburg (2000: 30-31).

8   The examples in row 1 were retrieved by searching for all adjectival uses of *committed* which immediately precede the following contexts: *to* *.*to* *.*to* *,*to* *,*to* *;*to* *;\. Since the construction type *provide x with y* – unlike other uses of the verb *provide* – does not occur in extraction contexts it was decided to exclude such cases from the analysis of the remaining straightforward structures.

9   Capital letters are used to refer to all uses of the verb *behave*.

10   For further details see Rohdenburg (forthcoming c).

Primary Sources

BNC	*British National Corpus*
d91-d00	*The Daily Telgraph and The Sunday Telegraph* on CD-ROM (1991-2000). Chadwyck-Healey.
DFP92-DFP95	*The Detroit Free Press* on CD-ROM (1992-1995). Knight Ridder Information Inc.
g90-g00	*The Guardian* (including *The Observer* 1994-2000) on CD-ROM (1990-2000). Chadwyck-Healey.
L92-L95	*The Los Angeles Times* on CD-ROM (1992-1995). Knight Ridder Information Inc.
M93-M00	*The Daily Mail and The Mail on Sunday* on CD-ROM (1993-2000). Chadwyck-Healey.
OED	*The Oxford English Dictionary*, 2nd edition, Version 1.13 (1995). Oxford University Press.
t90-t01	*The Times and The Sunday Times* on CD-ROM (1990-2001). Chadwyck-Healey.
W90-W92	*The Washington Times* (including *Insight on the News*) on CD-ROM (1990-1992). Wayzata Technology.

References

Givón, T. (1991), 'Isomorphism in the grammatical code: cognitive and biological considerations', *Studies in Language*, 15: 85-114.

Hawkins, J.A. (1999), 'Processing complexity and filler-gap dependencies across grammars', *Language*, 75: 244-285.

Hughes, A. and P. Trudgill (1979), *English Accents and Dialects. An Introduction to Social and Regional Varieties of English*. London: Arnold.

Joseph, B. (1980), 'Linguistic universals and syntactic change', *Language*, 56: 345-370.

Kjellmer, G. (1985), 'Help to/help Ø revisited', *English Studies*, 66: 156-161.

Mair, C. (1993), 'A cross-linguistic functional constraint on *believe*-type raising in English and selected other European languages', *Papers and Studies in Contrastive Linguistics*, 28: 5-19.

Mair, C. (1995), 'Changing patterns of complementation, and concomitant grammaticalisation, of the verb *help* in present-day British English', in: B. Aarts and C.F. Meyer (eds.) *The Verb in Contemporary English*: *Theory and Description*. Oxford: Oxford University Press. 258-272.

Mair, C. (2002), 'Three changing patterns of complementation in Late Modern English: a real-time study based on matching text corpora', *English Language and Linguistics*, 6: 105-131.

Rohdenburg, G. (1995), 'On the replacement of finite complement clauses by infinitives in English', *English Studies*, 16: 367-388.

Rohdenburg, G. (1996), 'Cognitive complexity and increased grammatical explicitness in English', *Cognitive Linguistics*, 7: 149-182.

Rohdenburg, G. (2000), 'The complexity principle as a factor determining grammatical variation and change in English', in: I. Plag and K.P. Schneider (eds.) *Language Use, Language Acquisition and Language History: (Mostly) Empirical Studies in Honour of Rüdiger Zimmermann*. Trier: Wissenschaftlicher Verlag. 25-44.

Rohdenburg, G. (2002), 'Processing complexity and the variable use of prepositions in English', in: H. Cuyckens and G. Radden (eds.) *Perspectives on Prepositions*. Tübingen: Niemeyer. 79-100.

Rohdenburg, G. (2003a), 'Cognitive complexity and *horror aequi* as factors determining the use of interrogative linkers', in: G. Rohdenburg and B. Mondorf (eds.) *Determinants of Grammatical Variation in English*. Berlin: Mouton de Gruyter. 205-249.

Rohdenburg, G. (2003b), 'Aspects of grammatical iconicity in English', in: W. Müller and O. Fischer (eds.) *From Sign to Signing: Iconicity in Language and Literature* 3. Amsterdam and Philadelphia: Benjamins. 263-285.

Rohdenburg, G. (forthcoming a), 'Functional constraints in syntactic change: the rise and fall of prepositional constructions in Early and Late Modern English', *English Studies*.

Rohdenburg, G. (forthcoming b), *The Role of Functional Constraints in the Evolu-tion of the English Complementation System*.

Rohdenburg, G. (forthcoming c), 'Irregular plural allomorphs of the *hooves*-type and derived adjectives like *(cloven-)hooved* in British and American English', in: G. Rohdenburg and J. Schlüter (eds.) *Grammatical Differences between British and American English*.

Rohdenburg, G. and B. Mondorf (eds.) (2003), *Determinants of Grammatical Variation in English*. Berlin: Mouton de Gruyter.

Ross, J.R. (1974), 'Three batons for cognitive psychology', in: W.B. Weimer, D.S. Palermo (eds.), *Cognition and the Symbolic Processes*. Hillsdale, N.J.: Laurence Erlbaum. 63-124.

Sammon, G. (2002), *Exploring English Grammar*. Berlin: Cornelsen.

Vosberg, U. (2003a), 'Cognitive complexity and the establishment of *-ing* constructions with retrospective verbs in Modern English', in: C. Jones, M. Dossena, M. Gotti (eds.) *Insights into Late Modern English*. Bern: Lang. 197-220.

Vosberg, U. (2003b), 'The role of extractions and horror aequi in the evolution of *-ing* complements in Modern English', in: G. Rohdenburg and B. Mondorf (eds.) *Determinants of Grammatical Variation in English*. Berlin: Mouton de Gruyter. 305-327.

Vosberg, U. (2005), Determinanten grammatischer Variation: Verschiebungs-prozesse bei satzwertigen Komplementstrukturen im Neuenglischen. Diss., Paderborn.

Recalcitrant problems of comparative alternation and new insights emerging from internet data[1]

Britta Mondorf

University of Paderborn

Abstract

This paper adduces novel support for the claim that a theory of processing efficiency is best suited to explain the morpho-syntactic variation involved in comparative alternation, i.e. the choice between the synthetic comparative form fresher *and its analytic variant* more fresh. *It introduces three studies investigating semantic, cognitive and pragmatic determinants that have hitherto not been subjected to empirical investigation. In order to arrive at a sufficiently sized database, conventional mega-corpora comprising 600 million words will be supplemented by web data. The first study takes as its starting point independent psycholinguistic evidence showing that abstract concepts require a higher processing load than concrete ones. As regards the choice of comparative form, the analytic variant is favoured for abstract rather than concrete meanings. Thus, the comparative of a* fresh approach *is more often formed analytically than that of a* fresh taste, *etc. Secondly, the paper provides indications that even historical analyses can benefit from using web data. Cases of gradual increase (e.g.* they became friendlier and more friendly *vs.* ?they became more friendly and friendlier) *appear to reflect an iconic ordering in which more form encodes more meaning. And finally, the choice between comparative variants in compounds / derivatives such as* broader-based *vs.* more broad-based *will be shown to correlate with the entrenchment of a parallel ADJ + N structure (e.g.* a broad base).*

1.   Introduction

When forming the comparative degree, we are faced with the option of choosing between the synthetic comparative form (*friendlier*) and its analytic variant (*more friendly*).[2] There is general consent in the literature that trisyllabic words take the historically more recent analytic comparative, while monosyllables take synthetic variants, with disyllabic words being subject to variation. Recent analyses, however, show that the true extent of variability in this area appears to have been underestimated in the past (cf. e.g. Fries 1993, Kytö 1996, Leech and Culpeper 1997, Kytö and Romaine 1997, 2000, González-Díaz 2004 and Mondorf 2000, 2002, 2003, 2004, forthc.). The present paper first sets out to provide support for the hypothesis that semantic and pragmatic factors constrain the choice between the morphological and syntactic comparative variant. Secondly, it aims to demonstrate how web data can further our understanding of synchronic and most remarkably even diachronic variation.

The article is structured as follows: Section 1 introduces the research question explored and the structure of the article. Section 2 presents the state of the art, while section 3 outlines some theoretical assumptions concerning the relation between processing complexity and comparative alternation. Methodological prerequisites and information on the database will be provided in section 4. The subsequent sections present three semantic and pragmatic determinants of comparative alternation that have hitherto not been subjected to empirical testing. Section 5 investigates the comparative formation strategies of concrete vs. abstract adjectives. Cases of gradual increase will be dealt with in section 6, where a data retrieval in the web illustrates how diachronic research can benefit from using web data. Moreover, this section aims to show that the choice of comparative forms is constrained by iconic motivations. In section 7 the availability of web data allows us to revisit the issue of comparative alternation in adjectival compounds / derivatives such as *broader-based* vs. *more broad-based* (cf. Mondorf 2000). In particular the impact of the entrenchment of a parallel ADJ + N structure (e.g. *a broad base*) which had to remain an open issue for want of sufficiently large databases can now be subjected to empirical analysis. Finally, section 8 summarizes the results and makes a case for combining conventional corpora with web data in linguistic research.

2.   The state of the art

The literature largely attributes variation in the choice of comparative forms to length and final segment (cf. e.g. König 1994: 540, Bauer 1994: 51 and the comparison of several grammar books in Fries 1993: 25f.). Strictly data-driven research on the issue of comparative alternation has been introduced by Fries (1993: 30) and Kytö (1996: 340) who both show that the synthetic *-er* form is preferred over its analytic variant in 98-99% of more than one thousand monosyllabic adjectives investigated, a finding that is confirmed in Leech and Culpeper (1997: 355).

Particularly relevant for present purposes is Braun's (1982: 112) postulate of a connection between the semantic complexity of an adjective phrase and the choice of comparative variant. He explains the different behaviours of *early* (predominantly synthetic) and *subtle* (predominantly analytic) by conceiving of the former as a semantically simple adjective and the latter as semantically complex. He gauges the degree of semantic complexity on the basis of the length of glosses provided in dictionaries and the availability of antonyms. Semantically complex adjectives according to Braun (1982: 112) prefer the analytic variant.

This claim will be tested against both conventional corpus data and web data in the following analysis.

3. Theoretical prerequisites

The argumentation pursued here assumes that a theory of processing efficiency is best suited to explain comparative alternation. Drawing on Hawkins (2003), language users can be considered to weigh the pros and cons between

> [...] less form processing [...] but more dependent processing on the one hand, and more form processing (explicit marking) with less dependent processing on the other.
>
> (Hawkins 2003: 200)

They can thus be conceived of as aiming at a trade-off between the explicit *more* and the inflected *-er* variant. Rohdenburg's (1996) *Complexity Principle* states:

> In the case of more or less explicit grammatical options, the more explicit one(s) will tend to be favoured in cognitively more complex environments.
>
> (Rohdenburg 1996: 151)

In accordance with this principle, the analytic comparative appears to be resorted to whenever a structure requires more processing capacity (cf. Mondorf 2003, 2004). Language users prefer the analytic form in environments that are for some reason more difficult, more complex, less entrenched / frequent, and less accessible or in any way cognitively more complex.[3] Cognitively complex environments are for instance

- bimorphemic rather than monomorphemic words, e.g. *more awful* vs. *gentler*
- instances of argument complexity, e.g. *He was more proud of her* vs. *He was prouder*
- identity effects, e.g. *modestest* vs. *most modest*, etc. (cf. Mondorf 2002, 2003, 2004).

The mechanisms by which the *more*-variant mitigates complexity effects have been subsumed under the notion of *more*-support.

> In cognitively more demanding environments which require an increased processing load, language users tend to make up for the additional effort by resorting to the analytic rather than the synthetic comparative.
>
> (Mondorf 2003: 252)

The advantages offered by *more*-support are threefold:

1.)   The analytic variant can unambiguously signal at the beginning of the degree phrase that a comparative follows, thereby rendering phrase structure easily identifiable.

2.)   The *more*-variant is more explicit and presumably easier to parse since it disentangles a complex lexeme consisting of a base plus inflectional suffix by assigning each function a separate form.

3.)   Simply by using the degree marker *more* as a signal, addressees can be alerted to the fact that a cognitively complex adjective phrase follows, so that some extra processing capacity can be allotted to that phrase (cf. Mondorf 2003: 254).

These three assumptions are in line with functional processing theories which predict that early recognition of phrase structure demands less processing from working memory than late recognition and thus facilitates language processing.[4] Hawkins' *Principle of Mother Node Construction* (1994: 60ff.) states that in the left to right parsing of a sentence a word that can uniquely determine or classify a phrase will immediately be used to construct a representation of that phrase. If we extend this principle to the competing comparative variants *more* and *-er*, we find that an early occurrence of *more* is a relatively – though not completely – safe signal that a degree phrase follows.

If *more*-support is able to at least partly counterbalance complexity effects, this compensatory strategy can be hypothesized to be also observable in semantics and pragmatics. This hypothesis will be empirically validated against conventional mega-corpora supplemented by web data in subsequent sections.

4.   Methodology

Depending on the sample required for the respective analysis, either parts or all of the following corpora (roughly totalling at 700 million words) have been selected in order to ascertain the determinants that constrain the choice between the synthetic and analytic comparative form.

The synchronic research introduced here is predominantly based on newspaper data, the only exception being the *British National Corpus* (BNC).[5] A list of the corpora together with information on their approximate size is provided in table 1.

Table 1: British English synchronic corpora used in this study[6]

Corpus	Million Words
British National Corpus (BNC)	100
Guardian 1990–94 (incl. *Observer* 1994)	141
Daily Mail and *Mail on Sunday* 1993–94	38
Daily Telegraph and *Sunday Telegraph* 1991–94	128
Times and *Sunday Times* 1990–94	192
Total	599

The diachronic analyses are based on the following British English historical corpora. This leads to a grand total of almost 100 million words for the historical data (cf. table 2).

Table 2: British English historical corpora used in this study

Corpus	Period*	Million Words
Early English Prose Fiction	1460 – 1682	10
Eighteenth Century Fiction	1660 – 1752	12
Nineteenth Century Fiction	1728 – 1869	40
Mid Nineteenth Century (British)	1800 – 1829	10
Late Nineteenth Century (British)	1830 – 1869	21
Early Twentieth Century (British)	1870 – 1894	5
Total		98

* birth dates[7]

As we will witness below, even relatively large-sized corpora can prove too small to permit meaningful analyses of some instances of grammatical variation. A case in point are comparatives in general and in matching semantic / pragmatic contrasts in particular. Since the conventional linguistic corpora fell short of qualifying as a useful database for the questions under investigation, I have resorted to using the world wide web with its unparalleled size of tens of billions of words to supplement the data. All web-based analyses reported here are based on internet retrieval by means of the search engine Google.

Obvious caveats for web-based linguistic analyses reside in the following aspects:

- The web is unspecifiable in terms of size
- The web is unspecifiable in terms of contents
- The web is a highly dynamic corpus, so that web-based analyses do strictly speaking not satisfy the scientific requirement of being repro-ducible.

For the present purposes of investigating comparative alternation, the unspecifiable size of the web data poses no problem. In addition, elimination of typically occurring 'waste entries' in concordances, such as quantifier uses of *more* etc. has largely been made redundant in this study by restricting the search to highly specific syntactic and lexical environments.

5.   *More*-support with abstract rather than concrete meanings

The present section draws on the assumption that concrete adjectives are easier to process than abstract ones. Consequently, they should require less *more*-support.

5.1   Psycholinguistic evidence on concreteness effects in language processing

Walker and Hulme (1999: 1258) propose that concreteness can be gauged "as an index of how directly the referent of a word can be experienced by the senses." In addition, Gilhooly and Logie (1980) discern a considerable degree of unanimity among people rating words as concrete or abstract. While e.g. *ball and ship* have been judged highly concrete, *logic and conscience* are rated as highly abstract (1980: 396).

At least three psycholinguistic experiments adduce independent empirical support for the claim that abstract entities require more processing effort than concrete ones.

Firstly, lexical decision tasks have produced faster reaction times for concrete than for abstract words (cf. e.g. Moss and Gaskell 1999).

Secondly, EEG measurements by Weiss and Rappelsberger (1996: 18) have monitored neurological differences in the processing of concrete vs. abstract lexemes. Concrete words, according to the authors, are easier to memorise or retrieve since they refer to objects that can be perceived via highly diverse channels: by seeing, hearing, feeling, smelling or tasting (Weiss and Rappelsberger 1996: 17). If we assume a neural network model, the learning of concrete nouns should correspondingly affect more and more widely distributed neurons than that of abstract nouns. Neurophysiological evidence indicates that the processing of concrete words implies the simultaneous activation of more and more widely spread sensory-based features and pathways than that of abstract words (cf. Weiss and Rappelsberger 1996: 17).

Thirdly, Walker and Hulme (1999) devised serial recall experiments in which subjects tried to verbally repeat a list of seven words. The accuracy of serial recall was statistically significantly higher for concrete than for abstract words. Quite similar results were obtained when recall was written rather than spoken, which provides support for the view that the "[...] locus of these effects is earlier in the language system than the point at which written and spoken output become separated" (Walker and Hulme 1999: 1263). The authors conclude that

> [...] concrete words benefit from a stronger semantic representation than do abstract words and [...] the quality or strength of a word's semantic representation contributes directly to how well it can be recalled.
>
> (Walker and Hulme 1999: 1261)

This conception of semantic complexity ties in with network models that assume that strong activation thresholds need to be activated for a neuron to fire. Hence, the concrete meaning of e.g. *fresh taste* might be more immediately accessible to the senses than its abstract counterpart *fresh approach*. And this difference in processing complexity should be reflected in the choice between the synthetic and the analytic comparative variant.

5.2 Corpus study on concreteness effects in comparative alternation

We have argued in section 3 that compensation for an increased processing load can take the form of greater explicitness, i.e. *more*-support. We can thus derive the following hypothesis:

Hypothesis 1: The analytic comparative variant is more likely to occur with abstract than with concrete meanings.

Seven adjectives have been analysed with respect to concreteness effects in the choice of their comparative form: *blunt, clear, cold, dark, fresh, tight, round.* These adjectives qualify for the investigation because they are equal in length, i.e. monosyllabic and they are sufficiently numerous in matching concrete and abstract uses. Given the scarcity of comparatives in general and of semantic contrasts in highly specific matching contexts in particular, even large conventional corpora (comprising more than 900 million words) proved to fall short of qualifying as a useful database for the question under investigation (cf. Mondorf 2004). The conventional corpus data has therefore been supplemented by internet data. After retrieving the comparative forms by means of Google, the vast quantity of resultant entries (with over 22,000 entries for *a dark colo(u)r*) meant that the general procedure of manually editing each entry had to be abandoned for the sheer reason of economy. This generally 'reprehensible' neglect of methodological rigour appears, however, justified in view of the following compensatory measures. In order to minimize waste entries and to isolate interfering factors that also have a bearing on comparative alternation the following restrictions have been imposed:

All adjectives
- are equal in length (i.e. monosyllabic),
- occur in attributive position,
- are immediately preceded by the indefinite article, and

- are immediately followed by two selected nouns.

The selected nouns had to be numerous enough to provide meaningful results and to differ with respect to concreteness. For instance, *fresh* has been googled for the *-er* and *more* comparative in the concrete NP *a fresh taste* (*a fresher taste, a more fresh taste*) and the abstract NP *a fresh approach* (*a fresher approach, a more fresh approach*).

What remains is the general messiness of web data, which is bound to include doublets and errors. Moreover, search strings can occasionally render crucially different constructions ("*a cleaner room*" provides instances of "*a cleaner's room*"), a problem that did, however, not occur with the adjectives analyzed in the present investigation. While far from belittling the methodological data-related problems involved in web-based linguistic analyses, the use of web data can nevertheless be argued to gain some provisional insights into the operation of *more*-support in semantics. Even for the most frequent pair investigated, i.e. *a fresh taste* (62 entries in the internet) no single entry has been found in 11 years of *The Guardian* (1990-2000).

Before we proceed to interpret the figures it is important to bear in mind that according to the vast majority of grammar books the *more*-variant should not occur at all with these monosyllabic adjectives. In addition, their occurrence in attributive rather than predicative use should additionally shrink the chances of occurrence of the *more*-variant, because previous research shows that analytic comparatives are significantly rarer in attributive than in predicative uses (cf. Braun 1982: 89, Leech and Culpeper 1997: 366, Lindquist 2000: 125 and Mondorf 2003: 275). Neither do frequency, syntactic complexity, end-weight, etc. promote the choice of the analytic comparative form for these adjectives (on the effects of these factors see Mondorf 2003, 2004). All seven adjectives should be marked domains of the *-er* variant. The results of the retrieval procedure are shown in figure 1.

Figure 1 gives the percentages for the analytic comparative form. For example with the adjective *fresh* expressing concrete meanings (i.e. used with the concrete noun *taste* in *a fresher/more fresh taste*) the analytic comparative is used in 8% of the cases. Each column is additionally labelled with the absolute figures for the analytic and the synthetic comparative form, i.e. *a more fresh taste* occurred 5 times as opposed to *a fresher taste* with 62 hits. As soon as abstract meaning is conveyed, however, the synthetic form *fresher* loses ground (136 occurrences) and *more fresh* becomes increasingly used (909 cases). Similarly, *clearer, colder* and *tighter* lose their knock-out status in abstract uses, where they become increasingly ousted by *more clear, more cold* and *more tight*. For all seven adjectives analysed we consistently observe higher percentages for the *more*-variant in abstract than in concrete uses. For five of the seven adjectives the concreteness effect is statistically significant. For the aggregate of all seven adjectives the concreteness effect is statistically very highly significant. Crucially, there is not a single reversal to the observed pattern.[8]

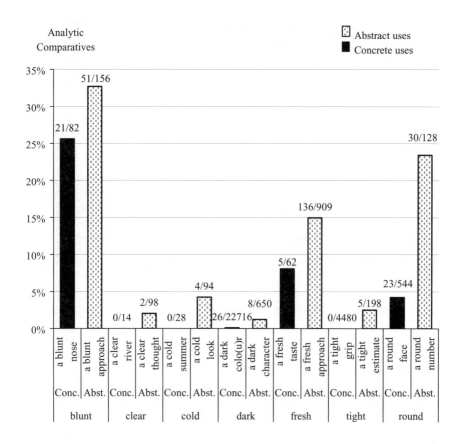

Figure 1: Analytic comparatives of concrete vs. abstract adjectives ($N_{Analytic} = 311$)[9]

The present study thus provides first indications that language users attempt to compensate for the added processing load of abstract concepts by resorting to the more explicit analytic comparative variant.

Some matching research results support the postulated negative relation between explicitness and concreteness effects. Morton (1991) reports that in earlier stages of English, which allowed variable adverb marking by *-ly* vs. *-Ø*, the more explicit variant systematically denoted abstract concepts, while the unmarked variant conveyed more concrete or primary meanings. She provides the following contrasts (1991: 4):

(1) *foul*   'how pigs root'   concrete
     foully   'how men sin'   abstract
     bright   'how the moon shines'   concrete

brightly	'how anchoresses should see and understand God's runes'	abstract
heavy	'how prisoners are fettered with iron'	concrete
heavily	'how men are burdened with God's command'	abstract
high	'how a sword is raised'	concrete
highly	'how ladies are attired'	abstract
narrow	'how closely captives are bound'	concrete
narrowly	'how severely sinners are judged'	abstract
dear	'how something is bought'	concrete
dearly	'how someone is kissed'	abstract

Kjellmer (1984: 18) in explaining ADJ–ADV productivity also provides support for the claim that the choice between explicit and zero adverb marking is semantically motivated. He attributes the existence of the contrast of e.g. *great - greatly* but not *big - *bigly* to the fact that *big* is far less often used with a secondary, dynamic meaning than *great*. In line with the *Complexity Principle* (cf. Rohdenburg 1996), explicit marking thus appears to be preferred in cognitively complex – in this case more abstract – environments.

6.   Diachronic research by means of the world wide web: gradual increase

Another factor constraining comparative alternation that has only recently been made amenable to empirical investigation through the availability of web data are iconic motivations operative in what has been termed 'gradual increase' (cf. Jespersen [1909] 1956: 390-391). Two comparatives of the same adjective can be connected by *and* in order to encode increasing degrees of intensity, e.g. *friendlier and friendlier*, *more and more safe*. It has repeatedly been claimed that adjective combinations expressing a gradual increase either opt for the synthetic or the analytic variant but never for a mixture of both (cf. König 1971: 105; Fillmore 1968: 3fn.), as in:

(2)   She became friendlier and friendlier.
   She became more and more friendly. (Based on Fillmore 1968: 3fn.)

Such a mixture was, however, possible in earlier stages of English. What can we hypothesize with respect to the ordering of both comparative forms in such mixed constructions?

   According to Rohr (1929: 64), if – as is only very rarely the case – a mixture of both variants occurs at all, the *-er* variant prevails for the lower and the *more*-variant for the higher degree of intensity. Jespersen ([1909] 1956) has provided the following examples indicating that *more* is able to create additional semantic intensity.

(3) drawn nearer and more near
grow bolder and still more bold
The strong fantasy had made her accents weaker and more weak
the visits became rarer and more rare.
Caleb's scanty hairs were turning greyer and more grey.
the screams grew fainter and more faint. (Jespersen [1909] 1956: 390-391)[10]

Here the weaker degree of intensity is expressed by *-er*, the stronger by *more*. Assuming that the reversed order will rarely if ever be found, an iconic correlation between form and meaning (i.e. intensity) can be postulated. Such an ordering would neatly tie in with the following iconic principles:

- Ross' maxim according to which more form encodes more meaning (1980: 39), and
- Givón's *Quantity Principle*, which states "A larger chunk of information will be given a larger chunk of code" (1991: 87).

It has repeatedly been implied that analytic comparatives can serve to create additional emphasis (cf. e.g. Rohr 1929: 21, 24; Curme 1931: 504; or Biber et al. 1999: 522). More than seven decades ago Rohr (1929: 21, 24) and Curme (1931: 504) stressed that the analytic comparative has a stylistic advantage over the synthetic form in that the extra lexeme puts additional emphasis on the comparative.

From the assumption that an increase in meaning is paralleled by an increase in form, we can thus derive the following hypothesis:

Hypothesis 2:   If both comparative formation strategies occur in constructions of gradual increase, the ordering is more likely to be synthetic + analytic than analytic + synthetic.

Owing to the extreme scarcity of gradual increase constructions on the one hand and the restriction to monosyllables on the other, it is not possible to systematically investigate this determinant in the conventional historical corpora described in section 4, table 2. Retrieval in the 100 million-word sample rendered merely five hits, which are listed below (my emphasis):

(4) [...]; I strove to escape from thought ---; vainly ---; futurity, like a dark image in a phantasmagoria, came **nearer and more near**, till it clasped the whole earth in its shadow. (Mary Wollstonecraft Shelley. *The Last Man*, 1826).

(5)   But how shall I tell you the things I felt, and the swelling of my heart within me, as I drew **nearer, and more near**, to the place of all I loved and owned, to the haunt of every warm remembrance, the nest of all the fledgeling hopes---; [...] (Richard Doddridge Blackmore. *Lorna Doone*, 1869)

(6)   [...] ; but when these visits became **rarer and more rare**, and when the void was filled up with letters of excuse, not always very warmly expressed, and generally extremely brief, discont and suspicion began to haunt those splendid apartments which love had fitted up for beauty. (Sir Walter Scott. *Kenilworth*, 1831)

(7)   The moonbeams grew **fainter and more faint** as the time proceeded, and the sharp distinction between light and shade faded fast from the marble floor; [...]. (E. G. Bulwer-Lytton. *Rienzi, Last of the Roman Tribunes*, 1803 (author's birth-date)[11])

(8)   And ever as she whispered, the spoken words of the two in the shut bed grew **fainter and more faint**, till at length they died away, and a silence fell upon the place. (H. H. Rider. *Eric Brighteyes*, 1856 (author's birth-date))

A sketch retrieval of the five adjectives in the web by means of Google supports the view that the vast majority of such examples stem from historical sources reaching up to the 1920s:

(9)   And now the tramp, tramp, tramp of the great army sounded **nearer and more near**, and through the dimly-lighted water the children could see the great Deep Sea [...] (E. Nesbit. *Wet Magic*, 1913)

(10)   [...] the first the doctor told me that his heart was weak; he got better of the bronchitis, but day by day, without pain, he became **weaker and more weak** until the [...] (C. J. Bloomfield-Moore. *Robert Browning*, 1890)

(11)   The darkness grows thicker around us, and godly servants of the Most High become **rarer and more rare**. (Martin Luther. *Table Talk*)

(12)   We could only hear the hoofbeats passing, boldly and steadily still, but growing fainter, **fainter, and more faint**. (Hough E. *The Passing of the Frontier*, 1918)

Supplementing the five hits found in conventional historical corpora with a sketch retrieval by means of Google provides the distribution printed in table 3. Table 3 also contrasts the findings for the conventional historical corpora and the web data (the abbreviations EEPF, NCF, etc. refer to the respective corpora investigated in each of the time periods, cf. the list of primary sources in the references).

Table 3: Gradual increase with five selected adjectives in conventional historical corpora and the web[12]

	EEPF 1460-1682	ECF 1660-1752	MNCBr 1800-29	NCF 1728-1869	LNCBr 1830-69	Web Data Historical	Web Data Present-day	TOTAL
nearer and more near	0	0	0	2	0	7	1	10
more near and nearer	0	0	0	0	0	0	0	0
wilder and more wild	0	0	0	0	0	1	0	1
more wild and wilder	0	0	0	0	0	0	0	0
weaker and more weak	0	0	0	0	0	1	0	1
more weak and weaker	0	0	0	0	0	0	0	0
rarer and more rare	0	0	0	1	0	3	0	4
more rare and rarer	0	0	0	0	0	0	0	0
fainter and more faint	0	0	1	0	1	2	0	4
more faint and fainter	0	0	0	0	0	0	0	0
synthetic before analytic	0	0	1	3	1	14	1	20
analytic before synthetic	0	0	0	0	0	0	0	0

(overall total $df = 1$, $p \leq 0.001$, very highly significant)

After manually editing all hits, multiple occurrences and those cases that were not instances of gradual increase have been excluded. Likewise, poetry texts, in which the choice of comparative is likely to be motivated by concerns of rhyme and metre, have been eliminated from the tally. The difference between both orderings is statistically very highly significant.

With a total of 20 instances, the results are merely some first and at this stage still highly tentative indication that Jespersen ([1909] 1956: 390-391) and Rohr (1929: 64) correctly assumed a synthetic before analytic ordering in gradual increase constructions in historical stages of English. The validity of the results is, however, further confirmed by the fact that there is no single case of a reversal of this iconic ordering.

7.   Parallel structures of compound adjectives

The third and final determinant of comparative alternation that has hitherto presented itself recalcitrant to empirical testing for want of sufficiently sized databases is the entrenchment of the base in adjectival compounds / derivatives. I have suggested in Mondorf (2000: 40fn.) that the existence of parallel structures in the form of ADJ+N combinations might increase a compound's proclivity towards the -*er* comparative.

> Parallel Structures: e.g. *broad base, high price*
> Synthetic comparative: e.g. *broader-based, higher-priced*
> Analytic comparative: e.g. *more broad-based, more high-priced*

Hypothesis 3:   The less entrenched the parallel structure, the higher will be the use of the analytic comparative variant.

20 compounds / derivatives in -*ed* have been analysed with regard to their choice of comparative form in relation to the frequency of their corresponding parallel structure.[13] As an index for the frequency of parallel structures I have ascertained the corresponding $a(n)$+ADJ+N sequence.[14] For instance, for *broad-based* the comparatives *broader-based* and *more broad-based* have been retrieved from the web as well as the string *a broad base*. In order to work with meaningful quantities the frequencies of the parallel structures of the 20 adjectives have been bundled in the following fashion:

Shorter adjectives (rendered trisyllabic in the synthetic comparative form):

1.   Rare Parallel Structures: *hard nose, fine grain, high pitch*
      less than 100 cases in the conventional corpora or
      less than 1 million cases in the www

2.   Frequent Parallel Structures: *broad base, low price, short life, long life,*
      high price
      more than 100 cases in the conventional corpora or
      more than 1 million cases in the www

Longer adjectives (rendered quadrosyllabic in the synthetic comparative form):

3.   Rare Parallel Structures: *tough mind, long wind, sure foot, full blood, high mind, far sight, broad mind, deep root*
less than 10 cases in the conventional corpora or less than 10,000 cases in the www

4.   Frequent Parallel Structures: *old fashion, full body, short sight, full flavour*
more than 10 cases in the conventional corpora or
more than 10,000 cases in the www

The results for shorter adjectives in conventional corpora are contrasted with those in the web in figure . The black columns provide the percentages for the analytic comparative form, e.g. *more hard-nosed, more fine-grained*, etc. The solid lines illustrate the frequency of parallel structures, e.g. *a hard nose, a fine grain*. While the first diagram is based on conventional corpora, the second is based on web data.

We witness that for both types of corpora a low degree of entrenchment of the parallel structure is accompanied by a high occurrence of the analytic comparative form. By contrast, well-entrenched parallel structures go hand in hand with lower percentages for the *more*-variant and concomitantly higher values for the -*er* variant. These effects are statistically very highly significant for the conventional as well as the web data ($p \leq 0.001$). This distribution is indicative of a greater need for *more*-support with adjectives that rarely occur in their parallel structure. *Hard-nosed* might require *more*-support to a greater extent (*more hard-nosed*), because its parallel structure is weakly entrenched (*a hard nose*). By contrast, *high-priced* often occurs with the synthetic comparative form (*higher-priced*), presumably because the parallel structure (*a high price*) is well entrenched.[15]

Let us now contrast long adjectives in the two corpus types, i.e. adjectives that would be rendered quadrosyllabic after attachment of the -*er* comparative. Again, the www data mirrors the results ascertained for more conventional linguistic corpora and even renders the observed patterns slightly more pronounced: while the parallel structure effect for conventional corpora produces statistically significant differences ($p \leq 0.05$) that for web data even turns out to be very highly significant ($p \leq 0.001$). In both corpus types the use of *more*-support is negatively correlated with the frequency of the parallel structure. Adjectives that rarely occur in their parallel structure trigger high percentages for the analytic comparative variant and vice versa. The fact that the difference between rare and frequent parallel structures is less marked than that observed for shorter adjectives in figure 3 can easily be ascribed to length effects. The variation spectrum for longer adjectives is narrower. The attachment of the -*er* suffix would render a long adjective even longer. This explains why the decline in the columns for the *more*-variant is less marked for longer than for shorter adjectives.

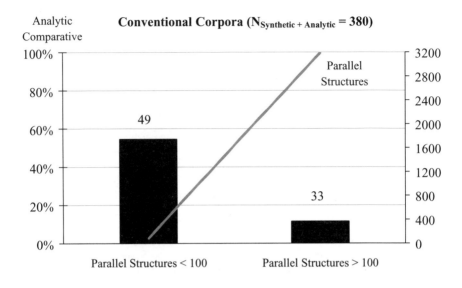

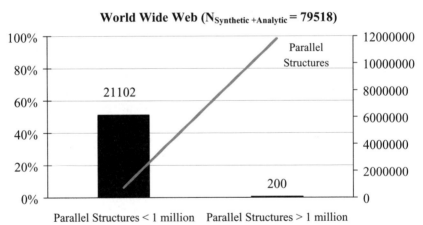

Figure 2:   Analytic comparatives and parallel structures of shorter adjectives in conventional corpora vs. the world wide web

Rare parallel structures investigated: *hard nose, fine grain, high pitch*
Frequent parallel structures investigated: *broad base, low price, short life, long life, high price*

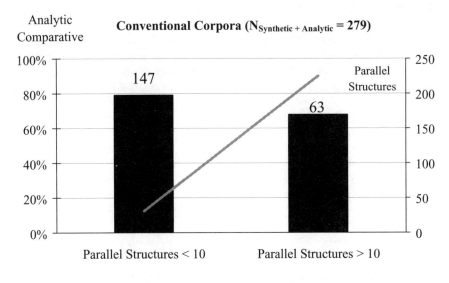

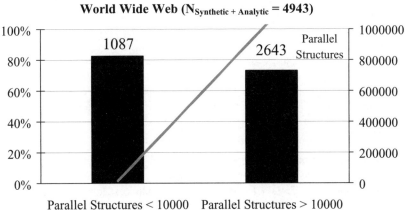

Figure 3: Analytic comparatives and parallel structures of longer adjectives in conventional corpora vs. the world wide web

Rare parallel structures investigated: *tough mind, long wind, sure foot, high mind, far sight, broad mind, deep root*
Frequent parallel structures investigated: *old fashion, short sight, full body, full flavour*

8.   Conclusion

The world wide web allows us to isolate several semantic, pragmatic and cognitive factors that do not lend themselves to analysis even in conventional mega-corpora. The shortcomings emerging from the messiness of web data are to some extent counterbalanced by the benefit of working with sizeable data. The possibility of searching for highly refined syntactic and lexical templates helps to reduce the methodological hazards of working with messy web data, thereby providing new insights into the operation of less salient factors that proved recalcitrant to analysis in smaller samples.

When it comes to contrasting the results arrived at by using conventional linguistic corpora with web data, we find that there is considerable overlap between the patterns observed for relatively homogeneous conventional corpora and those provided by internet data (cf. also the parallel results observed by Rohdenburg, this volume). While far from belittling the methodological data-related problems involved in web-based linguistic analyses, these are strong indications that accessing the web for linguistic purposes will open up promising avenues for future research.

Note

1   This paper is based on work within the Paderborn research project *Determinants of Grammatical Variation English: New Perspectives*, which is supported by the German Research Foundation (Grant RO2271/ 1-2). I would like to thank the participants of the International Symposium *Corpus Linguistics – Perspectives for the Future,* Heidelberg, 21-23 October 2004, for stimulating comments and suggestions.

2   The terms 'synthetic / analytic' are preferred over 'inflectional / periphrastic' here, since firstly synthetic comparatives lack some properties of inflections (cf. e.g. Zwicky 1989: 146) and since secondly the synthetic / analytic dichotomy is better suited to grasp aspects of cognition and typology that come into play in the explanation of comparative alternation.

3   On the problem of defining cognitive complexity cf. Mondorf (2004: 9f.).

4   Cf. Hawkins (1994, 2000, 2003).

5   The written part of the BNC includes, for example, academic books and popular fiction, letters, school essays, as well as many other kinds of text. The spoken part comprises informal conversation, the language used in formal business meetings, radio shows or phone-ins.

6   For bibliographical details on all corpora used see the references.

7   As publication dates are not available for all historical corpora, authors' birth dates have been chosen for locating the individual texts in time.

8   Based on retrieval of English language texts by means of Google (09.08.2004 and 12.10.2004). The statistical significance for the overall total was very highly significant (p ≤ 0.001, i.e. the probability of the difference to be a chance result lies below 0.001 in 100). The same holds for the adjectives *dark, fresh* and *round* (p ≤ 0.001). The results for *cold* and *tight* were still highly significant (p ≤ 0.05, i.e. the probability of the difference to be a chance result does not exceed 5 in 100), while for *blunt* and *clear* the differences were not significant.

9   Note that frequency analyses in Mondorf (2004) have shown that the adjectives investigated differ in terms of whether they are most frequent in their abstract or their concrete use. The general pattern concerning *more*-support with abstract concepts can thus be assumed to hold irrespective of frequency effects.

10   The above instances are also cases of end-weight, so that they cannot unequivocally be attributed to gradual increase.

11   Publication dates are not always available for the all historical corpora; examples thus marked are dated according to the author's birth date.

12   Based on an internet search by means of Google (18.08.04). 'Web Data Historical' refers to hits that on closer inspection turned out to stem from historical texts. 'Web Data Present-day' accordingly reflects Present-day English usage.

13   The selection process for these 20 adjectives and their occurrence in the synthetic vs. analytic comparative is described in Mondorf (2000). The present analysis merely considers compounds/derivatives that are rendered tri- and quadrosyllabic in the synthetic comparative form.

14   The restriction to the syntactic template $a(n)$+ADJ+N is firstly motivated by the fact that the entire amount of www hits was too numerous for manual editing and secondly by the intention to hold the factor position constant.

15   On the relation between frequency and choice of comparative formation strategy see also Mondorf (2003, 2004).

References

Primary Sources

British National Corpus (BNC) 1995 BNC Consortium/Oxford University Computing Services.

Early English Prose Fiction (EEPF) 1997 Chadwyck-Healey, Cambridge.

Early Twentieth Century Corpus (ETC) Selection of British and American fiction texts by authors born between 1870–1896. Source: Project Gutenberg.

Eighteenth-Century Fiction (ECF) 1996 Chadwyck-Healey, Cambridge.

Late Nineteenth Century Corpus (LNC) Selection of British and American fiction texts by authors born between 1830–1869. Source: Project Gutenberg.

Mid Nineteenth Century Corpus (MNC) Selection of British and American fiction texts by authors born between 1803–1828. Source: Project Gutenberg.

Nineteenth-Century Fiction (NCF) 1999–2000 Chadwyck-Healey, Cambridge.

The Daily Mail and the Mail on Sunday on CD-ROM 1993–1994 Chadwyck-Healey, Cambridge.

The Daily Telegraph and Sunday Telegraph on CD-ROM 1991–1994 Chadwyck-Healey, Cambridge.

The Guardian (including *The Observer* 1994) on CD-ROM 1990–1994 Chadwyck-Healey, Cambridge.

The Times and Sunday Times Compact Disk Edition 1990–1994 Chadwyck-Healey, Cambridge.

Secondary Sources

Bauer, L. (1994), *Watching English Change: An Introduction to the Study of Linguistic Change in Standard Englishes in the Twentieth Century*. London: Longman.

Biber, D. (1999), *Longman Grammar of Spoken and Written English*. London: Longman.

Braun, A. (1982), *Studien zur Syntax und Morphologie der Steigerungsformen im Englischen*. (*Schweizer Anglistische Arbeiten* 110) Bern: Francke.

Curme, G.O. (1931), *A Grammar of the English Language, Volume 2: Syntax*. Boston: Heath.

Fillmore, C. (1968), 'The case for case', in: E. Bach and R.T. Harms (eds.) *Universals in Linguistic Theory*. New York: Holt, Rinehard. 1-88.

Fries, U. (1993), 'The comparison of monosyllabic adjectives', in: A.H. Jucker (ed.) *The Noun Phrase in English: Its Structure and Variability*. Heidelberg: Universitätsverlag Winter. 25-44.

Gilhooly, K.J. and R.H. Logie (1980), 'Age of acquisition, imagery, concreteness, familiarity, and ambiguity measures for 1,944 words', *Behavior Research Methods, Instruments, and Computers*, 12: 395-427.

Givón, T. (1991), 'Isomorphism in the grammatical code: cognitive and biological considerations', *Studies in Language*, 15 (1): 85-114.

González-Díaz, V. (2004), *The Evolution of the Comparative Degree in English: A Corpus-Based Study*. Unpublished PhD Dissertation, Manchester University.

Haiman, J. (1983), 'Iconic and economic motivation', *Language*, 59: 781-819.

Hawkins, J.A. (1994), *A Performance Theory of Order and Constituency*. Cambridge: Cambridge University Press.

Hawkins, J.A. (2003), 'Why are zero-marked phrases close to their heads?', in: G. Rohdenburg and B. Mondorf (eds.) *Determinants of Grammatical Variation in English*. (*Topics in English Linguistics* 43). Berlin: Mouton de Gruyter. 175-204.

Jespersen, O. (1956), *A Modern English Grammar on Historical Principles*, VII. Copenhagen: Ejnar Munksgaard. [1909]

Kjellmer, G. (1984), 'Why *great: greatly* but not *big: *bigly*?: On the formation of English adverbs in -ly', *Studia Linguistica*, 38: 1-19.

König, E. (1971), 'Transitive adjectives', *Linguistische Berichte*, 14: 42-50.

König, E. (1994), 'English', in: E. König and J. van der Auwera (eds.) *The Germanic Languages*. London: Routledge. 532-565.

Kytö, M. (1996), '"The best and most excellentest way": The rivalling forms of adjective comparison in Late Middle and Early Modern English', in: J. Svartvik (ed.) *Words: Proceedings of an International Symposium, Lund, 25-26 August 1995*. (*Koferenser* 36) Stockholm: Kungl. 123-144.

Kytö, M. and S. Romaine (1997), 'Competing forms of adjective comparison in Modern English: What could be more quicker and easier and more effective?', in: T. Nevalainen and T.L. Kahlas (eds.) *To Explain the Present: Studies in the Changing English Language in Honour of Matti Rissanen*. (*Memoires de la Societe Neophilologique de Helsinki* 52). Helsinki: Societe Neophilologique. 329-352.

Kytö, M. and S. Romaine (2000), 'Adjective comparison and standardization processes in American and British English from 1620 to the present', in: L. Wright (ed.) *The Development of Standard English 1300-1800: Theories, Descriptions, Conflicts*. Cambridge: Cambridge University Press. 171-194.

Leech, G. and J. Culpeper (1997), 'The comparison of adjectives in recent British English', in: T. Nevalainen and T.L. Kahlas (eds.) *To Explain the Present: Studies in the Changing English Language in Honour of Matti Rissanen*. (*Memoires de la Société Néophilologique de Helsinki* 52.) Helsinki: Société Néophilologique. 353-373.

Lindquist, H. (2000), '*Livelier* or *more lively*? Syntactic and contextual factors influencing the comparison of disyllabic adjectives', in: J.M. Kirk (ed.) *Analyses and Techniques in Describing English: Papers from the Nineteenth International Conference on English Language Research on Computerized Corpora, ICAME 1998*. Amsterdam: Rodopi. 125-132.

Mondorf, B. (2000), 'Wider-ranging vs. more old-fashioned views on comparative formation in adjectival compounds/derivatives', in: B. Reitz and S. Rieuwerts (eds.) *Proceedings of the Anglistentag 1999, Mainz.* (*Proceedings of the Conference of the German Association of University Teachers of English* 21). Trier: Wissenschaftlicher Verlag Trier. 35-44.

Mondorf, B. (2002), 'The effect of prepositional complements on the choice of synthetic or analytic comparatives', in: H. Cuyckens and G. Radden (eds.) *Perspectives on Prepositions.* Tübingen: Niemeyer. 65-78.

Mondorf, B. (2003), 'Support for *more*-support', in: G. Rohdenburg and B. Mondorf (eds.) *Determinants of Grammatical Variation in English.* (*Topics in English Linguistics* 43). Berlin: Mouton de Gruyter. 251-304.

Mondorf, B. (2004), *More Support for* more-*Support: The role of Processing Constraints on the Choice between Synthetic and Analytic Comparative Forms.* Habilitationsschrift, Paderborn University.

Mondorf, B. (forthc.), 'Comparatives', in: G. Rohdenburg and J. Schlüter (eds.) *One Language – Two Grammars: Grammatical Differences between British and American English.* Cambridge: Cambridge University Press.

Morton, D. (1991), 'Adverb form in Middle English', *English Studies*, 72: 1-11.

Moss, H.E. and M.G. Gaskell (1999), 'Lexical semantic processing during speech', in: S. Garrod and M.J. Pickering (eds.) *Language Processing.* Hove: Psychology Press. 59-100.

Rohdenburg, G. (1996), 'Cognitive complexity and increased grammatical explicitness in English' *Cognitive Linguistics*, 7 (2): 149-182.

Rohdenburg, G. (this volume), 'Determinants of grammatical variation in English and the formation / confirmation of linguistic hypotheses by means of internet data'.

Rohr, A. (1929). *Die Steigerung des neuenglischen Eigenschaftswortes im 17. und 18. Jahrhundert mit Ausblicken auf den Sprachgebrauch der Gegenwart.* Ph.D. Dissertation, University of Gießen.

Ross, J.R. (1980), 'Ikonismus in der Phraseologie', *Zeitschrift für Semiotik*, 2: 36-56.

Walker, I. and C. Hulme (1999), 'Concrete words are easier to recall than abstract words: Evidence for a semantic contribution to short-term serial recall', *Journal of Experimental Psychology: Learning, Memory and Cognition*, 25 (5): 1256-1271.

Weiss, S. and P. Rappelsberger (1996), 'EEG coherence within the 13–18 Hz band as a correlate of a distinct lexical organisation of concrete and abstract nouns in humans', *Neuroscience Letters*, 209: 17-20.

Change and variation in present-day English: integrating the analysis of closed corpora and web-based monitoring

Christian Mair

University of Freiburg

Abstract

Working styles in corpus-linguistic research are changing fast. One traditional constellation, close(d) communities of researchers forming around a specific corpus or set of corpora (the "Brown / LOB community", "the BNC community"), is becoming increasingly problematical – particularly in the study of ongoing linguistic change and recent and current usage. The present contribution argues that whenever the possibilities of closed corpora are exhausted, it is advisable to turn to the digitised texts which – at least for a language such as English – are supplied in practically unlimited quantity on the world wide web. Web material is most suitable for studies for which large quantities of text and/or very recent texts are required. Specialised chat-rooms and discussion forums may additionally provide an unexpected wealth of material on highly specific registers or varieties not previously documented in corpora to a sufficient extent. On the basis of selected study examples it will be shown that, contrary to widespread scepticism in the field, web texts are appropriate data for variationist studies of medium degrees of delicacy – provided that a few cautionary procedures are followed in the interpretation of the results.

1. The study of grammatical change in progress: the limits of closed corpora

The starting point for early corpus-based work on grammatical change in progress in English were unsystematic or partially systematic observations in the linguistic literature, complemented by a wealth of educated guesses published in newspapers or "state-of-the-language" books addressed to a lay reading public. A typical late-20th-century consensus list of suspected ongoing changes in present-day English might pinpoint the following phenomena as subjects potentially worth systematic and detailed scrutiny on the basis of corpora:[1]

- demise of the inflected relative / interrogative pronoun *whom*
- use of *less* instead of *fewer* with countable nouns (e.g. *less people*)
- regularisation of irregular morphology (e.g. *dreamt* → *dreamed*)
- a tendency towards analytical comparison of disyllabic adjectives (*politer, politest* → *more polite, most polite*)
- spread of the *s*-genitive to non-human nouns (*the book's cover*)

- revival of the "mandative" subjunctive, probably inspired by formal US usage (*we demand that she take part in the meeting*)
- elimination of *shall* as a future marker in the first person
- development of new, auxiliary-like uses of certain lexical verbs (e.g. *want to* → *wanna* – cf., e.g., *the way you look, you wanna see a doctor soon*)
- further auxiliation of semi-auxiliaries and modal idioms such as *be going to* (→ *gonna*) or *have got to* (→ *gotta*)
- extension of the progressive to new constructions (esp. modal, present perfect and past perfect passive progressives of the type *the road would not be being built / has not been being built / had not been being built before the general elections*)
- use of *like, same as*, and *immediately* as conjunctions
- omission of the definite article in combinations of premodifying descriptive noun phrase and proper name (e.g. *renowned Nobel laureate Derek Walcott*)
- increase in the number and types of multi-word verbs (phrasal verbs, *have / take / give a* + verb)
- placement of frequency adverbs before auxiliary verbs (even if no emphasis is intended – *I never have said so*)
- *do*-support for *have (have you any money?* and *no, I haven't any money* → *do you have / have you got any money?* and *no, I don't have any money / I haven't got any money*)
- spread of "singular" *they* (*everybody came in their car*) to formal and standard usage.

Now, after almost three decades of corpus-based work on many of these phenomena, we can say that such lists, and the educated guesswork that they are based on, are hardly ever without any foundation in linguistic fact, at all. Nevertheless, the picture they paint of current changes in English is certainly incomplete, and in parts also a seriously distorted and flawed one. Anecdotal observation unaided by corpora over-emphasises rare, unusual or bizarre usages, and discontinuity with the past. Corpora show how innovations spread slowly and gradually, and at differential rates in different varieties / text-types, thus emphasising a powerful groundswell of continuity in usage. Unsystematic and impressionistic observation also tends to lead to an unduly narrow focus on just one type of ongoing change, namely innovations affecting the "shibboleths" of proper and correct usage which educated speakers are aware of and which prescriptivists resist. A systematic analysis of corpora, on the other hand, will also document large-scale developments which proceed below the level of conscious awareness, and very often it is these rather than isolated high-profile instances of change which are re-shaping the core grammar of the language. The strongest and most general argument for the necessity of corpora, however, is that, viewed at close historical range, almost all grammatical change will manifest itself in shifting statistical preferences in usage rather than categorial re-structurings in the underlying system. As Denison puts it in his survey of morphosyntactic changes in English during the past two centuries:

Since relatively few categorial losses or innovations have occurred in the last two centuries, syntactic change has more often been statistical in nature, with a given construction occurring throughout the period and either becoming more or less common generally or in particular registers. The overall, rather elusive effect can seem more a matter of stylistic than of syntactic change, so it is useful to be able to track frequencies of occurrence from eModE through to the present day.

(Denison 1998: 93)

A general defence of the corpus-based approach is one thing, but the availability of suitable data for specific investigations is another. Even in the study of a language such as English, with its rich corpus-linguistic working environment, it is a regular source of frustration to the linguist to note that the available corpora are too small for the study of many particularly interesting possible changes. Our closed corpora need to be complemented by other resources, and the question is whether full-text data bases and archives, "self-updating" digital dictionaries such as the *OED Online* or, ultimately, the textual riches of the world wide web can be used to fill this gap, in spite of the obvious shortcomings that they have in comparison to true linguistic corpora, i.e. those collections of digitised text which were expressly compiled for linguistic analysis, and with the linguist's needs in mind.

2.   The web – the unwanted corpus?

The world wide web has made life easy for linguists in many ways. Where in the not-too-distant past, say a mere 15 years ago, it would have been rather difficult to obtain a specimen of Singaporean or Indian newspaper English for purposes of demonstration in a survey lecture on World Englishes, today portals such as Refdesk.com (http://www.refdesk.com/paper.html) put thousands of digitised newspapers from all over the world at the reader's disposal. Samples of spoken English are accessible through web-based broadcasting, and specialised discussion forums run by or for groups as different as New Zealand motor bikers or Jamaican emigrés in the UK and the USA produce language of a degree of informality which would be difficult to come by in traditional written genres. But even those who make liberal use of web data in their teaching frequently remain wary of using the web for purposes of serious linguistic research.

Attitudes towards the web as a corpus span the whole range from enthusiasm to distinct reserve, with the former dominating outside the profession. "Corpus colossal" is the headline of a recent celebratory article in the *Economist* (20 Jan. 2005) which argues among other things that:

The easy availability of the web also serves another purpose: to democratise the way linguists work. Allowing anyone to conduct his own impromptu linguistic research, some linguists hope, will do more to popularise their notion of studying the intricacy and charm of language as it really exists, not as killjoy prescriptivists think it should be.[2]

Technical papers in corpus-linguistics tend to be more cautious, focussing as much on the potential as on the hazards of using the web as corpus. The "accidental corpus" (from the title of Renouf et al. 2004) seems an appropriate phrase to capture a widespread ambiguous mood: the web will have to be used because it is there, but clearly it is not the corpus that linguists would have compiled. Outside the corpus-linguistic community, the mood tends to be even more reserved, as expressed in Brian Joseph's "caveat googlator", a sternish warning addressed to the community from the prestigious position of the *Language* editor's column (Joseph 2004: 382).

In the present paper, I will show that despite its obvious drawbacks the English-language web is an inevitable source of data for studies on change in present-day English. By its very nature, work on this topic always requires recent data, and in many instances, in particular those involving ongoing grammatical changes, it also requires more data than even the bigger available linguistic corpora such as the *British National Corpus* (BNC) can provide. As will be demonstrated, the best way to minimise the risk of relying on a self-accumulating vast and ill-defined monitor corpus such as the world-wide web is to use it not as a stand-alone source of data, but in conjunction with tried and tested closed corpora. In diachronic work, such corpora are positively indispensable because they add the necessary element of time depth to the web. In a first study example, prepositional usage with the adjective *different*, I will show that a regionally selective search of the web replicates the distribution found in closed corpora. This is taken as a good prognostic for the validity of results from web-based studies of similar phenomena. On the strength of this, web data are used to study regional variability in two further grammatical constructions for which results from existing corpora are suggestive but not conclusive, namely certain extremely infrequent types of progressive and the variable complementation of the verb *save*.

3. *Different from/to/than*

Use of prepositions with *different* has been variable in English at least since the 16th century (cf. OED, s.v. *different* 1b). Present-day formal usage generally prefers *from*, and there is a suspected regional differentiation such that *different to* is said to be common in Britain whereas *different than* is assumed to be more prevalent in the United States:

> The comparative adjective *different* is usually followed by *from* (and sometimes *to*) in EngEng, while in USEng it is more usually followed by *than*.   (Trudgill and Hannah [4]2002: 74)

It is more difficult to credit the following unsupported claim by Jenkins, according to which *different from* would by now be largely absent from American English:

> The comparative adjective 'different' is followed by 'than' in US-Eng and by 'from' (or more recently, 'to') in EngEng.
>
> (Jenkins 2003: 75)

Even though this statement is factually incorrect, it is interesting because it expresses a widely held perception that in addition to regional variability there is ongoing change in this matter.

As the three adjective-preposition combinations are ideal search items in concordancing programs, it is not surprising that the phenomenon has been much studied by corpus-linguists. It has been investigated (using slightly different search routines with slightly different numerical results) by Kennedy (1998: 194) and Hundt (1998: 106). Concentrating on the clearest instances, i.e. those in which the preposition occurs immediately adjacent to the adjective,[3] the following results are obtained in the Brown quartet of reference corpora of 20th-century written British and American English.

Table 1: Prepositions following *different* in the Brown quartet

	Brown (US 1961)	LOB (Britain 1961)	Frown (US 1992)	F-LOB (Britain 1991)
different from	29	29	20	35
different to	-	-	1	3
different than	-	1	1	-

The data investigated – roughly four million words – is sufficient to demonstrate the overwhelming dominance of *different from* in written usage, both in British and American English, and in 1961 and 1991/92. For the two minority options it is impossible to draw any conclusions – a clear instance of the kind of corpus-linguist's frustration described above. Various corpora of spoken English help to some extent. Table 2 has the returns from the spontaneous conversations of the British component of the *International Corpus of English* (ICE-GB, c. 180,000 words), the spoken-demographic portions of the BNC (c. 4 million), the public release of the American Santa Barbara corpus (c. 70,000 words), the *Longman Corpus of Spoken American English* (c. 5 million)[4] and the *Corpus of Spoken Professional American English* (c. 2 million):

Table 2:   Prepositions following *different* in selected corpora of spoken English

	from	*than*	*to*
ICE-GB conversations	4	-	5
BNC spoken-demographic	21	4	42*
Santa Barbara	1	-	-
Longman CSAE	97	64	6*
CSPAE	91	82	-

* genuine instances from totals of 46 and 15, respectively

As predicted, there is a preference for *different than* in the American material, and for *different to* in the British data. As usual in such instances of prescriptively salient variation, anecdotal comment has proved partially correct. A regional contrast in usage has been identified correctly, but what has been vastly underestimated is the continuing vitality of *different from*, which extends to clear dominance in all varieties of written English. How do these findings compare with a rough-and-ready regionally differentiated Google "advanced mode" search in selected top-level national domains?[5] Tables 3a and 3b give the results. The search was conducted at two successive intervals in order to give an idea of the phenomenal growth of web content in a period of slightly more than two years.

Table 3a: Prepositions following *different* in regionally stratified web material I (Google, 30 May 2004)

	from	*than*	*to*
total	8,160,000	2,500,000	825,000
.us	194,000	85,200	6,060
.edu	1,450,000	343,000	33,100
.gov	787,000	152,000	6,050
.nasa.gov	11,000	3,180	235
.ca	253,000	68,700	11,200
.uk	469,000	33,000	157,000
.au	171,000	14,800	98,800
.nz	45,400	4,290	17,700
.za	28,700	2,910	11,600
.ie	25,600	2,330	11,600
.cn	18,700	921	729
.de	94,500	16,000	13,500

Table 3b: Prepositions following *different* in regionally stratified web material II (Google, 10 April 2002)

	from	*than*	*to*
total	2,790,000	1,110,000	410,000
.edu	892,000	217,000	21,900
.gov	282,000	43,600	2930
.nasa.gov	6,420	1,770	199
.ca	194,000	36,300	5,380
.uk	316,000	12,200	89,400
.au	140,000	7,090	64,300
.nz	16,300	1,660	6,270
.za	11,500	1,660	6,270
.ie	14,500	770	4,170

With American English being the default language of the Web, it is difficult to target it in such a simple search. As can be seen from table 3a, the '.us' top-level national domain is not representative because it is little used. The '.gov' domain may have a bias towards the language of government and administration, and the '.edu' domain contains material produced by a number of institutions of higher learning located outside the United States. Between them, however, the three domains provide a good record of contemporary US usage, and, what is even more important, the large amounts of material required for some searches.

    Web data are dirty, and in this search the results have not been cleaned up. That means that no attempt was made to eliminate spurious hits of the type *it was different from the start*, or *it is one thing to write to them but different to tell them to their face*. Nevertheless, the results are robust and fully confirm expectations. Being a dominantly written medium, the web is expected to attest dominance of *different from* in all regional varieties, and this is what we see. As for the two informal variants, they pattern as expected, too – *than* being more prominent in US and related Englishes, and *to* being more prominent in British English and those former colonial varieties which were under strong British normative influence until fairly recently. Table 3a contains the findings for the German ('.de') and Chinese ('.cn') top-level domains. These offer material of British, American and learner provenance and can thus be expected to follow no clear regional norm but merely to share the preference for the internationally dominant *different from*. This is precisely what is reflected in the inconclusive "in-between" figures that we get for *different than* and *different to*.

    In sum, known regional preferences established in closed linguistic corpora are replicated on the web, and this is an encouraging finding for anyone wishing to use the web as a source of data for the study of further, and possibly more complicated, instances of variability.

4.   Aspect: 20th-century changes in the structure and use of the progressive

Since the Early Modern English period the frequency of the progressive has increased greatly, and its functional range has expanded. Available corpora are generally sufficient to document the increase in frequency. Denison summarises the developments to the end of the 19th century as follows:

> The progressive construction, as in *I was swimming*, has undergone some of the most striking syntactic changes of the lModE [late Modern English] period. By early in the ModE period the BE + -*ing* pattern was already well established, and its overall frequency has increased continuously ever since. Dennis (1940) estimates an approximate doubling every century from 1500, though with a slowing down in the eighteenth century and a spurt at the beginning of the nineteenth (Strang 1982: 429). Arnaud, working from a corpus of private letters and extrapolating to the speech of literate middle-class people, estimates a threefold increase during the nineteenth century alone (1983: 84).
>
> (Denison 1998: 143)

There is no sign that the trend has abated. A number of publications based on the Brown quartet of corpora (Brown, LOB, Frown, F-LOB), for example Mair and Hundt 1995 or Smith 2002, have demonstrated a general increase both in British and American English over the thirty-year period studied.

When it comes to certain rare innovative forms or highly specialised uses, however, even corpora much larger than Brown quickly fail to yield conclusive data. Cases in point are the present perfect passive progressive, the past perfect passive progressive or all those modal passive verb phrases which contain at least three auxiliaries and the series *be being* (such as *the road will be being built*). There is, for example, not a single present or past perfect passive progressive in any of the four Brown-quartet corpora, and the one-hundred-million words of the BNC contain exactly one relevant example, namely:

(1)   That er, er, little action has been taken in the last thirty forty years since this *has been being discussed*, erm, I think the first international conference erm, produced their own report in nineteen sixty. (BNC, JJG 542)

As this was produced in a spoken text under natural conditions, the construction can be considered authentic in late 20th-century English. Beyond this, however, no conclusions can be drawn, in particular none concerning the distribution of such forms across genres or national varieties. The situation is little better for modal passive progressives. The Brown quartet yields three instances, all from British data (2 LOB, 1 F-LOB). Compare, for example:

(2)   We have also to notice that while the entropy of our given system will increase with external or given time, this relation is not reciprocal, for, if we first choose our time, a rare state in our stationary process *will just as likely be being approached as being departed from.* (LOB, J18: 197ff.)

In the BNC, constructions of this type are rare (< 100) but attested regularly.

It would obviously be foolhardy to conclude from all this that the construction is more at home in British English than in American English. The distribution of the three examples in the Brown quartet might be accidental, and there is no American database to match the BNC.

In such a situation it is tempting to try the method which was shown to work well in the case of *different*, namely look at the distribution of *been being* and *be being* in top-level national domains (and the largely American .edu-domain) on the web. Table 4 gives the results:

Table 4:   *been being* and *be being* on the English-language web (Google, 23 July 2003)

Database:	*been being*	*be being*
.uk	960	10,900
.ie	36	264
.au	368	4,210
.nz	80	862
.za	37	236
.us	330	783
.edu	1,320	4,640
.ca	333	1,710
total of 8 top level domains covered	3,464	23,605
www / total English language web	21,200	80,700

Given the uncertain and ever-changing nature of the "accidental corpus", the as yet ill-understood operations of the search engine, and also the fact that the data have not been cleaned up,[6] it is pointless to attempt to interpret these figures in absolute terms. What we can do is to compare the observed distribution against an expected "normal" one, as was done in a recent study on collocational profiles of national varieties of English (Mair forthcoming).

Eight top-level domains ('.uk', '.edu', '.au', '.ca', '.us', '.nz', '.ie', '.za') were checked for the frequencies of a set of ten regionally neutral and diachronically stable collocations in order to assess the relative "weight" of each of the eight domains in the total. On average, the '.uk' domain accounted for 32.9 per cent, '.edu' for 29.6, '.au' for 12.6, '.ca' for 10.2, '.us' 6.9, '.nz' for 2.9, '.ie' for 2.3, and '.za' for 1.7 (see Mair forthcoming: appendix for the precise calculations). Subsequently, a number of possible regionalisms were investigated, with the assumption being that a regional bias in the distribution of a particular form would show up as a fairly drastic deviation from the expected averages. For example, the '.uk' domain might yield 60 per cent of all occurrences rather than a value close to the expected "neutral" average of 32.9 per cent.

There is no principled reason why grammatical colligations such as *be being* and *been being* should not be analysed in the same way. Figure 1, based on the results reported in table 4, visually represents the distribution found in the eight domains:

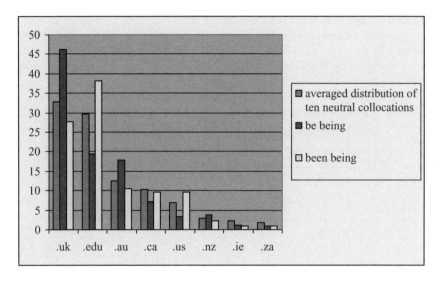

Figure 1:   Distribution of *be being* and *been being* in comparison to ten neutral collocations (frequencies given as percentages)

It is interesting to note that the three North American domains ('.edu', '.ca', '.us') show a similar distributional profile, by under-representing *be being* and over-representing *been being*. This is the reverse of what is found in the UK and Australian domains. The web data could be read as tentative support for the view that modal passive progressives are more common in British English and some British-influenced national varieties, which was suggested by the figures from LOB and F-LOB. However, given the many imponderables of web-based descriptive linguistics, deviations from the norm of between 10 and 20 per cent must be interpreted with caution. The problem requires further investigation.

The major result of this particular experiment is thus not any definitive new insight into the English progressive, but the realisation that in addition to Google we urgently need linguistically sophisticated retrieval software, which will make it possible to semi-automatically "clean up" the search output[7] or target more specific textual domains on the web through non-linguistic or text-internal linguistic criteria (or, even better, a combination of both).

5. Save (from) V-ing

In the preceding experiment the web data did not yield conclusive results, probably because the search items *been being* and *be being* did not target the intended grammatical constructions narrowly enough. This is not so in the following case, in which lexical sequences identify the intended construction with a very high degree of reliability. The construction in question is a particular use of *save*, in which the use of *from* before the gerund seems to be optional in British English.

The following example from the BNC illustrates the international common-core construction, available equally in British English and other national standards:

(3)   You can also print documents in the background while editing a second document which *saves you from* waiting around while your printer catches up with your typing speed. (BNC HAC 8936)

The same BNC text contains the following *from*-less construction, which is not current in all standard varieties:

(4)   This *saves you* having to exit one program to start another, and you can move freely between open programs using either the Hot Keys or CTRL + ESC keys. (BNC HAC 3755)

Judging by the evidence from the BNC, the latter, *from*-less type is more common in contemporary British English. For example, a search for *saves you + V-ing*[8] yields 13 instances, while *saves you from + V-ing* is attested only three times (cf. Appendix for the full set of examples). What is the situation in the web? Table 5 gives the frequencies of the construction for four common verbs, *have, pay, get* and *be*:

Table 5:   *Save NP V-ing* in selected top-level web domains (Google, access date 6 June 2003)

Search items	.gov	.uk	.us
saves you having	1	759	3
saves you from having	38	208	39
saves you paying	-	10	-
saves you from paying	1	1	1
saves you getting	-	41	-
saves you from getting	-	18	3
saves you being	-	21	-
saves you from being	-	12	2

The conclusion to be drawn from these figures could not be clearer: Apart from isolated instances, the *from*-less construction is absent from the North American '.gov' and '.us' domains, but extremely frequent in the '.uk' domain. The constructional variant with *from* is spread evenly. Web data, accessed at a level no more technical than the Google advanced-search mode, provides robust support for a grammatical Briticism. Of course, the initial data suggesting the hypothesis were provided by a closed corpus, the BNC. But as the BNC still lacks a suitable American equivalent, the comparative analysis required use of the web – at least as a temporary solution.

6.   Conclusion

The present paper wishes to encourage more web-based research into morphosyntactic variation and change in present-day English. I hope to have shown that such research can be successful in spite of the tremendous odds. In particular, the following three major factors must be reckoned with as having an obvious distorting influence on the results:

(1)   The amount and quality of the material looked at is uncertain.
(2)   The lexically based search options available in the Google advanced-search mode make it difficult to target grammatical constructions.
(3)   We as linguists still know far too little about the detailed mode of operation of the search engine (see Lüdeling, this volume).

The demonstrated practical success of some of the experiments in web-based language description described here can only be explained by the fact that the effects of these and many other potential distorting factors tend to cancel each other out. Obviously, the nature of the web as a corpus and the rough-and-ready procedures which currently have to be employed mean that web-based variation studies will have to investigate problems of low and medium levels of delicacy for some time to come. But robust evidence for crude claims is not a bad thing in the study of problems for which existing closed corpora do not even provide the data.

What is more, some of the gaps in this rough-and-ready type of linguistic description are already being filled as linguistically sophisticated web-compatible retrieval software graduates from the experimental stage and moves into wider use in the corpus-linguistic community (see the review in Fletcher, this volume).

Notes

1   The following list is based on Barber (1964: 130-44), with some modifications and additions.

2   Quoted from the *Economist* website at http://www.com/science, access date 24 Jan. 2005.

3   Thus, *A is different to B* is included, whereas the more difficult-to-analyse cases of the type *A is different and sometimes hostile to B* or *a different X than we had yesterday* are excluded.

4   This corpus is not publicly accessible. I am grateful to Sebastian Hoffmann, of Zurich University, for allowing me access to the material.

5   A language restriction was set to "English", and the search was restricted to the relevant top-level national domain, for example '.nz' for New Zealand.

6   For example, by eliminating instances in which *be* and *being* accidentally occur in adjacent position rather than constitute a construction, e.g. *my task will be being the adviser*.

7   In this particular instance, the major problems could be removed by simple part-of-speech tagging, because narrowing down the search to *be / been being* + PAST PARTICIPLE would target the relevant passive progressives with a satisfactory degree of precision.

8   This search and the following one were carried out using the tag-sequence search option of the BNC Web interface developed at Zurich.

References

Barber, C. (1964), *Linguistic Change in Present-Day English*. London and Edinburgh: Oliver and Boyd.

Denison, D. (1998), 'Syntax', in: S. Romaine (ed.) *The Cambridge History of the English Language, Vol. IV: 1776-1997*. Cambridge: Cambridge University Press. 92-329.

Fletcher, W.H. (this volume), 'Concordancing the web: promise and problems, tools and techniques'.

Hundt, M. (1998), *New Zealand English Grammar – Fact or Fiction? A Corpus-Based Study in Morphosyntactic Variation*. Amsterdam: Benjamins.

Jenkins, J. (2003), *World Englishes: a Resource Book for Students*. London: Routledge.

Joseph, B.D. (2004), 'The editor's department', *Language*, 80: 381-383.

Kennedy, G.D. (1998), *An Introduction to Corpus Linguistics*. London: Longman.

Lüdeling, A., M. Baroni and S. Evert (this volume), 'Using web data for linguistic purposes'.

Mair, C. and M. Hundt (1995), 'Why is the progressive becoming more frequent in English? A corpus-based investigation of language change in progress', *Zeitschrift für Anglistik und Amerikanistik*, 43: 111-122.

Mair, C. (forthcoming), 'Varieties of English around the world: collocational and cultural profiles', in: P. Skandera (ed.) *Idioms in World English*. Berlin: Mouton de Gruyter.

Renouf, A., A. Kehoe and D. Mezquiriz (2004), 'The accidental corpus: some issues in extracting linguistic information from the web', in: K. Aijmer and B. Altenberg (eds.) *Advances in Corpus Linguistics: Papers from the 23rd International Conference on English Language Research on Computerized Corpora (ICAME 23), Göteborg 22 – 26 May 2002*. Amsterdam: Rodopi. 403-419.

Smith, N. (2002), 'Ever moving on? The progressive in recent British English', in: P. Peters, P. Collins and A. Smith (eds.) *New Frontiers of Corpus Research: Papers from the Twenty-First International Conference on English Language Research on Computerized Corpora, Sydney 2002*. Amsterdam: Rodopi. 317-330.

Trudgill, P. and J. Hannah. [4]2002. *International English: a Guide to Varieties of Standard English*. London: Arnold.

Appendix: *Saves you from V-ing* and *saves you V-ing* in the BNC

It *saves you from* becoming under-insured as a result of inflation, with the risk of having to find thousands of pounds out of your own pocket in the event of a serious claim. (AYP 1603)

He *saves you from* a beating with remarkable ease and skill, yet you remain as blind and dull-witted as an earthworm. (C85 1656)

You can also print documents in the background while editing a second document which *saves you from* waiting around while your printer catches up with your typing speed. (HAC 8936)

His text explains: "And with this funeral goes a rented coffin -- it *saves you* buying one." (CES 1202)

"It *saves you* weaving through all those tables and chairs," Kolchinsky replied. (ECK 2037)

Oh well, it *saves you* penning. (GYT 157)

Because er i-- from the management point of view if you have got four hundred people and you work a lot of overtime that *saves you* having six or seven hundred people. (H03 329)

This *saves you* having to exit one program to start another, and you can move freely between open programs using either the Hot Keys or CTRL + ESC keys. (HAC 3755)

Saves you buying one. (KB6 1427)

It *saves you* having a holdall <unclear>, organise it more <pause> to heavy if we put that in there, right, what about, will they fit in the bag? (KBF 9660)

Saves you carrying it in the bag. (KCA 2765)

Yeah that *saves you* making a payment don't it? (KD2 2203)
It *saves you* running into the living room. (KE4 2264)

<pause dur=11> I mean, that thing is with Argos Mick it *saves you* walking round the blasted town! (KE6 3147)

Yeah, but then it *saves you* getting all the bits and (KP1 3465)
Saves you leaving all them taters. (KSU 245)

The dynamics of inner and outer circle varieties in the South Pacific and East Asia

Marianne Hundt and Carolin Biewer

University of Heidelberg

Abstract

Southern Hemisphere varieties such as Australian English (AusE) and New Zealand English (NZE) have fairly recently been codified as separate national standard varieties of English. This development may be of some importance for the dynamics of English varieties in the South Pacific and East-Asian region. With increased political, economic and personal contact between Australians and New Zealanders on the one hand and second-language speakers of English in countries such as the Philippines, Singapore or Fiji on the other hand, the latter may start modelling their speech on AusE and NZE rather than on the formerly more prestigious varieties of American and British English.

To test this hypothesis, the world wide web was used as a source to compile the SPEA-Corpus[1] – a collection of articles from on-line newspapers which were chosen to represent the different inner and outer circle varieties in question. The paper describes the compilation of SPEAC and presents the results of a case study – variation between the present perfect and the past tense. It discusses the results as a first step to modelling the dynamics of inner and outer circle varieties in the South Pacific and East Asia and the suitability of on-line newspapers on the world wide web as a source for corpus compilation.

1.   Introduction

The relation of different Englishes in the global village has been described in various models. Earlier approaches still took the predominance of British and/or American English for granted (cf. Greenbaum 1990: 194 or Algeo 1991). The underlying rationale of these models is that British (BrE) and American English (AmE) are the more prestigious varieties; additional arguments are based on the political, economic and cultural influence of Britain and the US as colonial powers. But the example of AmE itself shows that former colonial varieties can gain prestige and even become the centre of gravity for ongoing language change (cf. Kahane 1982 or Bauer 1994). This aspect is taken up by models that perceive of English as a pluricentric language with various interacting national standards. In Clyne's (1992) version of the model, the different national standards do not necessarily have the same status. When applied to English, this accounts for the special role of AmE and BrE – AmE is not only important because of the huge number of speakers whose first or second language it is, but also because of the socio-economic role of the US, whereas the prestige of BrE is mainly due to its role as the original 'home' of the English language. More importantly for us, the advantage of the pluricentric over a traditional model is that it allows linguists to account for the influence that more recent standard varieties of the language may exert on outer circle[2] varieties like Indian or Singaporean English. Australian (AusE) and New Zealand English (NZE) have developed from 'semi-centres' to 'nearly' or even 'full centres' over the past few decades.[3] In other words, they are not only perceived as separate national standard varieties of English but they have also been codified. This development may also be of some importance for the dynamics of Englishes in the South Pacific and East-Asian region: with increased political, economic and personal contact between Australians and New Zealanders on the one hand and second-language speakers of English in countries such as the Philippines, Singapore or Fiji, on the other hand, the latter may – consciously or sub-consciously – start modelling their speech on AusE and NZE. The hypothesis that we want to apply to the South Pacific and East Asian region has been phrased in a general way by Bailey (1990: 85):

> Language spreads from the center to the periphery; the periphery develops independent 'standards' that first compete and then coexist with those of the homeland, and these new standards may in their turn become new centers of radiating influence.

In other words, we postulate that AusE and NZE as inner circle varieties might have become or be in the process of becoming new epicentres[4] in the South Pacific and parts of East Asia: they function as a model for outer circle varieties like Philippine and Fiji or Singaporean English. Grammatical and lexico-grammatical patterns will be used to test this hypothesis. We would like to argue that grammatical features are particularly suitable for this purpose because they are less likely to be used as markers of a regional identity than accent or lexical items.

In order to test the hypothesis, grammatical variation in four inner circle varieties – British, American, Australian and New Zealand English – will be compared with patterns found in outer circle varieties of the Pacific and East Asia. Of the outer circle varieties that would be of potential interest, we selected Philippine English (PhilE) because of its historical connection with AmE, Singaporean English (SingE) as a variety with strong British roots, and Fiji English (FE) as a variety with particularly close connections with New Zealand. In addition to exonormative influence from any of the inner circle varieties, FE, SingE and PhilE could of course also exhibit a certain amount of substrate influence from Fijian, Chinese or Tagalog, for instance, which we will have to reckon with.

An obvious source of information for our purpose would be the parallel corpora of the ICE family. But not all of the sub-corpora that we need have been completed – we are still missing the American, Australian and Fijian members of the family. An alternative place to look for available material is the world wide web, in particular the regional newspapers that are available on-line.

In the following, we will briefly describe the compilation of our makeshift SPEAC, and present the results of a case study – variation between the present perfect and the past tense, almost a shibboleth of British and American grammatical differences. In our conclusion, we will discuss the results as a first step to modelling the dynamics of inner and outer circle varieties in the Pacific and the suitability of the world wide web as a source for corpus compilation.

2. Corpus compilation

The SPEAC consists of a collection of newspaper articles that were downloaded from the internet on the five working days of the week, first between the 15th of July and the 15th of August 2004 (SPEAC-1). We repeated the process between the 15th of November and the 15th of December (SPEAC-2). For the inner circle varieties we selected *The Sidney Morning Herald* (AusE), *The New Zealand Herald* (NZE), *The New York Times* (AmE) and *The Guardian* (BrE).[5] *The Singapore Straits Times*, *The Manila Times* and *The Fiji Times* represent the outer circle varieties in our corpus. In order to cover more formal and more informal journalistic styles, we decided to sample front page news (leading articles) and editorials. The target for the size of individual samples was 4,000 words per variety and day, and 2,000 per genre (i.e. a total of approximately 1.4 million words). We were careful always to collect a little more than required, with the result that the corpus now comprises 1.52 million words, a little more than 200,000 words per variety. The SPEAC-1 consists of 746,682 words and the SPEAC-2 comprises a total of 768,371 words. The reasons to keep the two sub-corpora separate will be discussed below.

In the compilation of the SPEAC, we encountered several problems concerning (a) the sample size and stylistic variation, (b) the availability of data, (c) the conversion of data and (d) the retrieval of extra-linguistic information. We will look at these in turn, with a view to the question whether our approach – to use the world wide web as a source for corpus compilation – is a feasible one.

(a)   Sample size and stylistic variation

One problem was that *The Fiji Times* provided us with fewer editorials than the other newspapers. This made it difficult to reach the sample size we had decided on. We had to include other kinds of material with a comparable informal journalistic style. What we decided to do was to include letters to the editor in our sample of editorials. It was easier to reach the daily target of 2,000 words per genre and variety with leading articles. These, in turn, posed the problem that we could not simply select the first three articles on the web page as it was very likely they had similar topics. Selecting from among different topics meant to tolerate individual preferences. For our sample of leading articles we could not but accept individual preference to some extent. In other words, the regional sub-corpora of the SPEAC are not as comparable or 'parallel' as we would have liked them to be.

(b)   Availability
Some newspaper issues were neither available on a day-to-day download nor could they be downloaded from the archives and therefore had to be replaced by other issues. The web pages of the newspapers also change continuously. Most issues are only available for a couple of days. We downloaded more articles than needed for each day, in case we lost some data during the compilation or conversion and would not be able to access it again at a later stage. Another particular problem occurred with *The Sidney Morning Herald* which sometimes provided tomorrow's issue under today's date, depending on the time of day we were downloading the material (as Australia is 12 hours ahead of time). This means that, apart from the danger of confusing dates, there was the danger that the issue we wanted had already been replaced.

(c)   Conversion of data
We had decided to save the downloaded data as word documents but also convert them into ASCII code. This surprisingly caused problems with *The Fiji Times* as some articles were doubled in the process, apparently due to some HTML codes that had been included in the download material. Another unexpected hitch occurred with the text samples from *The Manila Times*: in the converted files, apostrophes had been changed into question marks. This caused problems for the search of present perfect constructions with contracted forms of *have*.

(d)   Retrieval of extra-linguistic information
Background information on the author of an article is rare (not only with internet sources). We tried only to choose articles written by native speakers, judging from their names. Obviously, absolute certainty as to the authors' background is impossible to achieve. Some articles may have been written by a foreign correspondent from Great Britain or the U.S. But on the whole, newspaper articles downloaded from the internet probably provide more reliable data than many other downloads.[6] Ideally, the download would be done automatically rather than manually, but this requires a solution of how to deal with the available metalinguistic information in an automated way.

A problem related to the question of authorship is the question of the ultimate source of the articles. It is sometimes difficult to detect whether an article is not to some extent a repetition of a report from an international press agency. Only after the compilation of the SPEAC-1 did we realize that some newspapers made considerable use of international press reports, sometimes without acknowledging it.[7] Whereas the SPEAC-1 still includes articles written on the basis of international press agency releases, great care was taken to exclude such material in the compilation of the SPEAC-2. Comparison of data from the two sub-corpora will thus enable us to discuss the possible skewing effect that the inclusion of material based on international press releases may have on the data. This is an important methodological consideration for our ultimate goal, the automatic compilation of corpora from on-line newspapers.

3.   Case study: present perfect vs. past tense

For our case study we chose variation between the present perfect and the past tense, a pattern that is of interest from a diachronic, a regional and a stylistic perspective. Tottie (2002: 161), for instance, points out that "the perfect aspect is more common in British English than in American English, especially in newspaper language." The distinction between past and perfect is a fairly recent development in English. As it had not been fully grammaticalised when the first settlers arrived in America, its scarcity in AmE has been interpreted as an instance of colonial lag (cf. Görlach 1987).[8] Various corpus-based studies have shown that there is, indeed, a tendency for AmE to use the preterite more frequently than BrE, particularly with certain adverbials like *already* and *just* – the so-called 'colloquial preterite' (cf. Quirk et al. 1985:194, Biber et al. 1999: 462f.,[9] Meyer 1995, Hundt 1998:70-75, and Tottie 2001, 2002). Its patterning in AusE and NZE as well as the outer circle varieties we are looking at has not been studied systematically so far.[10] Another reason why we chose this variable is its frequency even in relatively small corpora.

3.1   Hypotheses

The hypotheses that we are going to test are the following:

a)   The overall frequency of the present perfect is higher in BrE than in AmE, which shows a higher rate of the colloquial preterite;

b)   NZE and AusE are either between AmE and BrE in their use of the colloquial preterite or lagging behind BrE in the development towards a more frequent use of the past with adverbials like *just, already* and *yet*;

c)   SingE and FE pattern like AusE and NZE;

d)   PhilE is moving away from its original 'parent' (AmE) and moving closer to AusE and NZE, i.e. it is using the present perfect more frequently than AmE while at the same time having a lower rate of the colloquial preterite.

'Unexpected' distributions of past or present perfect VPs in the outer circle varieties might have to be attributed to substrate influence. Fijian, a Malayo-Polynesian language, is not a prototypical isolating language but it nevertheless uses particles or function words for both tense and aspect marking.[11] Mandarin Chinese and Tagalog have no tense marking but aspect marking.[12] Note also that there is no 1:1 correspondence of the English present perfect and the Mandarin Chinese perfective marker:

> Chinese has a number of verbal suffixes with aspectual, or combined aspectual and temporal, value, for instance Progressive *-zhe*, Perfective *-le* (the latter combining perfective meaning and relative past time reference).   (Comrie, 1976: 128)

Alsagoff and Lick (1998: 139f.), for instance, point out that in colloquial SingE (CSE), aspect is marked with adverbials rather than with morphological marking on the VP. If marking within the VP occurs, it does so in the form of the past participle rather than the perfective auxiliary *have*:

(1)   a. She eat her lunch already.
       b. She eaten her lunch already.[13]

These patterns in CSE have been attributed to substrate influence (cf. Platt and Weber 1980, and Bao 1995). They are used in colloquial rather than standard SingE, but we still have to bear these and other differences between the inner and outer circle varieties in mind when we look at the data.

Sand (2005: 95) mentions the possibility that a levelling of present perfect and past tense may even be an 'Angloversal', i.e. a feature common to the contact varieties among the new Englishes.

3.2   Defining the variable

As far as the overall frequency of the present perfect is concerned, it is possible to use the Mossé coefficient, i.e. the frequency of the construction per 10,000 words.[14] To assess the general perfective-friendliness of the corpora, we used this approach, retrieving finite present perfect VPs on the basis of the auxiliary. This meant that we missed all the nativised patterns (for instance the CSE constructions) that were mentioned in the previous section.

Verb phrases with two or more lexical verbs (as in example 2) were counted as one instance of a present perfect VP. Similarly, elliptical constructions as the one in (3) were not counted as separate occurrences.

(2)   [...] where up to 1 million people have been displaced and about 50,000 killed. (SPEAC-1, 07-30-lead-AusE)
(3)   As they have for the past seven years, sisters Jenny Beckett and Philippa Robertson have been sorting donated books [...] (SPEAC-1, 08-05-ed-NZE)

Furthermore, we also excluded modal VPs, such as *He may have seen her* as these do not have past tense counterparts (*He may saw her*). Yet another pattern that we discounted was the lexical use of HAVE *got(ten)* [15] and *have*-passives of the type *have sthg. done*.

In a second step, we investigated the relative frequency of present perfect and past tense VPs by manually counting all past tense VPs in a small sub-set of texts. Instances of resumptive *did* as in example (4) were excluded in this approach.

(4)   Mr. Hawkins did not respond [...] Nor did Jack Roady, the prosecutor who
        has been supervising the testing. (SPEAC-1, 08-05-lead-AmE)

Again, VPs with coordinated verbs were counted only once. We also disregarded
instances of past tense VPs in conditional contexts as these do not allow for the
use of the present perfect (cf. *If I were you* ...vs. **If I have been you* ...). The
results of this manual search were then extrapolated to the size of the SPEAC-1
and SPEAC-2, respectively, to give us the relative frequency of past tense and
present perfect VPs.

        Contexts in which the present perfect or the past tense occurred with
typical adverbials (such as *recently* or *just* with the perfect, or *yesterday* with the
past) were included in our data. In the case of typical perfect adverbials this was
done because these were precisely the contexts of variable use that we were
interested in. But even past-denoting adverbs like *yesterday* and *ago* do not
categorically require a past tense VP, as examples (5)-(7) illustrate.

(5)   I am told he has had another execution in the house yesterday (Sheridan,
        School for Scandal, I.1; quoted from Meyer, 1995: 226)
(6)   There have been more deaths in Northern Ireland yesterday (radio news;
        [R. Huddleston, *Introduction to the Grammar of English*, Cambridge:
        CUP, 1984: 159]; quoted from Meyer, 1995:226)
(7)   Sanctions have been imposed by the UN thirteen years ago. (Radio New
        Zealand news, 12/79; quoted from Bauer, 1989)

Finally, we investigated the co-occurrence of the present perfect or past tense
with certain temporal adverbials, namely *already, just* and *yet*. In this case, the
data were retrieved from the complete SPEAC. Ambiguous examples, for
instance where *just* could also be taken to mean 'simply', were excluded from the
counts.[16]

3.3   Results

The results of the Mossé coefficient (present perfect VPs per 10,000 words) for
the seven sub-corpora are given in figure 1a. This coefficient, as we said,
measures the general perfective-friendliness of the texts. The data from the
SPEAC-1 do not confirm the first part of our first hypothesis – the overall
frequency of the present perfect is not higher in BrE than in AmE.[17] We do not
see a split between more American varieties (such as PhilE) and more British
varieties (like FE and SingE), either. Instead, the data show a split between inner
circle varieties and outer circle varieties as far as the overall frequency of the
present perfect is concerned. Of the inner circle varieties, the texts from New
Zealand surprisingly show the highest use of the present perfect, while the
Australian sub-corpus has the lowest number of present perfect VPs. The results
from the AmE and BrE newspapers are very similar. The least present-perfect

friendly variety in our corpus is FE, followed by PhilE and SingE, but they all cluster around a frequency of 50 present perfect VPs per 10,000 words.

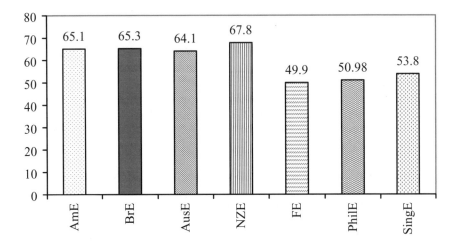

Figure 1a: Present perfect VPs in the SPEAC-1 (relative frequency per 10,000 words)[18]

To test for the possible skewing effect that the inclusion of material based on international press releases may have on the data, we also obtained the Mossé coefficient for our second sub-corpus (the SPEAC-2), represented in figure 1b. Surprisingly, once the press-release material from international agencies is screened out, the results still do not confirm our hypothesis that the overall frequency of the present perfect is higher in BrE than in AmE. The fact that the New Zealand and Australian newspapers now yield relative frequencies that position the two varieties on an equal level are intuitively more plausible than the results we obtained from our SPEAC-1. As far as the relation between inner and outer circle varieties is concerned, however, we still do not see a split between more American varieties on the one hand and more British varieties on the other hand. In other words, the SPEAC-2 also shows a split between inner circle varieties and outer circle varieties, albeit with a different ordering of the outer circle varieties. Somewhat unexpected, however, is the fact that the relative frequency of perfect constructions in the Philippine newspaper is very low and that, as a result, the outer circle varieties form a less homogeneous group in the SPEAC-2 than they do in our first sub-corpus.

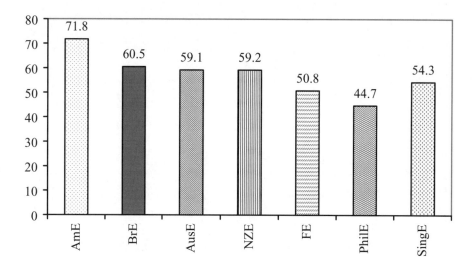

Figure 1b: Present perfect VPs in the SPEAC-2 (relative frequency per 10,000 words)[19]

The surprising result that AmE is the most prefect-friendly variety in this Mossé diagram goes against previous research (cf. Meyer (1995)), which was based on larger and more varied but also older text collections. This suggests that our makeshift corpus from the internet may be too small to use the Mossé index. On the other hand, textual genre or diachronic change will have to be considered as possible explanatory variables.

That the outer circle varieties emerge as less present-perfect friendly than the inner circle varieties in both SPEAC-1 and SPEAC-2 and that they further-more show no imminent connection with the inner circle varieties seems to present a relatively stable result. This might have to be attributed to substrate influence from the indigenous languages. Further studies on the use of the present perfect in inner and outer circle varieties using Mossé are needed to validate this result. But the results might also have to be attributed to the way the variable was defined. Let us therefore turn to the alternative methodological approach we outlined above.

The results that we obtained for the analysis of potential equivalents (i.e. past vs. present perfect VPs) on the basis of the SPEAC-1 are given in figure 2a. Note that the bars in this figure have been arranged in order of frequency.

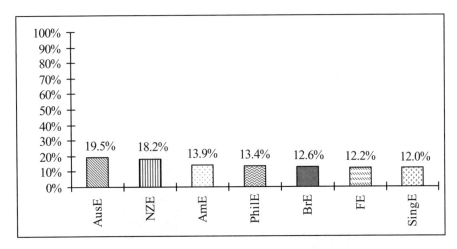

Figure 2a: Relative frequency of present perfect VPs as potential equivalents of past tense VPs in the SPEAC-1[20]

The findings from our first sub-corpus suggest that AusE and NZE might be the most conservative varieties – the relative frequency of present perfect VPs in the two southern-hemisphere inner circle varieties is higher than in both BrE and AmE, a result that seems to contradict our findings in the SPEAC-2. Furthermore, it comes as a bit of a surprise that AmE shows a slightly higher relative frequency of present perfect VPs even than BrE. As far as the relation of inner and outer circle varieties is concerned, we find that PhilE patterns like AmE, whereas both FE and SingE resemble BrE in their distribution of present perfect and past tense VPs. In other words, the data on this variable from the SPEAC-1 do not indicate that the two southern-hemisphere inner circle varieties are a centre of radiating influence for South Pacific and East Asian outer circle varieties like PhilE, FE and SingE. Again, however, we may question whether the results from the SPEAC-1 might have been skewed by the inclusion of material from international press agencies. Figure 2b provides the results for the same variable from the SPEAC-2.

In some respect, the results from our second sub-corpus again appear to be more intuitively plausible: the American newspaper texts in the SPEAC-2 yield a lower percentage of present perfect VPs than the British paper. It is also plausible that SingE should closely resemble BrE. But the relative frequencies of present perfect VPs in the SPEAC-2 still present some puzzles, namely that firstly, AusE and NZE are no longer grouped together and that secondly, SingE is now no longer the most innovative variety but ends up at the 'conservative' end of the ranking order, next to AusE. The solution to these puzzles is to be found in the method of data retrieval.

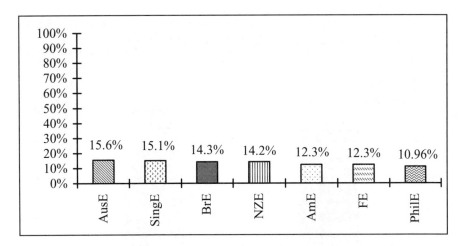

Figure 2b: Relative frequency of present perfect VPs as potential equivalents of past tense VPs in the SPEAC-2[21]

Recall that we manually counted all past tense VPs in a small sub-set of texts and then extrapolated the figures to the size of our sub-corpora. Extrapolation from small data sets, however, runs the risk of exaggerating skewing effects. At the same time, manual data retrieval has the advantage that it leaves the analyst with a good 'feel' of the sampled texts. We therefore suspected that individual texts differed quite markedly in their use of past tense VPs. This was actually the case: the frequency of preterite forms turned out to depend, among other things, on the topic of the respective text but also on whether the author felt the need to provide the reader with some background knowledge on previous events. Two randomly chosen days from the Fiji subcorpus of SPEAC-2 (the 9th of December and the 19th of November) yield 157 and 131 preterite forms, respectively, i.e. a difference of only 26 instances. The extrapolation of these numbers to the size of SPEAC-2 results in an estimation of 4,126 and 3,206 preterite forms, respectively, i.e. a difference of almost 1,000 occurrences of the variable. This clearly shows that skewing effects from individual texts are magnified through extrapolation, leaving us with a distorted picture of the whole situation. Extrapolation of manually retrieved data from small samples thus appears to produce fairly unreliable results. Let us therefore turn to the third definition of the variable, the co-occurrence of the present perfect and the preterite with temporal adverbials.

The search for co-occurrence patterns with temporal adverbials in our corpus (SPEAC-1 and SPEAC-2) produced rather different results for *already*, *yet* and *just*, as table 1 shows:

Table 1:   Co-occurrence of present perfect vs. preterite with *already*, *yet* and *just*[22]

	already	*yet*	*just*
NY Times (AmE)	25:6	7:2	7:1
Guardian (BrE)	28:7	11:1	12:1
SM Herald (AusE)	29:9	7:2	10:4
NZ Herald (NZE)	15:5	6:2	4:1
Fiji Times (FE)	24:2	3:0	9:2
Manila Times (PhilE)	25:14	4:1	6:4
SStraits Times (SingE)	29:1	8:2	4:2

With *already*, it would seem as if the colloquial preterite was an occasional variant in all varieties of English in our corpus. On closer inspection, however, nearly all the instances occur in contexts (like reported speech) that regularly require the past tense, i.e. they are variants of the past rather than the present perfect, as the following examples show:

(8)   Islanders already were fearing the murder could further dent the holiday destination's reputation, he said. (SPEAC-1, 07-19-lead-AusE)
(9)   [...] Trinh claimed the two women were already dead when they were thrown into the river. (SPEAC-1, 08-03-lead-AusE)
(10)   [...] those who were already young adults in 1989 and had a deep impression of the man and his work. (SPEAC-1, 02-08-ed-BrE)

There are only very few examples that are instances of the 'colloquial' preterite with *already*, which often co-occur in first-person pronouns:

(11)   We already did 6.4 [for the first quarter] and expect to grow more than 5 percent this second quarter, Neri said. (SPEAC-1, 08-09-lead-PhilE)
(12)   But then, I guess George W. already proved that. (SPEAC-1, 07-30-ed-NZE)
(13)   Either somebody 'choped' it already because there really is another film called The Woods this year, or Tiger said, 'Sorry, I want it for my golf movie'. (SPEAC-1, 08-06-ed-SingE)

The concordances also produce instances where the present perfect is used in a clear past-tense context.

(14)   We have stated our fears six years ago [...]. (SPEAC, 01-17-ed-PhilE)
(15)   We have run out of antibiotics like Cloxacillin months ago. (SPEAC-1, 08-04-lead-FE)[23]

Remember that *ago* also occasionally combines with the present perfect in NZE (see example 7). The constructions in (14) and (15) may receive further encouragement from instances of reported speech without back shifting, which are attested in the inner circle varieties:

(16)   Many an eyebrow will be raised at a report yesterday that the Government has quietly bailed out, for the second time, a Northland forestry venture that no bank will touch. (SPEAC-1, 07-21-ed-NZE)

(17)   Meanwhile the World Food Programme (WFP) said yesterday that it has begun using specialised all-terrain trucks to get food to Darfur [...]. (SPEAC-1, 07-29-lead-NZE)

(18)   The water companies, complaining yesterday that the Ofwat regulator has only allowed average price increases of 13% over the next five years [...]. (SPEAC -1, 08-06-ed-BrE)

The question therefore remains whether examples (14) and (15) have to be interpreted as instances of 'incorrect' learner English, whether we might count them as evidence of a newly emergent epicentre in the Pacific and East Asia, or whether it is simply an aspect of ongoing language change. On the basis of more systematially collected evidence, Sand (2005: 105-107) argues that the usage patterns in the contact varieties she studied is different from that found in New Zealand English:

> While the examples from ICE-NZ describes a resultant state (charges against a suspected murderer), most of the examples from the contact varieties simply describe events that took place the day before, such as an athlete's performance or a fishing excursion.
>
> (ibid.: 107)

Table 1 shows that *yet* and *just* collocate more strongly with the perfect than with the past tense in all varieties. Interestingly, the preterite is used more often with *just* in AusE and PhilE than in AmE. But again, on closer inspection, most of these are not occurrences of the 'colloquial' preterite:

(19)   [He] was just leaving the church after attending the Mass when his bodyguard [...] suddenly shot and killed him [...]. (SPEAC-2, 01-17-lead-PhilE)

(20)   "I wasn't even aware of what I just said," he said. (SPEAC-2, 02-01-lead-AusE)

(21)   Six fire engines were expected to bring the blaze under control quickly and no injuries had been reported, he said. The cause of the fire was not yet known. (SPEAC-1,08-06-lead-AusE)

But there are also occasional instances of the 'colloquial' preterite with *just*, often in instances of quotations of direct speech:

(22)   "I am being released. It is a surprise. They just came to get me now. I am a free man." (SPEAC-2, 02-02-lead-BrE)

(23)   "This group just returned from Samoa." Mr Cai said the teams were on a trip to foster goodwill. (SPEAC-1, 08-18-lead-FE)

(24)   "They said, 'It took China more than 20 years. We need more time. We just started,'" Mr. Shim said. (SPEAC-1, 08-20-lead-AmE)

There is no evidence in our data that *yet* is used with the colloquial preterite. Note, moreover, that the fairly low number of occurrences, especially with *yet* and *just*, make it very difficult to draw any definite conclusions, especially with respect to regional variation.

3.4   Discussion

It appears that the different ways in which we defined our variable reflect slightly different aspects on the use of the present perfect and past in the inner and outer circle varieties we investigated: the Mossé coefficient which measures the overall perfective-friendliness of the texts shows that, at the least conscious level of grammatical variation, the outer circle varieties appear to be subject to a strong element of substrate influence (nativization) or patterns that could be described in terms of 'naturalness' if the mother-tongue usage were to be taken as the yard-stick of comparison. Interestingly, the newspapers in the more carefully compiled SPEAC-2 also yield overall lower frequencies for the outer circle varieties. However, larger and more varied corpora (e.g. of the ICE-type) are required to use the Mossé index for this kind of study (cf. also discussion in Biewer (forthcoming)). The question remains whether the Mossé index is a suitable measure for this kind of study, in the first place. The problem with this definition of the variable is that it measures the frequency of one construction in relation to corpus size and does not relate its use to other (competing) constructions. Biewer (forthcoming) shows that the investigation of the present perfect : preterite-ratio for frequent verbs in a corpus produces more promising results.

The second definition of the variable in terms of relative frequency of present perfect and past tense VPs did not provide reliable results. Our method of extrapolating the results of small-scale manual analysis to the size of our sub-corpora turned out to be subject to skewing effects in the data sets. This approach to the definition of the variable can only be fruitfully explored on the basis of tagged corpora that allow for an efficient retrieval of all preterite verb forms.

The question is whether the third variable – lexico-grammatical variation of temporal adverbials in their preference for either perfect or past – is likely to give us reliable information on regional variation and change. The use of the past with adverbials like *already* has also been referred to as the 'colloquial' preterite. Our results are therefore more likely to reflect house-styles or, at best, regional differences in the willingness to adopt colloquial patterns in written language use.

4.   Conclusion

The results we obtained from our SPEAC could be referred to as the lottery effect in corpus linguistics. Our case-study was not a ticket to win us a prize – it did not confirm the hypothesis of a growing influence of NZE and AusE in the Southern hemisphere. But this does not mean that the hypothesis will turn out to be wrong. We need to collect data on a large number of grammatical and lexico-grammatical variables and piece them together in a big jig-saw puzzle. Only the completed picture or at least a large part of the puzzle will tell us the whole story. All we have done in our pilot study is to provide the first small piece. What this small piece suggests is

a)   that some usage patterns will be examples of traditional, exo-normative orientation, (i.e. BrE for SingE, AmE for PhilE), i.e. the relative ranking of the outer circle varieties

b)   that others will have to be attributed to nativization, i.e. patterns that might eventually be adopted as endo-normative rules (for instance the overall low frequency of the perfect in our case),

c)   and yet others may be examples of a new, regional exo-normative orientation towards AusE and NZE. An example of the latter type of 'radiating influence' might be that PhilE and FE – just like NZE – occasionally use the present perfect in traditional past tense contexts.

These different and competing norms will "manifest themselves patchily" – to use Leech's (2004: 75) words – they are unlikely to produce a clear overall trend pointing in a single direction. First and foremost, we need to collect data on a large number of grammatical and lexico-grammatical variables and piece them together.

With respect to the methodological issue at hand, we might ask whether the points we took care of in manually compiling our make-shift corpus from the web could and should be considered in an automatic retrieval of data from the web. The exclusion of material based on international news agency releases, for instance, produced – at least to some extent – intuitively more plausible results for the Mossé coefficients, for instance. Automatic data retrieval, however, seems to be the only solution to the compilation of large corpora that are necessary for the study of lexico-grammatical phenomena. In automatic data retrieval, the exclusion of press agency material is possible as long as it is openly (and systematically) flagged (for instance through the use of abbreviations such as dpa).[24]

Notes

1   The acronym stands for '*S*outh *P*acific and *E*ast *A*sian'-Corpus (SPEAC).

2   The term is adopted from Kachru (1986).

3   The terms are borrowed from Clyne (1995).

4   The term 'epicentre' is adopted from Leitner (1992) .

5   Our selection was partly based on the free availability of the respective papers. Some newspapers charge for the download, which is why we did not include *The London Times*, for instance. Obviously, the papers differ quite markedly in terms of their distribution and readership (see table 1 in the appendix).

6   Especially in the Pacific region, commercially interesting domain names such as '.tv' (Tuvalu), '.fm' (Federation of Melanesia) or '.vu' (Vanuatu) are quite common. The governments of countries with such domain names often charge money for the use of the name (cf. Neales, 2000). See also Mukherjee and Hoffmann (2006).

7   Whenever larger chunks of sentences or text occurred in more than one of our regional sub-corpora, it was obvious that they must originate in a press agency release. In the compilation of our second sample (SPEAC-2) we therefore preferably selected articles with the author's name to avoid this problem.

8   Vanneck (1958) claims that the use of the past tense in perfective contexts (i.e. with certain temporal adverbials) is a new development. Among the factors that might have contributed to the development of the 'colloquial preterite' in AmE, he mentions Irish English and interference phenomena in the speech of immigrants with mother languages other than English (ibid., p. 241). The most detailed longitudinal corpus-based study on the development of the present perfect / preterite opposition is Elsness (1997).

9   Biber et al. (1999: 463) found that the BrE preference for the perfect was more pronounced in news than in other registers. They suggest that "[i]t might be relevant that American newspapers are renowned for a space-saving drive towards stylistic economy, and that the simple past usually requires one less word than the perfect." Note, however, that their frequency data on the overall difference between BrE and AmE is based on both present and past perfect constructions. They also point out that the colloquial preterite "does not seriously affect the frequencies in conversation" (ibid.).

10   Hundt (1998) only looks at the co-occurrence of the perfect and preterite with a small number of temporal adverbials in BrE, AmE and NZE.

11   It has to be pointed out that the Fijian aspect markers *sā* and *se* have no direct equivalent in English. Whereas *sā* denotes a change from a previous

stage, *se* is used for a previous but continuing state that may possibly end in the future. *Sā/se vuli na luvequ* could both be translated by *My child is at school.* The first version has the additional meaning that she has just gone to school, whereas the second implies that she has been at school for a while and will come home soon. In other words, the English translation does not require a present perfect. The additional meaning transported by *sā/se* can be rendered in English by adverbials of time such as *now* and *still* (cf. Schütz 1985, Geraghty 1994; the examples are taken from Geraghty 1994).

12   For Mandarin Chinese, cf. Comrie (1976) and for Tagalog, cf. Schachter (1991).

13   The examples are taken from Alsagoff and Lick (1998).

14   An alternative approach taken by Meyer (1995: 206), namely to calculate the ratio of non-modal present perfect VPs per sentence, is only possible with tagged corpora.

15   Biber et al. (1999: 466) include *have got* among the perfect forms, but we would like to argue that *I have got a problem* and *I have had a problem* should not be treated as equivalents since they have completely different aspectual meanings.

16   Sand (2005: 98) defined the variable use of present perfect and past tense differently, again, considering only forms of the verb *to be.* This approach did not yield any quantifiable differences in the contact varieties of English she studied. She also concedes, however, that the irregularity of the verb might have led to masking differences between the varieties (ibid.: 99). In addition, she also used the Mossé coefficient (ibid.: 102ff.).

17   Unlike AmE, however, BrE appears to have a more pronounced preference for the present perfect in editorials (75.8 per 10,000 words) than in leading articles (54.2 per 10,000 words) in our data. Similar text-type-based preference patterns as in BrE can be found in the Australian, Fijian and Singaporean newspapers; in the New Zealand and Philippine data, they are almost negligible.

18   For absolute frequencies, see table 2a in the appendix.

19   For absolute frequencies, see table 2b in the appendix.

20   For absolute frequencies, see table 3a in the appendix.

21   For absolute frequencies, see table 3b in the appendix.

22   Sand (2005: 108-110) also looked at the co-occurrence of present perfect and past (among others) and the temporal adverbial *since.* Even though

she notes a slightly more frequent use of past tense VPs with this adverbial, she does not discuss qualitative evidence. It is therefore not clear what the proportions of colloquial preterites with this adverbial are in her data.

23   Note that in Indian English, present perfect is also used with past tense adverbials like *yesterday* (cf. Sand 2005: 94) and that this might be another source of influence for English in Fiji, where 44% of the population is of Indian origin.

24   For problems and challenges of automatic data retrieval from archives, see Hoffmann, this volume.

References

Algeo, J. (1991), 'A meditation on the varieties of English', *English Today*, 27: 3-6.

Alsagoff, L. and C.L. Ho (1998), 'The grammar of Singapore English', in: J.A. Foley (ed.) *English in New Cultural Contexts. Reflections from Singapore*. Singapore: Oxford University Press. 127-151.

Bailey, R.W. (1990), 'English at its twilight', in: C. and L.M. Ricks (eds.) *The State of the Language*. London: Faber and Faber. 83-94.

Bao, Z.M. (1995), 'Already in Singapore English', *World Englishes*, 14: 181-188.

Bauer, L. (1989), 'The verb *have* in New Zealand English', *English World-Wide*, 10: 69-83.

Bauer, L. (1994), *Watching English Change. An Introduction to the Study of Linguistic Change in Standard Englishes in the Twentieth Century*. London and New York: Longman.

Biber, D., S. Johansson, G. Leech, S. Conrad and E. Finegan (1999), *Longman Grammar of Spoken and Written English*. Harlow: Longman.

Biewer, C. (forthcoming), 'South Pacific Englishes - unity and diversity.' *Papers from the 27th International Conference on English Language Research on Computerized Corpora (ICAME-27)*, Helsinki 2006.

Clyne, M. (ed.) (1992), *Pluricentric Languages. Differing Norms in Different Nations*. Berlin and New York: de Gruyter.

Clyne, M. (1995), *The German Language in a Changing Europe*. Cambridge: Cambridge University Press.

Comrie, B. (1976), *Aspect: An Introduction to the Study of Verbal Aspect and Related Problems*. Cambridge: Cambridge University Press.

Elsness, J. (1997), *The Perfect and the Preterite in Contemporary and Earlier English*. Berlin and New York: de Gruyter.

Geraghty, P. (1994), *Lonely Planet Phrasebooks: Fijian*. Footscray, Victoria: Lonely Planet Publications.

Görlach, M. (1987), 'Colonial lag? The alleged conservative character of American English and other "colonial" varieties', *English World-Wide*, 8: 41-60.

Greenbaum, S. (1990), 'Whose English?' In C. Ricks and L. Michaels (eds.), *The State of the Language*. London: Faber and Faber. 15-23.

Hoffmann, S. (this volume), 'From webpage to mega-corpus: the CNN transcripts'.

Hundt, M. (1998), *New Zealand English Grammar. Fact or Fiction?* Amsterdam and Philadelphia: Benjamins.

Kachru, B.B. (1986), 'The power and politics of English', *World Englishes*, 5: 121-140.

Kahane, H. (1982), 'American English: From a colonial substandard to a prestige language', in: B.B. Kachru (ed.) *The Other Tongue: English Across Cultures*. Urbana: University of Illinois Press. 229-236.

Leech, G. (2004), 'Recent grammatical change in English: data, description, theory', in: K. Aijmer and B. Altenberg (eds.) *Advances in Corpus Linguistics. Papers from the 23rd International Conference on English Language Research on Computerized Corpora (ICAME 23)*. Göteborg 22-26 May 2002.

Leitner, G. (1992), 'English as a pluricentric language', in: M. Clyne (ed.) *Pluricentric Languages. Differing Norms in Different Nations*. Berlin and New York: de Gruyter. 179-237.

Meyer, M. (1995). 'Past tense and present perfect in the Brown and the LOB corpora', in: W. Riehle and H. Keiper (eds.) *Anglistentag 1994 Graz. Proceedings*. Tübingen: Niemeyer. 201-228.

Mukherjee, J. and S. Hoffmann (2006). 'Describing verb-complementational profiles of New Englishes: a pilot study of Indian English', to appear in *English World-Wide*, 27 (2): 147-173.

Neales, S. (2000), 'Internet: Kapitale Beute im Netz.' *Geo Spezial 'Südsee'*, April/Mai: 40-1.

Platt, J.T. and H. Weber (1980), *English in Singapore and Malaysia: Status, Features, Functions*. Kuala Lumpur: Oxford University Press.

Quirk, R., S. Greenbaum, G. Leech and J. Svartvik (1985), *A Comprehensive Grammar of the English Language*. London: Longman.

Sand, A. (2005) *Angloversals? Shared Morpho-Syntactic Features in Contact Varieties of English*. Habilitationsschrift. Freiburg im Breisgau.

Schachter, P. (1991), 'Tagalog', in: B. Comrie (ed.) *The World's Major Languages*. London: Routledge. 936-958.

Schütz, A. J. (1985), *The Fijian Language*. Honolulu: University of Hawaii Press.

Tottie, G. (2001), 'Non-categorical differences between American and British English: some corpus evidence', in: M. Modiano (ed.) *Proceedings from the Conference on Mid-Atlantic English*. Gävle: Gävle University College Press. 37-58.

Tottie, G. (2002), *An Introduction to American English*. Oxford: Blackwell.

Vanneck, G. (1958), 'The colloquial preterite in modern American English', *Word*, 14: 237-242.

On-line Sources

NY Times	www.nytimes.com
Guardian	www.guardian.co.uk
SM Herald	www.smh.com.au
NZ Herald	www.nzherald.co.nz
Fiji Times	www.fijitimes.com.fj
Manila Times	www.manilatimes.net
SStraits Times	straitstimes.asia1.com.sg

Appendix

Table 1:   Daily circulation of newspapers (print version)

	average copies per day	average daily readership
NY Times	1,100,000	no information available
Guardian	378,199	1,095,000
SM Herald	221,000	882,000
NZ Herald	213,334	603,000
Fiji Times	27,124	no information available
Manila Times	no information available	no information available
SStraits Times	384,597	1,230,000

Table 2a: Present perfect VPs in the SPEAC-1 (relative frequency per 10,000 words)

	# pres. perf.	# words	Mossé
NY Times (AmE)	790	121,289	65.134
Guardian (BrE)	720	110,276	65.291
SM Herald (AusE)	649	101,221	64.117
NZ Herald (NZE)	718	105,962	67.760
Fiji Times (FE)	476	95,362	49.915
Manila Times (PhilE)	554	108,675	50.978
SStraits Times (SingE)	560	104,074	53.808

Table 2b: Present perfect VPs in the SPEAC-2 (relative frequency per 10,000 words)

	# pres. perf.	# words	Mossé
NY Times (AmE)	813	113,252	71.787
Guardian (BrE)	677	111,823	60.542
SM Herald (AusE)	646	109,252	59.129
NZ Herald (NZE)	639	107,853	59.247
Fiji Times (FE)	515	101,364	50.807
Manila Times (PhilE)	514	114,961	44.711
SStraits Times (SingE)	597	109,866	54.338

Table 3a: Present perfect vs. past (potential equivalents) in the SPEAC-1 – based on extra-polated frequencies of past tense VPs

	# past tense	# pres. perf.	total	past : pres. perf.
NY Times (AmE)	4883 (86.1%)	790 (13,9%)	5673	6.181 : 1
Guardian (BrE)	4985 (87.4%)	720 (12.6%)	5705	6.924 : 1
SM Herald (AusE)	2687 (80.5%)	649 (19.5%)	3336	4.14 : 1
NZ Herald (NZE)	3228 (81.8%)	718 (18.2%)	3946	4.496 : 1
Fiji Times (FE)	3440 (87.8%)	476 (12.2%)	3916	7.227 : 1
Manila Times (PhilE)	3575 (86.6%)	554 (13.4%)	4129	6.453 : 1
SStraits Times (SingE)	4101 (88.0%)	560 (12.0%)	4661	7.323 : 1

Table 3b: Present perfect vs. past (potential equivalents) in the SPEAC-2 – based on extra-polated frequencies of past tense VPs

	# past tense	# pres. perf.	total	past : pres. perf.
NY Times (AmE)	4650 (87.67 %)	654 (12.33 %)	5304	7.11 : 1
Guardian (BrE)	4058 (85.7 %)	677 (14.3 %)	4735	5.994 : 1
SM Herald (AusE)	3487 (84.37 %)	646 (15.63 %)	4133	5.398 : 1
NZ Herald (NZE)	3859 (85.79 %)	639 (14.21 %)	4498	6.039 : 1
Fiji Times (FE)	3663 (87.67 %)	515 (12.33 %)	4178	7.113 : 1
Manila Times (PhilE)	4177 (89.04 %)	514 (10.96 %)	4691	8.126 : 1
SStraits Times (SingE)	3364 (84.93 %)	597 (15.07 %)	3961	5.635 : 1

'He rung the bell' and 'she drunk ale' – non-standard past tense forms in traditional British dialects and on the internet

Lieselotte Anderwald

University of Freiburg

Abstract

On the basis of data from the new Freiburg English Dialect Corpus (FRED) and data from the internet, this paper investigates the use of non-standard past tense forms for a group of verbs similar in shape to (and including) drink *and* ring. *In traditional dialect data from across Great Britain, non-standard past tense forms are highly frequent for these verbs and often even constitute the majority option. Their existence can on the one hand be traced back to historical forms. Investigations of present-day informal language as documented on the internet confirms that these non-standard forms are still in (frequent) use. Historical continuity alone does not, however, explain their extremely frequent occurrence in traditional dialect data, nor their occurrence today. In the framework of natural morphology, I propose abstract analogy as a functional principle that can be seen to work on this class of verbs, increasing overall system congruity (in the sense of Wurzel 1984, 1987) and thus stabilizing the inflectional system(s) of these dialects.*

1. Introduction

This paper is exploratory in character. I will compare new results from a new corpus with even newer data culled from the internet.

Non-standard past tense forms are a well-known feature of non-standard English around the world: Chambers includes levelling of verb paradigms as one of his "vernacular primitives" (Chambers 1995: 242; 2003: 255) or even as a "vernacular universal" (Chambers 2004: 129).[1] While patterns are different for individual verbs or groups of verbs (cf. Anderwald, in progress, for a detailed examination of several verb paradigms; Cheshire 1994 for a possible classification), this paper will concentrate on a subgroup of verbs, verbs like *drink, sing* or *begin*. These verbs form a coherent group and, despite all historical and synchronic variation, are in the majority levelled to a similar variant. This fact has in particular been noted by Bybee (Bybee 1985, 1995; Bybee and Slobin 1982), which is why I would like to provisionally call these verbs "Bybee verbs".

2. Bybee verbs

In a series of articles, Joan Bybee and co-writers have expanded the notion that in the English past tense system, there seems to be a semi-productive strong verb paradigm which can still attract new members – this is the pattern *string – strung – strung*. This newly productive pattern has been growing since Middle English; it is structured in terms of family resemblances (each member resembling the central, prototypical member *string – strung* more or less) and contains the following fourteen simplex verbs (in alphabetical order): *cling – clung – clung, dig – dug – dug, fling – flung – flung, hang – hung – hung, sling – slung – slung, slink – slunk – slunk, spin – spun – spun, stick – stuck – stuck, sting – stung – stung, strike – struck – struck, string – strung – strung, swing – swung – swung, win – won – won,* and *wring – wrung – wrung.*[2]

These verbs have in common that they form their past tense as well as their past participle with <u>, prototypically pronounced /ʌ/ in the South of England and /ʊ/ in the North.[3] The complete template for the past tense forms is given in (1):[4]

(1)   [C (C) (C) ʌ velar / nasal]$_{past}$

These Bybee verbs have attracted a number of different verbs historically; of the list above, six verbs did either not exist in Old English, or were conjugated differently: *dig, fling, hang, stick, strike* and *string. Strike* for example was an Old English class I verb which switched verb classes during Middle English; *dig, fling* and *string* only entered the English language in Middle English times and became strong – unusual for loan words; *hang* goes back – among other things – to an Old English weak verb that became strong between the thirteenth and fifteenth centuries, and *stick* was also an Old English weak verb (for individual histories cf. the *OED*: s.v. *dig, fling, hang, stick, strike, string*). These Bybee verbs thus acted as a powerful attractor already in earlier times.

Today, this influence is still visible in the non-standard systems, where the Bybee verbs attract another complete group of verbs, verbs like *drink – drank – drunk*. These verbs constitute a (sub)class of verbs that used to belong to the same Old English class III as *string – strung – strung* etc. This group of verbs is slightly smaller than the first group mentioned above and today contains these nine verbs in Standard English: *begin – began – begun, drink – drank – drunk, ring – rang – rung, shrink – shrank – shrunk, sing – sang – sung, sink –sank – sunk, spring – sprang – sprung, stink – stank – stunk* and *swim – swam – swum.*

3.   History

The Old English verb class IIIa is characterized by the fact that verbs had quite different preterite stems, which seems to have been responsible for their different historical development as well as century-long variation: the preterite I stem (i.e. used for singular past tense forms) was generally formed with <a>, whereas the preterite II stem (used for the plural past tense forms and in these verbs identical to the vowel found in the participle) was formed with <u>. A typical Old English paradigm for these verbs is exemplified by *drink* in (2).

(2)   drincan – dranc, druncon – druncen

During Middle English, when inflectional endings were progressively lost, the difference between past tense singular and past tense plural forms became increasingly obscured and as a consequence, past tense forms for these verbs became variable between <a> and <u>. In the North, typically the singular stem was chosen as the past tense marker (Wyld coined the term "Northern preterite" for this phenomenon, cf. Wyld 1927: 268). Görlach also notes this kind of levelling for Scots: "in some contrast to English, Scots almost invariably chose the former singular as the base form for the preterite - where there was a choice" (Görlach 1996: 168-169). In the West, on the other hand, the "Western preterite" used the past participle vowel to level the past tense paradigm (Wyld 1927: 268); according to Lass, "this begins to appear as a minority variant in the fourteenth century, and stabilizes for many verbs only in the period EB3 [i.e. 1640-1710] and later" (Lass 1994: 88).

Although Wyld claims that "the dialects of the S[ou]th and Midlands preserve, on the whole, the distinction between the Singular and Plural of the Pret[erite], where this existed in O.E., with fair completeness during the whole M.E. and into the Modern Period" (Wyld 1927: 268-269), both patterns seem to have spread geographically across the country, and were either dominant in different verbs, or indeed in direct competition. With standardization and concomitant codification of verb paradigms in Early Modern English, the former coherent verb class IIIa was thus essentially split between those verbs displaying the Western preterite (our first group of verbs, or Bybee verbs proper, e.g. *string – strung – strung*) and those following the Northern preterite pattern, resulting in a three-part paradigm today (*drink – drank – drunk*).

Considering this long-standing variation, it is perhaps not surprising to find that even today in non-standard dialects, these three-part verbs (e.g. StE *drink – drank – drunk*) show a very strong trend towards merging with two-part verbs, substituting the StE past tense *drank* by *drunk*. This results in a partially levelled paradigm *drink – **drunk** – drunk*, as noted by Bybee herself. In addition, Bybee verbs seem to be the only possible target group for the otherwise extremely unlikely pattern of weak verbs switching into the strong verb class (documented particularly for American English). The two new strong verbs documented in the dialectological literature, *sneak – snuck* and *drag – drug*, follow this same past tense pattern (cf. Hogg 1998; Murray 1998).

4.   Bybee verbs in FRED

4.1   FRED

The Freiburg English Dialect Corpus (FRED) was compiled at the University of Freiburg under the direction of Bernd Kortmann between 1999 and 2005. It sets out to document traditional dialect data from across Great Britain in order to make possible – for the first time – quantitative comparisons across dialects. At the time of writing, FRED comprises over 2.4 million words (excluding interviewers' utterances) from all the major British dialect regions.[5] FRED is transcribed orthographically and is available in machine-readable format so that automatic searches with the usual text retrieval tools are possible. In particular, all searches conducted for this paper were executed with the help of WordSmith. It is clear, however, that even in a large corpus like FRED, not all of the verbs mentioned above will appear equally frequently. Only the five most frequent ones are therefore investigated in detail here. They are (in order of descending frequency): *begin, sing, drink, ring,* and *sink.*

4.2   The investigation

For the investigation, all instances of past tense forms of the five verbs *begin, sing, drink, ring,* and *sink* were collected from all dialect areas. They were classified as being standard or non-standard (*began* vs. *begun*), and whether they had a singular or plural referent (*I begun* vs. *we begun*). (All instances of the participle as well as – some few – unclear instances are excluded in the following discussion.) Some examples are provided in (3) to (7) (emphasis added).

(3)   We used to work long hours haying time, work at night till it *begun* to get dark, and that, and the hay *begun* to get dark with the dew. (FRED KEN 011) (Kent, South East)

(4)   I heard a Gospel group singing. They *sung* The Rugged Cross, and they *sung* some more, more hymns. (FRED LAN 006) (Lancashire, North)

(5)   He never *drunk* much. (FRED CON 001) (Cornwall, South West)

(6)   I *rung* him up and told him. (FRED NTT 003) (Nottinghamshire, Midlands)

(7)   Now the Ocean people had the selling rights of that pit see, and the Powell Duffryn *sunk* it see, that is what happened. (FRED GLA 002) (Glamorgan, Wales)

Table 1:   "New" Bybee verbs in FRED

	nStE	StE	sum	% of nSt forms
sink	24	14	38	63.2
drink	18	18	36	52.6
sing	15	15	30	50.0
ring	13	16	29	44.8
begin	6	13	19	31.6
Total	76	76	152	$\varnothing$ 50.0

In contrast to many other verbs, which only appear rather sporadically in non-standard forms, these new Bybee verbs are surprisingly frequent in their non-standard forms, as table 1 indicates. Figures from FRED show that these non-standard forms are in fact used in around or over 50 per cent of all cases; this means they are in many cases the dominant option for these verbs for speakers of traditional British dialects.

4.3   Functional motivation

The functional motivation that offers itself when one looks at these verbs is analogy. Not only may historical continuity have played an important role in these verb forms – in some speech communities, long-standing variability may simply never have been standardized into the familiar 3-part-paradigm –, but the comparatively large group of fourteen verbs with a past tense vowel <u> even in Standard English (*string – strung – strung* and friends) may serve as an "attractor" for the formally very similar smaller group of nine verbs with a past tense vowel in <a>, as depicted in figure 1 below.

In the framework of natural morphology (Wurzel 1984, 1987), it can be shown that the dominant pattern of English verb paradigms is an identity of past tense and past participle, with a different present-tense form (consider the dominant pattern of weak verbs: *hunt – hunted – hunted*), as schematized in (8).

(8)   PRESENT $\neq$ PAST = PAST PARTICIPLE

While many historically strong verbs have indeed simply become weak since Old English times (cf. Krygier 1994 for a detailed analysis until Early Modern English), in this way stabilizing the inflectional system, a switch into the weak verb class has not happened for verbs like *drink* or *ring*. Instead, as Wurzel points out, inflectional systems can also stabilize if a dominant pattern is taken over, without verbs having to change over into the dominant class completely (Wurzel 1984: 79). In addition, as Bybee stresses, the vowel /ʌ/ has become the marker of 'past tense' in these verbs (Bybee 1985: 130), and this marker has become so stable through various additions to the verb class that it, in turn, confers stability on the verb paradigms themselves. This is the underlying motivating factor that can explain verb paradigm levelling for verbs like *drink – drunk – drunk*: we are dealing with a language-specific "natural" process (in the technical senses of increasing system congruity as well as inflectional class stability, cf. Wurzel 1984, 1987).[6]

Unfortunately, the percentages in table 1 alone cannot tell us whether this feature is still stable today, or whether it might be undergoing further change. Although figures look surprisingly well aligned if one considers the verbs' absolute frequencies (the most frequent verbs also appear in the non-standard forms most frequently), it has to be noted that frequencies overall are comparatively low, and indeed are quite similar. A statistical analysis confirms this impression: none of the differences between these verbs are in fact significant statistically.[7] Much larger amounts of data would be necessary if one wanted to find statistically robust differences between these verbs, in order to determine whether this group of verbs is still stable in its non-standard usage, or whether – despite all pressures from analogy and history – it may in fact be undergoing change towards the more standard forms today. Although FRED is a large corpus, for medium-frequency items like lexical verbs (in the past tense) it is obviously not large enough to warrant detailed hypotheses on lexical differences, or overall frequency relations.

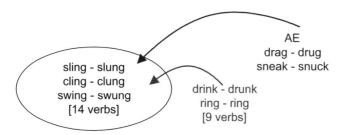

Figure 1:   Stable word class as attractor

5.   Bybee verbs in WebCorp

5.1   Background and search procedure

For exploratory reasons, the internet was chosen as a possible additional data source which is obviously much larger than any carefully compiled corpus so far – a recent estimate in fact speaks of the internet containing perhaps as much as 10 trillion words, a figure unimaginably large for a "corpus".[8] Whether the internet is also a useful source for non-standard data is an interesting question that has to my knowledge not been explored yet. For this reason, in a next step, the candidate verbs were investigated in their occurrence on the internet with the help of the meta tool WebCorp. WebCorp has been developed by Antoinette Renouf and others and is currently hosted by the University of Central England in Birmingham.[9] Treating the internet as a giant corpus, WebCorp allows the analyst to view KWIC concordances for specified search terms. "Piggy-backing" on conventional search machines, WebCorp accesses all matching web sites and displays all matching search terms in (specifiable) context. No doubt because of the size of the web, but perhaps also due to the fact that it is still being developed, WebCorp is comparatively slow – compared, that is, to simple search machines or usual corpus tools. On the other hand, WebCorp in fact accesses hundreds of web pages automatically – a procedure that is so extremely laborious if done "by hand" it is not worth attempting.

In order to make results at least regionally comparable to results from FRED, I decided to restrict my searches to the first order domain '.uk'. It is clear that not all texts produced in the UK actually enter the internet in this domain. However, the reverse is probably also true, and in this case more relevant: in this domain, we can be relatively certain that the huge majority of texts was in fact produced in the UK (although little of course is known of the actual regional provenance).

In order to facilitate searches and especially to make results more manageable, I decided to look only for combinations of a personal pronoun and the respective past tense form. Although this procedure is laborious and time consuming (instead of simply searching for *sung* vs. *sang*, for example, twelve different searches have to be conducted: *I sung, I sang, he sung, he sang, she sung, she sang, we sung, we sang, you sung, you sang, they sung, they sang*), it provides comparatively "clean" results from big corpora where wholesale search procedures are not viable, eliminating in particular <u> forms used as participles (*she has sung; we were drunk*). All remaining mis-hits were excluded manually. These were in particular inverted forms (*were you drunk?*), but also direct quotations, particularly frequent in discussion groups where the reply includes the original message; metalinguistic comments, including for example university web sites on the grammar of non-standard English or language teaching materials with built-in "mistakes" (in particular several pages on learning Welsh kept turning up in the results).[10] A serious restriction of WebCorp that only became apparent after a number of searches will be discussed below.

5.2   Results from WebCorp

Bearing in mind that results for individual verbs only include the combination of a personal pronoun with the verb in question, and are thus not directly comparable to results from FRED above, consider table 2.

Table 2:   Bybee verbs in WebCorp

verb	nStE	StE	sum	% of nSt form
sink	557	876	1,433	38.9
spring	517	824	1,341	38.6
stink	148	335	438	30.6
sing	724	1,753	2,477	29.2
shrink	210	511	721	29.1
ring	274	982	1,256	21.8
drink	270	1,032	1,302	20.7
begin	556	2,356	2,912	19.1
swim	72	1,336	1,408	5.1
Total	3,328	10,005	13,288	∅ 25.0

Table 2 offers some surprises. The first surprise is the extremely high average. It is indeed unexpected that a non-standard feature as noticeable as a past tense for these verbs in <u> should occur, on average, in around 25 per cent of all cases – that is, every fourth past tense form published on the internet (in the domain '.uk'). As nicely as this would complement my argument, these results are not really credible – in the light of the fact that the domain '.uk' includes such respectable institutions as the BBC, government web sites, university sites and similar doyens of Standard English.

Secondly, in table 2 a look at the absolute frequencies could raise an observant researcher's suspicions. Apart from the more frequent *sing* and *begin* and the comparatively rare *shrink* and *stink*, all other verbs occur with practically the same absolute frequency (between 1300 and 1400 occurrences). Judging by published frequency lists, reliable corpus results as well as intuition, this result is not very convincing. For example, in the balanced British National Corpus, (Standard English) past tense forms of these verbs have very different frequency ranks, from *began* at rank 15 (of all past tense forms) and *rang* at rank 138 via *drank* (rank 236), *sang* (rank 262) and *sank* (rank 280) to the rarer *sprang* (rank 408) and *swam* (rank 538).[11] As is clear from this ranking, these past tense verbs do not form clusters around certain frequencies, but are relatively evenly distributed between very high frequencies for *began* and rather rare ones for *swam*.

Thirdly, as mentioned above, many searches accessed exactly 200 web pages, or just under (199 or 198). This is enough to make any corpus linguist suspicious, and a clarifying e-mail in fact confirmed my suspicion that WebCorp searches are being capped. This means that whenever hits from 200 pages were reached, WebCorp automatically stopped accessing further web pages. In this way, WebCorp accesses a maximum of 200 pages (although the number of concordance lines generated from these pages is not restricted). According to one of the developers, this is due to the developmental status of WebCorp at the moment (Andrew Kehoe, UCE, personal communication 14 Jan 2005) and although the limit may be raised in the future, it is not foreseeable that it might be lifted altogether. What are possible ramifications of this capping? Remember that I searched for standard and non-standard past tense forms individually (*she sung* vs. *I sung*, but also *she sung* vs. *she sang*), and also excluded wrong hits manually. In this respect, a capping of actual hits does not distort the ratio of hits to mis-hits. However, when we compare the absolute frequency of, say, a non-standard strategy with a standard one, a capping of access to web pages can be expected to seriously distort results. Imagine a very frequent standard strategy, giving a – hypothetical – return of 900 hits on a total of 900 pages, and a comparatively infrequent non-standard strategy, giving only 100 hits on a total of 100 pages. "Really" the ratio of non-standard to standard verb forms would be 100 / (900+100), i.e. 100 / 1000 or 10 per cent. If, however, results are capped at the 200 mark, we would be given a WebCorp type result of 200 hits for the standard form, but again all 100 hits for the non-standard form. Only the standard form exceeds 200, so only the very frequent strategy is capped. It is clear that a resultant percentage (in our example, 100 / (200+100), i.e. 100 / 300 or 33.3 per cent) is seriously skewed, in favour of the non-standard form. I would suggest that this is exactly what has happened in table 2, resulting in implausibly high frequencies for non-standard strategies on the one hand, and in very similar overall absolute frequencies on the other.

While WebCorp is a wonderful and necessary corpus-linguistic tool, serious frequency analyses even of medium frequency words are thus simply not feasible with it at the moment.

6.   Bybee verbs in Google

To get an impression of the "real" relations of non-standard and standard English verb forms on the internet, I therefore resorted to a rather un-linguistic search tool, the search machine Google[12] (which is, however, increasingly used by linguists for decidedly linguistic aims, cf. several other contributions in the volume, but also the cautioning words *caveat googlator* by Joseph 2004). Searches here are incredibly fast (even large scale searches as a rule take less than a second), but not always suited to linguistic questions (cf. Fletcher, present volume). While the advanced search strategies available in Google go some way to customizing results, manual checking is still necessary in all cases. Again, I restricted all searches to the domain '.uk', and again I only looked for a combination of personal pronouns and the verb form in question. Some typical results are given in (9) to (11) (my emphasis).

(9)   *i drunk* caffeine-free coffee and tea in my 1st pregnancy and normal coffee and tea in my 2nd and 3rd pregnancies. (http://www.babycentre.co.uk/tips/4195.html)

(10)   You're quite welcome about the avatar compliment. It is a picture of you that *you shrunk* down isn't it? (http://www.gorjuss.co.uk/forum/index.php?act=Print&client=printer&f=10 &t=529)

(11)   The audience couldn't get enough of her [Gwyneth Herbert], *she sung* all songs from her new album – Bittersweet & Blue. (http://www.amazon.co.uk/exec/obidos/ASIN/B0002U4EIM/ref=pd_sxp_f/202-5635476-7841441)

Google is of course much less accurate as a corpus retrieval tool than WebCorp in that it typically only gives one instance of the search term per web page, while the WebCorp designers are careful to stress that WebCorp retrieves any and all instances of the search term from the web page accessed. On the other hand, in my case this is not too much of a discrepancy, as most results in WebCorp only amounted to one instance per page anyway. Where they did not, this was usually the result of unwanted repetition, direct quotations in replies, etc.

Another, linguistically more serious problem with Google is that even in the advanced settings, it does not treat clitic '*s* as a separate word, even in the "exact match" mode. While there may be very good – even linguistic – reasons for doing so, it is rather annoying from a practical corpus linguistic point of view: I ended up having to manually exclude dozens of instances of *she's sung* that the choice of the query string *she sung* should have eliminated automatically, as example (12) shows (my emphasis)

(12)   *She's sung* on everything from Talking *Telephone Numbers* to *Jonathon* [sic!] *Ross' Big Big Talent Show* to The Prince Of Wales' 50th birthday party. (http://www.users.globalnet.co.uk/~madeira/charlotte_church.htm)

Apart from these caveats, Google is fast and comparatively reliable and does indicate a certain amount of context for all hits, which for my purposes was almost always adequate, so that I did not have to visit individual sites frequently.

Nevertheless, I resorted to one other simplification. Obviously, it is not feasible, in the light of sometimes thousands of actual hits, to exclude all mis-hits manually from the Google results. A typical strategy in the light of such high numbers of occurrences is the careful analysis of one or several random samples (say, of 100 of 200 hits each) (cf. Krug 2000). However, as I had already manually excluded all mis-hits from the WebCorp data, I decided to use this as my sample study (remember that the ratio of hits to mis-hits is unaffected by the capping of pages accessed, as this is only an "internal" measure inside pages, not across pages or searches). From all Google results, I therefore deducted the ratio of excluded hits that my WebCorp searches had indicated. This is a complicated undertaking and can most emphatically not be recommended as a standard procedure. I only resorted to it because I had already conducted the laborious WebCorp searches without knowledge of the distorting influence of the page capping. In principle, sample counts of hits vs. mis-hits would have been my preferred strategy. However, where I checked the estimated results (based on the rate of WebCorp exclusions) with manual exclusions from Google, results were very accurate. All results from this extended procedure are displayed in table 3.

Table 3:   Bybee verbs in Google

verb	nStE	StE	sum	% nSt form
stink	505	1,024	1,529	33.0
shrink	673	1,557	2,230	30.2
sink	3,299	16,133	19,432	17.0
spring	1,673	22,396	24,069	7.0
sing	6,027	83,712	89,739	6.7
drink	3,854	60,299	64,153	6.0
ring	2,085	69,329	71,414	2.9
begin	2,349	665,225	667,574	0.4
Total	20,465	919,675	940,140	∅ 2.2

Taking into consideration that these figures only mirror the number of pages, not the number of instances on these pages, and are thus not directly comparable to figures from WebCorp above, the distribution (both absolute and relative) of frequencies here is much more plausible. The relatively low overall average of 2.2 per cent non-standard forms is mainly due to the huge absolute numbers of *begin*; as we have seen before, *begin* is a highly frequent verb and in these results from Google, dwarfs all other past tense verbs. Excluding *begin*, the average of non-standard past tense forms rises to about 6.5 per cent.

Let us now look at the relative ordering of these non-standard verb forms. Re-ordering the verbs in terms of their absolute frequencies, we can see a most extraordinary patterning (cf. the last two columns in table 3, which compare absolute and relative frequencies), which is also statistically robust.[13]

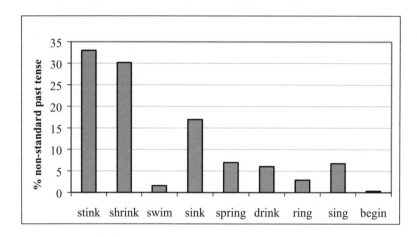

Figure 2:   Bybee verbs in Google

In figure 2, verbs have been ordered in terms of increasing absolute frequency, with the least frequent verb (*stink*) on the left, the most frequent one (*begin*) on the right. The columns indicating the relative frequency of the non-standard past tense (*stunk* or *begun*, respectively) form a neat curve with just two exceptions, namely *swim* and *sing*. Although *sing* is a relatively frequent verb (at almost 90,000 occurrences in Google the second most frequent verb of this group after *begin*), it patterns with the less frequent verbs *drink* and *spring*. While *drink* (around 64,000 occurrences) and *spring* (only around 24,000 occurrences) are clearly used less frequently overall, they are found with a non-standard past tense form with almost identical (relative) frequencies of 7.0% (*spring*), 6.7% (*sing*) and 6.0% (*drink*) respectively. In fact, *sing* is so strikingly more frequent in Google than in the BNC (where it is situated in fact between *drank* and *sprang*) that one might assume that the verb *sing* is perhaps a little over-represented on the internet. Impressionistically, this can be confirmed, as a huge number of web pages is dedicated to pop stars' fan clubs, concert reviews, album presentations etc., and the higher absolute frequency of *sing* might in fact mirror this skewing. There is no simple explanation why *swim* patterns differently, though. It is a relatively infrequent verb and non-standard forms should therefore be relatively frequent. *Swum* is not encountered frequently on the internet, however. Internal analogy might play a role here. Clearly, *swum* is phonologically quite different from the similarly frequent *stunk, shrunk, sunk* or *drunk* as it ends in a simple nasal, not in a combination of a velar nasal and another velar consonant. In fact, it is phonologically most similar to *begun*. Although *begin* is much more frequent in absolute terms, the relative frequencies of *begun* and *swum* on the internet are in fact comparable.

The overall pattern (with the exception of *sing* and *swim*, as discussed above), however, is clear and persuasive: the more frequent a verb is, the less frequently it occurs in a non-standard form. This distribution might hint at on-going standardization which these verbs are subject to. The rather rare verbs *stink* or *shrink* occur very frequently in their non-standard forms *stunk* or *shrunk* (around 33 per cent for *stink*, just over 30 per cent for *shrink*). Possibly, these verbs are so rare that normative pressures are not strong enough (should we say *he shrunk* or *he shrank*? Does *stink* pattern like *drink* or rather like *string*?)[14] to evoke the StE past tense in <a> consistently, and the competing non-standard form has a better chance of surviving in these rarer verbs.

Nevertheless, averages of over 6 per cent (if we exclude *begin*) show that non-standard past tense forms are alive and well in Great Britain today even in a written medium like the internet that mostly adheres to written norms and contains only a minority of texts that can be characterized as being more typical of spoken language. It is these "nearly spoken" texts (in news groups, discussion forums or of course web logs, or "blogs"), however, that are potentially the most interesting, as they approximate unmonitored speech most closely. Collecting huge amounts of authentic data based on these sources might be a promising avenue for investigating informal, unmonitored language use today.

7. Conclusion

This exploratory investigation has shown that a feature of traditional British dialects as pervasive as verb paradigm levelling of the pattern *drink – drunk – drunk* is also found on the internet in the (geographically comparable) first order domain '.uk' today, and is therefore a feature that is still very much a part of present-day non-standard British English. It could be shown that the linguistic retrieval tool WebCorp is still unsuitable for larger-scale quantitative work of certain kinds, due to built-in restrictions that cannot be overcome at the moment. However, WebCorp might be useful for smaller-scale studies, or for pilot investigations. Searches with Google, although linguistically much less accurate, can help to document that language on the internet is authentic and contains - at least in parts - texts whose production is little monitored. The internet may thus be quite suitable for linguistic analysis for researchers interested in very current informal language, avoiding the observer's paradox to some extent. In the absence of reliable extraction tools, however, quantification over the whole domain (though possible) is not very meaningful, as it cuts across very different genres. Nevertheless, this exploratory study has shown that at least some traditional dialect features are continuing to be used today in non-negligible quantities – a result that may be related to the fact that they are functionally well-motivated.

Notes

1 Chambers' list of vernacular "universals" has recently been criticized for being heavily biased towards pervasive features of non-standard American English, and apparently does not take much account of other English dialect regions and certainly not of other languages, cf. Kortmann and Szmrecsanyi (2004).

2 This list is based on Quirk et al. (1985: 103-120), but excludes morphologically complex forms like the derivational *restring* or *overhang*.

3 In addition, there are some intermediate, especially "fudged" forms between these extremes (Chambers and Trudgill 1998: 110-113). This does not affect my argument.

4 Cf. Bybee (1995: 431).

5 For a detailed break up of speaker profiles, regions, etc. cf. Anderwald and Wagner (to appear 2006) or consult the project home page on http://www.anglistik.uni-freiburg.de/institut/lskortmann/FRED, where sample texts and audio files are also available.

6 This is not to deny the importance of socio- and geolinguistic variables involved in the *spread* of this change. I do think, however, that the original change can be functionally interpreted (and in fact is re-interpreted so by its speakers), and that features which are functionally (re-)motivated stand a better chance of spreading and stabilizing than those that are not.

7 Judging by Pearson's chi square test at df=4, p is much larger than 0.05.

8 'Corpus colossal', *The Economist* Jan. 20, 2005.

9 Cf. Renouf et al. in the present volume.

10 All searches were conducted between November and December 2004 and should thus represent a relatively homogeneous stage of the internet.

11 These figures are based on VIEW (Variation in English Words and Phrases) provided by Mark Davies at Brigham Young University (http://view.byu.edu/).

12 I conducted all searches from http://www.google.de. All searches were conducted at the beginning of January 2005. For differences in search results depending on the Google site where one conducts one's searches from cf. the contribution by Fletcher (this volume).

13 Running a curve estimation on these figures in SPSS, the logarithmic curve turns out to fit the data very well at df 5 with an F=76.26. P here is <0.001, and the curve fit is thus highly significant.

14 Consider also the title of the blockbuster film *Honey, I Shrunk the Kids* (and sequels).

References

Anderwald, L. (in progress), *Naturalness and dialect grammar: evidence from non-standard past tense paradigms*. Post-doctoral dissertation (Habilitationsschrift), English Department, Freiburg University.

Anderwald, L. and S. Wagner (to appear 2006), 'FRED - the Freiburg English Dialect corpus', in: J. Beal, K. Corrigan and H. Moisl (eds.) *Papers from the 20th Sociolinguistics Symposium at Newcastle, April 2004*. Vol. 1: *Synchronic Corpora*. London: Macmillan:

Bybee, J. (1985), *Morphology: A Study of the Relation between Meaning and Form*. Amsterdam and Philadelphia: John Benjamins.

Bybee, J. (1995), 'Regular morphology and the lexicon', *Language and Cognitive Processes*, 10: 425-455.

Bybee, J.L., and D.I. Slobin (1982), 'Why small children cannot change language on their own: suggestions from the English past tense', in: A. Ahlqvist (ed.) *Papers from the 5th International Conference on Historical Linguistics*. Amsterdam and Philadelphia: John Benjamins. 29-37.

Chambers, J.K. (1995), *Sociolinguistic Theory: Linguistic Variation and its Social Significance*. Oxford: Blackwell.

Chambers, J.K. ([2]2003), *Sociolinguistic Theory: Linguistic Variation and its Social Significance*. Oxford: Blackwell.

Chambers, J.K. (2004), 'Dialect typology and vernacular universals', in: B. Kortmann (ed.) *Dialectology Meets Typology*. Berlin and New York: Mouton. 127-145.

Chambers, J.K. and P. Trudgill (1998), *Dialectology*. 2nd edition. Cambridge: Cambridge University Press.

Cheshire, J. (1994), 'Standardization and the English irregular verbs', in: D. Stein and I. Tieken-Boon van Ostade (eds.) *Towards a Standard English: 1600-1800*. Berlin and New York: Mouton de Gruyter. 115-133.

Görlach, M. (1996), 'Morphological standardization: the strong verbs in Scots', in: D. Britton (ed.) *English Historical Linguistics 1994*. Amsterdam and Philadelphia: John Benjamins. 161-181.

Hogg, R.M. (1998), '*Snuck*: the development of irregular preterite forms', in: G. Nixon and J. Honey (eds.) *An Historic Tongue: Studies in English Linguistics in Memory of Barbara Strang*. London and New York: Routledge. 31-40.

Joseph, B.D. (2004), 'The editor's department: on change in language and change in *Language*', *Language*, 80: 381-383.

Kortmann, B. and B. Szmrecsanyi (2004), 'Global synopsis: morphological and syntactic variation in English', in: B. Kortmann and E.W. Schneider (eds.) *A Handbook of Varieties of English*. Vol. 2: *Morphology and Syntax*. Berlin and New York: Mouton de Gruyter. 1142-1202.

Krug, M.G. (2000), *Emerging English Modals: A Corpus-Based Study of Grammaticalization*. Berlin and New York: Mouton de Gruyter.

Krygier, M. (1994), *The Disintegration of the English Strong Verb System*. Frankfurt a. M.: Lang.

Lass, R. (1994), 'Proliferation and option-cutting: the strong verb in the fifteenth to eighteenth centuries', in: D. Stein and I. Tieken-Boon van Ostade (eds.) *Towards a Standard English: 1600-1800*. Berlin and New York: Mouton de Gruyter. 81-113.

Murray, T.E. (1998), 'More on drug/dragged and snuck/sneaked: evidence from the American Midwest', *Journal of English Linguistics*, 26: 209-221.

OED. 1994. *Oxford English Dictionary on CD-ROM*. 2nd edition. Oxford: Oxford University Press.

Quirk, R., S. Greenbaum, G. Leech and J. Svartvik (1985), *A Comprehensive Grammar of the English Language*. Harlow: Longman.

Renouf, A., A. Kehoe and J. Banerjee (this volume), 'WebCorp: an integrated system for web text search'.

Wurzel, W.U. (1984), *Flexionsmorphologie und Natürlichkeit: Ein Beitrag zur morphologischen Theoriebildung*. Berlin: Akademie-Verlag.

Wurzel, W.U. (1987), 'System-dependent morphological naturalness in inflection', in: W.U. Dressler, W. Mayerthaler, O. Panagl and W.U. Wurzel (eds.) *Leitmotifs in Natural Morphology*. Amsterdam and Philadelphia: John Benjamins. 59-96.

Wyld, H.C. (1927), *A Short History of English: With a Bibliography and Lists of Texts and Editions*. 3rd edition. London: John Murray.

Diachronic analysis with the internet? *Will* and *shall* in ARCHER and in a corpus of e-texts from the web

Nadja Nesselhauf

University of Heidelberg

Abstract

This paper investigates the potential of a quick-and-dirty corpus compiled from the web for diachronic analysis. The development of the future time expressions will, shall, *and* 'll *in 19th century British English is first studied on the basis of a "traditional" diachronic corpus, ARCHER, and then on the basis of a corpus of fiction texts created from electronic texts available on the internet.*

In addition to the overall changes in the relative occurrences of the three forms, the changes in three types of linguistic contexts (person, negation, and if-clause environments) are investigated. One of the main differences found in the results based on these two (types of) corpora is the development of 'll: *While the results from ARCHER point to a decrease in this expression in the 19th century (both in fiction texts and overall), the results from the fiction corpus point to an increase. Closer investigation reveals considerable inter-textual variation in the use of this form. The analysis demonstrates that, although not reliable as the only source for diachronic analysis, a quick-and-dirty corpus from the web can yield insights that can supplement those gained by a traditional corpus.*

1.   Introduction

Two types of diachronic analyses based on data from the internet are conceivable: an analysis of short term changes (in the past 15 years of so) in texts produced specifically for the internet, and an analysis of changes in larger and/or earlier time-spans based on texts written for other media and later made available on the internet.[1] Both types of investigation have only rarely been attempted to date; it is the latter type that will be carried out here (for a discussion of some issues connected with the former type of approach cf. Kehoe 2006; one of the few examples of the latter type of approach is Hoffmann 2002).

The number of texts from earlier times now electronically available on the internet is vast. English texts can – to name just two prominent examples – be found on the "Project Gutenberg" site from where around 13,000 e-books of all kinds (fiction, drama, scientific and religious writing, biographies, dictionaries, encyclopaedias, etc.) can be downloaded (http://www.gutenberg.org/)[2] or on the "Renascence Editions" site with around 200 fiction and non-fiction texts in English from 1477 to 1799 (http://darkwing.uoregon.edu/~rbear/ren.htm).[3] Not all e-texts are freely available, however, and not all registers are equally well represented on the net. In particular, literary works from earlier centuries are freely available in large quantities, and many of these can be easily downloaded and searched automatically (as opposed to some other registers, for which often only scanned page-images are available, cf. for instance JSTOR at http://www.jstor.org/, where scholarly journals are thus archived). For the present study, fiction texts (which, in contrast to drama-texts, usually contain both speech-based and non-speech based language) from Project Gutenberg have been used.

The potential of a corpus of fiction texts from the web is explored by analysing the development of the three future time expressions *will*, *shall*, and *'ll* in 19th century British English. While the use of these three expressions has been investigated fairly intensively for Present Day English (e.g. Berglund 1997, Szmrecsanyi 2003) and for Early Modern English (e.g. Gotti 2001, Kytö 1992), their development in the 18th and 19th centuries has been neglected to date. The analysis presented in this paper takes into account not only the relative overall frequencies of the three expressions, but also their potential development in some linguistic contexts which have been shown to influence the choice of future time expressions (person, negation, and *if*-clause environments, cf. e.g. Kytö 1992, Szmrecsanyi 2003).

First, the analyses will be conducted on the basis of ARCHER (*A Representative Corpus of Historical English Registers*), a traditional corpus (for a definition of 'traditional' cf. section 4). In section 3, the compilation of an e-text corpus is described and the same analyses are then performed on the basis of this corpus. In section 4, possible reasons for the differences in the results from the two analyses are investigated. On the basis of this investigation, the potential of a quick-and-dirty corpus from the web for diachronic analysis is discussed in the final section.

2.   Investigating *will* and *shall* with ARCHER

2.1   Corpus composition

ARCHER (*A Representative Corpus of Historical English Registers*) consists of British and American English texts from a variety of registers between 1650 and 1990.[4] The corpus is subdivided into periods of 50 years. Registers are typically represented with about 10 extracts of about 2,000 words (for a detailed description of ARCHER see Biber et al. 1994). Only a subcorpus of ARCHER was used for the present investigation, which will be referred to as S-ARCHER in what follows. S-ARCHER comprises British texts from the two periods 1800-1849 and 1850-1899 from the following categories (with the letter in brackets indicating the abbreviation occurring in the codes of the corresponding corpus files): news reportage (n), journals (j), fiction (f), drama (d), medical writing (m), (other) science writing (s), sermons and homilies (h), private letters (x). Table 1 shows the number of words in each category.

Table 1: Number of words in the different registers of S-ARCHER

	n	j	f	d	m	s	h	x	total
1800-1849	23101	21897	52793	29525	26167	18942	11107	13876	197408
1850-1899	23336	22785	48487	33256	32095	22061	10981	10795	203796

The category of fiction contains extracts considerably longer than 2,000 words, the category of private letters contains 26 letters per period with mostly far fewer than 2,000 words, and the category of sermons and homilies contains only 5 texts per period. In total, S-ARCHER comprises around 400,000 words, with around 200,000 words in each of the two periods.

2.2 Overall results

In the analysis, only those occurrences of *will* and *shall* were considered whose main function is future time reference. For *will*, therefore, instances primarily expressing volition as in *burn it if you will* (ARCHER, 1819miln.d5) were disregarded (as well as instances of *will* as a noun etc.). Instances of *shall* were disregarded if they express the function of addressee's volition or obligation (cf. Coates 1983: 186). As the distinction between the uses of *shall* as prediction and intention on the one hand and of addressee's volition or obligation on the other is often difficult, only fairly clear instances of the latter types such as the following were excluded (the first example illustrating addressee's volition, the second obligation):

> {=M HARDUP:} Send Mr Garrick's dresser to him directly, with my best sword and the ribbon.
> {=M UNDERTONE:} Yes, sir. Shall I ring in the overture?
> {=M HARDUP:} Not yet! not yet!
> (ARCHER, 1839plan.d5; my emphasis)

> Art. 4.--If in the interval of the Session of the Chambers grave circum-stances should momentarily render insufficient the measures of guarantee and repression at present established, the censorship shall be immediately restored to activity, in virtue of a royal ordinance, counter-signed by three Ministers.   (ARCHER, 1822eval.n5; my emphasis)

The forms *shal*, *shalbe*, and *shall-be* were also checked, but not found to occur.

Table 2 shows the overall numbers of (future uses of) *will*, *shall*, and *'ll* found in S-ARCHER.[5]

Table 2:　Occurrences of *will*, *shall*, and *'ll* with future time reference in S-ARCHER

	will	shall	'll	total
1800-49	551 (57.2%)	244 (25.3%)	169 (17.5%)	964
1850-99	477 (65.3%)	150 (20.5%)	104 (14.2%)	731

These results indicate that the overall number of these three expressions has decreased in the 19th century – probably due to the increase of other future time expressions, in particular of *BE going to* (cf. e.g. Mair 2004). They also indicate that, unsurprisingly, the use of *will* increased and *shall* decreased during the century and that, perhaps somewhat surprisingly, *'ll* decreased.

2.3　Register differences

Table 3:　*Will*, *shall*, and *'ll* in the different registers represented in S-ARCHER

	will	shall	'll	total
journals:				
1800-49	20 (76.9%)	5 (19.2%)	1 (3.8%)	26
1850-99	37 (68.5%)	14 (25.9%)	3 (5.6%)	54
letters:				
1800-49	65 (67.7%)	31 (32.3%)	-	96
1850-99	54 (66.7%)	23 (28.4%)	4 (4.9%)	81
fiction:				
1800-49	149 (58.4%)	61 (23.9%)	45 (17.6%)	255
1850-99	109 (58.3%)	55 (29.4%)	23 (12.3%)	187
news reportage:				
1800-49	92 (82.9%)	19 (17.1%)	-	111
1850-99	83 (96.5%)	3 (3.5%)	-	86
medicine:				
1800-49	18 (69.2%)	8 (30.8%)	-	26
1850-99	38 (76%)	12 (24%)	-	50
science:				
1800-49	42 (79.2%)	11 (20.8%)	-	53
1850-99	23 (88.5%)	3 (11.5%)	-	26
drama:				
1800-49	140 (39.9%)	88 (25.1%)	123 (35.0%)	351
1850-99	99 (48.1%)	33 (16.0%)	74 (35.9%)	206
sermons:				
1800-49	25 (54.3%)	21 (45.7%)	-	46
1850-99	34 (82.9%)	7 (17.1%)	-	41

If the occurrences *will*, *shall*, and *'ll* are regarded separately for each of the registers represented in S-ARCHER, the results indicate that there are considerable differences in the different registers, both with respect to the relative frequency of the three expressions in a given period and with respect to the ways their relative frequencies develop (cf. table 3). The form *'ll* only occurs in some of the registers, and in larger numbers only in the categories of fiction and drama. While *will* is more frequent than *shall* in all registers, the *will-shall* ratio is by no means the same across the categories, with news reportage, for example, displaying a particularly low share of *shall*. As to the diachronic development, medical and science writing as well as drama very much reflect the overall development, with a certain decrease of *shall* and an increase of *will*. News reportage and especially the category of sermons and homilies display the same tendency, but stronger. In the category of private letters, the relation of *will* and *shall* has remained fairly stable; in journals the opposite tendency, a decrease of *will* and an increase of *shall* can be observed. In the category of fiction, the relative frequency of *will* has remained stable, *shall* has increased and *'ll* decreased. In the category drama, the relative frequency of *'ll* has remained stable. The different proportions and developments seem to be connected to the degree to which the individual registers are speech-based or contain speech-based language (particularly in the case of *'ll*) and on the amount of first person use in the different registers (cf. section 2.4.3 for the correlation of the three expressions with grammatical person and section 4 for a discussion of the results in the category of fiction).

2.4 The influence of linguistic context

2.4.1 Negation

To investigate the influence of negative contexts on the choice of *will*, *shall*, and *'ll* and potential change in this area, only *not*-negated forms were considered and in addition only those where *not* immediately follows the expression under investigation. The contracted forms *won't* and *shan't* were also included in the investigation. The results are displayed in table 4.

Table 4: *Will*, *shall*, and *'ll* in contexts of negation in S-ARCHER

	will not	won't	shall not	shan't	'll not	total
1800-49	43	20	16	5	6	90
	(47.8%)	(22.2%)	(17.8%)	(5.6%)	(6.7%)	
	70.0%		23.3%		6.7%	
1850-99	28	29	12	7	1	77
	(36.4%)	(37.7%)	(15.6%)	(9.1%)	(1.3%)	
	74.0%		24.7%		1.3%	

The table reveals that in both periods *'ll* occurs very rarely in negative contexts, possibly with decreasing tendency (the 6 occurrences in the first half of the century occur in 5 texts), but numbers are too small for more definite conclusions. *Will not* and *won't* are greatly preferred over *shall not* and *shan't* in both periods – in the first period this preference is stronger than the general preference of *will* over *shall* (cf. section 2.2). The patterns in the first and second half of the century are fairly similar. The data also indicates a change in the relation of *will not* and *won't* in the 19th century (for *shall not* and *shan't*, numbers are too small and additionally skewed for conclusions of any kind – the 7 occurrences in the second period occur in only three texts). The contracted form clearly gains ground in the time span investigated: while the ratio of *will not* to *won't* is 2.1 to 1 in the first half of the century, it is 1 to 1 in the second half.

2.4.2 *If*-clause environments

For the analysis of the distribution of the *will*, *shall*, and *'ll* in *if*-clause environments, a span of +/- 10 was investigated and the relevant instances extracted manually. Again, the numbers are rather small for definite conclusions, but possibly suggest a decline of *shall* and an increase of *'ll* in *if*-clause environments (cf. table 5).

Table 5:   *Will, shall,* and *'ll* in *if*-clause environments in S-ARCHER

	will	shall	'll	total
1800-1849				
if-clause	10	1	3	14
main clause	22	14	5	41
total	32 (58.2%)	15 (27.3%)	8 (14.5%)	55
1850-1899				
if-clause	7	0	2	9
main clause	26	10	9	45
total	33 (61.1%)	10 (18.5%)	11 (20.4%)	54

2.4.3 Person

For the analysis of the correlation of *will*, *shall*, and *'ll* with grammatical person, only occurrences with one of the Present Day English personal pronouns directly preceding the future time expression were considered (other personal pronouns occurred very rarely, with a few instances of *thou* and *ye*).

Table 6: *Will, shall,* and *'ll* following the different personal pronouns in S-ARCHER[6]

	00-49 will	50-99 will	00-49 shall	50-99 shall	00-49 'll	50-99 'll	00-49 total	50-99 total
I	86 32.2%	70 34.0%	83 31.1%	93 45.1%	98 36.7%	43 20.9%	267	206
you	70 56.5%	71 60.2%	24 19.3%	11 9.3%	30 24.2%	36 30.5%	124	118
he	19	10	10	4	7	7	36	21
she	8	7	2	1	4	2	14	10
it	44	42	6	4	-	1	50	47
he/she/it	71 71.0%	59 75.6%	18 18.0%	9 11.5%	11 11.0%	10 12.8%	100	78
we	9 17.6%	4 12.9%	27 52.9%	17 54.8%	15 29.4%	10 32.3%	51	31
they	12 48%	6 60%	5 20%	1 10%	8 32%	3 30%	25	10

The analysis shows that in the first half of the century the first person singular is followed by *will, shall,* and *'ll* in roughly the same number of cases, while in the second half, there is a considerable increase of *shall* and a considerable decrease of *'ll*, with *will* being used, as before, in about a third of the cases. For the first person plural, there also seems to be an increase in *shall*, though only a very slight one. *You*, on the other hand, is already in the first period followed by a high proportion of *will* (around 55%) and by an even slightly higher proportion (around 60%) in the second half, with *shall* decreasing and *'ll* increasing. The third person singular pronouns *he/she/it* also display a slight increase of *will* and a decrease of *shall* (this tendency emerges both when these pronouns are considered together as well as when considered individually). The same development can also be observed for *they*, but the numbers are very small here.

3. Investigating *will* and *shall* with a corpus of e-texts from the web

3.1 Compilation of the corpus

Since a major advantage of electronic texts available on the internet is that large quantities of them can be quickly prepared for automatic analysis, the corpus of electronic fiction texts was designed to be larger than the S-ARCHER corpus, with around 500,000 words for each of the two periods 1800 to 1849 and 1850 to 1899. Since the degree of representativeness of a corpus decreases with the inclusion of fewer texts but since, at the same time, the present aim is to explore the potential of corpora from the web that can be created with a reasonable investment of time, it was decided to use (extracts from) at least 20 works by individual authors of up to 50,000 words each. Each decade of the 19th century was to be represented by 100,000 words. Unfortunately, the Project Gutenberg site does not allow searches according to date of publication, which meant that a more time-consuming approach had to be adopted in order to find electronic versions of relevant works. Two works of literary history were consulted (Fabian 1991 and von Wilpert 1997), on the basis of which novels by British authors from the two periods in question were selected, and their availability in Project Gutenberg checked (with a positive result in most cases). An effort was made to include mainly texts by English authors (or authors who had spent most of their lives in England) in the corpus. This requirement, as well as the one that all decades were to be covered with a roughly equal number of words, were largely, though not completely, met.[7] The composition of the corpus, which will be referred to as WebFict (*Corpus of Fiction from the Web*), is presented in table 7.

Table 7:   Composition of WebFict

Year	Author	Title	Words
1813	Austen, Jane	*Pride and Prejudice*	50004
1818	Shelley Wollstonecraft, Mary	*Frankenstein*	50015
1822	Peacock, Thomas Love	*Maid Marian*	35964
1824	Mitford, Mary Russell	*Our Village*	14050
1826	Disraeli, Benjamin	*Vivian Grey*	50005
1834	Bulwer-Lytton, Edward George	*The Last Days of Pompeii*	50016
1834	Marryat, Frederick	*Peter Simple*	50027
1834	Carlyle, Thomas	*Sartor Resartus*	50017
1837	Dickens, Charles	*The Pickwick Papers*	50022
1847	Thackeray, William M.	*Vanity Fair*	50010
1847	Brontë, Emily	*Wuthering Heights*	50006
			500136
1853	Gaskell, Elisabeth	*Cranford*	50054
1859	Collins, Wilkie	*The Woman in White*	50004
1861	Eliot, George	*Silas Marner*	50035
1865	Carroll, Lewis	*Alice in Wonderland*	26698
1872	Carroll, Lewis	*Through the Looking Glass*	23312
1872	Butler, Samuel	*Erewhon*	50040
1879	Meredith, George	*The Egoist*	50010
1880	Trollope, Anthony	*The Duke's Children*	50005
1889	Conan Doyle, Arthur	*Micah Clarke*	50016
1895	Wells, H.G.	*The Time Machine*	32479
1896	Wells, H.G.	*The Island of Dr. Moreau*	17544
1896	Hardy, Thomas	*Jude the Obscure*	50006
			500203

If the selected novels were shorter than 50,000 words, an extract from another work by the same author was added (Carroll, Wells), in one case an extract from another work published around the same time (Mitford).[8]

After the selection had been made, the selected novels were downloaded as plain text files from the Project Gutenberg site. The Gutenberg-header (which provides information on the project and legal issues connected with the use of the e-text) was then removed as well as introductions and tables of contents. All words exceeding 50,000 were also removed (keeping intact the sentence within which this limit was reached). The corpus could then be used with WordSmith, which was also used for the analyses with S-ARCHER.

3.2   Overall results

The same principles as in the analysis with S-ARCHER were followed in all investigations (i.e. the same semantic types of *will* and *shall* excluded, the same types of negative context considered etc.). Older forms of *shall* (*shal* etc.) were not found in WebFict either (although this might be a consequence of spelling regularization, cf. section 5). Table 8 displays the overall results.[9]

Table 8:   Occurrences of *will*, *shall*, and *'ll* with future time reference in WebFict

	will	shall	'll	total
1800-49	1112 (57.6%)	511 (26.4%)	309 (16.0%)	1932
1850-99	822 (54.7%)	326 (21.7%)	354 (23.6%)	1502

As in S-ARCHER, the overall number of the three forms decreases in the course of the century. The occurrences of the three expressions relative to the number of words in the two corpora is, however, overall lower in WebFict, with about 386 per 100,000 words in the first half of the century and about 300 in the second, as opposed to about 488 per 100,000 in the first period and 359 in the second in S-ARCHER. The relative proportion of the three forms is very similar in both corpora in the first half of the century. However, with respect to the development of these future time expressions, the results of WebFict only correspond to those of S-ARCHER with respect to *shall*. The proportion of *will*, which increases in S-ARCHER, displays a slight decrease in WebFict, and the proportion of *'ll*, which decreases in S-ARCHER, displays an increase.

3.3   The influence of linguistic context

3.3.1   Negation

As in the previous investigation, *'ll* is only occasionally followed by *not*, and there is an indication that *'ll not* might additionally be decreasing in the course of the century. The proportion of negated *will* to negated *shall* is also very similar to the results obtained with S-ARCHER, with a slightly clearer preference for *will* in WebFict. As in S-ARCHER, the apparent increase in *shan't* might be due to skewing, as 15 out of the 16 instances occur in only 3 different texts. As in S-ARCHER, *won't* increases in the course of the century. In WebFict, however, the preference for *will not* over *won't* in the first period is not as pronounced as in S-ARCHER (the ratio is 1.6 to 1 as opposed to 2.1 to 1), and *won't* is used more frequently in the second half (with a relative frequency of about 3 to 2), whereas in S-ARCHER both forms occur with roughly equal frequency then.

Table 9:   *Will*, *shall*, and *'ll* in contexts of negation in WebFict

	will not	won't	shall not	shan't	'll not	total
1800-49	127 (46.7%)	79 (29.0%)	42 (15.4%)	3 (1.1%)	21 (7.7%)	272
	75.7%		16.5%		7.7%	
1850-99	68 (31.5%)	104 (48.1%)	24 (11.1%)	16 (7.4%)	4 (1.9%)	216
	79.6%		18.5%		1.9%	

3.3.2   *If*-clause environments

The analysis of *will*, *shall*, and *'ll* in *if*-clause environments also displays similar tendencies to those observed in S-ARCHER (cf. table 10). While *shall* appears to be decreasing in *if*-clause environments, *'ll* appears to be increasing (both in relative and absolute terms and – only in WebFict – in both main clauses and *if*-clauses). In absolute terms, the number of occurrences of *will* remains stable in *if*-clause environments in both WebFict and S-ARCHER; in relative terms there is a difference in the two corpora, as in WebFict there is a relative decrease of *will* and in S-ARCHER a slight increase.

Table 10:   *Will*, *shall*, and *'ll* in *if*-clause environments in WebFict

	will	shall	'll	total
1800-1849				
if-clause	11	2	6	19
main clause	54	26	17	97
total	65 (56.0%)	28 (24.1%)	23 (19.8%)	116
1850-1899				
if-clause	12	2	11	25
main clause	52	21	43	116
total	64 (45.4%)	23 (16.3%)	54 (38.3%)	141

3.2.1 Person

The distribution and development of *will*, *shall*, and *'ll* after the different personal pronouns as evidenced by WebFict partly coincides with the previous analysis, and partly deviates from it. With respect to the first person, the data from WebFict, like the data from S-ARCHER reveals an increase of *shall*, though to a much lesser degree (cf. table 11). In contrast to the previous analysis, however, *will* decreases and *'ll* increases after *I*, and whereas S-ARCHER has roughly equal proportions of the three expressions in the first half of the century, WebFict reveals such an equal distribution in the second half of the century. The results for *you*, on the other hand, are very similar, both with respect to the proportion within the periods and the change from one period to the other (increase of *will*, decrease of *shall*, increase of *'ll*). For the third person singular, the two corpora only share the decrease of *shall*, whereas in contrast to the previous analysis, *will* decreases and *'ll* increases in WebFict, and the proportions of *'ll* are higher in both periods. For the first person plural, WebFict reveals the same overall tendencies, though partly of different strengths as compared to the S-ARCHER data: *will* decreases (to a greater degree), *shall* increases (to a similar degree), and *'ll* increases (to a greater degree). For *they* (which occurs infrequently in S-ARCHER), WebFict has an increase of *will*, a slight increase of *shall*, and a decrease of *'ll*.

Table 11: *Will, shall,* and *'ll* following the different personal pronouns in WebFict[10]

	00-49 will	50-99 will	00-49 shall	50-99 shall	00-49 'll	50-99 'll	00-49 total	50-99 total
I	250 41.7%	158 31.1%	185 30.8%	182 35.9%	165 27.5%	167 32.9%	600	507
you	151 61.6%	164 64.6%	42 17.1%	14 5.5%	52 21.2%	76 29.9%	245	254
he	63	54	12	12	43	25	118	91
she	38	23	8	6	13	14	59	43
it	68	53	15	8	2	24	85	85
he/ she/it	169 64.5%	130 59.4%	35 13.4%	26 11.9%	58 22.1%	63 28.8%	262	219
we	42 30.4%	14 18.4%	79 57.2%	45 59.2%	17 12.3%	17 22.4%	138	76
they	16 51.6%	36 61.0%	4 12.9%	8 13.6%	11 35.5%	15 25.4%	31	59

4.   Investigating the differences in the results

While some of the investigations conducted with the two corpora have yielded identical or similar results with respect to the use and development of *will*, *shall*, and *'ll*, a number of – partly substantial – differences have also been observed in the above analyses. These must be the consequence either of one of the ways in which S-ARCHER and WebFict differ and/or of skewing effects in at least one of the corpora.[11] The differences between these two corpora are partly connected to the fact that S-ARCHER is what has been termed a traditional corpus above (section 1) while WebFict consists of e-texts downloaded from the internet. 'Traditional' with respect to a corpus is taken to mean that the corpus has been compiled for the purpose of linguistic investigation, on the basis of careful sampling, by typing or scanning in the original sources, and usually by adding some degree of annotation. The e-texts from the internet on the other hand were converted into electronic form (by volunteers) for a different purpose, namely the availability of literary texts for a wide readership. Other differences derive from the (quick-and-dirty) style of compilation of WebFict rather than from the fact that the texts this corpus consists of were taken from the internet. In contrast to S-ARCHER, which contains eight registers, WebFict only contains one. WebFict also contains far fewer texts, and the individual texts included are much longer than in S-ARCHER. An additional difference, which is indirectly connected to the fact that texts that already were in electronic form have been used, is corpus size, with WebFict being more than double the size of S-ARCHER (and about ten times the size of the fiction part of S-ARCHER).

Whether the differences in the overall results of the two corpora are due to the differences in the (number of) registers represented was checked by comparing the results from WebFict to the occurrences of *will*, *shall*, and *'ll* in the fiction texts in S-ARCHER (cf. tables 3 and 8). This comparison indicates that the different behaviour of *will* in the two corpora (a fairly large increase in S-ARCHER versus a slight decrease in WebFict) might largely be a consequence of the different representation of registers, since in the fiction texts of S-ARCHER the proportion of *will* stays about the same in the two periods. For *shall* and *'ll*, however, the development in WebFict and in the fiction texts in S-ARCHER is exactly the reverse, with an increase of *shall* and a decrease of *'ll* in the fiction texts of S-ARCHER. Indeed, when the development of *'ll* in the different registers (cf. section 2.3) is examined, it turns out that it is this decrease in fiction that leads to the overall decrease of *'ll* found in S-ARCHER, as in drama (the only other register with more than an insignificant number of occurrences of this expression), the proportion of *'ll* remains stable in the two periods.

In order to investigate whether the reason for the difference in the overall results lies in the composition of the corpora, the number of times *will*, *shall*, and *'ll* occur in the individual texts included in WebFict and in the fiction part of S-ARCHER is investigated. Table 12 shows this distribution for WebFict.

Table 12: *Will*, *shall*, and *'ll* in the individual texts in WebFict[12]

	will	shall	'll	total
Austen	171	69	-	240
Shelley Wollstonecraft	114	60	-	174
Peacock + Mitford	127 + 33 (160)	90 + 11 (101)	5 + 3 (8)	222 + 47 (269)
Disraeli	131	43	6	180
Bulwer-Lytton	99	41	3	143
Marryat	97	37	76	210
Carlyle	83	39	-	122
Dickens	71	31	53	155
Thackeray	88	29	35	152
Brontë	98	61	128	287
Total:	1112	511	309	1932
Gaskell	51	17	17	85
Collins	117	35	4	156
Eliot	40	25	107	172
Carroll	47 (33 + 14)	37 (25 + 12)	123 (57 + 66)	207
Butler	95	19	-	114
Meredith	135	39	2	176
Trollope	165	61	23	249
Conan Doyle	103	58	14	175
Wells	43 (37 + 6)	7 (7 + 0)	12 (5 + 7)	62
Hardy	26	28	52	106
Total:	822	326	354	1502

The table reveals that while there naturally is some inter-textual variation with respect to the use of all three expressions in the two periods, this variation is far greater for *'ll* than for *will* and *shall*. For *will*, the lowest number of occurrences for an author in the first period (disregarding Mitford, as she is only represented with far fewer than 50,000 words) is 71, the highest 171; in the second period the lowest is 26 the highest 165. For *shall*, in the first period the lowest number of occurrences in the text(s) of an author is 29 and the highest 90 (in the 36000 words from Peacock) or 101 in an 50,000-word extract (if Mitford and Peacock are considered together). In the second period the lowest number is 7, the highest 61, although in the shorter extract from a novel by Wells (17,500 words) there is no occurrence. In the case of *'ll*, on the other hand, there are texts (of 50,000 words) in each period without any occurrence (three in the first, one in the second period), as well as more than one text in both periods with very few occurrences (3 and 6 occurrences in the first, 2 and 4 in the second period). At the same time, there is a text with 128 occurrences in the first period, and one author in the second period has 123 occurrences in 50,000 words. This means that while for *will* the highest number of occurrences in a text is about six times the one in the text with the lowest number of occurrences, and for *shall* this factor is nine, the factor for *'ll* – even disregarding the texts with zero occurrences – is around 40 in the first and around 60 in the second period (with an additionally much more uneven distribution of the number of occurrences in the other texts). As only few (around 10) texts per period were included in WebFict, the results of *'ll* in particular might therefore be skewed to a great extent. If, for example, instead of the texts by Carroll, another one with very few, say 3, occurrences had been chosen, the increase of *'ll* would be very slight (from 16% to around 18.5% assuming the same number of occurrences of the other forms as in the Carroll texts); if such a text had been chosen for the first period instead of the Brontë text, the observed increase of *'ll* would have been more drastic (from around 10.5% to 23.6%).

The danger of the great inter-textual (or probably inter-author)[13] variation of *'ll* distorting the results does not only apply to the WebFict corpus but also to the fiction section of the S-ARCHER corpus, as almost the same number of texts (and authors) are represented there as in WebFict. The distribution of *'ll* of the S-ARCHER fiction texts is as follows: in the first period, the expression occurs in five (out of 11) texts altogether, with the frequencies 5, 7, 7, 12, 14; in the second period, the expression occurs in 8 (out or 11) texts, with the frequencies 1, 1, 2, 2, 3, 3, 4, 7. Again, the replacement of a single stretch of text would have yielded fairly different results (if, for example, instead of the extract with the 14 occurrences an extract without any occurrence of *'ll* had been selected, the decrease of *'ll* in fiction would only have been from 13.8% to 12.3% , all other things being equal). On the basis of the S-ARCHER results alone, however, the considerable inter-textual variation would not have been discovered, as the stretches of text included in the corpus are too short and the number of occur-rences too low for an investigation of this phenomenon. With respect to the development of *'ll*, neither of the two corpora thus provide a clear answer, as due to the great degree of variation between texts around 10 texts per period is too low a number for firm conclusions (and as *'ll* additionally occurs in very few registers in S-ARCHER).

The finding of the great inter-textual variation of *'ll* is of course interesting in its own right and not merely because it potentially explains the differences in the results. Apparently, in the periods investigated, the frequency of *'ll* is not (only) dependent on the amount of conversation in a text (cf. e.g. *Pride and Prejudice*, which contains a great amount of conversation but not a single occurrence of this form), but on other factors such as the author's (or possibly in some cases the editor's) preferences, the style of narration, the social milieu described etc. These factors would be worth pursuing further, which is, however, beyond the scope of the present paper.

For *shall*, the factor of inter-textual variation which surfaces due to the low numbers of texts and, in the case of S-ARCHER fiction, also due to the low numbers of occurrences might also have contributed to the differences. The degree of (possible) influence of this factor will probably be lower than in the case of *'ll*, however (as there is less inter-textual variation, and the absolute numbers are higher for *shall*), and it is likely that other factors are also responsible for the difference. Considering that in both corpora there is an increase of *shall* with the first person singular, it appears possible that – perhaps again due to the low numbers of texts – the distribution of *I* is different in the two corpora. If the number of occurrences of *I* per 1,000 words is investigated, this is indeed found to be the case. In S-ARCHER fiction texts, the rate of first person singular pronouns is 15.6 per 1,000 words in the first period, and 22.8 in the second; WebFict has 19.5 first person singular pronouns per 1,000 words in the first and 21.6 in the second period (for comparison, S-ARCHER as a whole has 15.2 and 18.1 per 1,000 words). As owing to the inclusion of only short extracts the danger of distortion is even greater in the fiction category of S-ARCHER than in WebFict, it can be speculated that the WebFict results, which show an overall decrease in *shall*, are closer to representing the development of *shall* in 19th century fiction (but again the number of texts does not allow firm conclusions).

With respect to negation, the major difference in the results from the two corpora is the relation of *will not* to *won't*, with *won't* occurring (both absolutely and relatively) more frequently in WebFict. As *won't* occurs more frequently in more informal contexts in Present Day English (cf. e.g. Szmrecsanyi 2003: 304) a hypothesis is that the rise of *won't* in the 19th century starts out from conversation (at least as represented in literature) and therefore is particularly frequent in WebFict, as conversation is represented to a greater degree there than in S-ARCHER (where conversation in all likelihood only occurs to a significant degree in two of eight registers, drama and fiction). A cursory glance at the instances of *won't* in WebFict seems to confirm that they occur mainly in conversation. In addition, if the register-specific variation in S-ARCHER is examined, it turns out that in the first period, 7 of the 20 occurrences of *won't* are in fiction, 13 in drama, in the second period 2 out of the 29 are in private letters, 11 in fiction and 16 in drama. The difference in the results is thus a consequence of the difference in the (number of) registers in the two corpora.

As to the differences in the results obtained for the distribution of *will*, *shall*, and *'ll* with regard to grammatical person, some of these probably derive from the low numbers of occurrences, especially for S-ARCHER. In addition, preferences by individual authors or in individual texts which surface as a consequence of the low numbers of texts might again play a role. For example, if the striking rise from 2 to 24 occurrences of *it'll* in WebFict is examined, it turns out that this is due to two texts only, of which one has 16 occurrences and the other 8. Had another text without any occurrences of *it'll* been selected instead of the one with 16, the overall increase of *'ll* after third person singular pronouns would have been negligible in WebFict and would thus have corresponded to the development as evidenced by S-ARCHER.

5.   The potential of a corpus of e-texts from the web for diachronic analysis

As the investigation of possible reasons for the differences in the results of the traditional ARCHER corpus and the quick-and-dirty fiction corpus from the web has shown, these differences are largely consequences of the difference in the (numbers of) registers covered by the two corpora, of the small number of texts included in WebFict and in individual categories in ARCHER, of the short extracts in S-ARCHER, and of the difference in size (with S-ARCHER being too small to yield meaningful results for certain kinds of investigation). The limitations of WebFict therefore largely result from the quick-and-dirty style in which it has been compiled rather than from the fact that the corpus is based on e-texts downloaded from the internet. For the type of linguistic phenomenon investigated here, potential problems deriving from the fact that these texts were turned into electronic form by non-linguists for non-linguistic purposes did seem to play any significant role. During the analysis, spelling errors or other errors and oversights (such as doubling of lines and paragraphs as can occasionally be found in traditional corpora) caused by producing electronic versions of the texts were not encountered at all. The printed versions of the texts therefore seem to have been represented with a high degree of accuracy. A disadvantage of the electronic texts found in the Gutenberg project is that they are often based on editions other than the original publication and there is, moreover, in many cases no information on which one (cf. also Hoffmann 2002). The spelling has mostly been regularized, which is an advantage for grammatical and or lexical analysis, but would render such a corpus useless for phonological analysis.[14] Whether and, if so, to what extent archaic lexical items and grammatical constructions have been adapted to Present Day English in the editions used is unclear (cf. ibid.). The additional absence of linguistic annotation might be a problem for some kind of analyses but not for an approach like the one taken in this paper where single grammatical items are analysed.

The obvious advantages of a corpus from the web are the easy availability of large quantities of texts from many earlier periods and from many registers, so that a researcher has access to data for which a traditional corpus has not been compiled yet or is not available Disadvantages correspondingly are the lack of availability of texts from certain periods – in particular very early ones and, due to copyright reasons, many from the 20th century – and the lack of availability of texts from certain registers a researcher might be interested in (cf. section 1). A further advantage of a corpus compiled from e-texts is the comparative speed of compilation. Although, like all corpus production, the compilation of a corpus of texts already available in electronic form even in a quick-and-dirty approach as described above is still fairly time-consuming if a certain level of representative-ness is aimed at, this approach still allows a single researcher to create a corpus in a reasonable amount of time, which, if compiled in the traditional way, would probably require collaborative effort, or at least many months of work. A researcher can thus in many cases create a corpus which exactly meets his/her needs with respect to size and composition; for example if a large amount of text from a certain period or register is required, or if whole texts or certain parts of texts (e.g. introductions) are required (e.g. for a study of discourse). A corpus containing fewer texts of great length can, despite its shortcomings, also be useful for some kinds of analysis, in particular, as was seen above, for the investigation of inter-textual or inter-author variation. In addition, a corpus created by the researcher has the advantage that the he or she is more aware of its exact composition and the possible problems and/or skewing effects connected with it.

Three – not totally separable – approaches in the use of corpora of e-texts from the web for (diachronic) linguistic analysis seem particularly promising. First, a corpus compiled in a style similar to the one described in this paper (or perhaps even quicker and dirtier) can be used for a fast exploration of whether a certain phenomenon is worth investigating in a certain period. Second, a corpus from the web can be compiled on the basis of sampling standards comparable to that of a traditional corpus. This seems particularly sensible if no traditional corpus is available for a particular research question and the researcher's resources are limited. As most of the limitations of corpora from the web derive from their composition and not from the quality of the texts itself, such a corpus has great potential for many types of linguistic analysis; on the other hand, its compilation also takes a fair amount of time. Third, a corpus from the web compiled in a quick-and-dirty style can be used in combination with a traditional corpus (cf. also Mair, present volume). As was seen in the above investigation, such an approach has the potential to point to possible limitations of the results of the traditional corpus and to alert the researcher to areas where further investigation is necessary. In some cases, the corpus from the web can, because of its different composition, yield results that go beyond those of the traditional corpus, as the finding of the great amount of inter-textual variation in the use of *'ll* has demonstrated. In many cases, a combination of the second and the third type of approach seems promising: the compilation of a fairly carefully sampled corpus restricted to one (or very few) registers and periods to supplement a traditional corpus in areas where the amount of text of that particular type and/or period is too small to answer a certain research question. (In the investigation above, for example, the traditional corpus would have been too small to investigate the distribution of *shall, will,* and *'ll* following the different personal pronouns in a certain register.)

Corpora compiled on the basis of e-texts from the internet therefore clearly have some potential for diachronic linguistic analysis. While only a more carefully designed corpus from the web can serve as the primary source of a linguistic investigation, a quick-and-dirty corpus consisting of e-texts from the internet can provide valuable insights in a diachronic study if combined with other resources.

Notes

1   I would like to thank David Allerton, Carolin Biewer, and Marianne Hundt for comments on earlier versions of this paper.

2   All internet addresses cited in this paper were accessed on 7 February 2005.

3   For a collection of links to such sites see, for example, http://www.sil.org/linguistics/etext.html.

4   In this paper, ARCHER refers to the corpus as originally compiled by Douglas Biber and Edward Finegan between 1990 and 1993.

5   According to the chi-square test, this distribution is significant at $p \leq 0.01$.

6   The forms *won't* and *shan't* are included in the counts for *will* and *shall* in this table.

7   Carlyle is Scottish; for the first decade of the 19th century (1800-09) no novels are included, the 1830s are overrepresented, the 1870s slightly overrepresented and the 1860s slightly underrepresented, cf. Table 7.

8   *Our Village* by Mitford was actually published between 1824 and 1832.

9   The distribution is significant at $p \leq 0.001$ according to the chi square test.

10   The forms *won't* and *shan't* are included in the counts for *will* and *shall* in this table.

11   Some of the differences might also be the consequence of chance results, in particular where low numbers are involved (cf. below). The overall results of the two investigations, however, are statistically significant (cf. above).

12   For those 50,000-word extracts stemming from more than one work, both the sum of the occurrences in both works and the number of occurrences in each work are given.

13   To what degree the observed variation is due to individual preferences of the authors and to what degree the texts by a single author also display such variation must be left open here. It is assumed, however, that an author's preference plays at least some role.

14   Spelling has, however, also been regularized in some of the texts included in ARCHER.

References

Berglund, Y. (1997), 'Future in present-day English: corpus-based evidence on the rivalry of expressions', *ICAME Journal*, 21: 7-20.

Biber, D., E. Finegan and D. Atkinson (1994), 'ARCHER and its challenges: compiling and exploring a representative corpus of historical English registers', in: U. Fries, G. Tottie and P. Schneider (eds.) *Creating and Using English Language Corpora. Papers from the Fourteenth International Conference on English Language Research on Computerized Corpora, Zürich 1993*. Amsterdam and Atlanta: Rodopi. 1-13.

Coates, J. (1983), *The Semantics of the Modal Auxiliaries*. London and Canberra: Croom Helm.

Fabian, B. (1991), *Die englische Literatur*. 2 Vols. München: Deutscher Taschenbuch Verlag.

Gotti, M. (2001), 'Semantic and pragmatic values of *shall* and *will* in Early Modern English Statutes', in: M. Gotti and M. Dossena (eds.) *Modality in Specialized Texts. Selected Papers of the 1st CERLIS Conference*. Frankfurt: Lang. 89-111.

Hoffmann, S. (2002), 'In (hot) pursuit of data: complex prepositions in late modern English', in: P. Peters, P. Collins and A. Smith (eds.) *New Frontiers of Corpus Research. Papers from the Twenty First International Conference on English Language Research on Computerized Corpora Sydney 2000*. Amsterdam and New York: Rodopi. 127-146.

Kehoe, A. (2006), 'Diachronic linguistic analysis on the web with WebCorp', in: A. Renouf (ed.) *The Changing Face of Corpus Linguistics*. Amsterdam and Atlanta: Rodopi. 297-307.

Kytö, M. (1992), '*Shall (should)* vs. *will (would)* in early British and American English: a variational study of change', *North-Western European Language Evolution*, 19: 3-73.

Mair, C. (2004), 'Corpus linguistics and grammaticalisation theory: statistics, frequencies, and beyond', in: H. Lindquist and C. Mair (eds.) *Corpus Approaches to Grammaticalisation in English*. Amsterdam: Benjamins. 121-150.

Szmrecsanyi, B. (2003), '*Be going to* versus *will/shall*: Does syntax matter?' *Journal of English Linguistics*, 31 (4): 295-323.

Wilpert, G. von (1997), *Lexikon der Weltliteratur*. 3rd edition. München: Deutscher Taschenbuch Verlag.